JEWISH
IRELAND

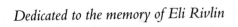

Dedicated to the memory of Eli Rivlin

JEWISH IRELAND

A SOCIAL HISTORY

RAY RIVLIN

The History Press Ireland

Jewish Ireland is an updated version of *Shalom Ireland* published in 2003.

The History Press Ireland
119 Lower Baggot Street
Dublin 2
Ireland
www.thehistorypress.ie

British Library Cataloguing in Publication Data.
A catalogue record for this book is available from the British Library.

ISBN 978 1 84588 708 7
Typesetting and origination by The History Press
Printed in Great Britain
Manufacturing managed by Jellyfish Print Solutions Ltd

CONTENTS

PREFACE

When John Wilson TD, then Minister for Tourism and Transport, officially opened the upper floor of the Irish Jewish Museum, Dublin, on 1 January 1988, a report in the *Jewish Chronicle* concluded with the words, 'For that final touch all that is required is a scholar who will dedicate himself to an up-to-date history of Irish Jews.'

I lay no claim to so exalted a title, but *Shalom Ireland* published in 2003, was the result of three years' intensive research and updating it to *Jewish Ireland* took the best part of another year. The material was drawn from the archives of the Irish Jewish Museum, the library of the London School of Jewish Studies (Jews' College), the Dublin Diocesan Archives, Drumcondra, the National Library of Ireland and Dublin's Civic Museum as well as from private memoirs, a myriad of books and newspapers, school records and minute books, unpublished letters and legal documents, communal publications and works in progress. An even greater source of information has been the oral testimony gleaned from hundreds of Irish Jews around the world through personal interview, telephone, correspondence and cyberspace.

Though every effort has been made to establish accuracy, records can be inaccurate and memory selective. Where divergent accounts of the same event were presented to me, I chose the version that could best be corroborated; but readers may well recall yet a different set of circumstances, and I apologise if factual errors and misspelt names have inadvertently crept in.

It would be impossible to name all the people in Ireland and abroad who contributed personal histories, communal information or anecdotes, or even those who simply pointed me in the right direction. I thank them all and offer sincere apologies to those who find little or no reference to themselves or their families after giving lengthy interviews. Many wonderful people and fascinating stories have been omitted for lack of space. With more material than I could use, selection had to be made in the interests of presenting not a blow-by-blow account but a panoramic, entertaining and accurate view of Irish Jewry.

I thank Cecil Calmonson for making available to me an almost complete set of the *Irish-Jewish Year Book* and the many people who entrusted me with documents and photographs they greatly value; my good friend Roberta Collins for acting as a continuous sounding-board; and the many people who answered my numerous queries. The late Raphael Siev was invaluable both for checking the accuracy of historical data and allowing free access to the photographic archives of the Irish Jewish Museum. I thank my editor at The History Press, Ronan Colgan, for having the faith to reprint this updated version of *Shalom Ireland* and Beth Amphlett for her general assistance in the editorial process of *Jewish Ireland* and for her patience in dealing with each one of my 'final' changes.

The nineteenth-century Russian immigrants to Ireland merged the characteristics of the *heim* (homeland) with those of their adoptive country to produce that quaint hybrid, the Irish Jew. Overcoming problems that included poverty, communal dissension and covert anti-Semitism, they made a remarkable contribution to Irish society while establishing a way of life that was unique within the Diaspora. The decline in numbers that began mid-way through the twentieth century eroded the traditional life-style of Irish Jewry, so that today's young people have never experienced it. When the nostalgic remembrance of older generations inevitably fades from living memory, I look to this book to keep the past alive.

Ray Rivlin
Dublin, 2011

1

CLANBRASSIL STREET

Anyone wishing to meet a microcosm of Irish Jewry in the first half of the twentieth century would have turned first to Dublin, home to 90 per cent of the Irish Jewish community. There they could choose between visiting one of the many synagogues on a Saturday morning, the day of the Jewish Sabbath, and a trip to Clanbrassil Street on a Sunday morning. Those who chose the second option were transported to scenes more in keeping with nineteenth-century Russia than with twentieth-century Ireland.

Clanbrassil Street, on the south side of the River Liffey, was the hub of Jewish Dublin, the pivot from which densely-Jewish streets and terraces radiated as far as the South Circular Road and across it to the enclave of narrow streets known locally as Little Jerusalem. Like many Dublin streets, it divides into two sections. Lower Clanbrassil Street runs from New Street near St Patrick's Cathedral to Leonard's Corner on the South Circular Road; Upper Clanbrassil Street from Leonard's Corner to the Grand Canal. Emmet Bridge at Harold's Cross where the street terminates, held a double significance for Jews of that era. In life, going 'over the bridge' meant moving to a residence in a south Dublin suburb, a definite step up the social ladder; in death, it meant the inevitable last journey to the Jewish cemetery at Dolphin's Barn. Dubliner Michael Coleman always refers to it as Dublin's Bridge of Sighs, from the countless mourners who have passed over it.

There was nothing mournful or lifeless about Clanbrassil Street. The kosher shops that lined both sides of the short route from St Kevin's Parade to St Vincent Street South – both side streets off Lower Clanbrassil Street – had a constant stream of customers to buy the meat and fish, the groceries and delicatessen, the drapery and haberdashery, the bread and confectionery on display in the different outlets. Only rarely did anyone make a purchase and go straight home: Clanbrassil Street shopping meant calling on family and friends, meeting acquaintances, exchanging recipes and gossip, giving and receiving advice and complaining to anyone who would listen. It even meant making a date, as Anne Samuel, *née* Isaacson, used to do when young Eric Chaiken delivered a hen from Goldwater's on a Thursday and asked, 'Are you all right for Saturday night at the Metropole?' (then a popular Dublin ballroom). Geoffrey Goldberg, who married Eric's sister, Eileen, and eventually settled in Manchester, enjoys telling how his Uncle Gerald, on a visit from Liverpool in the 1950s to see his grandparents, went into Shapiro's, the tobacconists, looking for twenty Woodbines and found a wife. The couple

Butcher's shop in Clanbrassil Street, 1984, once owned by Janie and Isaac Goldwater.

Baile Ehrlich in her butcher's shop, Clanbrassil Street, 2000.

were introduced by the relative of the bride-to-be who served him. Clanbrassil Street was vibrant, colourful, alive. It was a street where people lived and socialised. Children were born and brought up there. It saw laughter and tears, hardship and prosperity, humour and pathos, rivalry and amazing solidarity in time of need.

It was probably the Jewish character of the street when Joyce was writing *Ulysses* (1914-21) that led him to choose 52 Upper Clanbrassil Street as the birthplace of Leopold Bloom, the book's fictional Jewish hero, 'born' 18 May 1866. With no Jews then living in that area, it was as unlikely a combination of time and place for the birth of a Jewish child as it was for Bloom to be categorised as a Jew on the basis of his father's faith; Jewish lineage traditionally passes through the mother.

The small number of Jewish families living in Dublin in the 1860s, all descendents from an earlier immigration, were well ensconced across the River Liffey on the north side of the city. *Thom's Directory*, which has been recording the occupants of Dublin street premises, albeit with some inaccuracies, since 1844, lists no likely Jewish residents for either stretch of Clanbrassil Street until the 1890s, when they concentrated in Lower Clanbrassil Street.

The first to take up residence in Upper Clanbrassil Street appears to have been Fossell Mitafaki (spelt 'Mitafaky' in the 1892 edition of *Thom's Directory* and 'Mitawfsky' by 1893), who went to live at number 57 in 1891. This forefather of a Mitofsky family still represented in Dublin, left Upper Clanbrassil Street in 1898 to settle in nearby Raymond Street. By that time Upper Clanbrassil Street had the shopping amenities offered by David Rosenberg, greengrocer, at number 42A and Lazarus Golding, draper, at number 55. By the turn of the century they were both gone and only a scattering of Jewish settlers continued to locate in that section of the street.

The distinction of being the first Jew in Lower Clanbrassil Street specifically designated a trader seems to belong to a Mr Miller, a picture-frame maker at number 98. In 1894 he moved to number 18, where he continued trading for another ten years. In that time the street saw many Jewish comings and goings, with families moving in and out or simply changing premises, as Mr Miller did. It was not easy for early arrivals to settle down in a land whose very language was a mystery to them. Some moved on within a few months, some stayed a few years but there was a nucleus that established roots, stability increasing as the new century advanced. Weinrouck's Bakery opened in 1904 and continued trading into the 1940s. It produced its goods under the long-term management of Mr Moiselle in a laneway off Rosedale Terrace at the back of the Clanbrassil Street shops and sold them at number 42A Lower Clanbrassil Street, a corner shop where street and terrace meet. The pervasive aroma of their 'real crusty brown breads with a dinge in the middle,' their bagels and fresh yeast, together with the miniature loaf they occasionally made for her, were lovingly remembered by Doris Waterman, *née* Fine, whose family ran a grocery shop next door at number 40 from 1924 until 1971.

Fine's grocery shop, Terenure, Dublin 1984. Doris Waterman (second left), Helen Green (second right) and proprietor Hilda White (right) serve customer Leslie Baker.

Although it involved only nineteen premises, that early documented Jewish presence, augmented by unrecorded sub-lettings, probably amounted to well over 100 people and must have made a significant impact on the run-down, working-class, hitherto Catholic neighbourhood. In later years, certainly, Jewish influence there was out of all proportion to the number of Jewish-occupied premises. Brian Smith, who left Dublin in 1965 to settle in Canada, even had the childhood fancy that 'Clanbrassil' was a Jewish name; others of the community still imagine the street was once predominantly Jewish. It never was.

The street numbers in Lower Clanbrassil Street run from 1 to 55 along the left-hand side as one approaches the South Circular Road, and from 56 to 121 on the opposite side, going back towards New Street. The status of some of its dilapidated housing changed from time to time, but from the beginning of the twentieth century, in any one year, at least twenty-five of the buildings and sometimes more than thirty were listed as tenements, a form of dwelling with which Jews in Clanbrassil Street were rarely associated. Of the ninety or so premises that remained for private occupation, no more than twenty-five were ever occupied simultaneously by Jews, and that was only once in the peak year of 1923. The overall highest density of Jewish residents was between 1921 and 1943, when an average of twenty-three premises were occupied by Jews, concentrated between numbers 28 and 46 on the one side and between 78 and 98A on the other, a pattern of occupancy that was to continue with only minor deviations until the street's decline as a Jewish area.

On a percentage basis, the comparatively few Jewish families established in the street should never have been enough to give it the ethnicity it acquired, but the majority of those families were traders in kosher products whose shops attracted into the street the entire local Jewish community as well as visitors to Dublin from elsewhere in Ireland and abroad.

Kosher trading is unlike any other. The dietary laws imposed on Observant Jews and embedded in a code of law called *kashrut*, encompass almost all food products, regarding both their permissibility as food and their methods of production, preparation and consumption. Because all early Dublin traders were accepted as being traditionally and genuinely Orthodox, much was taken on trust, and rabbinic supervision to ensure *kashrut* compliance could be quite perfunctory. Only butchers were subjected to stringent regulation and regular inspection. Dr David Rubinstein, now living in London, is a grandson of Myer Rubinstein, who opened a butcher's shop at number 82 in 1905, and a son of Philly Rubinstein, who eventually took over his father's business. He still remembers Dayan Alony, a rabbi qualified to serve as a rabbinical judge, calling to check the kosher stamp on carcasses after every delivery.

Laws relating to the consumption of meat are laid down in Leviticus 11:3 enjoins the Jews, as a Holy people, to eat only animals designated as 'clean', defined as those that chew the cud and have cloven hooves. Verses 13-19 proscribe a wide variety of winged creatures, mostly birds of prey, as 'detestable fowl'. Of the birds permitted in Leviticus, many could not be identified by the rabbis interpreting the words into a Code of Practice; as a result, the Observant eat only a small selection of common farmyard poultry.

Because the consumption of blood is prohibited, even permitted fowl and animals must be ritually slaughtered and as much blood as possible drained away. As a further safeguard against the infringement of this edict, meat and fowl must be soaked in water and then salted to remove any residual blood before cooking can take place. This *kashering*, traditionally undertaken by the housewife, was later offered as an optional service by some butchers. It is now done commercially before the product is sold. Because they contain veins that only great deftness and butchering skill can successfully remove, the hindquarters are never used, and even the forequarters will be rejected after slaughter if the lung or any other organ appears diseased. Rejection of cattle was so uncompromising in Dublin that carcasses finally stamped as kosher were considered *glatt kosher*, the highest level of *kashrut* that can be applied to meat.

The ritual killing of fowl and cattle is known as *shechita*. The issuing of trading licenses to kosher butchers, the supervision of slaughter houses and butchers' shops and the stamping that indicates acceptability within the dietary laws lies with the Central Board of *Shechita* of Ireland. The command in Exodus 34:26 and Deuteronomy 14:21 not to 'seethe a kid in the milk of its mother' is interpreted as an injunction to separate milk and meat foods. Separate utensils are kept for their preparation and serving and the consumption of meat after milk requires an interval of one to six hours, depending on family custom.

The story of the Creation (Genesis 1:29) declares all fruit and vegetables permissible, so Clanbrassil Street greengrocers faced few restrictions. General grocers too were once free to sell popular branded goods believed to contain no animal fat and kosher shops displayed items such as Campbell's vegetable soups, Jacob's biscuits and Kennedy's bread. All were legitimately purchased by Orthodox customers. One trading family remembers Rabbi Herzog, Chief Rabbi of Ireland from 1926 until 1936, as a regular customer for a Kennedy's batch loaf. Only at *Pesach* (Passover) did more stringent rules apply. Because the Israelites were freed from bondage by a somewhat ambivalent Pharaoh (Exodus 8:24-14:8), who could easily have changed his mind again and refused to let them go, the Exodus from Egypt, which the Passover commemorates, began in something of a rush, leaving no time for newly baked bread to rise. The hasty departure is immortalised in the annual obligatory eating of unleavened bread, similar in texture to water biscuits, and the restriction of other products freely consumed during the rest of the year. Food permitted for Passover use must be prepared in domestic and commercial settings with equipment that is newly purchased, kept exclusively for Passover usage or ritually cleansed for that purpose. Rabbis or their appointed representatives, rarely, if ever, seen in groceries where their womenfolk shopped regularly, called into every outlet before Passover to ensure that year-round stock was either removed from the premises or hidden behind sheets of paper, and that each shop was appropriately cleaned and re-stocked for the eight-day period. Passover fare had to be manufactured under supervision and stamped *Kosher for Passover* by a rabbinical authority. Sometimes the *hechsher* or official stamp was placed on the product at the place of manufacture; sometimes the labels were delivered separately, to be affixed to the goods by the trader.

In the second half of the twentieth century some of the stringency of Passover production that had passed into products used throughout the year in ultra-Orthodox communities elsewhere, began to affect Irish kosher-trading practice. The growing use of additives and preservatives in food manufacturing, many of animal origin, also helped exclude a range of previously acceptable popular brands. As alternatives became increasingly available, Ireland began importing foodstuffs made under supervision mainly from England, America, Israel and Holland. Tinned and packet soups, soup cubes, cooking oils, cheese, biscuits, sweets, chocolate and ice cream, all certified as kosher, were just some of the products that began to appear regularly in Clanbrassil Street shops, alongside local and imported nationally-used commodities whose manufacturers guaranteed animal-free ingredients and allowed Jewish inspection of their plant. McDonnell's of Clarendon Street, for instance, produced kosher margarine under the supervision of Dayan Alony. The *Irish-Jewish Year Book*, published annually since 1950, apprised community members of permissible products in any given year. The quality of the *hechsher*, of extreme importance to the ultra-Orthodox, never troubled the Irish conscience. What was passed as kosher was accepted as kosher and used by the most Orthodox of Irish customers, irrespective of any outside claims that one stamp indicated a greater degree of supervisory vigilance than another.

During his period of office as Chief Rabbi of Ireland, Rabbi Jakobovits overcame local resistance to establish the practice of serving only kosher-labeled wine at kosher functions, a custom soon extended to its exclusive use for wine benedictions in the home and, ultimately, even for social consumption among Observant Irish Jews. Bread also fell victim to the new zeal among Irish religious leaders for greater *kashrut* compliance. As unsupervised bakers might conceivably be using non-permitted substances for greasing tins, for glazing loaves or even as an ingredient, *challahs* (the plaited or round loaves traditionally used for bread benedictions on Sabbath and Festivals), or other kosher loaves, became the daily bread of Orthodox Irish homes.

An early supplier was Clein's Bakery at 1A Lennox Street. Started by Zalman Seftl Clein in 1920 when his family moved from Cork to Dublin, it was run by various managers, including Zalman's son-in-law, Syd Barnett, until 1936 when it was sold to Barney Stein. In 1948 an unrelated Harry Clein became associated with it through his marriage to Barney's widow, Ida Stein, *née* Herman. Her son, Bevan Stein, who later moved to France, remembered working there part-time as a schoolboy and student. The head baker then was Fred Keane, with Christy Hackett his second-in-command. Neither was Jewish. For a few years after Frank retired, a Mr Benson ran the bakery, trading as Benson's, but his return to England left Christy in sole charge. In 1964 he rented the business from Mrs Clein and changed its name to Bretzel. Though no written agreement was ever signed, it was an amicable arrangement that continued beyond Christy's retirement when his son, Morgan Hackett, took over the tenancy. He bought the bakery after Mrs Clein's death in 1996. Though Jewish-owned from 1920 until 2000, it was not always certified as kosher and other firms intermittently supplied Dublin's kosher bread. In 1955-6 it was available from Robert Roberts of 44 Grafton Street; in 1962-3 the official supplier was Gerrard's Cakes Ltd.

As with Kosher shops elsewhere, the Clanbrassil Street outlets, irrespective of the product sold, were obliged to close from before sunset on Friday night, when the Sabbath began, until after sunset on Saturday, when it ended, and for the duration of all Holy days on which work was forbidden.

With all the exclusively kosher shops in Dublin now closed, claiming association with a Clanbrassil Street trading family carries the same kind of prestige as an alleged place on the *Mayflower* passenger list. 'It seems that we all had a shop in Clanbrassil Street at one time or another,' quips Israeli-resident Maerton Davis, trebly connected through his great-grandfather, Myer Rubinstein, his grandfather, Barney Rubinstein, who ran his own butcher's shop at number 31 from 1939, and his uncle, Barney Davis, a Clanbrassil Street grocer. 'It's no wonder we never made a living!'

Some of the shops must indeed have yielded lean enough pickings, for few of the traders had specific skills or resources to support a business venture.

Dr Sam Davis, another London-based grandson of Myer Rubinstein, described his grandfather as an expert judge of cattle, which he bought 'off the hoof' at the Dublin Cattle Market. Gerald Baigel remembered the barter arrangement between his father, Harris Baigel, who bought Margolis's grocery business, with its wine and spirit license, in 1913, and Mr Atkins, the shoe-repairer at number 87 since 1917. In return for Baigel groceries and the odd bottle of whiskey, Mr Atkins supplied Mr Baigel with an annual pair of leather, hand-made boots, whose excellent quality testified to his skill as a boot maker. Despite the general contention that butchery was 'slavery work', almost all the butchers eventually garnered some degree of butchering skills, mostly from their non-Jewish employees. The womenfolk among the grocery families had the traditional culinary arts brought from the *heim* and handed down. In time, Clanbrassil Street had its first and only professional enterprise in Sam Citron's pharmacy, which opened at number 80 in 1934, but by and large the owners of the shops in and around Clanbrassil Street began trading with little or no experience of buying or selling, no cash reserves and minimal stock. Many were women, some young widows with children to rear. The only assets they all shared were the courage to take risks and the determination to make a living independent of non-Jewish employers, most of whom did not want their services.

Clanbrassil Street shops were no emporiums. The late Ethel Freedman, in her unpublished memoirs, written in 1970 at the request of her son, Allan, remembers the street as:

> ... a whole row of small shops ... occupied by grocers, greengrocers, drapers, dairy, butchers, general mixed stock, all in a state of confusion. One old lady had in her window grocery, pots and pans, small drapery items and kitchen utensils.

Equipped with no more than some sort of counter and minimum shelving, with bare or shabby linoleum-covered floor – except for the butchers, who sprinkled sawdust to absorb the spills of blood and other fluids – and often in dire need of a coat of paint, almost all doubled as home and income. Some had living accommodation above and behind the small shop space; others were no more than small dwellings whose front room had been converted to shop use. Mr Werzberger's shop, previously owned by an M. Freedman, unrelated to Ethel, and aptly listed in *Thom's Directory* as number 42½, was so narrow that three customers standing abreast could span its width.

Sam Davis described his grandfather's shop at number 82 as stone-floored with 'a small, pokey room at the back', not much larger than the ice cabinet it accommodated, a device kept cold by specially delivered ice blocks hooked up inside it. Lynda Garber remembers the little shop run by her grandmother, Sarah Rick, at the corner of Lombard Street West, beside Barney Rubinstein's shop. Left to bring up a family of seven children when her husband died prematurely in 1935, Mrs Rick began selling groceries and cigarettes from the front room of her home. The club she ran, with accumulated weekly contributions that could be cashed in at time of need or extra expense, may have attracted some trade, but Lynda reckons Mrs Rick's five daughters and twin sons, grown and married, were eventually her best customers. Just the whiff of a *schmaltz* herring still evokes for her the pungent barrel that had a permanent place on the shop floor and the years of hardship her grandmother endured.

Herbie Kay's father also died young, in 1944, leaving his mother Sadie with no means of support to rear her four children, the youngest only eleven weeks old. Rejecting any suggestion that the family be separated, she accepted help to pay key money for the rented house and shop at 29 Lombard Street, which the Shenkman family wanted to vacate, and there she slaved, from morn till night, to make a living. Once or twice a week she took an early-morning 54 bus to Christchurch from where she made her way downhill to the Central Market behind Capel Street to buy her stock of fruit and vegetables, trudging back up the hilly street with whatever she could carry to catch another 54 bus and be back in the already-opened shop by 9 a.m. What she and, later, Herbie could not transport on the messenger bicycle had to be delivered by paid carriers, an expense she could ill afford, until Gerald Madden of Madden Brothers, a market wholesaler, called one day to collect payment for goods supplied. Invited in for a cup of tea, he spotted her wedding photograph, recognised Herbie's father and exclaimed, 'That's Max Kay!' Gerald and Max had been friends in their 'dancing days'. After that, no matter which market firm supplied Mrs Kay, Madden's delivered her produce free of charge.

Officially, her shop closed at 6 p.m. but, apart from the stragglers who called freely at all the shops after hours for forgotten or urgent purchases, Mrs Kay was busily engaged, evenings and night-time, in preparing her own range of the delicatessen items – such as chopped herring and pickled cucumbers – that were made in almost all the kosher grocery shops. In the weeks leading up to Passover all the kitchens became mini food-processing plants, as quantities of *imberlich* and *tagelich* (seasonal sweetmeats), sponge cakes made with potato starch instead of forbidden flour, mead (an alcoholic drink fermented from honey), and *chrane* (a strong horseradish sauce) were turned out in abundance.

Mrs Kay obtained her horseradish from the Robinson family, who made weekly trips to Dublin from their home in Carlow. Each stick had to be scraped and then minced or grated, when the emanating pungency brought tears to the eyes. Herbie almost has tears in his own eyes, tears of laughter, when he recalls the evening he was sent with excess sticks of horseradish to Mrs Kronn, whose family owned Jackson's, the grocery shop at number 39 Lower Clanbrassil Street. Her daughter, Leila, told him, 'She's in the back. Take it in to her'. Herbie found Mrs Kronn, her back towards him, busily grating. As he called her name, she turned and he saw she was wearing a Second World War gas mask to protect herself from the fumes – an unwitting perfect defense against a plant now said to contain mustard gas.

The kitchen work before Passover was exhausting. Fay Dehan, *née* Cohen, a niece of Sadie Kay, who now lives in Manchester, was brought up in her mother's 'front-room' shop in Walworth Road, off the South Circular Road. She remembers her aunt being so tired near the completion of a large order for *imberlich* that she put pepper into the mixture instead of ginger and had to throw out the whole batch. If the sponge cakes flopped or the sweetmeats failed to set, they were discarded too, with the loss of ingredients as well as potential profit – and profit, for Sadie Kay, was hard to come by.

Accounts for goods given on credit were supposed to be settled in full each week, and many were. One esteemed patron even paid on behalf of a neglectful customer she had recommended; but too many debts were partially settled and immediately topped up to an even higher figure with new purchases. When Mrs Kay finally closed the shop to join her children in England in 1966, there were outstanding accounts that would never be settled, despite the oft-repeated assurance, 'Don't worry, Mrs Kay, I won't die in your debt!'

Even in Clanbrassil Street, where trade was brisker, many hard-working shopkeepers struggled for survival, often because, as David Rubinstein declares in relation to the family butcher's shop, 'They didn't know how to run a business!' A part-time delivery boy during his student days, he recalls the waste of time in frequently delivering twice to the same house on the same day, the second delivery often being made by his father late at night on his way home from a day's work that had begun at 6 a.m. David's mother, Sessie, worked alongside his father, starting a little later, finishing a little earlier, but always having to cook the family meals on the premises and take them home to be eaten.

Ethel Freedman's husband, Woulfe (Wolfe), using good business sense, rented number 35 Lower Clanbrassil Street, a shop, 'with good living accommodation upstairs and downstairs', for his parents, after he encouraged them to move to Dublin from Limerick during the First World War. She writes in her memoirs:

> He had the whole place re-decorated, he had the windows properly fitted out to display the merchandise which was grocery, confectionery, etc … The Dublin community had never seen a shop like that in Clanbrassil Street. He dressed the windows properly. In the centre he had a glass shelf, hanging from chains, on which he displayed boxes of chocolates and it was soon the centre of attraction in the street.

Other traders eventually earned an adequate, and some a comfortable living through a combination of ingenuity, growing expertise and total indifference to the number of hours they worked.

Lithuanian-born Masha Ordman was brought to Ireland at the age of six. None of her three daughters, Lydia Haffner, *née* Birzansky, and Gertrude and Edna Telzer, who settled in Manchester, could ever fathom how a single girl in her early twenties had the acumen to raise a bank loan and the courage to start a business at 80 Lower Clanbrassil Street in 1917. They cannot say for certain whether that original premises was a tiny shop with living accommodation or the front room of a small dwelling, but they do know the entire opening stock was 'a few sweets'. As trade progressed Masha diversified into tea, sugar, cheese, bread and other light groceries and the little produce she could carry back from the market at what they describe as 'some unearthly hour of the morning'. Then, in her ill-equipped kitchen, she turned out the delicatessen designed to tempt customers. When she married and moved to Cork in the 1920s her sisters, Sophie and Edie, took over the business, helped by Sophie's husband, Harry Sakarov. They were able, in time, to dispose of number 80 to Mr Citron, the pharmacist, and erect a fine double-fronted shop next door at number 81, the site of a demolished tenement, on the strength of the business Masha had built from nothing.

Baigel's was another success story. The only Jewish outlet officially licensed to trade as a, 'tea, wine and spirit merchant', it had the Irish rights to Palwin kosher wines which arrived from Rishon-le-Zion in Palestine graded in different casks to denote quality. The Baigels bottled and labeled it themselves, as they did with Guinness, delivered in smaller casks. Gerald remembered as a ten-year-old using a funnel to help fill the bottles obtained from the Irish Glass Bottle Company and corking them with the aid of a corking machine, supplied by a firm in Aungier Street. The washed and filled bottles were held under a small aperture which supported the cork, already softened by immersion in water. At the press of a lever, the cork slotted into the bottle neck and within a few hours expanded to seal it. The wine was labeled *Kosher for Passover*, the Guinness *Bottled by Harris Baigel*. Baigel's also sold groceries and delicatessen, often home-made, but in contrast to Mrs Kay's later experience, their less well-to-do customers paid cash in full for their purchases; it was the affluent who tended to run up accounts that were settled only after visits to their home.

The Fines also built up a business they could be proud of and clearly were, since Hilda White, *née* Fine, who succeeded Mrs Fine in running it, has the words *Kosher grocer for 57 years* inscribed on her tombstone. Doris Waterman never worked in her mother's shop but she recalled the selection of groceries and delicatessen delivered there by suppliers – barrels of pickled cucumbers and pickled cabbage imported from England, locally obtained barrels of *schmaltz* herrings and salt herrings, large tins of *gaffelbitter* herrings, drums of nut oil, wooden boxes of butter, pound bags of different spices, boxes of smoked salmon and sacks of flour, sugar and coarse salt. In addition to 'bread and butter' items and some fresh market produce, her mother also sold a range of cakes, home-made with the help of her older daughters and an employee, Kathleen Plunkett.

Mrs Fine, grey hair tied in a bun at the back, overall crossed in front, began baking at 3 a.m., strenuously beating mixtures with a wooden spoon to fulfil customer demand for cheese cake, *milchige* (a yeast cake), *mandel* (almond) bread and *kichlach* (a type of biscuit). In summer a hand-operated churn was used to make ice-cream, which was spooned into cornets that sold at a ha'penny or 1*d* each, according to size.

Diversification was also the key to other successes. Sam Citron, in addition to dispensing, 'Prescriptions, Drugs, Ethical Products, Sundries, Proprietary Articles, Disinfectants, French Polish, Cellulose, Paints, etc., etc.,' advertised himself as 'Sole selling agent in Éire for Gerald Carter and Co. London, Contractors to the Principal Furniture Manufacturers'. Baigel's wine and spirit license was sold on to Freedman's when Baigel's closed in 1939, but other traders began selling ready-bottled kosher drink, especially at Passover time. Mr Werzberger elevated his confined space to greater earning potential by wholesaling cigarettes and acting as an agent in Ireland for Palwin bottled wines and a small range of kosher liqueurs. But no one in Clanbrassil Street made an easy living.

Thelma Cowan, daughter of Cissie Robinson, who took over the Arnovitch grocery shop at number 69 when her father died in 1943, was taken out of school at the age of fourteen to help her mother in the shop. Asked almost fifty years later what it was like to work there, she spontaneously groans, 'Hard! So hard' and then goes on to describe the endless hours when, living on the premises, they were always on call with 'no lunch-time, no holidays'. When the messenger boy took a day off, Thelma had to cycle round with orders demanded for delivery before lunch-time. Her mother worked 'from early morning till late at night', snatching time between customers to prepare the usual appetising delicacies, including *smetena* (rich sour cream) and *kaese* (soft cream cheese) for which Thelma carried gallons of unpasteurised milk, in covered pails, from Smullen's Dairy at number 57. After the Leopolds at number 71 emigrated to South Africa, A. and R., as her mother renamed the shop, was the only kosher grocery in the street selling fresh fish.

Only fish with fins and scales are permitted for kosher consumption. A. and R. stocked a full range, including fresh salmon, which could be sold only under licence to offset possible poaching. Any infringement could result in a fine, and inspectors called at the shop repeatedly to spot check the validity of the licence, which had to be renewed every year. Mrs Robinson went every Tuesday and Thursday morning to the Fish Market, making sure to be there by 6 a.m. when the best selection was offered at the cheapest price.

Even at busy Passover time Mrs Robinson did not want Thelma involved in the cooking sessions, but she was allowed to take turns at mincing the horse-radish – as long as she kept well away from the hot stove, where Auntie Edie's mead was fermenting. Whether from superstition or old wives' tale, Mrs Robinson subscribed to Pliny's first-century contention in his *Natural History* that, 'contact with menstrual blood turned new wine sour', and no one would buy sour wine.

Sadie Baigel, *née* Rosenfield, Gerald Baigel's widow, who was a shop assistant in Ordman's from 1946 to 1948, remembers the messiness of pushing up her sleeves to delve into the barrels, with bare hands, for cucumbers and herrings. She also recalls the incessant grind of slicing the smoked salmon, bottling the nut oil which froze in the drum in the heart of winter, and weighing the spices into one-ounce packages and the sugar, flour, coarse salt and other dry goods into brown paper bags. Two people, one at each end of a wire cutter, were needed to divide blocks of butter into halves, then quarters, then eighths. Smaller slabs were then cut off with wet patties and shaped to customer requirements before being weighed and wrapped in greaseproof paper. Table salt, packed by the Steinberg family and sold at 1*d* per packet under the trade name of the Capital Salt Company, was one of the few ready-packed items in the shop. Even when she moved next door to Betty's, the drapery shop at number 38 run by Becky Daniels, another daughter of the grocer, Mrs Fine, she found the work tiring. Mrs Daniels, like Mrs Rick, ran a weekly club that attracted customers, but at Betty's the accumulated shillings had to be spent on items from the shop. There was plenty to choose from. Betty's was an Aladdin's Cave of knitting wools, patterns, children's wear, knickers, hosiery, tablecloths, towels, boxed gifts for engagement and wedding presents and every sort of haberdashery. Always by the door hung a selection of pretty aprons, skilfully machine-made by her husband, Syd, from bolts of patterned cotton and reckoned a bargain at 1*s* or 1*s* 6*d* each. A popular item, they needed frequent replenishing and Sadie remembers Mrs Fine's constant reminder, 'Syd, have you got the aprons ready?' In her spare time, between serving customers, Sadie sorted boxes and boxes of miscellaneous buttons into homogeneous colours, shapes and sizes.

The obligatory closing on the Sabbath and Holy days must have come as a blessed relief to these traders whose shops were open for business, through the side or back door if not through the front, at all hours, including public holidays, church holidays and Christmas Day. In winter, when the sun set early, they even opened after the Sabbath to take in merchandise left outside by delivery men during the Sabbath closure and to serve customers for as long as they kept coming.

Preparation for all festivals brought additional custom. Pre-Passover, when the Birzansky sisters describe Lower Clanbrassil Street as 'black with cars' as people collected their orders, was the 'Christmas' of the kosher trading year. Otherwise the busiest days were Thursdays when housewives prepared for the Sabbath, and Sunday mornings, often extended into early afternoon, when their men folk frequently joined them to replenish the larder.

Shopping in Clanbrassil Street was an experience that activated all five of the senses. The ear was immediately caught by the mixture of English and Yiddish spoken by customers and traders alike. It was in Mr Werzberger's shop that Brian Smith learnt to count in Yiddish as his parents' purchases of religious goods, wine and candles were totted up for payment. Allan Freedman, taken on Sunday mornings to visit his grandparents, munched a selection from the box of broken biscuits while his father joined the group in front of the shop counter, already involved in the weekly all-Yiddish discussion of politics or current affairs which might well have passed over a child's head in any language. Adults who were children into the 1950s and '60s recall their own limited understanding of the bi-lingual conversations around them. Perhaps it was just as well they could not understand everything that was said for the concept of *losh inhora* (precepts against slander) was by no means rigidly observed; personal, private and communal affairs, friends, family, community leaders and neighbours as well as the latest engagements, marriages, births and deaths, all came under general review.

Lower Clanbrassil Street was a kaleidoscope of movement and colour as stylish shoppers, like the three French sisters, Mrs Citron, Mrs Silverstein and Mrs Harrison, the last usually accompanied by her French poodle, mingled with the traditionally-garbed elderly and the less fashion-conscious. Together they wove their way along the crowded narrow streets, greeting each other and meandering, almost as an afterthought, in and out of the shops. Fishwomen added local colour every Tuesday and Thursday morning. Some draped in black shawls, they piled their crates of fruit on the pavement and sold their fresh fish from the depths of ancient baby carriages covered with wooden boards, which served as counters. Their pitch was on the opposite corner from Barney Rubinstein's, just outside number 32, a general grocery and drapery shop run successively by the Wolfes, the Gredsteins and the Goldsteins. Rabbi Hool in London remembered his mother, Janie Hool, *née* Feldman, who died in 1945, bringing the fishwomen a big jug of tea. Before every Jewish Festival and even late on Saturday nights, they plied their wares around Jewish homes. A roving eye in the early 1950s might have caught young Herbie Kay, barely into his teens, on his Sunday morning round, taking orders for presentation boxes of fifty or 100 cigarettes, then popular as gifts, and selling packets of ten or twenty to men waiting in the street for their wives. When his mother, busy in her own shop around the corner, discovered his activities through finding a cache of cigarettes in his bedroom, she warned Mr Werzberger, who was supplying him on credit, that she would not be responsible for her son's debts. He was not concerned. 'I wish I had more customers like Herbie', he told her. On one occasion shoppers saw Myer Rubinstein rush out of his shop in blood-stained apron, brandishing his butcher's knife, to stop people in the street and collect urgent donations for someone in desperate need who had just sought his help. Others might have seen that same man, on the opening day of number 31, pacing up and down one side of Lombard Street West, while his son, Barney Rubinstein, the father of three daughters, paced up and down on the other side in the opposite direction, as they both awaited news of a fourth imminent birth. Word reached Myer first, and he shouted across, 'Eileen had another girl. You're no bleddy good!' – a story that Rhona, the fourth daughter, now living in Israel, never tires of hearing or repeating.

Smells permeated the street. The pungent and aromatic flavours from the grocery shops of the *schmaltz* herrings in brine, the pickled cucumbers, the *smetena*, the *kaese*, the smoked salmon and the kippers merged with the yeasty aroma of Weinrouck's freshly-baked bread and the sometimes overpowering odour of freshly-killed, hanging poultry, meat carcasses, garlic salami, sausages, pressed beef, pickled meats, liver and the whiff of sawdust that escaped from the butchers' shops. Doris Waterman identified some customers by their perfume when she was still too small to see over the counter without standing on a chair.

Touching was endemic. Drapery was handled to test quality of fabric, held up for size, examined for strength of seams and fastness of buttons. Fruit, vegetables, bread, fish and fowl were poked and prodded, pinched and squeezed to ensure freshness, crispness, plumpness, or whatever specific quality was sought by each discerning housewife. Mrs Lev, wife of the Hebrew School headmaster, had the unnerving habit of poking fresh meat still on the cutting board, even while Barney Rubinstein was chopping it. Rough and ready in his language, Barney warned her, time and time again, 'Jaysus, one day yill have that finger chopped off yih!' And one day she did! 'I told yih, yih feckin eejit!' Barney cried. 'Where's that bleddy finger?' He found the severed tip on the cutting board, stuck it back with plaster, packed some ice around it, covered the lot with a bag and rushed her to the Meath Hospital, where the tip was sewn back.

With no food safety regulations to conform to, standards of hygiene varied from shop to shop but customers were unconcerned where they found it lax. Producers of *smetena* and *kaese* skimmed the sour cream from the pails of unpasteurized milk that had been left to set, then poured the curd into muslin bags, which they hung out-of-doors, with no protective covering, until the whey dripped through to leave only the delicious soft cheese. Baigel's and Jackson's invested early in fridges. The majority continued to store perishables in outdoor safes whose wire-meshed doors kept out flies and insects. An American relative visiting Fine's in the mid-1940s was amazed that the shop had no fridge and presented one as a gift before her return journey. One chain-smoking shopkeeper, prone to disposing of cigarette butts in the ubiquitous barrel of *schmaltz* herrings, regularly delivered orders wrapped in newspaper that contained as many butts as herrings.

Nearly every customer loved a free nibble. Mrs Fine's customers knew she always made the family a 'quick dinner' of chips on busy Thursdays; several timed their shopping so they could grab a few from the kitchen while they waited to be served. Another shop had a customer who regularly scooped a fat cucumber out of its pickling brine and consumed it, on the spot, free of charge. Others enjoyed a morsel of pressed beef to try out a new recipe, a sliver of smoked salmon that had escaped the uncut mass, a taste of cheese newly in stock, or whatever happened to be on offer or within grasp. Few children left the A. and M. Butchers at number 42 without a free slice of *wurst*. Carol-Ann Sevitt, *née* Barling, recalls one such offering from Abe Samuels, a joint owner of the shop with Mr Walzman, when she was about six years old. 'This is gorgeous', she told him, to which he replied, 'No meat is gorgeous. Women are gorgeous!' Jonathan Tolkin, now in Toronto, received his slice in a little package, beautifully wrapped, first in white paper, then in brown, and tied with a looped string for ease of carrying. The sense of importance he felt in carrying it down the street remains a highlight in his life.

Customers were demanding. Thelma Cowan remembers how they turned over the 'giant plaice' they insisted on having, to inspect the gills for freshness, and how she was made to forage, again and again, in the barrel of *schmaltz* herrings for 'a bigger one', 'one with milk' or 'one with roe', till she produced one to the correct specifications – but those same customers would sit at the counter and confide all their problems and tales of woe to her mother. 'Cissie, what am I going to do? My boy won't study and I want him to be a doctor', from one ambitious but frustrated mother. 'Cissie, I must have a boy!' from the despairing, pregnant mother of six daughters.

The indispensable chicken soup, traditional to Jewish Sabbath and Festival cuisine, was made in Irish homes from hens, when that breed was still the natural parent of a chicken. Men who travelled the countryside to earn their living often brought live hens home for killing at the hen-house, located first in deplorable premises behind Ordman's shop in Lower Clanbrassil Street. Rats darted about freely, devouring any bird left behind in error. Pluckers, sorting and bagging the feathers that sold at 4s per stone for hens and chickens, £1 10s per pound for ducks and £3 per pound for geese, had to probe warily. When that hen-house allegedly burnt down, it was replaced by another, equally dilapidated and vermin-ridden, in St Vincent Street South, with an approach via hilly waste ground. It served until 1954 when a 'state of the art', purpose-built hen-house with plucking machines was erected at 45 Lower Clanbrassil Street under the auspices of the Board of *Shechita*.

It was often children who took the fowl to the hen-house for killing. Even with their legs tied, the birds sometimes escaped from their bag or sack, with amusing consequences. Frightened by tales of their tendency to kidnap children, Eleanor Lewis Silverman, who left Dublin in 1955 to settle in America, remembers running past the shabbily-dressed gypsies who sometimes camped on vacant ground nearby. Berra Levi, a respected community member, 'rescued' one Jewish child when he plucked him from a passing gypsy horse and cart, but whether he had foiled a kidnap attempt or spoiled a proffered joyride is not recorded. Their weekly visit to the hen-house afforded the children, many with few playthings, the opportunity of collecting the coloured farm-identification rings attached to the legs of each live bird and scattered in the killing.

Over the years the charge for killing a hen which could be bought live for 1s 6d rose from 2d to 4d to 6d, with plucking always an optional extra for those who could afford a few pence more. At one time Henry Bernstein sold tickets in advance for slaughtering services from the *Shechita* house behind Ordman's. Succeeding generations, in more settled employment, relied on butchers' shops to provide a ready-killed bird, bought live from dealers and stored in the back of shops until morning when messenger boys took them in hand-carts to be killed. Customers would wait, sometimes impatiently, sometimes with time to spare for noisy gossip, until the dead birds arrived and were thrown onto the counter, when they pressed forward, *en masse*, in search of one firm enough, soft enough, fat enough, lean enough, plump enough, clean enough to warrant purchase. Cheap as they were to buy, even from the butcher, some customers still haggled over price, and the odd one never paid. In one butcher's shop, after a long wait, Doris Waterman reached the counter to choose her hen just as someone announced the approach of Mrs ----- . Immediately the entire stock of fowl disappeared before her eyes as the butcher swept them all under the counter. 'She owes me £99,' was his doubtless exaggerated explanation, before she entered the shop and asked for a hen. 'We've none,' he told her, and the fowl were retrieved only after she left.

Pickled tongues were a favourite delicacy of the more affluent but each head of cattle had only one tongue and they were always in short supply. Myer Rubinstein solved the problem by promising a tongue to everyone who requested it and then placating the disappointed customers with promises for next week. His grandsons still have no idea how he decided on the lucky recipients. Rhona Rubinstein remembers her father employing a similar ruse in his own shop, promising the same tongue to four different people.

Not all the residents were traders and not all the traders were resident. Some premises, such as the Garber home at number 43, were exclusively residential, while proprietors who lived elsewhere let the upstairs or back of their shops to relatives or other families. From his charming cottage in Co. Wicklow, Maurice Factor, now into his nineties, recollects his boyhood home behind Betty's Drapery as 'a kitchen and three-bedroom flat that had no front door'. They entered from Rosedale Terrace, 'through a back door, down some steps into a yard and then into a kitchen.' He describes his family then as, 'very poor', a socio-economic condition shared with many of his neighbours. But life was good. The comparatively large families in the area, Jewish and Christian, meant no shortage of company, and the boys were happy to play in the street at hop-scotch and marbles without envying the Hornby trains and Meccano sets beginning to appear among the sons of more successful traders. The girls played skipping and ball games; Doris Waterman never forgot the chant that accompanied one street game of the 1930s, where a ball was bounced against a wall to different instructions:

Plaining (caught with both hands)
Clapping (hands clapped before catching)
Rolling (arms rolled before catching)
Backy (hands clapped behind back before catching)
Right hand (caught with right hand only)

Left hand (caught with left hand only)

O–X–O (ball bounced against the wall three times in succession)

Sometimes they played shop with invisible stock and currency that consisted of broken china pieces dug out of the ground on the sites of demolished tenements in Rosedale Terrace. Each child seemed to belong to everyone and found a welcome in every Jewish house and shop. Often the local youngsters were joined by customers' children, who escaped the boredom of protracted, half-understood conversations by running upstairs, into back kitchens or outside to play. Even adults could tire of the inevitable long wait for service as conversations dragged on. Iris Crivon, who left Dublin for London around 1970, has an abiding memory of her mother, Sylvia, an inveterate catnapper, leaning against the wall of a Clanbrassil Street shop, apparently fast asleep!

With parents lacking the means or the time for recreational pursuits, children found outings away from the district rare and precious treats. The highlight for Gerald Baigel was setting off in his father's horse and trap with a few chosen friends for a day-trip to the sea; Maurice Factor recalls the thrill of being among the lucky few sometimes rounded up for a picnic at Ticknock, near the Dublin Mountains, in one of the Model T Fords some traders had converted into tiny pick-up trucks. The 'mighty distance' he had to travel doubled the pleasure of frolicking 'on the rocky, grass mounds'.

Sometimes entertainment came, unsolicited, to the street. Len Yodaiken, now living in Israel, dates his love of toy soldiers from the late 1930s when he watched two successive St Patrick's Day Parades from the window of the family flat at number 39, above the shop run by his aunt and uncle, Celia and Ivor Kronn. No more than five or six years old, he describes himself as 'engrossed' by the pageantry of the cavalry and the stirring sight of the splendidly-uniformed brass and pipe bands as they marched with rhythmic step. Doris Waterman recalled from the same era the anticipation of young teenagers like herself every Saturday night, as they waited for a show that rivaled, 'spending money and dressing-up to go to the Gaiety Theatre'. Sent to bed early, they fell asleep in the certainty of being wakened, around midnight, by drunken brawls and shouting from the tenements across the road, where Saturday night disputes were almost a regular weekly feature. After watching it all with enjoyment from the safety of their front bedroom, they dressed and ran into Mollie Barron's for chips.

Mollie's shop, at number 37, doubled as a mini-deli and erstwhile take-away. Customers could buy chips, with or without *wurst* or sausages, from a hatch opening onto St Vincent Street West or eat at one of the few tables used by friends for card games when business was slow. Sarah Hyman, born in a Clanbrassil Street flat, remembers cats lazing, or even 'widdling', on the bag of potatoes stored in Mollie's backyard; but everyone loved Mollie's chips, and her Saturday late-night snacks were especially popular. By the late 1930s the café element was gone but Mollie continued to sell light groceries and delicatessen such as pressed beef, saveloys, *wurst* and *schmaltz* herrings. Her niece, Alma, sometimes helped behind the counter. Alma was no more than fifteen or sixteen when a customer of unusual bearing and elegance entered the shop to buy a *schmaltz* herring. 'I want one with milk,' she told Alma, but as often as Alma delved into the messy barrel the specimen she produced was unsuitable. 'One with more milk,' the lady kept repeating. 'One with more milk,' as she rejected each one. Alma finally lost patience. 'Go on, Missus,' she declared, 'it's a bleddy cow you want, not a herring!'

Relations with Christian neighbours were harmonious. Local children might play harmless pranks such as peeping round a shop door to ask, 'Have you any broken biscuits?' then running away with the injunction, 'Well, mend them!' but they were never disappointed when they made Communion collections around the Jewish shops. Nuns and priests calling for charitable donations were equally well received.

It took more than fifty years for the glory days of Lower Clanbrassil Street to develop, and another fifty years for its glory to be extinguished, yet the change was so gradual that the century emerges as an interweaving pattern, each generation feeding on the memories of the past as much as on the experience of the present.

Just as gaslight gave way to electricity, so the horse and cart that once delivered orders and provided family transport competed for a while with the sleeker bicycle until both were overtaken by the motor-car and Clanbrassil Street saw the first of several chauffeur-driven cars arrive to collect the orders of the well-to-do.

Towards the middle of the century, Irish Jews began leaving the South Circular Road, some to go 'over the bridge' to the suburbs of Terenure, Rathfarnham and beyond, others to more distant, foreign shores. The twenty-three kosher shops trading in 1943, became sixteen by the end of the 1950s, nine by the end of the '60s, five by the end of the '70s, two by the end of the '80s and one by the end of the '90s. The last to go, in May 2001, was Erhich's at number 35, just one of many competing butchers' shops when it opened there in 1952.

Borach Erhlich traded first near Leonard's Corner, from a dingy downstairs space in a tenement house that was soon condemned. The Erhlich's had a family of three to support and Barney Rubinstein offered a space within his own shop, with a separate entrance from Lombard Street West. Mr Erhlich traded there with the help of his daughter, Baila, for many years, making what living he could from the scanty premises. In 1952 Baila became aware that the Freedman's at number 35 wanted to sell their shop. With nowhere near enough capital, she took advantage of a bank strike to chance buying it. The strike lasted seventeen weeks, by which time she had accumulated the purchase price with the help of friends. When her father died in the 1970s, Baila took over the business. She was helped by faithful staff that included Paul Fields, trained by her father and with the family for fifty years, Dominick McKeown who did general butchering, Hannah Scott and her daughter, who made all the delicatessen sold in the shop, Alec Goldwater and a succession of shop assistants. Helen Green, who had previously worked both in Fine's and Barney Davis's grocery shops, was a walking encyclopedia of local Jewish affairs and personalities from the tales exchanged and confided over the counter.

Baila Erhlich, a small woman, became an institution. Despite her large ledgers, her apron pockets were always stuffed with scraps of paper and fragments of cornflake boxes, all scribbled reminders of orders taken, deliveries to be made, goods to be purchased, debts outstanding and tasks to be tackled. Her good works were legendary. Characters from within the community, many in poor circumstances, would congregate at the Bunch of Grapes, a pub now demolished, at the corner of Donovan's Lane. After one drink they would cross the road to Baila's shop for a 'square meal', sometimes cooked on the premises, sometimes brought, ready to serve, from her home in Terenure. Augmenting the small stipend paid to her by the Board of Guardians for distribution to alleviate hardship, she dispensed food to the needy, sweets and other treats to the Jewish Home of Ireland, cheques to charitable institutions of all faiths and perishable goods, unlikely to be sold, to selected convents. One poor soul from outside the community, who periodically pushed her baby in a baby carriage all the way from Ballyfermot, was never refused the free meat she came to collect. Her home, an extension of the shop, attracted young and old, stranger and friend, the joyful and the bereaved. It was open to anyone who needed a meal, a chat, an order they couldn't collect from the shop, a donation, a favour or an urgently-needed grocery item.

Nothing in the shop was ever priced. Customers she deemed able to afford it paid top price for everything; the struggling received a discount; the poor often paid nothing. Acerbic of tongue and brusque of manner, Baila could be extremely off-hand to customers. Asked to price an item coming in for Passover, a standard reply was, 'I don't know. If you want it, take it, if not, don't!' A comment about the high price of meat, brought the response, 'Would you rather give it to the doctor?' and one customer who made a mild protest at the lengthy delay for service while gossiping proceeded, was asked, 'Who sent for you?' But she sent chicken soup when that same customer was recovering from an operation.

Baila died in 1997. Rabbi Broder, then Chief Rabbi, described her in a eulogy as 'a queen in the community', and Baila certainly had her large court of admirers. But at heart she was more Robin Hood than queen and a fitting rearguard in the long line of hard-working, ingenious, charitable, humorous, strangely naive, *heimische* (homely) traditional Jews who marked the passage of time in Clanbrassil Street.

2

EARLY YEARS

In 1957, at the start of an American lecture tour, the then Chief Rabbi of Ireland, Rabbi Jakobovits, wrote an article for the New York *Jewish Forum* entitled 'Jews and Irishmen'. It contained a joke about three Jews who met somewhere in Europe to discuss emigration plans. The first said he was going to the United States where he would find comfort and security; the second that he was going to Israel to help build up the land of his forefathers. The third said he was going to Ireland. 'Ireland!' echoed the others. 'Why Ireland?'

'Because,' explained their friend, 'Ireland is the last country where the devil will look to find a Jew!'

Bernard Shillman in *A Short History of the Jews in Ireland* (1945) traces Ireland's first Jewish settlers back to 1232, shortly after the Anglo-Norman invasion. In 1290 Jews were expelled from Great Britain and Ireland. They were not readmitted until 1656 when Oliver Cromwell hoped to use them as a bulwark against rebellious Irish Catholics. According to Shillman, the Dublin Jewish community then formed is 'one of the oldest ... founded in Great Britain since the re-settlement.' James Harrington, in *Commonwealth of Oceana* (1737), even suggested that Ireland should become the national home of the Jews; but the number of Jewish settlers remained small.

In 1881, when Lithuanian Jews were desperately seeking asylum outside Russia, the census listed no more than 394 Jews in the whole of Ireland. Dublin, its capital, was the most important city in the British Isles after London but Lithuanians were largely unaware of it. Most of them had never heard of Ireland. South Africa, Canada and England were more familiar place names, and each had its own appeal as a possible sanctuary. So, too, had Palestine, the biblical Zion, especially after 1897 when Theodor Herzl inspired the first Zionist Congress to replace the dreams and prayers of the past eighteen centuries with a political movement for a

Sarah Aronovitz outside the family grocery shop in Collooney Street, Limerick, in the 1890s.

return to the Jewish national homeland. It was America, however, that became the *goldene medina*, the land of dreams. Reputedly both affluent and tolerant, it eclipsed every other potential haven for those who could travel the distance and afford the fare.

That so many Russian Jews reached Irish shores in the first waves of Russian emigration was often the result of mere chance. The Cohen brothers, with insufficient fare for the journey to America, were sold tickets as far as Ireland without realising the situation until they were forced to disembark at Cork. Siva Solomons' parents, the Millers, were so desperate to leave that they took the first available vessel, irrespective of its destination, while folklore abounds with tales of unscrupulous sea captains who accepted full fare for America and then hoodwinked refugees into going ashore at an Irish port, where they could easily find others seeking passage to America. Tales are also told of refugees who mistook the name Cork for New York and disembarked too soon. Others, better informed, regarded Ireland as a first stage in their journey, planning to move on to America when they could afford it.

Enid Mescon records in *From County Cork to New York with the Jacksons*, that the Zacks, as they were then called, left the boat at Queenstown (Cobh) because, 'it was out of kosher food'. Larry Elyan in *From Zhogger to Cork*, published in the *Jewish Chronicle* of August 1980, recounts that his grandfather, Meyer Elyan, was brought to Ireland to act as reverend to the Cork Jewish Community. Maurice and Fanny Goldwater, documented by their grandson, Maurice Moseley, in his unpublished book, *The Struggle*, were representative of many who went first to England. Disappointed with industrialised Liverpool and Manchester, they travelled on to Ireland, represented to them as, 'a bright, green country, mostly agricultural, where the air was good and clean and where a man could feel free'. It is thought that others arriving in cargo ships at Grimsby, Hull or Liverpool were directed towards Ireland by Jewish philanthropic societies and community leaders in England, who thought that immigrants should build up smaller Jewish communities rather than enlarge established centres. Many joined *landsleit* (friends or relations from the same area) already settled in Ireland, the fortunate few receiving the fare or the ticket in the post.

Whatever the quirks of fate that brought Russian Jews to Ireland, the journey for each one was traumatic. Agents or couriers could be employed to find them a safe route out of the country but their exorbitant fee of up to 200 roubles left most emigrants fending for themselves. Davida Noyek Handler, in her account of the Noyek family from 1798, records some of the hazards and delays that faced them. Reaching the port of embarkation could take several weeks. The poorest walked the whole way through the many border controls and across swollen rivers, carrying their small bundles of possessions on their heads to keep them dry. Others went by train, often for the first time in their lives. Ahead might be many weeks of waiting in barrack-like hotels before they were able to board a ship. The better off hired a bunk each night; the rest slept on the floor, eking out their meagre supply of food.

Even legal emigrants required tickets, exit papers and passports, none of which could be obtained expeditiously, if at all, without bribing officials. Those leaving illegally often had to hide in coal-berths in the hold while guards pierced the wooden planks looking for human cargo, before allowing the ship to sail. Some were confined to the hold for the entire period at sea.

Twenty-year-old Fanny Solomons was already a widow with a young child when she married Maurice Goldwater just before setting out in 1887 on 'the greatest adventure and challenge of their lives'. The hazardous journey overland, the border that had to be crossed in secret, the close watch that had to be kept on their light luggage to avoid loss or theft, all added to the tension of saying goodbye to relatives they might never see again. Both families had depleted their resources in the expenses of departure and the young couple left with very little. Their most precious possessions, Fanny's candlesticks and Maurice's religious books, had more spiritual than material value. More practical assets were the parting gifts of jewellery given to Fanny by her parents and the gold watch and chain given to Maurice by his father, in case they ran short of money. The journey to Liverpool, where Fanny had relatives willing to help them, took three weeks of discomfort that included standing in long lines each day for food.

Davida Noyek Handler, a descendent, claims the Noyek brothers, Abraham and Daniel, spent three years travelling, mostly by foot, through Poland, Germany, Holland and England, a distance of more than 1,500 miles. Speaking only Yiddish and Russian, they met with experiences so unspeakable that they could never recount them, even to their children. 'It was terrible! You don't want to know about it,' was to remain their only comment on the awful journey that lasted from 1894 until 1897.

For Raphael Siev's grandmother, the journey was never completed: she died by the roadside giving birth to his father, Albert. The bereaved husband, Maurice, left the infant with a woman willing to nurse him and continued on his own to Liverpool, where he set up home before sending for them. He married the nurse on her arrival. Albert was still a youth when he left Liverpool to try his luck in Ireland.

The more fortunate were able to leave Russia as a family or even as part of a neighbourhood group; more often the travellers were individuals, siblings or couples, some newly-married or expecting a first child. They all left hoping to send for loved ones as soon as they settled. Often children not yet into their teens left alone, their parents preferring them to have potential safety and happiness abroad rather than certain danger and misery at home, even if it meant the sacrifice of never seeing them again. Most arrived in very poor circumstances; some were penniless.

The Jews who came to Ireland in the late nineteenth and early twentieth centuries were true asylum seekers, fleeing from vicious edicts that deprived them of liberty and livelihood. Some were escaping from organised pogroms. In their mildest form, these recurring riots against Jews resulted in looting; at their worst, they could devastate whole towns and villages, leaving victims homeless, raped, maimed or dead.

A large number of the Irish immigrants were from the *shtetl* or small town of Akmiyan (Akmene), or similar townships in the province of Kovno (Kaunas) in Lithuania to where their ancestors had trekked from the Rhineland before Lithuania passed from Polish to Russian control in 1772. Invited in by Polish princes who wanted to colonise their lands, the Jews had brought the added benefit of trading expertise to areas where such commercialism was closed to serfs and considered too menial for high-born Polish participation.

Tolerated at best under Tsarist rule, more than 90 per cent of the almost 5 million Jews in Russia were obliged to live inside the Pale of Settlement,

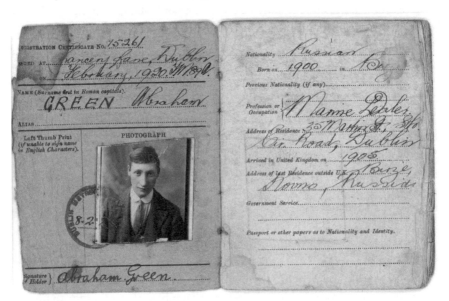

Registration papers issued to Abraham Green from Kovno, Dublin 1920.

designated areas with constantly changing borders. There they earned their living, keeping their own identity and religious customs and speaking Yiddish, a corrupt form of German traditionally spoken by Jews from eastern and western Europe, generically termed *Ashkenazim*. *Sephardi* Jews hail from the Iberian Peninsula, the Mediterranean lands and North Africa. Since one purpose of the Pale was to safeguard Russians from Jewish influence, the Jews' exclusive way of life should have been welcomed; instead their reluctance to assimilate was viewed with suspicion, and even liberals accused them of being 'a State within a State'.

Shtetls were small market towns where Jews predominated. Each one acted as a communal centre for the welfare and cultural life of its own Jews and those of neighbouring villages. From birth to death, no milestone along the pathway of life was regarded as a private matter. *Bris* (circumcision), *Bar Mitzvah* (confirmation), marriage, illness and tragedy, even individual or family conduct were considered communal affairs. The essence of *shtetl* life was family and community spirit, centred around home and synagogue.

The autocratic Tsars regarded all religious minorities as a threat to the established Church and penalised them accordingly. The accession in 1855 of Alexander II, more liberal than his predecessors, augured well but even concessions that included the emancipation of the serfs satisfied few of his subjects. The despotic nobles considered he had gone too far; the revolutionaries felt he was not going far enough. On 13 March 1881, just after he had sanctioned a commission to institute further reforms, Tsar Alexander II was assassinated by anarchists. The deed occurred shortly before the Jewish Festival of *Purim*, a day of celebration and rejoicing for the downfall of Haman, an arch-antagonist who sought the destruction of the Jewish people around 500 BCE. It was an unhappy coincidence. Six weeks after the assassination, the *Jewish Chronicle* reported that Russians charged the Jews with 'making merry in anticipation of the event'.

The Russians had long been jealous of the Jews. Under Alexander II some had become prominent in cultural and professional circles while a minority had grown rich through trading luxury items in great demand by Polish nobility. Some had become landowners. It made no difference that most of the *shtetl* population were living in poverty on a diet of potatoes and seasonal vegetables, as domestic servants, lowly-esteemed craftsmen or, in the words of writer Hannah Berman, as peddlers who, 'bent double under their heavy packs of the cheapest merchandise ... travelled scores of miles in search of customers ... mostly on foot'. The head of the Holy Synod, which governed the Russian Orthodox Church, was not without support when he expressed the wish that one-third of Russian Jews would convert, one-third die and one-third emigrate.

The opportunity to destroy the Jews came with the assassination of Tsar Alexander II. Revolutionaries blamed the Government and the Government found a convenient scapegoat in the Jews.

Hannah Berman was related to the Zlotovers, one of the first Russian families to settle in Ireland. Her account of the family, brought up to date by Dr Melisande Zlotover as *The Zlotover Story* (1966), records how the Zlotover brothers, prosperous before the assassination but made destitute by its aftermath, suddenly became aware of 'rude and aggressive' behavior from peasant neighbours. Driving Jewish-owned cattle from their owners' land and replacing them with peasant herds and other incidents of effrontery became so marked that the brothers eventually sought legal redress in Kovno. What they brought back instead was a copy of the Temporary Laws, passed in May 1882 and known as the May Laws. For the first time the family became aware of the new restrictive practices. No one inside the Pale was permitted to settle 'anew outside of towns and townlets'. They could no longer execute deeds of sale or mortgages or lease real estate, either for themselves or on behalf of others. It was forbidden to trade on Sundays or any Christian festival.

The 'temporary' May Laws were never rescinded by the Tsars. Interpreted ever more harshly, with new strictures constantly invoked until every freedom was eroded, they remained in force until 1917 when the revolutionary Provisional Government repealed them.

The custom of pressing Jewish boys from the age of twelve into military service in isolated military academies, where they were under pressure to convert, had mercifully lapsed, but from 1874 all Jewish males over twenty-one became eligible for conscription, which could last for twenty-five to thirty-five years. Bad experience had taught conscripts the harsh realities of being a Jewish soldier under the Tsars. Families who could afford it paid local Gentiles to take the place of their sons. Some hid their boys with relatives or friends in another village under false names, sometimes taking the identity of youths who had died. Benny Gruisin, interviewed in Alabama in 1977 by Elinor Gruisin and Celia Gruisin Goldberg, recalled that 'many young men would pierce their eardrums or cut off a finger' to evade military service which kept men 'captive, like you were in jail'.

Benny was one of the many thousands of Jews conscripted at the start of the Russo-Japanese War of 1904. As preparations were proceeding for departure to the Manchurian front, a family friend smuggled him out of his barracks in Plutz, Poland. Bribing any guard along the way who recognised Benny as a deserter, they fled first to Vienna, then on to the Baltic Sea, where they hid in a succession of small towns until they were able to board a train for Warsaw. From Warsaw they went to Riga, where a policeman was paid to bring Benny across the Russo-German border. 'We had to take off our shoes and walk for a mile,' he recalls, 'then go across the river in a small skiff with another [deserting] soldier,' but, at last, he was free. He sailed from Hamburg to join a cousin in Dublin.

David Rivlin, who eventually settled with his family in Ireland, watched Jewish recruits disappear one by one from the barracks where he was stationed. He decided to desert before he became the next victim. With no illusions as to the penalty if he was caught, he broke out of the barracks, only to find he had left without his cap. For a soldier to appear in public without full uniform was in itself a serious breach of military discipline and he would be arrested on sight. David had to break back into the barracks to retrieve his cap before breaking out a second time and making his escape. It is not clear whether his future wife, Jane Rapaport, left with him or met him *en route*, but they were married in Paris before they left for England.

At one time the pursuit of higher education had been accepted as grounds for exemption from military service and Jewish boys had flocked to educational institutions to escape conscription. With that loop-hole closed since 1874, the Government still decided in 1886 to admit only 10 per cent of Jews living within the Pale and fewer still from outside it, to high schools and universities, effectively excluding most Jews from the professions. Even a move to another village was restricted. With no right of redress against draconian laws or unprovoked attacks on Jewish property, with harassment and extortion by local police a regular occurrence, with the threat of expulsions and increasingly violent pogroms growing ever more frequent, life had become unbearable for Russian Jews. Even before their expulsion from Moscow in 1891, many knew it was time to leave. Between 1881 and 1914, 2 million fled the country.

Hannah Berman describes the arrival in Dublin of 'the first little batch of Lithuanians' who were 'taken in charge by the police and housed amongst other foreigners, in the same little square, Chancery Lane, where stood the police-station'. There they shared tenement-like accommodation with 'Italian organ-grinders, bear leaders and one-man band operators and makers of small casts of saints of the Catholic Church, to which they belonged.'

To the small local Jewish community, well-settled and influential beyond its size, the poverty-stricken immigrants, with their out-moded attire, Orthodox customs, Yiddish language and unfamiliarity with Irish life, were an embarrassment. 'Greeners', they called them. It was Meyer Elyan's contention that Akmiyan was 'notorious as a nest of horse-thieves and smugglers'. If so, the Akmiyani cunning can only have enhanced the other characteristics of the Lithuanian immigrants, described by Hannah Berman as 'of good stock, healthy in mind and body', whose adaptation to their new surroundings 'was a proof of their energy, their common sense and their intelligence'. The success stories that developed from the humble peddling activities initially adopted by most of the immigrants to earn a living seem to bear out this assessment.

Among the wider community the reaction to the influx of bearded, strangely garbed and impecunious foreigners ranged from tolerance through indifference to malevolence. Many met with extraordinary kindness and respect. Abe Benson remembered into his ninetieth year how his mother arrived in Dublin at the North Wall with a family of small children to join her husband, who was unable to meet her. Speaking only Yiddish, she presented a piece of paper bearing her husband's address in Clanbrassil Street to the first stranger she saw. Realising that the distance was too far for the children to walk and the impossibility of directing her by public transport without a common tongue, he generously hailed a cab, paid for the journey and sent the little group on its way.

Alexander Black from Poland experienced similar kindness in Northern Ireland. Shortly after his arrival in Manchester with his parents, he was sent to Bangor, Co. Down, to join relatives in business. Arriving by steamer at Donegall Quay in Belfast, he tried to find the railway station. Unable to ask directions, he wandered into Waring Street, close to the docks, and thought he had found it when he came to an imposing building with uniformed officials in peaked caps. It was actually a branch of the Ulster Bank, attended by bank messengers. The one he approached looked at the Bangor address written on a piece of paper. Taking Alexander by the arm, he guided him along the 'somewhat circuitous route' to the nearest bridge across the River Lagan and on to the station, where he seated him safely on the Bangor train. The story, retold in the Ulster Bank's company magazine for Christmas 1991, had a happy ending. Young Mr Black prospered in business but never forgot the kindness of the Ulster Bank messenger. When he needed a bank account, he opened it in the Ulster Bank in Waring Street and became one of its best customers.

The authorities too showed understanding and consideration. From 1897, when Tara Street baths opened in Dublin, until 1916, when the community built its own facility in Adelaide Road Synagogue, a section of the Baths was set aside for the sole use of the Jewish community as a *mikvah* (ritual baths). The approximately eighty women a month who used it were noted by Dublin Corporation to be 'exceptionally clean', resulting they believed in a healthier lifestyle and a comparatively low rate of child mortality. When a water shortage closed the Baths for six weeks in 1914, the *mikvah* was the only section kept open. For those who could not afford the 2s admission charge, Jewish charitable organisations issued tokens which the Baths redeemed for cash.

Revd Meyer Elyan, finding himself for the first time in his life, 'surrounded by *Goyim*' (Gentiles), spoke glowingly of the many acts of kindness he and his family received in Cork from their Catholic neighbours. 'To be able to go about unafraid was … a new-found pleasure,' he told his grandson, Larry Elyan, and he marvelled that 'they raised their hats to me, a foreigner, a *Yid*' (Jew).

Others were less tolerant. In 1997, during an interview with Rathnait Long for a school project entitled *A Question of Survival: The Jewish Community in Cork*, Des O'Driscoll, the librarian for Cork Examiner Publications, admitted, 'I know that my grandfather and uncles, who were all decent men in every other way, were fairly anti-Semitic.' Though certainly not representative of all Irishmen, their attitude would not have been unique. 'The Jews killed Christ!' was a lesson mastered by every child over generations of Catholic teaching;

now that the 'Christ-killers' were among them, the seeds of prejudice were bound to flourish.

Jews took few jobs from the native Irish. Employees who mostly refused to work after sunset on Fridays, irrespective of the hour, and would not work at all on Saturdays or designated Holy days, had little appeal in a society that often demanded long hours and a seven-day working week. Yet many regarded the Jews as a threat to the Irish economy. Every pair of shoelaces, every blanket, every holy picture bought from a Jewish shop or peddler could otherwise have been supplied from an Irish outlet; every suit of clothes, every suite of furniture, skillfully made by Jewish hands in back rooms or shabby workshops, deprived an Irishman of profit. Their involvement in money lending impinged on the trade of the non-Jewish financier, 'altogether a less agreeable chap', according to Eunan O'Halpin, Professor of Government and Society at Dublin City University, who compared the two in Louis Lentin's television documentary, *No More Blooms*. Oral testimony collected by Kevin C. Kearns in *Dublin Tenement Life: An Oral History* (1994) also suggests that Catholic moneylenders were less desirable to deal with than their Jewish counterparts. One mother of twenty children commented:

> The Jewmen, we couldn't do without them ... Oh, they'd fleece you. But they were a necessity of life ... The (Christian) moneylenders, they were the worst – and they were your own neighbours! Some of them, if you didn't pay them, you'd be met on the street and get a hammering off them.

Mickey Guy, in his seventies, recalled:

> Everyone had a loan off a Jewman ... on the QT [quiet] ... There was another woman in the tenement houses named Kelly and she was a moneylender and she'd be sitting in the pub drinking from ten in the morning till ten at night and the poor people'd be looking for money.

Incidents of early anti-Semitism are documented by Louis Hyman in *The Jews of Ireland: From earliest Times to the Year 1910* (1972) and by Dermot Keogh, Professor of History at University College, Cork, in *Jews in Twentieth Century Ireland* (1998). Placards in 1886 urging the public 'to have no truck with the foreign Jews of recent arrival' were bolstered by 'rancorous' letters in the *Telegraph* and the *Freeman's Journal* declaiming against the Jewish presence and their involvement in Irish society. The *Freeman's Journal* described the writers as 'hare-brained fanatics' or 'a set of ruffians' and the Jews as 'hardworking and inoffensive' while the *Evening Telegraph* reminded its readers that 'Ireland stands alone among nations in freedom from the odium of having ... persecuted the Jews'. Neither expression of support prevented attacks on individual Jews going about their lawful business. In July 1887, at the opening of Limerick Assizes by Mr Justice O'Brien, an application was made to exempt Jews from jury service 'owing to ill-will of which they are the victims'. The following 16 December the *Jewish Chronicle* reported a police prosecution against Thomas Punch who struck a Jew called King on the mouth with a heavy stick, 'causing blood to flow', as King was walking along Charlotte Quay in Limerick. Mr King's solicitor said the unfortunate Jews of Limerick were again 'being made the subject of attack' and asked the court for a sentence that would 'teach [Punch] to leave the Jews alone'.

On 28 October 1892, the *Jewish Chronicle* drew attention to the remarks of Frederick Falkiner, Recorder for Belfast City. Trying a case where a Jew refused to pay for a baby carriage, he declared, 'These fellows will swear anything.' Jewish citizens met in Dublin at St Kevin's Parade to pass a resolution of protest, supported by Belfast newspapers and, again, the *Freeman's Journal*. Challenged in open court, Falkiner admitted he had never known any Jewish men 'implicated at the criminal side of the court'. John Redmond, chairman of the Irish Parliamentary Party, wrote to a Jewish fellow-member of Parliament, Samuel Montague, in 1894, deploring 'any insult or annoyance' offered to the Jewish community after attacks in Cork that resulted in three years' imprisonment for the perpetrators.

The Aliens Act (1905) attempted to curb the immigration of Jews and other aliens into Britain. Medical inspections were instituted at ports and entry was refused to those who could not show sufficient means of support for themselves and any dependents. Isaac Black, who later brought his brother Alexander into Ireland, was refused entry when his ship docked in England in 1905. Unable to produce the statutory £5, he was sent back to Hamburg, his port of embarkation. Determined not to retrace the whole journey to his native Poland, he sought help locally. A philanthropic society in Hamburg gave him the £5 he needed and paid his fare back to England. Isaac Black, who was to establish a prosperous house-furnishing firm in Belfast in the 1930s, was escaping abject poverty. Had he been escaping religious persecution he would have been exempted from the payment, a humanitarian concession that doubtless saved Jewish lives. In one week alone in 1905, Dublin's *Evening Mail* carried horrendous accounts of Russian atrocities from Reuters correspondents abroad. A telegram of 8 November from Paris quoted a letter from Kiev detailing the massacre of 25,000 Jews, 1,000 of them women and children who were 'outraged and strangled'. On 9 November a telegram from Odessa reported seventy people killed and 120 injured after policemen in disguise spread rumors that the Jews had made an attempt on the life of the Bishop of Odessa. From St Petersburg came news on the eleventh of 'anti-Semitic rioting' that destroyed 300 Jewish shops and 130 homes; more than 200 Jews were killed or injured. On 13 November it was reported that 800 Jews were waiting to cross into Romania after vicious attacks in Bessarabia where Jews had been tortured and then drowned in large cages specially built on shore and trundled into the sea, laden with victims.

Sydney Curland moved from England to Ireland in 1921. He was still in Russia in 1912 when his father and brother absconded instead of reporting for military service. Seven-year-old Sydney was taken into the Russian army in reprisal, 'to learn how to use a gun and to groom horses'. His mother and nine-year-old sister were exiled to Siberia.

By comparison, the worst Irish outrage, the Limerick 'pogrom' of 1904, was mild indeed. A Catholic priest, Father John Creagh, declaiming from the pulpit against Jewish methods of trading, exhorted his congregation 'not to prove false to Ireland, false to your country and false to your religion, by continuing to deal with the Jews'. Joe Briscoe, son of Robert Briscoe, the prominent Jewish politician, describes the Limerick episode as 'an aberration in an otherwise almost perfect history of Ireland and its treatment of the Jews'. He believes the Limerick occurrence is too often 'blown up totally out of context' and that the attitude of Father Creagh, trained with the Redemptorists in France, reflected less of Irish opinion than of French clerical prejudice. French Redemptorists had been anti-Semitic since the 1870s when they blamed the insignificant number of French Jews for France's growing secularisation.

The family of Gerald Goldberg, a former mayor and leader of the Jewish community in Cork, lived in Limerick at the time of Father Creagh's campaign. In a letter to *The Irish Times* of 13 August 1984 he recounted how his father's house 'was attacked, its windows broken, its front door battered and the family driven into refuge in an upper room'. His father and a cousin, David Weinrouck, were viciously attacked on their way home from synagogue. When his father, gashed across the temple from ear to ear, asked a jarvey to assist his cousin whose leg had been broken, the jarvey also slashed him across the face. He also recalled that, 'David Weinrouck's wife was caught by the hair, swung around and dashed to the ground, while walking in the streets'. Raphael Siev, whose parents had a little shop in Collooney Street, Limerick, never forgot the hardships they suffered, together with other Jewish shopkeepers, as people followed Father Creagh's advice. Not only did Catholics start to shop exclusively in Gentile premises, they also refused to pay Jewish traders for any goods previously bought on credit, and to repay loans. With no money coming in, the family survived by eating the stock from the shop. Rapheal spoke of the boycott as 'robbery with even the basic costs never paid'. The Board of Deputies of British Jews attributed at least one death to the episode, not from physical assault but from 'stress and strain'.

The events decimated the tiny community. Of the thirty-two Jewish families then living in Limerick, several left because of the incident and, in the words of Fanny Goldberg, Gerald's sister, 'Everybody had been ruined'.

Michael Davitt, founder of the Irish National Land League and the first to apply the tactics of boycott to political circumstances, wrote *Within the Pale: The True Story of Anti-Semitic Persecution in Russia* (1903). Better informed than most contemporaries, he still tried to distinguish between anti-Semitic prejudice that was unjustified on purely religious grounds and that which was justified on economic grounds. After the Limerick episode, he came to realise the two are indistinguishable.

Anti-Semitism in Ireland was never universal and rarely physical, but it was State promulgated during the period of Nazi persecution in Europe and expounded by many prominent Irish people. It frequently went unchallenged. Manus O'Riordan, head of research at the Services, Industrial, Professional and Technical Union (SIPTU) and historian of Irish Jewry, was born and raised in Little Jerusalem. In 'Anti-Semitism in Irish Politics', published in the *Irish-Jewish Year Book*, 1984-5, he quotes numerous examples that span decades.

Arthur Griffith, reckoned by Gerald Goldberg to have been 'the most virulent anti-Semite in Ireland', was the founder of Sinn Féin and the newspaper, *United Irishman*, in which he published many anti-Jewish articles. On 23 January 1904 he wrote of the 'notoriously dishonest business methods of three-fourths of the Jews of Ireland'. An article of 23 April asserted that, 'the Jews of Great Britain and Ireland have united ... to crush the Christian who dares to ... point them out for what they are – nine-tenths of them – usurers and parasites ... and a grinder of the poor ... in every respect an economic evil'. Virginia Glandon in *Arthur Griffith and the Advanced Nationalist Press 1900-1922*, excuses Griffith's virulence as stemming from the suspicion and fear of foreigners which she regards as 'an inevitable aspect of the narrow creed of nationalism itself'. Griffith's biographer, Brian Maye, also seeking to mitigate his prejudice, concedes that Griffith had a 'wildly exaggerated notion of the extent of Jewish involvement in money-lending and devious business practice', but regards him as not generally antipathetic. He claims that Griffith admired the 'honest and patriotic Jews' seeking to establish a Jewish homeland, wrote nothing anti-Semitic after 1904 and numbered Jews among his friends. In 1910, Griffith's daughter, Ita, was a flower-girl at the wedding of Michael Noyk, a Jewish Irish patriot. She played with Noyk's children at the Griffith home, bought for him on his marriage by friends who included the Jewish gynaecologist, Bethel Solomons.

One of Griffith's acolytes was Oliver St John Gogarty, senator and man of letters, who declaimed to cheers at Sinn Féin's founding conference in 1905, 'We are the victims and tools of the most disgraceful and Jew-ridden Government in the world.' He told a similar audience in 1906, 'I can smell a Jew and in Ireland there's something rotten.'

The journalist, J.J. O'Kelly, generally known by his pen-name, *Sceilg*, founded the *Catholic Bulletin* in 1911. Chairman of Dáil Éireann (the Irish Parliament) during the War of Independence and a one-time Minister for Education, he warned the Sinn Féin *ardfheis* (general congress) more than once against imagined Jewish plots. In 1930, he accused 'Jewish masters' of 'once more' menacing world peace. Eoin O'Duffy, succinctly referred to as 'O'Duffy (fascist)' in the index to Richard M. Kain's book, *Dublin in the Age of William Butler Yeats and James Joyce*

(1972), was a former commissioner of the *Garda Síochána* (the Irish police force) when he formed the Blueshirt movement in emulation of Hitler's Brownshirts and Mussolini's Blackshirts and established the Irish Brigade that supported Franco in the Spanish Civil War. Writing in *Hibernia* in 1938, he declared that he organised his Irish Brigade to fight against 'Communism, Jewry and Freemasonry'. His extreme ideas found no lasting appeal, but no one questioned his prejudice against Jews. Maurice Manning, in his account of the Blueshirts, even denies that the movement was anti-Semitic.

O'Riordan concluded, 'It was the small size of the Jewish community which militated against the development of a mass anti-Semitic movement rather than any innate virtues of Irish society, during the 1930s and '40s.' Official policy would appear to support that view. As early as 1933, Leo McAuley of the Irish legation in Berlin reported:

> The legation has seen a marked increase in enquiries and applications, mostly from Jews of Polish or East European nationality. As far as possible, it has discouraged such people from going to Ireland as they are really only refugees. It assumes that this line of action would be in accordance with Government policy.

It was. In 1936, the Department of Justice stated, 'There have been for years numerous protests concerning the number of alien Jews who became established in this country and the Minister (for External Affairs) will not look with favour on any policy which might lead to an increase in that number.' In 1938, when the *Anschluss*, Germany's triumphant entry into Austria, rendered 120,000 Austrian Jews stateless, the Irish Government made entry into Ireland for holders of German or Austrian passports dependent on a valid visa – available only to applicants 'not of Jewish or partly Jewish origin' and 'without non-Aryan affiliations'. In 1946, when a London Jewish Society bought a refuge at Clonyn Castle in Delvin, Co. Westmeath, to house 100 Jewish war orphans aged from seven to sixteen, Gerry Boland TD (member of Dáil Éireann) and Minister for Justice, refused to admit them on the grounds that, 'it has always been the policy of the Minister for Justice to restrict the admission of Jewish aliens for the reason that any substantial increase in our Jewish population might give rise to an anti-Semitic problem.'

Raphael Siev was staying at Jury's Hotel in Cork in the 1980s when the porter took him to meet Martin Gotha, a practising Catholic in his eighties, who wanted to talk to a Jew. He told Raphael he was Jewish-born. Arrested by the Gestapo in 1938, he and other Jews at Dachau concentration camp, where prisoners were routinely beaten to death, were offered release and entry to Ireland if they would convert to Catholicism. Most agreed. In Ireland he was met by Christians who cared for him until he could speak English and take a job. He ended his story by declaring, 'I will die a Roman Catholic. They gave me my life.' His release papers from Dauchau and certificate of medical fitness to travel are now in the Irish Jewish Museum, Dublin.

Much of the responsibility for Ireland's negative response to Jewish immigration can be attributed to Charles Bewley, Ireland's representative in Berlin from 1933 until 1939. Watching the situation as it developed in Germany, he must have been fully aware of the consequences of inaction, yet he described the Nuremberg Laws which deprived Jews in Germany of every civil liberty and human right, as 'certain inconveniences', and deliberately delayed visa applications passing through his office. He described Jews as 'the chief supporters of communism', accused them of practising 'usury and fraud' in their commercial activities and claimed that they either caused or exploited Germany's 'appalling degradation before 1933'. They created 'grave moral scandals' in whatever country they entered and were 'a form of corruption'. It was 'beyond any degree of reason that they could be treated like ordinary citizens'.

Robert Briscoe in his autobiography, *For the Life of Me* (1959), written in association with Alden Hatch, attributed his first encounter with 'real anti-Semitism' to Charles Bewley. Bewley was Ireland's newly appointed trade commissioner in Berlin when Briscoe visited there in 1922 with his friend and political associate, Charley McGuinness. The three frequently met for coffee at a Jewish establishment, until the proprietor disclosed the racist insults levelled at him by Bewley the previous night. Outraged, the two friends went round to Bewley's office and vandalised it in his absence. They were still engaged in the process when he returned. Briscoe recalled that Bewley's face 'turned a lovely lavender shade' and that he conceded, 'quivering', to their demand that he go with them to the café and make a 'humble and abject apology'.

The attitude of Éamon de Valera, leader of the Irish Government from 1932 until 1948 and later President of Ireland, was less clear-cut. Louis Wigoder recalled hearing that de Valera emphasised the importance of the Old Testament while teaching at Blackrock College, and praised the Jews for their contribution to civilisation. The Constitution of Ireland (1937), drafted under De Valera's direction at a time when European Jewry was under dire threat, guarantees 'the free profession and practice of religion' to every Irish citizen. Both Robert Briscoe and Chief Rabbi Herzog considered him sympathetic towards Jews as well as a personal friend. In 1950, when de Valera was planning a trip to Israel with his sons, he told Briscoe, 'You know how interested I am in your people,' and urged him to accompany them, which he did. Joe Briscoe recalls that his father's last words were spoken to de Valera, who was known to his supporters as 'the Chief'. Asked to be kept informed of Briscoe's deteriorating condition, de Valera arrived at his bedside when the dying man had been in a coma and unresponsive to his wife, children and doctor for some hours. Briscoe opened his eyes in response to de Valera's voice. When de Valera asked, 'Do you know who this is?' he replied, 'The Chief,' before relapsing into a final coma.

De Valera's warmth and solicitude towards his Jewish friends as a private individual were in marked contrast to the determined wartime exclusion of Jewish refugees practised by the Irish Government while he was Head of State. It took a personal visit from Rabbi Herzog, then Chief Rabbi of Palestine, to persuade Gerry Boland to let the Clonyn Castle children enter Ireland and even then their stay was limited to a year. De Valera must also bear responsibility as both *Taoiseach* (Prime Minister) and Minister for External Affairs for maintaining Charles Bewley in his post during the critical pre-war Nazi era – a personnel decision considered by Dermot Keogh to be 'one of the worst ... made since the foundation of the State'. At the Evian Conference in July 1938, held to seek a solution to the Jewish refugee problem, Ireland's overcrowded professions and the need for Irish citizens to emigrate for employment were cited as reasons for refusing asylum. In October that year, a direct plea to de Valera from Chief Rabbi Herzog to admit six or seven refugee doctors and dentists – in strict proportion, population-wise, to the number admitted by Britain – fell on deaf ears. Gerald Goldberg, interviewed in 1982 by Maev-Ann Wren for *The Irish Times* after the broadcast of Peter Feeney's television documentary, *A Jew, an Irishman and a Corkman*, recalled that Robert Briscoe also appealed directly to de Valera on behalf of a refugee committee established by Gerald in 1939. De Valera promised his support but changed his mind within a week, without explanation. Not a single refugee was allowed into Cork and Briscoe was refused even a temporary visa for his own aunt, consigning yet another victim to a concentration camp and ultimate death. With the full horror of the extermination camps by then fully revealed, historians are still trying to account for the condolences expressed by de Valera on behalf of the Irish people when Hitler committed suicide.

Ireland was only one of many countries with an apathetic approach to saving Jewish lives but most accepted a quota of Jews on humanitarian grounds. Work in progress by a Dublin expatriate, Michael Brennan, records that Northern Ireland, under British control, had two associations dealing with the refugee situation, the Christian multi-denominational Belfast Committee of German Refugees and the Jewish Refugee Aid Committee, which established a Belfast home in Clifton Park Avenue. Owned by the Black family and run by Sam Korentyre, the house offered shelter to those sent on to Ireland when the *Kindertransport* brought 10,000 unaccompanied children, mostly from Germany and Austria, to Britain via Holland in 1939. About twenty more were placed with Jewish families. Adult refugees, denied work permits to practise their own professions, were employed freely in the north as maids, cooks and chauffeurs. From 1939 until 1946, more than 100 refugee children and adults were accommodated on a farm at Millisle, Co. Down, organised by the *Bachad* Fellowship, a Zionist group that prepared young people for pioneer work in Palestine.

Edith Kohner, a refugee from Czechoslovakia who lived there for a time, recalled the Refugee Settlement Farm in an article, 'Jews in the North', printed in the spring 1998 edition of *Causeway*. In 1939, Alec Berwitz, Maurice Solomon and Leo Scop were detailed to find a farm on behalf of the Jewish Aid Refugee Committee, but it was the president of the Belfast Hebrew Congregation, Barney Hurwitz, a native of Lithuania, who negotiated the lease 'over a pint of Guinness' on the '70 acres of arable land that had not seen a plough for years'. Financial and volunteer support from Jews north and south of the border and technical advice from officials of the Northern Ireland Ministry of Agriculture, transformed the land. The 'disused farm with nothing working ... a closed-up and musty house and a barn full of dung' became a working farm that won a Government prize for producing more wheat per acre than any other farm in Northern Ireland at that time. In addition to providing 'safety, education and training in agriculture', it offered a Jewish way of life for those refugees fortunate to reach it. Maurice Jaswon, a Dubliner who worked on the farm in student holidays, remembers attending a wedding and a *Bar Mitzvah* there.

A small group of refugee youngsters who arrived in Dublin from England were sent north to ensure their safety, and in 1946 Millisle acted as a six-month convalescent home for sixty young survivors of concentration camps, flown in from Prague to Sydenham Airport.

The Republic's stringent exclusion policy has since been officially recognised and regretted many times. Michael McDowell TD, Minister for Justice, apologised again at Ireland's first official Holocaust commemoration, held at Dublin Castle on 26 January 2003. What he described as a betrayal of the Constitution may also have damaged Ireland economically. Many of the Jewish refugees refused entry had exactly the kind of commercial and manufacturing experience that could have helped promote Irish industry. In 1936 the Council of German Jewry in England proposed that refugee businessmen be allowed to open small factories in Ireland, which would boost the economy and give badly needed local employment. The suggestion was rejected.

Marcus Witztum, a Polish Jew already living in Ireland, had a little more success. With the support of Fianna Fáil senator, John McEllin, he persuaded the Government to agree to the establishment of a hat factory in Galway, to be managed mostly by Czechoslovakian Jews. Opened in 1938 by Seán Lamass, TD, Minister for Industry and Commerce, and blessed by the Bishop of Galway, it employed more than 100 local people. Two years later Western Hats in Castlebar was built. A report in the *Connaught Telegraph* of 5 November 1997 claimed that it 'helped keep a fire in the hearth and food on the table in a time of grim austerity [by providing] valuable employment for over 200 lucky people [who] did not have to take the packet ship in search of employment'. Emile Hirsch bribed the German Government to transfer almost his entire ribbon factory from Vienna to a site in Co. Longford, where refugees worked alongside local workers to the advantage of both. Detractors such as Peter Kelly, a Fine Gael candidate who saw these mutually beneficial arrangements only as '£1,000 a year jobs going to Jews and foreigners who have been imported into this country', supported the Government's refusal to replicate the schemes elsewhere, underlining Marcus Witztum's contention that 'there is no such thing as a Jewish problem. It is a Christian problem!'

But even in Ireland there were Christians who felt differently. Sabina Shorts, *née* Wizniak, who told her story in Mary Rose Doorly's *Hidden Memories* (1994), was grateful to more than one of them. In 1936 she was sixteen and her sister only ten when fear of Nazis persecution drove their mother to abandon their luxurious home in Berlin for the comparative safety of the squalid, overcrowded Warsaw Ghetto. Under German occupation by 1939, their illusory refuge became 'a place of absolute terror'. It is believed her mother was murdered there. Her sister died later in a concentration camp.

Sabina's father had already left Germany and somehow 'managed to get himself to Ireland'. It was he who devised the pretext of a non-existent aunt in Ireland who could not die happy without seeing her favourite niece and in 1940 Sabina was granted a four-week visa to visit the 'dying woman'. Exactly four weeks later a deportation officer from the Department for External Affairs called to tell her she must leave. He would meet her at the railway station and escort her onto a Belfast train. They did meet, but the official, sympathetic to her plight, suggested she board the train, get off at the first station and return to Dublin. Then he advised her not to board at all: he would 'let on' he had seen her depart.

Now an illegal alien, she rented a room in the South Circular Road, where she lived happily with the Stapleton family until she discovered that her landlord was a policeman. 'Do you not like the room any more? Are you not happy here?' he asked when she told him she was moving elsewhere. 'I love it here,' she said. He winked. 'You can only leave if you don't like it here,' he told her, and Sabina realised he had known of her illegal status since she arrived.

Years later when she applied for full immigrant status, she was granted a residence permit on condition she did not continue to work. An official from the Aliens Office present at the hearing whispered to her, 'Don't change anything. Just carry on the way you are,' and she kept her job. The entire department, she realised, had known of her situation without doing anything about it. In *Dublin's Little Jerusalem* (2002), Nick Harris claims that Sabina was permitted to stay in Dublin because he pretended to the Hungarian Embassy, at her father's request, that she was his fiancée. Sabina was seemingly unaware of this ploy and never met Nick Harris. Whatever the subterfuge employed, official Irish involvement remained the same. By turning a blind eye the authorities saved Sabina's life.

The savior of many Jewish lives was Dr Robert Collis, an Irish physician who led a team of nurses into Belsen concentration camp as soon as it was liberated. His future second wife, Dr Han Hogerzeil, already involved in rescue work in Holland, assisted him and recalls in *Hidden Memories* the jubilation, four weeks after their involvement, when the daily death rate at Belsen fell from 800 to 300.

Dr Collis took responsibility for trying to keep alive the 500 surviving children, many desperately ill. One five-year-old whose Jewish father and Catholic mother had both perished, held his hand and told him, 'My father is dead. Now the doctor is my father,' so Dr Collis brought him and his sister back to Ireland, where he reared them with his own family. He also brought back three other orphans whose families could not be traced. Seven-year-old Terry Molnar and his two-year-old sister, Suzi, remained in Ireland as the adopted children of Willie and Elsie Samuels. Evelin Schwartz's adoptive family emmigrated with her to Australia.

Gerald Goldberg in Cork, fearing a Nazi invasion and subsequent arrest, arranged for a Christian family to care for his son if the need arose and return him to Jewish hands when the war was over. His nephew, David Marcus, a Cork schoolboy in 1940, recounts in *Oughterbiography* (2001) how his own fears of a German invasion kept him awake at night listening for the rattle of machine guns and the tramp of Nazi boots. After the Blitzkrieg he 'searched on the way to school in Mardyke's elms for Nazi paratroopers'. Both were spared the reality and by comparison with Jewish communities in occupied countries, Irish Jewry had a benign war.

Cushioned by neutrality and censorship from even the knowledge of Nazi excesses, Jewish children included Hitler in their play. Gloria Frankel, who settled in Manchester, remembered a skipping game in which two girls held a rope while two more skipped in and out to the chorus of:

> Vote, vote, vote for de Valera ('de Valera' runs in)
> In comes Hitler at the door-ay-oh ('Hitler' runs in)
> Hitler is the one that will have a bit of fun (both skip)
> And we don't want de Valera any more. ('de Valera' runs out)

But there were still casualties. Maurice Jacobson, born in Dublin in 1895, died when the Germans made a third ferocious air attack on Belfast in May 1941, bringing the overall toll of dead and injured into the thousands. He had left the comparative safety of an under-stairs cupboard to check for fire damage upstairs when the explosion hit his home in Eglington Street, trapping his wife, still in the under-stairs cupboard, and his two little girls crouching below a solid oak table. His legs took the weight of the debris and Fay, the younger of the daughters, clearly recalls that air-raid wardens had almost to demolish the house to release him. Both legs were amputated in a vain attempt to save his life. Many Jewish families evacuated for a time to safer towns such as Bangor, Lurgan, Newcastle, Donaghadee and Portadown. Some left the province altogether.

Less vicious but totally indefensible was the bombing of neutral Ireland by assailants identified as German from an unexploded incendiary bomb picked up near the Curragh, Co. Kildare. Drogheda, Co. Louth, and Enniskerry, Co. Wicklow, suffered no casualties but bombs dropped in Co. Carlow killed three people. Thirty died in the North Strand area of Dublin where Lena Curland's brother-in-law was on duty as an Air Raid Precautions (ARP) volunteer. He told her the first thing he saw was a headless body in the gutter.

The bombs that fell on the south side of the city, damaging Greenville Hall Synagogue and homes in Donore Terrace on the South Circular Road and Rathdown Park, Fortfield Road and Lavarna Grove in the suburb of Terenure, were described in *The Irish Times* of 3 January 1941 as 'heavy calibre'. Abe Benson, chief ARP warden for the district, lived at 23 Rathdown Park. His wife, Sylvia Benson, in *Down Memory Lane* (1977), recalls how, shortly before the attack, she was professionally advised against making an inventory of the contents of their house, as there was no danger of a raid. 'This is Ireland, not England', she was told complacently. Their other potential safeguard, a 'beehive shelter' in the back garden, served them no better. When the Terenure raid occurred without warning at 6 a.m, the shelter was buried in more than twenty feet of rubble before they could reach it. The Bensons' toddler, Leonora, aged two, was asleep in her cot when the bombs fell, bringing down part of her bedroom ceiling. Rescued by the maid, she asked, 'Mummy, has Santa Claus come down the chimney?'

Coincidentally, the most badly damaged houses in both Rathdown Park, which took a direct hit, and Lavarna Grove, were numbers 25 and 27. One of them belonged to the Plant family who had just moved in after selling 93 South Circular Road to Revd Roith. 'I bet Mr Plant's very upset he sold the house to us,' said the Roiths when they heard the news but at 2 a.m. next morning in a successive raid, their home, too, together with number 91, where the Leventhals lived, dissolved into piles of rubble. Thirteen-year-old Abraham Roith was one of several flung from their beds on to the floor and 'half-buried in wreckage' while Mrs Leventhal and her son, both injured, were so covered in debris they had to be dug out. A fire officer commented on 'the coolness and courage of the people who were trapped in the wreckage'. The Jewish community, in turn, praised the auxiliary services and donated a Chrysler ambulance to the Irish Red Cross Society in gratitude for rescue work. Its plaque was returned forty-eight years later for display at the Irish Jewish Museum. The bomb blast shattered hundreds of windows and the ceiling of Greenville Hall Synagogue collapsed to the floor.

Despite 'energetic protest' from Ireland's Chargé d'Affaires in Berlin, there is no evidence that the reparations demanded from Germany were ever paid in full. Restitution was made for the North Strand damage but the Department of Finance reimbursed Dublin Corporation for repairs to Greenville Hall Synagogue and houses on the south side.

The main cost of the war to Irish Jewry was the loss of extended if not immediate family through persecution and the death camps. Joe Briscoe lost 156 relatives. Zlate Werzberger, a concentration camp survivor, was featured in Irish newspapers when she arrived in Dublin after her release in 1945. She and her

Plaque on the Chrysler ambulance presented to the Irish Red Cross Society in grateful thanks for rescue work after German air raids on Dublin 1941.

mother had remained in Romania when her father fled to Ireland to save his life long before the outbreak of the Second World War. Now living in Canada, she will never forget watching her 'beloved mother being sent by the infamous Dr Mengele to the crematorium' at Auschwitz in 1944, nor the deaths of other beloved members of her family, still 'a loss beyond words'.

Elsa Hoefler, travelling on a Czechoslovakian passport in 1938, was granted permission to remain in Britain for forty-eight hours. She travelled on to Ireland to join her husband who was seeking refuge in Limerick and was there just four weeks before the isolation, loss and trauma became too much for her to bear. She shot herself in a room at the Crescent Hotel. Her grave in the Jewish cemetery remained unmarked until the Limerick Civic Trust erected a tombstone in 2001.

The only Irish-born victim of the Holocaust was Ettie Steinberg who married a Belgian in a Dublin synagogue in 1937. Forced by the Nazi advance to flee their home in Belgium, they sought refuge in France, moving from place to place for greater security with their little son, Leon, born in Paris. They were arrested in 1942 at a hotel in Toulouse and eventually sent to Auschwitz on a transport that took them straight to the gas chambers. A letter from the Steinbergs enclosing hard-won visas for entry to Northern Ireland arrived one day after their arrest. A plaque in memory of Ettie and Leon was erected in the Irish Jewish Museum in 2002.

A victim of a different kind was Mina Simons. Born in Germany, she and her family had been brought to Ireland in 1924 by Harris Baigel who had married Mina's sister. Mina was unhappy in Ireland and went to see the German ambassador, Georg von Dehn, about returning to Germany. He advised against it and offered her a job as secretary to the legation. She was still employed there in September 1933 when the ambassador sent for her. With tears in his eyes, he said the Nuremberg Laws obliged him to dismiss her. A year later he committed suicide. Her reference, signed by the ambassador, testifies to her 'highest sense of duty and a never-lacking attention to her work'. Rating her honesty as 'indisputable', it goes on to state, 'Mrs Simons leaves her position, as, for the employment in clerical positions, new regulations have been drawn up.'

Geoffrey Goldberg's mother was on her way to England in 1941 to marry his father when German planes strafed the boat. A bullet lodged in her leg and she had to walk down the aisle on crutches. Travel restrictions prevented Irish members of the family from attending the wedding.

Jews who were not refugees were never excluded from Ireland. Over the years some immigrated to marry into local families, some to join resident family members, some for specific employment. Others came in search of a better way of life. David Stein, who changed his name to Sam Brown on arrival in 1914, was typical of a small number of 'flyboys' who came to evade British conscription at the start of both world wars. By 1946, the Jewish population in Ireland had peaked at more than 5,000.

Even when standards of Orthodoxy began to relax, Irish employers were unenthusiastic about employing Jews. Siva Miller, later Solomons, after leaving school in the 1930s, took a course at the Technical College in Rathmines, Dublin, in shorthand, typing and bookkeeping. She never forgot her first interview at

Servicemen and women newly returned to Dublin after demobilization from the British forces in 1945, admiring the jewellery display at The Pillar House, Henry Street, owned by the Marks family.

the age of fifteen, when, having passed a test of her skills, the job appeared to be hers. Then she was asked her religion. Her reply charged the atmosphere and Siva became aware of prejudice for the first time in her life. 'If you hear from us in a few days, you'll know you have a job,' she was told. She never did hear from them – a rejection she anticipated by telling her parents immediately after the interview that she would never again seek employment in a non-Jewish firm. In the 1980s a Jewish secondary teacher who met anti-Semitism in every Dublin school she taught in, had a door slammed in her face by a colleague. 'I'm not talking to the likes of you!' he declared. Erasing her pupils' anti-Semitic graffiti from the blackboard became routine until her retirement in 1999.

Some racist comments were ludicrous and clearly arose from lack of education. Bess Romney, *née* Cristol, was born in Cork but her parents were living in Clonmel when a local woman knocked at the door one day asking to see their 'tails and horns'. Invited in, she became a friend. Lena Curland worked in a clothing workshop alongside a girl who remarked, 'I always heard the Jews had horns. You don't seem to have any.' Lena replied, 'My hair is so thick I can hide them!' Believing the answer, the girl then asked, 'Is it true Jews are buried standing up?' 'Of course,' said Lena. 'The men are stood facing the women. There's a window in the coffin. They're in evening wear. At night, they come out and dance.' The girl believed that answer, too!

Sometimes it was childish innocence. Ethna Golden, a Catholic, was born in Kingsland Parade and lived as a young child in Lennox Street, both locations within the Jewish belt of the South Circular Road. She remembers at the age of nine taking her friend, a little Jewish neighbour, to St Kevin's Church, pointing out the statue of Jesus on the cross and saying, 'That's what you did.' 'I did not!' replied the Jewish child, indignantly. Neither the accusation nor the denial marred the friendship. Mischievously helping themselves to church candles, the children lit them and ran happily out to play.

Many of the present generation of Jews are fortunate in experiencing little or no racial prejudice in Ireland, but an underlying element of latent if not blatant anti-Semitism has continued through the twentieth century and into the twenty-first – the dying kick, perhaps, of a nation described by Tom Garvin, Professor of Politics at University College Dublin, in reference to its war-time attitude, as 'very organisable into xenophobic movements … very much the pretty typical post-peasant society.'

Uncertain of their reception and prospects in their adopted land, homesick for the families left behind and determined to keep their identity as Orthodox, traditional Jews, the early Russian immigrants were somewhat isolated. Their bulwark against loneliness, vulnerability and insecurity, their safeguard against assimilation, was to recreate in Ireland the familiar *shtetl* life of the *heim*. No longer forced to live in segregated or specified areas, they elected to reside in

WARNING !

The JEWS started the War-Jewish people cannot
be trusted.

The must not occupy any responsible position or
Public Offices.

Jews are not democratic minded but opportunists,
Exploiters of Christians, these Parasites should be
excluded from any position where they can
influence the Nation's Economy and the People.
THROUGH THIS PARASITIC RACE THE WORLD
HAS BEEN CONTINUALLY INVOLVED IN WAR,
REBELLION AND MISERY, [HITLER WAS RIGHT]
DON'T HARM THEM BUT MAKE IT THAT THEIR
LIFE HERE COMPELS THEM TO RETURN TO ISRAEL.
Now that the Jews have Israel drive them back to
Israel and not allow them to have any control in
our affairs.

JEWRY is an organisation opposed to Christianity
THIS IS A CHRISTIAN COUNTRY AND *JEWISH*
INTERFERENCE IN OUR INTERNAL & EXTERNAL
POLICY MUST CEASE FORTHWITH.

Irishmen play your part in boycotting these Human
Leeches from OUR SOIL.

IRELAND FOR CHRISTIAN'S ONLY.

Warning against Jewish interference in Irish affairs circulated in Dublin 1956.

close proximity. Melvyn Sharpe and brothers Theo and Abe Garb, visiting Dublin in 2001 for a reunion, were foremost among the expatriates who could identify from memory almost every Jewish house they passed. Along the South Circular Road, where the Garb brothers had lived, they remembered Ellis Yodaiken at number 66, Ellie Marcus at number 68, Jacob Marcus at number 74, Itzik Marcus at number 88. In Donore Terrace they pointed out the homes of the Brass family, the Gittlesons, other Garbs, the Nurocks, Sefton Levy, Annie Danker, Betty Byrne, Revd Roith, the Lazaruses, the Noyeks, the Prices, Burack the dentist, and Revd Segal – all of them former residents, many in adjoining houses.

Affluence moved people onwards and upwards; emigration moved them across the seas and a growing laxity in religious practice made *shtetl*-type existence unpalatable to the young. Disregard for traditions had crept early into immigrant life. The religious Zacks, who refused to journey on to America without kosher food at the turn of the century, were riding New York trams on the Sabbath by 1911. Many Irish Jews remained true to the tenets of their faith and some young people became fired with new religious zeal under the influence of Orthodox mentors, but generally, succeeding generations wanted greater freedom to choose friends and even marriage partners from outside the community.

While ghetto-style living kept temptation at bay, strength of character or respect for parents often triumphed over failing religious belief to maintain conformity. It could not survive the dispersion of families to disparate addresses sometimes miles away from a synagogue or co-religionist. Leah Calmonson, now in her nineties, recalls when she and her husband 'couldn't sit down to a cup of tea without fifteen other couples sitting down with us.' Almost all Irish Jews past middle age recollect the same camaraderie: spontaneous family get-togethers, friends dropping in, neighbours all around willing to help, the concern of one the concern of all. Today, among the fewer than 1,000 Irish-born Jews that remain in Ireland, most of them middle-aged to elderly, quite a few feel lonely and isolated. The last bastions of Jewish Ireland are Dublin and Belfast with presence elsewhere reduced to single figures. In both cities the more Observant or traditional tend to live in the vicinity of the synagogue but the Little Jerusalem syndrome that was such a distinctive feature of Irish life is gone forever.

3

RABBIS AND FESTIVALS

The anglicised Jews who lived in Dublin before the Russian immigrants arrived had been designated the Dublin Hebrew Congregation in 1839. Their synagogue in Mary's Abbey, a commercially important street just north of the River Liffey, was at number 12, the original premises of the Bank of Ireland. Established in 1836 with a seating capacity that is variously estimated at between ninety and 220, it was conveniently placed and large enough for the small settled community on the north side of the city. For the hundreds of religious newcomers who settled two miles away on the south side and were obliged by Orthodox practice to walk on the Sabbath and Festivals, it was both inconvenient and too small. Its two-hour weekly service on Saturday mornings did little to meet their need for prayer facilities three times a day and even the ritual fitness of their Torah scrolls was questioned.

In 1876, Russian *Chevra* (religious groups) opened two small prayer houses for their own use in the vicinity of Lower Clanbrassil Street and the South Circular Road. The initiative was greatly resented by the Dublin Hebrew Congregation whose members perceived the new St Kevin's Parade and Lennox Street congregations as a direct challenge to their previously undisputed authority in matters relating to Dublin Jewry.

On 1 August 1889 a correspondent calling himself 'Spectator' suggested in a letter to the *Jewish Chronicle* that 'the authorities of the Mary's Abbey Synagogue should throw off their prejudice against their Russian brethren in Dublin and endeavour to create a united synagogue instead of the three congregations now existing'. A spirited reply on 8 August from Dr Ernest W. (Wormser) Harris, honorary solicitor to the Dublin Hebrew Congregation, refuted the implication that Mary's Abbey was to blame. The Mary's Abbey authorities, he alleged, in trying to effect such a union, had met with 'indignant refusal or outrageous demands' from the 'arrogant and overbearing Russians'. He deplored the 'sort of ghetto' the Russians had established and offered all the advantages of Mary's Abbey if they would come under its authority and pay a 'mite' towards its funds. In a subsequent letter on 30 August, Maurice E. Solomons, a *macher* (decision-maker) in the congregation, recognised the entitlement of the 'foreigners' to proportional representation on the Board of Management of a united synagogue but Mary's Abbey would not yield controlling power as the Russians demanded.

It would seem that the Russians were indeed contentious. Dr Alexander Carlebach, rabbi to the Belfast community from 1959 until 1967, records in *The Early Years of the Jewish Community in Ulster* that Belfast had a synagogue in Great Victoria Street, with its own minister and choir, from the 1870s when Russian immigrants began arriving. Quarrelsome and slow to integrate, they engaged in petty squabbling even among themselves. It took a new synagogue in Annesley Street, near Carlisle Circus, built in 1904, to bring the first semblance of unity. In Limerick, Russian arrivals increased the number of Jews from two in 1872 to ninety by 1892 but the Lithuanian immigrant Rabbi Elias Bere Levin found the tiny community 'riven with doctrinal differences' which often ended in the civil courts. The first Limerick synagogue, established in Rabbi Levin's home at 63 Collooney Street, was quickly challenged by a second at number 72, opened by Louis Goldberg. Rabbi Joseph Brown found community dissension so intolerable that he left Limerick to settle in Dublin. Cork with its 155 Jews by 1891 also had two congregations: a small prayer house at 1 Eastville and a larger synagogue at South Terrace, each with its own minister.

Attitudes in Dublin appeared to mellow after the newspaper correspondence. The newly-formed Montefiore Musical and Dramatic Club stressed the need for 'greater sociability' within the community and hoped to promote 'a greater feeling of friendship between the English and foreign residents'. In November 1889, when a deputation of *chevra* from Lennox Street Synagogue called at Mary's Abbey to discuss amalgamation, they were sympathetically received. Less than a year later the *Jewish Chronicle* reported the generous contribution of £100 from Sir Julian Goldsmid 'to the building fund of the new synagogue … at Dublin'. Building began in 1891 and was completed the following year. Dr Adler, Chief Rabbi of the United Hebrew Congregations of the British Empire, travelled from Britain for the consecration on 9 December 1892.

Described as 'Eastern Romanesque' in architecture, the new edifice in Adelaide Road was Ireland's first purpose-built synagogue. It seated 450 people with overflow accommodation in the basement, and was within easy walking distance of the South Circular Road, but it did not unite the Dublin Jewish community. Still remembered as 'the English *shul*' (synagogue), it tended to attract both the less Orthodox and the better educated, creating an 'us' and 'them' mentality. There are still Jewish Dubliners who feel the members of Adelaide Road Synagogue always thought themselves superior.

The exterior of Adelaide Road Synagogue, established 1892.

Mary's Abbey Synagogue held its last service the week before Adelaide Road Synagogue was consecrated but the synagogues at St Kevin's Parade and Lennox Street continued to function. By 1912 they had been augmented by others in Lombard Street, Oakfield Place, Heytsbury Street, Camden Street and Walworth Road, now home to the Irish-Jewish Museum. Even their combined facilities were inadequate for the growing immigrant community and some of the premises were in woeful condition.

With no desire to join the Dublin Hebrew Congregation, a group of men met at 42 Longwood Avenue on Sunday 10 October 1909 to discuss the situation. They arrived as representatives of four different synagogues; they left as founders of the Dublin United Hebrew Congregation. A.J. (Con) Leventhal in his *Dublin United Hebrew Congregation, 1909-1925: A Brief Survey* records how a building fund was opened with their collective subscription of 13s 9d – the first contribution towards the fine new synagogue they envisaged building on the South Circular Road. House-to-house penny collections over the next four years yielded a further £170 8d, by which time a suitable site had been found. Greenville House, Dolphin's Barn, was purchased in 1913 for £625. A community appeal for £5,000 caught the imagination of British Jewry. Dr J.H. Hertz, Dr Adler's successor as Chief Rabbi in Great Britain, wrote a letter of 'approval and sympathy' and the *Jewish Chronicle* upheld it as 'the united voice of Dublin Jewry ... sent in the cause of peace and our common faith'. Lord Rothchild sent a donation of £100; another benefactor promised £2,000. But it was now 1914. The outbreak of the First World War gave Britain more pressing priorities than Dublin's new synagogue.

Until funds would again be available for development, the upstairs of Greenville House was used for prayers that required a *minyan*, a quorum of ten post-*Bar Mitzvah* males. Small socials and communal meetings were held on the ground floor until 1916, when Greenville Hall was officially opened. Purpose-built within the grounds of Greenville House at a cost of £750, the assembly hall served the community for more than sixty years as a popular venue for every kind of private and communal function.

From the 1940s to the 1970s Greenville Hall was the domain of Annie Danker, Dublin's authorised kosher caterer. Her home, a kosher guesthouse, was portrayed in her obituary in the *Irish-Jewish Year Book*, 1976 as 'an oasis of hospitality to a stranger' as well as 'a happy centre of Jewish religious life'. Irrespective of what celebrants could afford to pay, an Annie Danker menu was never frugal. Every *simcha* (celebration) seemed to be a personal joy as course followed course, each plate overflowing with the traditional, often unhealthy, foods still dear to the Irish-Jewish palate. Her own rotund frame a tribute to her unstinting cuisine, 'Auntie Annie', as many called her, padded her way in slippers and apron around each table at every function to enquire, 'Is everything all right?' It was the rare celebration that did not end with the serving of pickled meat sandwiches, crusts neatly trimmed, just as guests were about to leave.

In 1949, when charges for the hire of Greenville Hall ranged from 3 guineas (lounge only) to 10 guineas (all facilities, Saturday or Sunday night), Mrs Danker adamantly refused to collect a proposed levy for the Board of Management by

The interior of Greenville Hall Synagogue.

adding 1s per head to her catering charges, even threatening to stop catering if the Board persisted. According to legal opinion, the Board had the right to charge Mrs Danker for preparation time in the kitchen, but even the threat of such reprisal failed to win her co-operation. In 1952, a circular letter informed the community of the 1s levy. When Mrs Danker had still not applied it by 1953, Chief Rabbi Jakobovits decided that 'some other form of collection' would have to be found.

Sonia Cheyette (*née* Woolfson) remembers Annie Danker as a 'lovely, generous lady' who served 'lashings of food' at her wedding in 1957 and forced a 'huge box' of it into her reluctant arms before she and her new husband set off on their honeymoon. 'Just for tonight,' said Mrs Danker. 'You might be hungry. You didn't eat much.' How to dispose of the food at the hotel was a predicament they finally solved by eating the lot with considerable relish.

In 1922, a new Building Committee raised a loan of £5,000 to erect the long-awaited synagogue. The *Irish Independent* covered the events of 28 April 1924 when Joseph Zlotover, president of the United Hebrew Congregation, laid the foundation stone on what he described as 'Irish soil which has never been stained with Jewish blood.' Greenville Hall Synagogue was consecrated in 1925. Its relatively speedy completion after so many years of planning owed much to the support of Dr Isaac Herzog, Chief Rabbi of Dublin from 1919.

As far back as 1899 Dr Wormser Harris had attributed much of the dissension between Dublin's anglicised and foreign Jews to Chief Rabbis of Great Britain. In his opinion their 'pastoral visits once in twenty years' and poor knowledge of Irish affairs rendered their ecclesiastical supervision of Ireland 'valueless' and he looked forward to a time when Ireland would have enough Jews in well-to-do circumstances to support its own spiritual leader. Autonomy in its religious affairs came with the War of Independence, 1921-2, which freed twenty-six of Ireland's thirty-two counties from British rule and led to the establishment of the Irish Free State. In a letter to the *Jewish Chronicle* of 3 March 1933, Jacob Zlotover rebutted a suggestion that Rabbi Herzog's title of Chief Rabbi of Ireland was 'self-assumed'. Zlotover averred, 'The communities of Cork, Limerick and Waterford formally accepted Herzog's ecclesiastical jurisdiction, together with Dublin.' On 23 March 1926, the Rabbinate Committee decided to change his official status from Chief Rabbi of the Dublin Jewish Community to Chief Rabbi of the Irish Free State.

Isaac Herzog, the son of a rabbi, was born in 1888 in Lomsha, a part of Poland under Russian control. He was nine when his family left to settle first in Massachusetts, then in Leeds, then in Paris, as his father moved from one rabbinical post to another. In his article, 'Rabbi Isaac Halevy Herzog', in the *Irish-Jewish Year Book*, 1965-6, Rabbi O. Feuchwanger claims the boy was already considered 'a budding genius' from his knowledge and understanding of the *Talmud*. Divided into sixty-three tractates, which vary in length from 25 to 250 pages, the *Talmud* constitutes the central structure of Jewish learning. By the time Isaac was sixteen he could recite the entire text by heart.

His brilliant mind absorbed secular subjects with equal ease. He studied Zoology for his doctorate and went on to become 'a renowned *Talmudist*, linguist, jurist, diplomat, scholar in many branches of secular knowledge, out-spoken Zionist, humanitarian, saint'. His address to a Nationalist meeting in fluent Irish within a few months of first hearing the native language earned him the courtesy title of *Sinn Féiner*.

Rabbi Herzog's call to Ireland initially was as communal minister to the Belfast Hebrew Congregation. The anonymous writer of 'Rav (Rabbi) Herzog – a Personal Portrait' in the *Irish-Jewish Year Book*, 1983-4 recalls his arrival there in 1916. The president of the Belfast Jewish Community went to the railway station expecting to find a 'polished and dapper Frenchman of dignified and imposing appearance' waiting on the platform; instead he found 'a physically frail, pallid man, without a trace of glamour' huddled over a book in the last carriage.

Relations between Ireland's Jewish citizens and its Gentile politicians were non-existent before Rabbi Herzog's arrival. As one observer put it, 'There was no central point of contact.' The meek and gentle rabbi changed all that through natural dignity and simplicity. According to his anonymous admirer, 'goodness shone from him along with humility and purity.' He is credited with changing Belfast and Dublin from 'a collection of Jews into a community, self-respecting and respected by their Gentile fellow citizens'. Éamon de Valera said of him, 'From the moment I met him, I felt in the presence of a good and holy man.'

Belfast claims to have shown its appreciation by 'tactfully' arranging a meeting between its bachelor rabbi and the 'charming, intelligent' Miss Sarah Hillman. Both sons of their marriage were born in Ireland, Chaim in Belfast and Yaacov in Dublin. Chaim, whose brilliant military and diplomatic career culminated in the Presidency of Israel (1983-93), records his parents' introduction rather differently in his autobiography, *Living History* (1997). However they met, the same anonymous source is certain that 'no finer life's partner, no more devoted a helpmate, could they or the rabbi have chosen'.

Chaim Herzog described his father as 'the absent-minded professor type' who never thought to replace a broken shoelace. Instead, he replaced the shoes. His new wife discovered a collection of discarded, broken-laced footwear under his bed at 2 Norman Villas, Belfast. Her good friend, Lady Jakobovits, recalled that Mrs Herzog also discovered her husband's tendency to write cheques and promissory notes he could not honour in favour of any poor person seeking his aid. When the National Irish Bank complained that he owed them £300, she confiscated his chequebook.

It seemed to Chaim that his father and mother were parents to the whole Jewish community. Anyone in dispute with a Jew, whatever his faith, took the problem to 33 Bloomfield Avenue. There it was settled to everyone's satisfaction by *Din Torah*, arbitration based on Jewish law, with the rabbi presiding. He was equally skilled in handling disputes within secular authority. His spirited defence of ritual slaughter before a *Seanad* (Senate) committee dealing with the Slaughter of Animals' Bill

(1935), earned him the respect of Senator M.F. O'Hanlon, who congratulated the Dublin Jewish Community on having 'so able and erudite an advocate'.

In 1936, Rabbi Herzog received a call from Palestine to become its Chief Rabbi. A deputation appointed by the Dublin Rabbinate Committee begged him not to accept. How could they ever replace him? He had already refused a similar call to Salonica but a call to Palestine he felt obliged to accept. When he left in 1937, the Herzog name was familiar to 'Jew, Gentile, Orthodox, Liberal, Agnostic, Freethinker', and his numerous friends included heads of Church and State. Among them was Cardinal Joseph MacRory, Primate of all Ireland. In *Living History*, Chaim Herzog recalls an occasion when the two religious leaders sat together at a State dinner in Dublin Castle. The cardinal reproached the rabbi for eating only fruit instead of the 'excellent ham' enjoyed by other guests. The rabbi smiled whimsically and said, 'Let us discuss this at your wedding!'

Despite the desire they had once expressed for a united synagogue, St Kevin's Parade, Lombard Street West, Lennox Street and Walworth Road continued as autonomous congregations alongside Adelaide Road even after Greenville Hall Synagogue was built. The Lennox Street congregation was so fiercely independent that even internal disputes could lead to fisticuffs. With such divisiveness already diminishing the community's resources, one of Rabbi Herzog's last duties in Ireland was to complete the writing of the *Torah* scrolls for Dublin's seventh synagogue.

The Terenure Hebrew Congregation traces its inception to a meeting in September 1936 when Simon Eppel pointed out 'the urgency of setting up a

Opening of Terenure Synagogue 1953. 'Cantor Gluck leads the procession of *Torah* scrolls ahead of Chief Rabbi Jacobovits. Kilted Joe Levy (Rovers) and Philip Turk (Scouts) attend the arrival.

place of worship conveniently situated for Jewish residents in Rathmines, Rathgar and Terenure.' Initially termed the Rathmines Hebrew Congregation, the new synagogue opened in rooms at 6 Grosvenor Place, rented at 35*s* per week from Boruch Citron.

Shortly after his departure, Rabbi Herzog sent Jewish New Year greetings to Dublin from his home in Palestine. He hoped the Jewish community would continue 'in perfect unity' and speedily appoint 'a spiritual leader worthy of the respect and confidence of the entire community'. Neither aspiration was fulfilled.

By 1940 the Rathmines Hebrew Congregation had outgrown Grosvenor Place, and larger premises at 52 Grosvenor Road were purchased with a loan from the Provincial Bank. Three years later the amalgamation of Dublin synagogues came under consideration yet again but the unanimous decision to bring them all under the control of one United Synagogue as quickly as possible was never effected. Negotiations dragged on until 'insurmountable obstacles' caused the scheme to be abandoned in 1947. With no consensus on any candidate, the post of Chief Rabbi remained vacant for almost thirteen years.

Immanuel Jakobovits, a young, single rabbi recently appointed to the Great Synagogue in London, arrived in Dublin to lecture at a summer school organised by the *Bnei Akivah* (children of *Akivah*) youth movement. His impressive performance galvanised the disparate congregations into instant and uncharacteristic unanimity. Nomination was followed by acceptance and in February 1949 Rabbi Jakobovits, who would later be knighted as Chief Rabbi of Great Britain, was inducted as Chief Rabbi of Ireland. The *Taoiseach*, John Costello TD, a guest of honour, announced Ireland's *de facto* recognition of the newly established State of Israel at the inaugural dinner.

In his article 'My 10 years with Irish Jewry' in the *Irish-Jewish Year Book*, 1958-9, Rabbi Jakobovits described his sojourn in Ireland as 'the most enjoyable and exciting period of my life'. It certainly brought him personal fulfilment, since he arrived alone and left with his effervescent French wife, Amelie, and their five Irish-born children. Professionally the post offered 'a scope of rabbinical activity as varied and challenging as any in the world'.

What others termed problems were challenges to Rabbi Jakobovits. Two he had to face in the wider community concerned reaction by the Catholic Church to Israel's perceived authority over Holy sites and a prospective calendar reform.

In *Amelie: The Story of Lady Jakobovits* by Gloria Tessler, Amelie Jakobovits recalled the meeting she and the late rabbi had with Archbishop John Charles McQuaid of Dublin regarding the sites. In what she describes as 'an unpleasant tone', he warned the rabbi of the unpredictable consequences from the Vatican and within Ireland 'if access to religious and holy places ... is not totally available and free of all possible unpleasantness.' Most of the Holy places were then in Jordanian hands and the few under Israeli control were already freely accessible. That Irish Jewry might be held responsible for Israeli actions they could neither control nor influence constituted, in her view, a new form of latent anti-Semitism that augured the beginning of anti-Zionism.

The proposed calendar reform was equally offensive to Jews. The Hebrew calendar predates *Anno Domini* (AD) by 3,761 years, placing the year 2000 in the Hebrew year 5761. Based on a lunar year of 364 days, evenly divisible by seven, it has been fixed since the fourth century, with every Festival falling on a specific Hebrew date and every Sabbath occurring on a Saturday. The conventional calendar is calculated on the solar year of 365 days. In an effort to standardise the dates of Christian festivals, a calendar reform movement proposed incorporating the awkward 365th day into one annual eight-day week. The adjustment would have created havoc in Jewish life with a 'wandering Sabbath' that occurred on a different day each year. Rabbis worldwide objected. In 1957, Rabbi Jakobovits travelled to Rome to meet the Papal astronomer who, coincidentally, was an Irishman. It was agreed that the Catholic Church would not pursue the issue.

Within the Jewish community the challenges were somewhat different. When plans to amalgamate the synagogues failed in 1947, the Rathmines Hebrew Congregation, expanding even beyond its Grosvenor Road premises, decided to erect a purpose-built synagogue in Terenure. Though they had no funds for such a structure, Wolfe Freedman and Erwin Goldwater initiated the project by acquiring a suitable site. 'Leoville' on Rathfarnham Road was bought for £1,490. Inspired by the example of the Arcadia Ballroom in Bray, which operated from a Nissun hut, the Building Committee erected one of its own in the grounds of 'Leoville' to serve as a temporary synagogue until it could afford a permanent structure. When the renamed Terenure Hebrew Congregation opened Terenure Synagogue in 1953, its seating capacity of 600 made it the largest synagogue to be built in Ireland in the past thirty-five years. Congratulated on its 'original, modern, commanding and attractive design', the architect said it conformed to the committee's specifications for a building that would 'cost less than half the normal cost, look as if it cost the full amount and be an example of good modern design.'

In the opinion of Rabbi Jakobovits, Dublin now had at least four synagogues too many. The census of 1946 rated the Jewish population in the Republic at no more than 3,907; by 1961 there were only 3,255. Emigration was taking its toll, intermarriage was on the increase and Jewish families had become fashionably small. Community debts were rising to a point where only drastic reorganisation could prevent collapse. Most unfortunate of all, in the rabbi's view, was the founding of Ireland's first Progressive synagogue by 'a new and potentially growing splinter group' spearheaded by Larry Elyan, its first chairman. Progressive Judaism accepts the divinity of G-d but not of the *Torah*, which it considers the work of various scribes. It moderates Orthodox obligations and traditions to conform to a more flexible, secular way of life.

Chaim Bermant, author of *Lord Jakobovits* (1990), records how on one occasion the Chief Rabbi stayed on a Liverpool ferry going back and forth across the Irish Sea from Thursday when it sailed, until the following Sunday. Delayed by fog, the ferry had first docked at Dun Laoghaire on Friday night after the onset of the Sabbath, when disembarkation was not permitted. Such a degree of orthodoxy had little in common with Progressive Judaism but Rabbi Jakobovits concentrated on containment rather than confrontation or criticism.

To the youth of the community he was an inspiration. Concerned with improving their standard of Jewish education and religious practice, he brought groups of teenagers to his home for lectures, study and debates. Lady Jakobovits remembered 'the group of *Bnei Akivah* kids' becoming more and more committed as they visited twice or three times a week. Isaac Bernstein, Maurice Hool and Edward Jackson from Cork went on to become rabbis; almost all the rest found careers in Jewish education. To the rabbi's regret, most of them emmigrated to Israel. He never discouraged them from leaving but in 1958 he wrote, 'Had we been able to retain this wonderful element here … Dublin would indeed be a model community today.' Instead, 'the drainage led to increased apathy and a growing dearth of communal workers'.

Lady Jakobovits denied that her husband was presiding over what Gloria Tessler describes as an 'ethnic minority waiting to emigrate'. Dublin social life was vibrant and exciting, with a wedding almost every week and a surfeit of functions to attend. The Jakobovits home, as remembered by neighbour Hazel Broch, *née* Rubinstein, now living in Israel, was open house to everyone: the community, Jewish tourists and officials of Church and State that included the Papal Nuncio. A man of commanding physical presence and an acknowledged expert in the field of Jewish medical ethics, Rabbi Jakobovits, like his predecessor, won the respect and affection of Dubliners. Passers-by raised their hats to him in the street. Honouring his gentleman's agreement with the Rabbinate committee to stay in Dublin for ten years, he moved on to a challenging position in America where a Texas newspaper had already hailed him as the Irish rabbi, Jack O'Bovits.

His successor, Dr Isaac Cohen, began his Hebrew education at the age of five in his hometown of Llanelli in Wales. The son of a strictly Orthodox shopkeeper from Lithuania, he grew up under his mother's constant injunction to be a *mensch*, a Yiddish term for someone who shows consideration for others and is worthy of general respect. From being a post-*Bar Mitzvah* boarder at Aria College, Portsmouth, he proceeded to Jews' College and the University of London on a scholarship. By 1935 he had his rabbinical diploma. The next four years were spent ministering to congregations in Harrow and District in London. In 1939, he moved to a post in Leeds where he also acted as a chaplain to the forces. In 1946, he resumed his rabbinical and university studies in London where, he told Veronica Kelly in an interview in the *Irish Times* of 4 January 1964, he and his wife, Fanny, lived 'like students in a rented two-roomed flat.' A call to Edinburgh enabled him to gain his doctorate at the University of Edinburgh and to represent Scottish Jewry at all State functions, including the coronation of Queen Elizabeth II in 1952. It was an excellent apprenticeship for a Chief Rabbi whose duties would be as much ambassadorial as spiritual. In 1959 he was called to Ireland.

Rabbi Cohen edited the *Irish-Jewish Year Book*, instituted by Rabbi Jakobovits as an annual catalogue of *kashrut* and communal information, from 1959-79. Succeeding issues became detailed accounts of all communal activities and clearly show his own increasing involvement in the wider community.

Almost every dignitary of Church and State on official business in Ireland either called upon or received the Chief Rabbi and he was a guest at every State function. At the start of every civil New Year, he conveyed greetings from the Jewish community to the President of Ireland at *Áras an Uachtaráin* (the presidential residence) and offered tributes as well as personal and community condolences on the deaths of Pope John XXIII and Pope John Paul I. He was among the religious leaders invited by the Papal Nuncio to meet Pope John Paul II on his visit to Ireland in 1979.

Special services were held within the Jewish community for events as diverse as the commemoration of the Irish members of the UN peacekeeping forces killed in the Congo, the fiftieth anniversary of the 1916 Easter Rising and the recovery of President de Valera from serious illness. The Chief Rabbi represented the Jewish community at the funeral of Roger Casement by accompanying the procession to Glasnevin Cemetery and was present at the entrance to the Pro-Cathedral as a mark of respect when a State funeral was held for President de Valera in 1975. Only the invitation to join other religious leaders in blessing the shamrock on St Patrick's Day nonplussed him. The fortunate coincidence of 17 March falling that year on the Sabbath prevented his attendance and spared him the embarrassment of explaining it was a benediction without precedent in Jewish religious practice.

In 1965, the Irish-Jewish community undertook to create a forest of 10,000 trees at Kfar Kanna near Nazareth in Israel in the name of President de Valera for his 'many years of devoted service in the cause of peace and freedom'. Eight years later, three of those trees were flown to Ireland by the Jewish National Fund Forestry Department. They were replanted, at a unique ceremony, in the presidential gardens at *Áras an Uactaráin* by the Chief Rabbi, Professor Leonard Abrahamson (chairman of the de Valera Forest Commission), and the President himself who was 'deeply moved by the significance of the occasion'. That same year, in a supplement on Ireland in the *Jewish Chronicle*, the *Taoiseach*, Sean Lamass, wrote, 'We cherish our Jewish community in Ireland as we do our other religious minorities.' The standing of the Jewish community was further enhanced when the Chief Rabbi was invited to deliver televised messages to the Irish nation. Begun in 1962 as a prelude to Passover and the Jewish New Year, they have continued ever since at those same Festival times and on numerous other occasions.

In the early 1960s, Lombard Street Synagogue closed and St Kevin's Parade Synagogue relocated. Renamed *Machzikei Hadass*, the small, Observant congregation continued to function from 77 Terenure Road North. Otherwise no attempt was made, despite general financial deficits, to rationalise Dublin's synagogues during Rabbi Cohen's period of office. Outside his ambit, a new synagogue was opened in 1965 at Somerton Road, the centre of Belfast Jewry, but it was a replacement for and not additional to the synagogue in Annesley Street and its attractive circular design lent itself to further reduction in size without detriment to its appearance or function. The man responsible for the achievement was Barney Hurwitz, president of the Belfast Hebrew Congregation since 1936. Described by Martin Wallace in the *Belfast Telegraph* of 20 July 1962 as 'the lay focus of Jewish life in Belfast', he went from door to door collecting subscriptions for the new synagogue. Sir Isaac Wolfson, in Belfast to perform the opening ceremony, offered a donation towards any outstanding debts. He was assured there were none. The president had raised every penny himself. Sir Isaac endowed the Wolfson Centre instead. The substantial cheque presented to Barney Hurwitz on his seventieth birthday was immediately passed on to the Belfast Abbeyfield Society, which cares for the aged. It paid for the centre they called Hurwitz House in his honour.

In 1966, an arson attempt was made on Terenure Synagogue. Prompt action by Dublin Fire Brigade saved the main structure and probably the life of the perpetrator who was found inside the building, but fire and water caused extensive damage to internal fittings and religious artefacts. The adjacent Samuel Taca Hall, which attracted many private and communal functions, was unscathed. Expressions of sympathy from the wider community were much appreciated by the congregation, as was the offer to make interim use of facilities at Adelaide Road Synagogue, but Terenure's claim for malicious damage failed. The culprit was found unfit to plead. The restored synagogue had the additional refinement of beautiful stained-glass windows designed by Stanley Tolmin and membership remained high. Sabbath morning services in the 1970s could attract several hundred adults and as many as seventy children.

Adelaide Road Synagogue, with its own Dr Leslie Golding Hall, renovated by Esther Golding in memory of her husband, also drew a large attendance. It had a male voice choir under the direction for many years of Isaac Bernstein and was the 'State occasion' synagogue. It was there in 1975 that Rabbi Cohen made history by reciting the traditional priestly blessing in Irish as well as Hebrew during the service of inauguration for Cearbhall O'Dailaigh as President of Ireland.

Greenville Hall Synagogue fared less well. Migration away from the South Circular Road had reduced its membership from 300 in 1951 to 150 by 1961. An increase in seat rental and the temporary commercial letting of the communal hall, then seldom used by the community, helped to keep the synagogue open, but it was clearly becoming redundant.

Although the 1979 census showed an increase in Ireland's total population, the Jewish community had halved over the previous twenty years. Rabbi Cohen maintained that the quality of the community remained high. He saw no good in adopting 'an attitude of defeatism' and rejoiced that he had been able to uphold 'the great traditions of Irish Jewry', which he defined as Jewish education, the maintenance of facilities for fulfilling religious obligations and care of the sick and needy. Dublin's popular Friendship Club, which continues to function as the Over Fifty-fives, was founded at his instigation to give 'some refreshment, a game, a gossip' to the 'appreciable number of elderly and lonely people in the community with few comforts and few friends'. Rabbi and Mrs Cohen left for retirement in Israel 'with deep feelings of sadness' at parting from so many of their own good friends.

David Rosen admits he became Ireland's fourth Chief Rabbi under the influence of Rabbi Jakobovits, who 'worked on his vanity' to encourage him to accept the post. Formerly rabbi in Cape Town to the 10,000 souls who formed the largest Jewish congregation in South Africa, he was on his way to a position in New York when Rabbi Jakobovits told him of Ireland's interest. The feeling was not mutual. America, with its extensive Jewish population, offered a much more attractive prospect to the dynamic young rabbi, and he asked Rabbi Jakobovits why he should prefer a community of 3,000 Jews to one of 3 million. Rabbi Jakobovits stressed the vibrancy of the Irish community and the substantial influence he would have over it. Being Chief Rabbi of Ireland was a 'unique position … with significance way beyond the small confines of the community.' It was a role that few rabbis in the world could fill effectively. A visit to Ireland convinced Rabbi Rosen of its possibilities; he withdrew from the American commitment and accepted the Irish appointment.

Though still in his twenties, Rabbi Rosen had already gained a reputation for being 'dangerously liberal'. What he himself describes as a 'Stop David Rosen' campaign was launched against him from Britain, as certain rabbinical authorities attempted to intimidate Ireland into revoking its call. The issue was debated for three months but the Representative Council of Irish Jewry withstood the pressure and he took up office in October 1979, the youngest Chief Rabbi in the world.

As an Orthodox rabbi he was certainly different. His striking features gave him the appearance of a patriarch; his command of English peppered his sermons with vocabulary outside the range of rank-and-file congregants; he heartily partook of refreshments in Jewish homes where predecessors had confined themselves to fruit and wine; his attractive wife, Sharon, made skilful use of cosmetics and they were both vegetarians. It was that last 'aberration' that upset Baila Ehrlich. A vegetarian rabbi was a poor example to any community from a butcher's point of view and when he also appeared unenthusiastic about deciding meat and fowl *sheilahs* (queries regarding their ritual fitness for consumption) she dubbed him 'the *Purim* Rabbi'. The term implied he was masquerading in the role but the five years he spent in Ireland were among the most progressive in the community's history.

With a few notable exceptions, Irish Jews were never totally observant. Influenced, however, by the ethos of staunch Catholicism that permeated the wider community, they strongly adhered to their own faith in tradition and thought. Generally more Orthodox in practise, too, than many United Synagogue congregations in Britain and elsewhere, they resisted change and, in Rabbi Rosen's view, held 'an attachment to often meaningless custom and superstition.' It was this 'combination of staunch traditionalism and Jewish ignorance' that made innovations a constant struggle.

In the early 1980s Lennox Street and Walworth Road Synagogues finally succumbed to depleting numbers and growing dilapidation of premises. Financial prudence dictated that Greenville Hall Synagogue should also close but what Rabbi Rosen calls 'over-indulgent nostalgia' triumphed over 'religious priorities and the wise use of resources' to delay the inevitable. The synagogue was still functioning when Rabbi Rosen left in 1984.

Already interested in the field of inter-faith diplomacy, which would form the basis of his career after leaving Ireland, he was instrumental in establishing a Council of Christians and Jews in Ireland and in setting up a programmeme in Christian-Jewish relations at the Irish School of Ecumenics. Sharon Rosen used her experience and skills to serve as the only non-Catholic counsellor on the Catholic Marriage Guidance Council. The good relationship Rabbi Rosen established with the Progressive community was enhanced when he became the first and only Chief Rabbi to address them on their own premises. He did not, however, advocate their beliefs. A small number of Gentiles in Dublin married to Jews had undergone a Progressive conversion. He encouraged and assisted those who wanted their children to integrate fully into Jewish life to go one step further and adopt Orthodox conversion.

Rabbi Rosen greatly enjoyed the diplomatic, social and cultural activities associated with his work and found a lively interest in Judaism among the wider community, where he was well received and respected. Having made his own useful contribution to the progress of Irish Jewry, he immigrated to Israel, where he negotiated the establishment of full relations between the Vatican and the State of Israel.

Ephraim Mirvis came to Ireland from Israel in 1982, on Rabbi Rosen's recommendation, to fill the position of communal rabbi at Adelaide Road Synagogue. Two years later he became Ireland's fifth Chief Rabbi and the first since Rabbi Herzog to be promoted from 'within the ranks'. A native of South Africa, he felt very much at home in Dublin where the community shared his Lithuanian background. Though its deep devotion to *Yiddishkeit* (Jewish ethos) was more in thought than in deed, the community impressed him as still vibrant with 'qualities of strength that belied its numeric smallness'. With no desire to be 'a mere functionary', Rabbi Mirvis strove to maintain religious standards throughout the community by making Judaism 'relevant, meaningful and exciting'. Young people especially were welcomed to his home for lectures, discussions and social gatherings.

Kept open by sentimental attachment long after its ability to muster a regular *minyan*, Greenville Hall Synagogue finally closed in 1984. Many of its displaced congregation joined *Machzikei Hadass*, which offered comparatively low seat rentals and a warm welcome even to newcomers less religiously Observant than its traditional membership.

The gradual departure of deeply committed adherents, such as the two Elzas families, the Bleirs, the Masars and the Yodaikens, to more religious communities elsewhere, and the death of religious stalwarts such as Aaron Zvi Steinberg, described in his obituary as 'a pillar of Orthodoxy', left Dublin with few who were strictly Observant. Driving to *Shabbat* services became commonplace for members of Adelaide Road and Terenure Synagogues and a growing number of congregants at all Orthodox synagogues infringed the Sabbath, ate non-kosher food in public places, and generally paid decreasing attention to religious practice regarded by their forefathers as sacrosanct. As Christian as well as Jewish society veered towards ever-increasing secularisation, the number of regular *shul*-goers continued to decline until Dublin could scarcely fill one large synagogue, let alone two.

It would take more than a decade to decide whether Terenure Synagogue, one of the last bastions of the Observant, or Adelaide Road Synagogue, the finer, more historic building, should be the one to close. Some of the *machers*, often continuing decades of committed family service, added to rank-and-file intransigence by resisting the potential loss of congregational positions that had earned them considerable *yichis* (community respect and prestige). Had the two synagogues pooled their resources in the 1980s and invested in a joint custom-made centre, it is Rabbi Mirvis's belief that the community might have been saved but the only show of solidarity was a spasmodic boost in attendance as members of each *shul* strove to demonstrate its viability. It was 1999 before obduracy and sentiment succumbed to the practicalities of demography and economics. Adelaide Road Synagogue was too far away for the Terenure Orthodox to walk there every Sabbath and Festival, and its prestigious city location made it the more valuable property to sell. Despite the contention of Hubert Wine, then its honorary secretary, and Gerald Gilbert, estate agent, in the Dublin Hebrew Congregation's annual report of 1971 that the synagogue site was 'incapable of development and valueless', it was sold in 1999 for around £6 million.

Progressive Synagogue membership remained steady, with converted non-Jewish spouses and occasional defectors from the Orthodox communities replacing members who emigrated or died. With its own burial grounds at Woodtown, Rathfarnham, its own Hebrew classes, its own communal magazine and youth club and no permanent resident rabbi to rival the Chief Rabbi, it posed no threat to Orthodox Jewry, and Rabbi Mirvis continued the cordial relations established by Rabbi Rosen.

Like all his predecessors, Rabbi Mirvis entered wholeheartedly into his wider community commitments, enjoying them as much for their humour as for their pomp. He recalls one State occasion at Dublin Castle when he queued in the rain with other guests for admission. Ushers went to and fro selecting the especially eminent among the distinguished gathering for preferential admittance under the shelter of an umbrella. When Rabbi Mirvis and his wife, Valerie, were chosen, someone complained, 'Chief Rabbi, that's a very un-Christian thing you are doing!'

Rabbi Mirvis's request in 1985 that Peter Menton be denied admission to Ireland was his first representation to the Government as Chief Rabbi. Menton, a convicted Nazi war criminal newly released from jail in Holland, had expressed his intention of returning to a house he owned in Co. Waterford. An expulsion order was issued against him and Rabbi Mirvis felt highly gratified at the respect shown by the State for the safeguarding of Jewish interests. He noticed the same respect on a personal level when he travelled to a seaside town in Co. Kerry in an effort to develop kosher outlets around the country. The firm he was inspecting had sent him a ticket to Tralee and an invitation to lunch, which he declined in favour of his own kosher sandwiches. At lunchtime his hosts insisted that he accompany them home. He was escorted to the kitchen, where he found a freshly caught kosher fish beside new plates, new cutlery and a new frying pan. 'Now,' said the hostess, 'please tell us how to do it.'

The strong friendships developed by Ephraim and Valerie Mirvis within the Jewish and the wider communities encompassed members of the Government and diplomatic corps, the media and the business world. As part of a group aptly named 'Labour of Love', Valerie Mirvis used those social contacts to raise funds for the Rotunda, one of Dublin's main maternity hospitals. She and the rabbi had arrived in Ireland with one small daughter; they left with four additional sons, all born at the Rotunda, and a conviction shared with Rabbi and Sharon Rosen that Ireland was the perfect place to raise a young family. Rabbi Mirvis speaks of his Irish sojourn as 'enriching' and 'the most wonderful thing that could have happened to a young rabbi starting out, for the experience it gave.' Their departure in 1992 for the fuller religious life of the Marble Arch Synagogue in London brought to an end Ireland's unbroken chain of Chief Rabbis who, despite factional opposition and even hostility at times, had committed themselves, over a prolonged period of time, to the welfare and strengthening of the Irish Jewish community.

Important as they were, the Chief Rabbis did not serve Irish Jewry alone. For many years a stalwart of Jewish life in Dublin was Dayan Zalman Alony, born in Russia in 1915. When his father, Rabbi Dubov, left Russia with the rest of his large family for a post in Manchester, Zalman Dubov remained behind to complete his rabbinic studies; he, too, was forced to leave when conscription loomed. Changing his name from Dubov (the Russian for tree) to Alony (its Hebrew equivalent), the young rabbi moved to Palestine. He was on a visit to his parents in Manchester when he met his future wife, Leah (Lily) Matlin, from Dublin, where he eventually succeeded her father as rabbi to Walworth Road Synagogue. Rabbi Alony's daughter, Mrs Winer, from her home in London, remembers that ministry as only one of his many responsibilities. As well as travelling the country to supervise factories making kosher products, he frequently visited the communities in Cork and Limerick, took morning assembly at Zion Schools in the 1960s when Mr Lev was headmaster, and acted as Jewish chaplain to the hospitals, the Boy Scouts, the Prison Service and the Lord Mayor (when the incumbent was Robert Briscoe). He assisted at numerous services and functions around the many synagogues, held study groups, answered religious queries and tried to solve every problem brought to him. With 'the phone going day and night', his wife sometimes suggested taking it off the hook but the Dayan, who studied *Torah* into the early hours anyway, would not hear of it. Every phone call was important, and no one was ever turned away. He regarded those busy years as the best time of his life and still managed to publish a substantial volume of work, which included *The Essence of Judaism*, seven books in Hebrew on religious topics and numerous articles for European, South African and American publications.

Remembered by most Dublin adults for his playful and sometimes painful practice of pinching their childhood cheeks by way of fond greeting, Rabbi Alony was the essence of kindness. Eleanor Silverman in America recalls him as 'the nicest, wisest man' and Zerrick (Jerry) Woolfson in Canada, as 'one of the kindest, most congenial men I ever met, highly erudite and intellectual.' Philippa Blatt *née* Robinson, now living in Israel, remembers from childhood his annual visits to Carlow to supervise Passover arrangements at the sugar factory. She would watch with excitement for his black car and listen with wonder to the Bible stories he told the children round the fire. Before he left Ireland in the 1980s to join the London *Beth Din* (ecclesiastical court), a reception was held in his honour at the Samuel Taca Hall in Terenure. One of the guests was the governor of Mountjoy Prison, where the Dayan had acted as chaplain to the occasional Jewish prisoner. In a farewell speech, the governor admitted there had been little contact between them but he wished Rabbi 'Maloney' well in his new office.

The last minister at Mary's Abbey and the first at Adelaide Road Synagogue was Rabbi Israel Leventon, whose family of more than 100 descendents gathered in Dublin in 2002 to rededicate the *Sefer Torah* (*Torah* Scrolls). He spent ten years of his 'spare time' scribing, even as he carried out the multifarious duties of serving a growing community single-handedly.

Over the years, Dublin's many other excellent rabbis included Theodore Lewis and the fiery, charismatic Isaac Bernstein, whose brilliant mind won him an Exhibition (scholarship) to Trinity College in Mathematics. Born in Dublin, they served their own community before respectively securing more prestigious posts in America and London. Among other Irish-born rabbis who took their skills abroad were Ivan Watchman, Monty Miller, Yehudah Copperman, Robert Hodes, Jonathan Yodaiken and Gideon Golding.

Outside the jurisdiction of the Chief Rabbinate of Ireland, the longest-serving and most renowned of the rabbis that ministered to the Belfast Hebrew Congregation were Jacob Shachter and Alexander Carlebach. Rabbi Shachter, described by the *Belfast Telegraph* of 19 August 1967 as 'a scholarly and dignified man', arrived in Belfast in 1926 with thirteen years' rabbinical experience. When he retired to Israel in 1953, the Governor General of Northern Ireland, Lord Brookborough, wrote from England, 'You and the Jewish community have always been of the greatest assistance and it has always been a pleasure to work with you.' The Minister of Labour, Major Ivor O'Neill, who represented the Northern Government at Rabbi Shachter's farewell reception, said he had woven himself into the character of Northern Ireland and won a place in the hearts and affections of the people. Academically distinguished as a writer and expert in Jewish jurisprudence with an honorary degree from Queen's University, Rabbi Schachter's two main objectives were to disseminate learning and religion among the Jewish Community and to keep close contact with the leaders of other faiths. He met the Moderator of the General Assembly weekly. Generous with his own time, he encouraged Northern Ireland's Jews to support non-Jewish charities and was chairman of the Lord Mayor's Coal Fund when he left Ireland.

His successor, Rabbi Carlebach, who studied international law and wrote several books on Jewish education, was born in 1908 in Cologne, where his father and brother were both rabbis. As chaplain to the Jewish Students' Society, he was particularly concerned with the youth and he and his wife regularly welcomed students and other young people to their home for *Shabbat* meals.

Behind the rabbis was a cohort of religious ministers, readers, *chazanim* (cantors), *shochtim* (who ritually slaughtered meat), *mohelim* (who performed circumcisions), Hebrew teachers, choirmasters, one person often performing many of the roles simultaneously. The dedicated service they gave was often poorly rewarded. On one of his return visits to Dublin, Rabbi Lewis was reminded by a young mother that he had once given her *6d* for answering a question correctly in class. He smiled and said, 'Carol, that *6d* represented an important part of my salary.'

Aubrey Moher, from his home in London, describes his father's involvement in Irish religious life as multi-functioned. Trained as a *shochet*, he had moved from Poland to London, where there were so many other immigrants seeking similar employment that local *shochtim* objected to foreigners encroaching on their trade. Revd Moher had no option but to move on. Informed by the London *Beth Din* of vacancies in Argentina, several weeks' journey away, and in Waterford, just hours away, he opted for Waterford.

In addition to his slaughtering and synagogue duties, Revd Moher had to visit Jewish prisoners in Waterford Jail. There were none to visit until some English

Jews, found guilty of fraud, asked for a rabbi. The handsome fee paid for each prison visit was a welcome supplement to his comparatively meagre salary and Revd Moher was happy to go as often as required. He also benefitted, as a *shochet*, from a supply of some of the meat from the animals he killed.

The Mohers moved to Dublin in 1938, where they employed a young maidservant, a common practice even among struggling Jewish families. She lived in and was satisfied with a few shillings a week and her keep. Daily outings with baby Aubrey brought her into contact with other nursemaids whose more affluent employers supplied them with uniforms. So badly did she want a similar uniform for herself that she saved her wages to buy one. Community dignitaries immediately objected to a *shochet* living above his station to the extent of debating the matter at a Board of *Shechita* meeting in the early 1940s.

Revd Abraham Gittleson was born in Dublin in 1915. He spent a number of years studying at Gateshead *Yeshiva* (Jewish religious seminary) before returning to Dublin to train as a *shochet* for the Board of *Shechita*, where he became its Head *shochet*. Further training in ritual circumcision by the medical team of the Jewish Memorial Council qualified him as a *mohel*. In the 1950s, he became minister to the United Hebrew Congregation at Greenville Hall Synagogue and devoted the rest of his life to the community. In February 1953, both he and his colleague, Revd Roith, appealed to the Chief Rabbinate of Ireland for a *Din Torah* against the Board of *Shechita* of Ireland in respect of their salaries and working hours. The dispute was heard before Chief Rabbi Jakobovits, Dayan Alony, the chairman of the Jewish Representative Council and Dr Charles Spiro, a legal member of its committee. Rabbi Shachter from Belfast acted as rabbinical judge. The reverend gentlemen won their case. Hours of *shechita* were to be adjusted to allow them time for ministerial duties within their respective synagogues, they were to be paid travelling expenses and an extra fee for emergency *shechita* outside Dublin and each was to receive a wage increase of more than £3 per week. When Revd Gittleson died in 1984, the United Hebrew Congregation honoured his memory by establishing a fund in his name for the benefit of Jewish pupils at Stratford College, Dublin's Jewish secondary school, a gesture officially acknowledged in 2003 when a testimonial to him was unveiled within the school.

Revd Solly Bernstein was reader at Grosvenor Place Synagogue and a *shochet* when he requested a rise in 1936. 'Why?' he was asked. When he explained he had just got married, the response was, 'So who told you to get married!'

Revd Segal, *chazan* at Greenville Hall Synagogue from 1946, was earning £12 per week when he was called to Glasgow in 1957. To supplement their livelihood in Dublin, his wife kept a guest house and her husband acted as *shomer*, an obligatory supervisor who ensures compliance with dietary laws at all kosher functions.

Isaac Fine held a diploma in Hebrew teaching from Jews' College in London. A native of Lithuania, he had lived in Manchester from the age of six and was teaching there in 1952 when he married Edna Davis from Dublin and moved to Ireland. Dublin had no vacancy for a Hebrew teacher. To qualify for a better income than he was earning in his father-in-law's failing business, he began a four-year diploma course in Accountancy at Rathmines Technical College, studying at night. His excellent results won him money prizes each year but qualification was to earn him little. Nearly every community organisation from the *Chevra Keddisha* (Holy Burial Society) to the *Talmud Torah* (the organisation responsible for religious education) used his services free of charge until payment became essential to his survival. His son, Mordechai, a dentist in Manchester, recalls his father as 'too bogged down' with community work to undertake private commissions. Already teaching *Bar Mitzvah* boys privately, he eventually joined the *Talmud Torah* as a teacher.

Jewish life in Ireland centred around the Hebrew calendar, the degree of ritual in each household varying with its *frumkeit* (degree of observance). In most homes preparations for the Sabbath began on Thursday with the cooking of traditional favourites such as chopped liver, *gefüllte* fish (chopped and fried or boiled in brine), chicken soup with *lockshun* (vermicelli, often home-made), potato *kugel* (pudding) and *tzimmis* (a kind of carrot-based compote) or *chollent* (a concoction of meat, potatoes and possibly beans that cooked overnight in bakery ovens). Its initiation before sunset on Fridays, even with minimalist observance, required the blessing of candles, wine and *challahs*. In more Orthodox homes parents blessed their children, hands were ritually washed with water poured from a vessel, Sabbath melodies pervaded the evening and grace was recited after meals.

Any act construed as work was forbidden so there could be no use of transport, no cooking and no handling of money. Observant families had a *Shabbos goy* (Sabbath Gentile), usually a friendly neighbour, who called to switch off lights or poke the fire. President Ó'Dálaigh, credited by Rabbi Cohen as having fashioned 'unbreakable ties of affection, esteem and honour in the hearts of Jewish citizens in this country', was one of many *Shabbos goys* who grew up on the South Circular Road.

Synagogue attendance on Saturday mornings was optional for women. Depending on the design of the synagogue, mothers, wives and daughters who chose to attend sat upstairs in a 'Ladies' Gallery' or downstairs, screened from male view. Everyone wore *Shabbos* best and the women certainly noticed each other. Hennie Bernstein remembered her circuit of synagogues as a teenager in the wake of *Rebbizin* Jakobovits (the rabbi's wife) so she could admire the *rebbizin's* stylish hats. Many families hosted a *Kiddush* after the service for friends and relations; some, like the Steinbergs, invited whole congregations. Wine was blessed and light refreshments served in a convivial atmosphere.

Shabbos afternoon was traditionally a time of rest but some young people preferred to go for walks, to rendezvous in St Stephen's Green or to visit each other at home. The older or more serious-minded might walk to Kevin Street Public Library to read the *Jewish Chronicle*, rated by some as much a part of *Shabbos* as the *challahs* and the wine. One Clanbrassil Street trader went regularly to the cinema without, in his view, violating any Sabbath law. Admission was free in return for his window display of their forthcoming attractions and he walked there and back.

The Jewish New Year, *Rosh Hashannah*, generally falls in September. It introduces the ten days of penitence that culminate in *Yom Kippur* (Day of Atonement), the holiest Festival in the Hebrew calendar. During those ten days, Jews believe the Almighty judges all humanity, inscribing each person in the Book of Life or Death. The traditional festive greeting translates as, 'May you be inscribed for a good year'. The ceremony known as *Tashlikh*, whereby sins are symbolically cast into natural running water, was performed by the Birzanskys in Cork at the Marina, a beautiful long walk that ended at the river bank. Their grandfather, Rabbi Avroham Seftal Birzansky, died on a nearby grassy hillock where he habitually sat to study *Torah*.

Yom Kippur, twenty-five hours of solemn prayer and total abstention from food and drink, which ends with the blowing of a *shofar* (ram's horn), begins with the hauntingly beautiful *Kol Nidrei* service. No one privileged to hear it in Greenville Hall Synagogue in September 1946 could forget the experience. The cantor was *Chazan* Garb, a native of Poland who had reached Ireland in the 1920s via London and Manchester. So magnificent was his singing voice that passers-by would stop to listen as he enthralled the congregation. On this night he sang with a poignancy that brought it to the sublime. Shortly before the service started, his ailing father, determined to be present, entered the synagogue holding the hand of his young grandson, Theo Garb. Moving to take his seat, he suddenly slid to the floor and died. In shocked silence, his body was removed to his home across the road but instead of accompanying it, *Chazan* Garb insisted upon conducting the service. His immediate personal sorrow transcended the natural heartfelt supplication of the prayer to make his performance unique.

Succot, the Feast of Taberacles, is a harvest Festival celebrated five days after *Yom Kippur*. It commemorates both the wanderings of the Israelites in the Wilderness and the use by Israelite farmers of makeshift structures in fields during harvesting. Each synagogue has a communal *Succah* or booth, and Orthodox families erect their own. Roofed only with leaves and branches and decorated inside with fruit, flowers and pictures appropriate to the festival, they are used for family meals and entertaining throughout the eight-day festival. Hardy males even sleep in them. The day after *Succot* is *Simchat Torah* (Rejoicing of the Law) when the *Torah* scrolls, read portion by set portion throughout the Hebrew year in perpetuity, are both concluded and re-started to noisy celebration of their everlasting continuity.

Chanucah, the Feast of Lights, is often mistaken for the 'Jewish Christmas' because children receive presents and it falls in December. The eight-day festival commemorates the retaking and rededication of the Holy Temple by Judah Maccabee in 165 BCE after the Syrians and Greeks had taken and defiled it. To symbolise the miracle of a lamp burning for eight days inside the temple on a one-day supply of oil, a *menorah* (eight-branched candelabra) is lit in every Jewish home. Beginning with a single candle, one more is added each succeeding night until all eight are alight. Particularly enjoyed by children, *Chanucah* was celebrated for many years with a parade of youth organisations in Adelaide Road Synagogue. Each of the many youth clubs, secular and religious, smartly turned out in their uniforms, marched behind their own flag before admiring parents, clergy and friends, in fierce competition to win the title for best presentation.

Purim falls in March. The *Magillah* (Book of Esther) is read in synagogue, and children noisily react to each mention of Haman's name by stamping their feet or shaking rattles. Many appear in fancy dress and families traditionally exchange gifts of fruit, sweetmeats, chocolates or wine.

Four weeks after *Purim*, Jews celebrate the most ritualistic and demanding of all the festivals. *Pesach* (Passover) involves the complete disruption of normal household procedure for weeks beforehand as every nook and cranny is cleaned of *chometz* (leaven), even to the turning out of pockets. Dishes and utensils used all year round are replaced by Passover ware, brought out of storage. In Siva Miller's home, dishes were changed over while the children slept. She never forgot the awe and excitement of seeing the kitchen dresser shrouded for maybe six weeks before the festival and that magical first glimpse each year of the beautiful Victorian ladies with large hats that decorated each of their Passover cups.

The focal point of Passover is the *Seder*, a set order of service for the first two nights, when the *Haggadah* (narration of the Exodus from Egypt) is chanted to age-old tradition and symbolism. As many as thirty people might sit down together, family, friends and strangers passing through, uniting in celebration of the colourful and joyous event, with the emphasis on child participation. Food preparation, which often included home-produced wine, is still prodigious. Zelda Pushinsky's family made their own mead. In her seventies she could still recall with hilarity the hens at her childhood home in 14 Raymond Street as they pecked at the spillage and staggered drunk around the backyard.

With Passover milk in bottles and cartons unavailable before the middle of the twentieth century, each family made arrangements for its own supply. Lydia Birzansky, aged fourteen, and her elder sister, Gertrude, used to be sent by bus from their home in Cork to a distant farm until they heard that a local African mission had a small herd of cows behind their church. To their amazement the children were admitted by a man in a long brown robe with a beaded cross suspended from his waist. He wore sandals but no socks and only a fringe of hair showed around his otherwise bald head. It was their first encounter with a monk. They still remember his gentle reply of, 'It's a pleasure,' when they paid and thanked him for milking directly into their gallon cans.

Despite the range of delicacies associated with Passover fare, the only product essential to the Festival is *matzo*, unleavened bread. It reached Ireland via London, mostly from Bonn's of Carlisle, until 1941, when war conditions interfered with normal commercial activity. Jack Steinberg, from his home in Manchester, recalled how his father, Aaron Zvi Steinberg, called an emergency meeting of the Jewish Representative Council, where the decision was taken to bake *matzo* in Ireland. Broderick's Bakery on the north side of the city hired out its plant for two weeks, and Mr Steinberg, Rabbi Alony, Rabbi Lewis and Rabbi Frankel koshered as much equipment as possible for Passover use. Wheels for pricking the surface of the *matzo* were made from old pennies notched at regular intervals around the circumference. Boards, rolling pins and an electric machine for grinding broken *matzo* into meal were bought from McKenzie's in Pearse Street.

Matzo must be made from white flour which was unavailable during the war years, but Government permission was obtained for a special milling. The Dublin Port Milling Company put new silks into its machines to grind the wheat. Speed is essential in producing *matzo*: each batch from start to finish must be completed within eighteen minutes. With the help of twenty female employees, the finished product was so acceptable that hardly anyone noticed that that year's *matzo* was home-made.

No one forgets the *matzo* made in Dublin in 1942. Flushed with success, community leaders expected even better results by moving their operation to Spratt's of Allingham Street. Best known for its production of dog biscuits, it was much better equipped than Broderick's, with up-to-date machinery and electric ovens. The results were catastrophic. Ettie Steinberg, Jack Steinberg's wife, loyally insisted it tasted 'delicious' and, ground down, 'made lovely pancakes' but its hard texture drew an immediate community analogy between the *matzo* made at Spratt's and its more usual product. Mrs Garber from Vincent Street South, unaware of Mr Steinberg's part in its production, told him the man responsible for making it, '*soll zich ausbrechen alle zehner*' (should break all his teeth). Passover was an opportunity for Jewish households to treat Christian friends to a box of *matzo*, then available only in kosher shops. A friend of Herbie Kay who tried sampling his gift in 1942 exclaimed, 'Jesus, Herbie, what did the Jews do to deserve this?' Importation fortunately resumed in 1943.

The last milestone of the Jewish year is *Shevuot*, translated as Pentecost or the Feast of Weeks. It commemorates the end of harvesting and the acceptance by Moses at Mount Sinai of the *Torah* and the Ten Commandments on behalf of the Jewish people. The festival is particularly associated with the eating of cheesecake attributed in Jewish humour to the milk having curdled because Moses spent so long on the mountain.

Outside *Shabbos* and festivals, the year was punctuated by community celebrations. The *Bris* of every baby boy, the *Pidyon-Ha-Ben* (Redemption of the First Born) six weeks later if the male infant was the first child conceived, *Barmtzvahs*, engagements and weddings were equally important events. The Progressive Synagogue always held a *Bat Mitzvah* ceremony for girls fully equivalent to the boys' *Barmtzvah* but it was 1973 before the Orthodox synagogues adopted a form of female initiation called *Bat Chayil*. Considered revolutionary at the time, the project was spearheaded by Nathan Elzas, then a part-time *chazan* at Adelaide Road Synagogue, with the full support of Maurie Gordon, a prominent member of the congregation. It gave groups of twelve-year-old girls the benefit of a structured confirmation-type preparation course and some of the attention previously reserved for their brothers.

The greatest sorrow within the community was death, with intermarriage a close second and often, in the eyes of the highly Orthodox, the equivalent of death as a loss to the family and the community. Only the lengthy and painstaking Orthodox conversion to Judaism of the non-Jewish partner could absolve the deed. Ann Sevitt, daughter of Abram and Lieba (Elizabeth) Shevitovsky, *née* Garmidir, married Tom O'Brien in the 1930s. They had met at political and social gatherings in support of the Republicans in the Spanish Civil War, gone hostelling together and carried their love affair way beyond what was acceptable for their time. Ann Sevitt's mother, the more Orthodox of her parents, accepted the situation when Ann arrived home with her infant daughter, Sonia. Her father never forgave her. In 1986, Sonia recorded the extraordinary dual relationship she had as a child growing up in a household where neither parent converted and where attendance at Mass with the O'Brien grandparents alternated with accompanying Granny Sevitt to Greenville Hall Synagogue on *Shabbos*. She never felt accepted by either faith. When the Protestant primary school she attended in Bray put her outside during prayers, her sense of alienation was complete.

All Jews, irrespective of status in life, are buried in identical deal coffins within hours of death. There are no floral tributes or adornments. Throughout their adult lives synagogue members will have paid a small annual fee to the Holy Burial Society so that funerals can be free of charge. Members of that society in Ireland are all volunteers, prepared to leave home or work, day or night, to attend the dead and perform funereal rites. Parents, children and siblings sit *Shiva*, seven days of prayers, mourning and condolence sustained by visits from friends and relations. *Kaddish* (a sanctification of G-d's name), one of the most ancient prayers in the Jewish liturgy, is recited by male mourners for eleven months and on each anniversary of the death, to speed the departed soul towards Heaven.

From birth to death Judaism is a way of life that can be sustained only so long as the infrastructures for its practice are in place and utilised. It is their rate of loss rather than depleting numbers that may finally decide the fate of Irish Jewry.

4

ENTREPRENEURS AND CRAFTSMEN

When Maurice and Fanny Goldwater sailed from Liverpool in 1886 to try their luck in Ireland, they had no idea that their future livelihood would be decided before the SS *Munster* docked at Cobh. It just happened that the Cohen brothers were on the same ship and the four became acquainted when the Goldwaters heard the welcome sound of Yiddish among the English of their fellow-travellers.

The Cohens, whose valid ticket to America had not been honoured eight years earlier, had never completed their journey to New York. Left penniless in Cork, they had turned for help to the local Jewish community who supplied them with clothes and drapery to sell from door-to-door on a weekly instalment system. Within a few years the Cohens had converted the hawking of merchandise into a successful wholesale business, which supplied other immigrants with cheap clothing to peddle around the countryside. They were more than willing to employ Maurice Goldwater on a wage and commission basis as one of their 'tallymen' – the name applied locally to the Jews who sold goods at 1*s* or so per week and kept a tally of each customer's balance.

Peddling had been the last resource of many an unskilled man in the *heim*. In Ireland, where 10*s* could buy a hawker's license and enough cheap stock to fill a basket, pack or tray, it became a source of income for both the experienced and the impoverished among the new arrivals. As in Russia, the peddler had to cover many miles each day on foot or by train, carrying heavy loads of slippers, blankets, assorted drapery, picture frames, holy pictures and a variety of other cheap goods. When some customers asked only for cash to buy commodities elsewhere or for living expenses, the more enterprising peddlers expanded into moneylending.

Peddlers had to travel in all weathers, and most were on the road by 4 a.m. Some went home each evening no matter how late they finished; others spent the night wherever darkness overtook them. There were even peddlers who stayed away all week, returning to their family only for the Sabbath. Those who could afford it took bed-and-breakfast accommodation; the rest slept in outhouses or barns. Almost all brought their own kosher food. As the early start was not conducive to synagogue attendance, the pious recited morning prayers wherever they happened to be. One landlady entering Philip Davis's bedroom one morning unannounced was startled to see her lodger draped in a prayer shawl, head and one arm bound in phylacteries (leather boxes containing scriptural passages), while he swayed to the rhythm of Hebrew litany. Recognising neither the language nor the appurtenances, she exclaimed, 'Jesus Christ! The Devil is here!' and promptly put him out.

Maurice Goldwater enjoyed plying his trade around the scenic countryside, where farming and artisan customers treated him with kindness and respect. An induction from Cohen canvassers into local business practice, his Russian experience of peddling and a modicum of broken English learnt in Manchester and Liverpool all combined to make him a successful salesman within his appointed circuit. By 1890 he was earning enough to move Fanny from their lodgings within a Jewish household to a rented house of their own in Jewstown, the Cork equivalent of Dublin's Little Jerusalem; but he was not earning enough to support a family. When Fanny became pregnant with their first child, it was time to branch out on his own.

The Cohens had no objection. They continued to supply him on a 'sale or return' arrangement or through credit, as they were doing for other erstwhile novices who had graduated to independence. A ready supply of new arrivals was always available to replace ambitious tallymen seeking advancement through wholesale trading, as the Cohens had done themselves, or through building their own retail connection, as Maurice was about to do. Either route or even a complete deviation could lead to that immigrant entrepreneurial dream – a successful business.

The paths initially taken by the Cohens and Goldwaters to secure a livelihood were replicated wherever Jewish immigrants settled in Ireland; but some found the work and the customers less congenial. It was especially difficult for those with poor or no English. Harold Mushatt could recall newcomers going from door to door trying to sell bootlaces, boot polish and tawdry jewellery with 'Good morning' and 'Thank you' as their only English vocabulary. Even their knowledge of coinage was perfunctory. Many used an abacus to calculate and most kept their accounts in Yiddish. In 1924, when Bernard Cherrick died in a Dublin street from a heart attack at the age of thirty-eight, his young Irish-born widow, Sarah, had to ask Rabbi Herzog to translate his accounts so she could continue his weekly business to support herself and her baby daughter.

Many were ridiculed. Children in Limerick would bend their backs in imitation of the laden peddlers and run after them shouting, 'A pitchie (picture) man, a tallyman, a Jew, Jew, Jew.' Con Leventhal, Jewish scholar and academic, records how Catholic boys in Lombard Street in the heart of Little Jerusalem chanted their own parody of the Jewish peddler as he sought payment for goods supplied or their immediate return.

Two shillies [shillings], two shillies, the Jewman did cry,
For a fine pair of blankets from me you did buy.
Do you think me von idjit [one idiot] or von bloomin' fool?
If I don't get my shillies, I must have my vool [wool].

Frequently the peddler got neither. Geoffrey Wigoder's book, *In Dublin's Fair City* (1985), describes how dishonest customers would buy goods for a modest down-payment and disappear before the first or second instalment of the balance fell due. Customers borrowing money used the same ruse. In *Dublin Tenement Life* (1994) by Kevin C. Kearns, May Hanaphy, in her mid-eighties, recalled:

... a relation of ours over on the north side. She'd get £20 off her Jewman ... And then she'd move. It was much easier to move than to pay the Jewman. My relative actually moved to England to escape the last loan.

Often the disappearance was illusory. Maggie Murray, a contemporary of May Hanaphy's, remembers how a friend of hers evaded payment:

When she'd get a loan off a Jewman the Jewman would knock and she'd put black crêpe on the door. See, years ago when you're dead they'd put a crêpe on the door ... She'd get a young fella to answer and say, 'Oh, she's dead.'

Noel Hughes, in his sixties, calls to mind a later version of the same ruse:

Some of the Jewmen, Harry Green and Mr Baker and Mr Spellman, they were moneylenders around here. But now they were done out of a lot of money too. Someone would go and get a lend of a few quid and when the Jewman'd come there'd be a make-up husband – or maybe the husband was in on it. He'd say, 'What are you borrowing money off Jews for?' And he'd give the 'wife' a dig. And the Jewman would run out the door. And he wouldn't come back.

His own grandmother had borrowed from a Jewish moneylender without his grandfather's knowledge. On collection day, 'Bill the Sailor' Connolly stood in as her husband and was shaving with an open razor when the moneylender called to request payment:

'You're borrowing money off them?' he says and gives a box to me granny. And he made a run for the Jewman and the Jewman runs down the street because

Bill has an open razor in his hand. And he never come back any more. That happened an awful lot.

Benny Matthews experienced no such dishonesty. His father, Isaac Matthews, was brought to Northern Ireland as a teenager in 1890 by a Latvian neighbour established in Lurgan as a general peddler. Isaac lived and worked with him and between them, Benny claimed, 'they practically clothed every kid in Lurgan,' for repayments of 3d to 6d a week. Isaac eventually bought the business through monthly instalments. When Benny took over, in 1936, he did the rounds on a bicycle that cost him £7 19s 6d. Every household in and around Lurgan welcomed him for his goods and his good humour.

When electricity reached Moira, five miles from Lurgan, in the 1950s, Benny lent a regular customer £5 to buy a cooker. She asked him to keep the transaction confidential and promised to repay on the first Thursday of the following month but she died of a stroke before the due date. Rather than betray her confidence, Benny said nothing about the loan when her husband settled other debts, though £5 was more than he could earn in a day's collection. Months later he met her daughter. She told him her mother, bereft of speech before she died, had mouthed what seemed to be 'Ben' and tried to hold up the five fingers of one hand. Could Benny account for it? Benny explained what had happened and the loan was repaid at 10s a week. He told this story in the *Belfast Telegraph* when it offered a prize of five premium bonds to anyone who could demonstrate true honesty. One of them won him £500. When tools were stolen from the boot of his parked car, the thief who tried to sell them cheaply in the local pub was forced to return them when he admitted their true ownership. No one was allowed to steal from Benny Matthews.

Where the interest charged on financial transactions was high enough to offset losses, peddlers and moneylenders became wealthy men, and many used their substantial income to finance more prestigious business ventures. The more easily intimidated were seriously out of pocket and forced to supplement their meagre earnings by other means. Geoffrey Wigoder's grandfather, Myer Joel Wigoder, was among them. Before he reached Ireland in 1891 his journey from Lithuania had taken him through Germany, Holland and Belgium where he left a trail of failed business enterprises. More scholar than businessman, he tried giving Hebrew lessons after his peddling day was over; but even for the modest fee of 1s per week per pupil for several hours' daily tuition – Fridays and Saturdays excepted – pupils were hard to find. Eventually he turned instead to making picture frames. Evening and night and all day Sunday, working in winter darkness by paraffin lamp or candle, he measured, sawed and nailed the frames, hoping they would earn him a higher profit than the pictures he sold from his pack by day. His eldest son, Saul Harris Wigoder (who also answered to Harry or Barney), did milk rounds before and after school from the age of ten to help feed the family of five children. By twelve, Harry's schooldays were over. During the day he hawked 'a bundle of draperies, ribbons, cottons, wools, blankets, shirts, stockings' around the houses; at night he helped make the picture frames, until framing took over from peddling. Myer Joel in his autobiography recalled Harry earning 12s in one day by making 144 frames for the trader they supplied. When the family moved to 33 New Street, a workshop with inadequate living space, Harry slept on a table in the shop with brothers, Philip and Louis, on either side of him.

Harry Wigoder was twenty when he opened a shop in 1901. He advertised it by paying boys 1s per thousand to put 'fancy coloured bills' through letterboxes. Wigoder's shop at 75 Talbot Street sold wallpaper, Catholic prayer books, statues, framed holy pictures and paint. Two years later his father opened his own Wigoder shop in rented premises at 27 Capel Street; it was twenty-five years before he could afford to buy the property. The two shops always operated independently, and expansion into other branches occurred only later under new ownership; but the family name remains a part of Irish trading history. More than 100 years later, Wigoder shops are still supplying paint and wallpaper to households all over Ireland.

For unskilled immigrants who failed at peddling or baulked at trying it, even as a stop-gap, one possible alternative was the collecting and reselling of waste, such as scrap metal or rags. Sam Yodaiken and his siblings, the first of the Yodaiken family to settle in Dublin, had a scrap-metal yard adjacent to their home at 34 Lower Clanbrassil Street from 1899. By 1907 they were operating as rubber merchants from number 98A. Philip Davis's youngest daughter, Sybil Roberts, now living in London, recounts that her father went from peddling into the scrap metal and rag business long before 1931 when she was born. His day's work still started between 4 a.m. and 5 a.m. when he set off to collect waste he had bought the day before. By breakfast time he had brought the load home, only to set off again immediately after the meal in search of further supplies. It was 7 or 8 p.m. before his travelling day was over and there was still waste to sort and his store to supervise.

The work was unremitting and attracted rats and fleas but by the 1920s Philip Davis owned his own butcher shop at 43 Lower Clanbrassil Street; number 44 where he lived with his wife and family; number 45 which was let to Jewish tenants; number 46 which was occupied by the Barrons who also ran a butcher shop in another Davis premises around the corner in St Vincent Street South; yet another property run by Harry Robinson, bookmaker, adjacent to Barron's shop and a very small premises next door to the bookmaker which Philip used as a store. The business is still owned and managed by the Davis family.

When Zorach Woolfson came to Ireland in the mid-1880s with his wife and four children, he earned his living collecting scrap from door to door. Solly Woolfson, his grandson, who became the head of Kayfoam Woolfson, described him and his own father, Willy Woolfson, Zorach's youngest son, as 'wealthy scrap merchants' by the end of the First World War. Working from several different premises, including a marine store in Bridgefoot Street on the quays, they specialised in collecting and sorting rags into large bales of specific natural fabrics, which were shipped for 'regeneration' to mills in Yorkshire; much of the resultant 'shoddy' was used to make cloth for British military uniforms. For a time financial success outstripped business acumen as the Woolfsons began investing in shoe shops, butcher's shops and similar enterprises, all of which failed for want of efficient management. Early market investments were equally unsuccessful when Joe Woolfson, Zorach's 'suave, debonair son', was sent to England with a large sum of money to buy strongly recommended Dunlop shares and returned instead with worthless German marks. By the mid-1950s, Solly and his father were exporting waste to Europe and America, and the output of their rabbit-skin drying process to felt hat manufacturers in Britain and Belgium. Already the largest waste dealers in Ireland, they bought a laundry in Fleming's Place in 1958 for washing and drying rags that were sold on as cleaning cloths to garages and engineering shops. By now Solly's brother, Louis Woolfson, had joined the firm, leaving Solly free to handle their latest venture, representing Japanese firms who were exporting textiles to Europe.

The advent of synthetic materials in the mid-1960s crippled the business of recycling natural fibres but the Woolfsons had already opened the first plant in Ireland to make core fibre padding and felt fillings for mattresses and upholstery. In the early 1970s, they moved the operation to a modern specialist plant at Bluebell Industrial Estate, Dublin, dedicated principally to the manufacture of flexible polyurethane foam, a new product that had begun to replace expensive latex rubber foam in mattresses. Manufacturing mattresses and beds was a natural progression. In 1981, a licence agreement was entered into with an American mattress company to manufacture King Koil mattresses under franchise. With the acquisition in 1987 of O'Dearest, Kayfoam Woolfson became the biggest bedding company in Ireland. It went on to develop visco elastic memory foam, registered under the trade-name Kaymed. Similar to material used in space exploration to cushion astronauts against the extraordinary pressure of take-off and landing, Kaymed is used throughout the world for pressure-relieving products, including medical mattresses. The firm that began with the door-to-door collection of scrap eventually employed 331 workers before it was sold in 2007.

Solly Woolfson enjoyed reminiscing about his less affluent days. He especially recalled the first time he hosted a celebration family dinner at a Dublin hotel. Still a young man with limited means, he had priced the set menu in advance and carried exactly enough money to pay for his party of eight. Then the waiter suggested a slight change of menu. Would the guests prefer delicious, newly delivered fresh strawberries with cream to the set dessert? The substitution added £1 per head to the bill and the guests who opted for it had to pay the excess themselves.

There were numerous other Jewish scrap-dealers but according to the oral testimony of Elizabeth (Lil) Collins in *Dublin Tenement Life*, the *nonpareil* of Ireland's waste-collectors was Harry Sive. Lil Collins was only sixteen – the same age as her Russian-born boss – when she started work in Harry's newly opened shop in Meath Street in 1916. She was still there when he closed, fifty-five years later. Technically operating a rag store, Harry bought 'bales of clothes and cloth, whiskey bottles, stout bottles, jam jars, brass and copper, kettles, aluminum pots.' His place was a hive of industry, with work often continuing into the early hours of the morning and all day Saturday. Some employees prepared the clothes by tearing out the linings and pockets with a knife, sorting the bales into different fabrics, and boiling them; others cleaned and hammered the copper and brass or scraped labels off bottles and jars before washing them. Harry would buy waste over the counter but most of his scrap was bought from 'tuggers', some as young as nine years old, who might walk as far as Newbridge or Bray pulling one of Harry's empty three-wheeled basket cars, which they tugged back to the store laden with items they had collected at big houses along the way.

When Harry Sive started in business his only bed was a wooden table in the shop. He ended with forty-eight basket cars lined up outside his shop and a staff of twenty-eight sorters and thirty or forty tuggers. Lil reckoned he was a millionaire, but generous. He paid good wages – 2s 6d to Lil when she started working for him - and a good price by weight for the scrap he bought. He never charged tuggers for the use of his basket cars and gave money 'to start the week' to any tugger who could not afford 'stock' – the cheap delph or ornaments distributed in exchange for scrap. If a tugger pawned a basket car, easily recognisable by WASTE SALVAGE and the initial S. printed on it, his only response was a mild, 'Go over and get it back.' He provided free pink and blue smocks for his female workers and dungarees for the men and allowed them to take any new or nearly new clothes that came in; any unclaimed money found in pockets or handbags was also theirs to keep. Employees arriving on winter mornings found Harry 'on his knees lighting the fire for us', as the shop was cold. 'Very, very charitable and very kind to children,' is Lil's assessment of him as she recalls his weekly contribution towards the restoration of the big bell on St Catherine's Church in Thomas Street. At Christmas he gave boxes of chocolates to the women, cigarettes to the men and a bottle of port and 'an envelope with a few bob in it' to everyone. His annual Christmas party had plenty of free drink, big cakes and fish and chips for all. He stood bail for any local resident in trouble with the law and always offered some kind of job to the miscreant.

Generosity to his workers did not stop arguments between Harry and Lil's sister, Kitty, who was his forewoman. She would shout at him, 'You crucified our Lord and you're not going to crucify me!' Otherwise staff relations were amicable and Lil remembers Harry's workers 'putting their arms around the women and kissing them and always singing [so] you could hear them out in the street, doing their work.'

Another alternative to peddling, or possibly an extension of it, was dealing in second-hand furniture. For some it provided mere subsistence, but those with a discerning eye might spot ornaments or household furniture with potential antique or design value as they called at different houses. Owners who regarded the pieces as unwanted items were happy to sell them at a reasonable price. The buyer sold them on at a profit, and Jewish immigrants had become antique-dealers.

David Cherrick had such a discerning eye. A native of Lithuania, he reached Ireland in 1891 at the age of seventeen, leaving behind parents he would never see again. Of rural background, he had neither trade nor money and spoke no English. Peddling seemed his only option. His 'little weekly' eventually supplied retail customers in Arklow with shoes, shirts, suits, blankets and bedding, bought wholesale from Ferrier Pollock in Dublin. By the time he decided to move to Dublin he also had a furniture shop in Arklow which he replaced with a successful antique business on the Dublin quays. It transferred to Nassau Street in the 1920s. David dealt mainly in silverware and gold sovereigns. His widowed sister-in-law enjoyed browsing there and David's greeting of 'Sarah, I have a bargain for you,' often tempted her to buy. The shop remained in business until 1953, by which time he also owned Rathmines Motors, which was run by two of his sons. It sold and repaired cars and operated as a petrol station, with Julius (Jules) keeping the books and Arthur selling the cars.

Described by his granddaughters, Barbara Davis and Vicky Rose, as 'a good businessman', David worked his Arklow weekly till he was almost eighty. Despite his easy access to cars, he never drove and carried all his own heavy parcels.

In 1957 Harold Lindy left Ireland to settle in America, where he became a successful antique-dealer. Kevin Tierney, the senior vice-president in charge of silverware at Sotherby in New York, recognised the Lindy name and was delighted to discover that Harold was the nephew of Albert Lindy, the Dublin antique-dealer. 'Does he still have the Queen Anne tea service?' he asked, and they both recalled the magnificent silverware dated 1700 that Albert liked too much to sell.

Albert's father, Samuel Lindy, was born in Lithuania. He reached Dublin from London in 1914 and opened a mattress factory on the North Circular Road. Remembered as a charitable man, he bought shoes at Christmas for poor children from the Coombe tenements and Harold recalls the large number of Jewish poor who were enjoying meals at his grandfather's home in Victoria Street each time he went there to visit.

Albert's first job was selling gas stoves in a shop in Lennox Street that became a synagogue. He opened his antiques business in the 1940s in a rented shop in Camden Street Upper beside Brady's pharmacy and opposite Mr Duffy, for years the Lindy's barber. In 1960, Harold Lindy was on a visit to Ireland when his uncle returned from a trip to Rome, intimating that he had met the Pope. Mr Duffy called to hear all about it. 'Albert, Albert,' he begged, 'tell me about His Holiness.' Albert told him how a limousine had brought him to the Vatican, where he waited alone in an office, with his back to the door, until he heard it open and the Pope came in. 'He whispered something in my ear,' said Albert.

The barber, hands together as if in prayer, urged, 'Go on, go on, what did he say?' 'He wanted to know who gave me such a terrible haircut!' said Albert.

Joshua (Sam) Honigbaum, who changed his German surname to Samuels at the outbreak of the First World War, was born in Hull in 1863 to immigrant parents, Solomon and Helena Honigbaum, the sixth of ten children. At thirteen he left school to work as a 'market man', a job as commonplace among the Jews in England as peddling was to the Jews of Ireland. Over the next twenty years he established himself as a trader in drapery and jewellery in Manchester and possibly also in Lancaster but he looked to Ireland for greater prosperity. In 1897, he went alone to Dublin, returning to Manchester every few weeks to attend to his business and visit his growing family. By 1905 he felt confident enough to close his outlets in England and move his wife and five children to Dublin. Three more children were born in Ireland.

The Irish business was established in rented premises which he later bought, at the top of Henry Street, close to Nelson's Pillar and the General Post Office (GPO). His daughter, Ethel Freedman, in her private memoirs, describes the premises as 'a very large building, three stories over basement [that] sold just about everything – gold and silver jewellery, watches, cheaper jewellery, musical instruments, toys, clocks, ornaments, tea-sets, anything he could buy and sell to make money.' The shop was on the ground floor but Samuels' Bazaar, as he called it, was much more than a retail outlet. The first floor was a music hall. Responding to the loud, repeated urging of a uniformed commissioner to visit 'Samuels' Bazaar and Variety Show! Entertainment every hour! Walk in, walk in!' passers-by paid at the door for immediate admission to each performance. There was no seating. To the piano accompaniment of Kate Levenston, 'member of a well-known musical family,' vaudeville acts of all kinds – 'singers, dancers, comedians, acrobats, jugglers, musicians' – delighted the standing audience with a stage performance that started anew every hour. The acts were changed each week and Ethel Freedman remembered her father poring over variety publications, such as the *Stage* and the *Star*, looking for new talent. Arthur Lucan (Old Mother Reilly) and his wife, Kitty McShane, were just two of the many variety stars of the time who began a successful music hall career at Samuels' Bazaar.

At the back of the music hall were the further attractions of wax figures 'à la Madame Tussaud' and slot machines. The replicas of the famous and infamous were hired from England, with displays changed as personalities fell into and out of favour. The slot machines were Samuels-owned. By inserting 1*d* a customer could watch amusing or dramatic pictures unfold before his eyes. One electric machine, claiming to be 'invigorating and good for rheumatism', passed electricity through the body when the patron inserted 1*d* and grasped two handles. Far-seeing as he was in entertainment and entrepreneurial opportunities, Mr Samuels made one surprising error of judgement. After introducing magic lantern pictures into his performances he decided this precursor of the cinema had no future and willingly let a friend 'take it away to try it'. The friend was Maurice Elliman, whose family name would become closely associated with the Irish film industry. .

The attractions of Samuels' Bazaar ended in 1916 with the Easter Rising. The event is recalled by Ethel Freedman in her memoirs and by her youngest sister, Gertie Shatter, in an interview given in 1990 to Susan Nolan and Damien Walker for the archives of the Dublin Jewish Museum. On Easter Monday an employee, known to the Samuels family only by his rank of sergeant in the Irish Volunteers, advised them against removing the heavy shutters from the shop windows. 'I think we should close,' he said. 'I'll try and see you home. They've already started at the Pillar.'

He guided them out of the shop to the sound of gunfire in Sackville Street (now O'Connell Street), just as the first casualty was being carried from the GPO towards Jervis Street Hospital. He walked them 'up Moore Street … into Parnell Street where we saw [the] prancing horses of the only British regiment … in the city when the rebellion started', and on for miles in a circuitous route to Grafton Street. A group of volunteers at St Stephen's Green called the sergeant to come and join them. 'Good-bye, Boss,' he said. 'Good-bye, Miss Ethel. G-d knows if we will meet again.' Warned by a volunteer to 'move away quickly or I'll shoot!' the family continued the hazardous journey to their home in Harold's Cross, passing several trouble spots and a 'tremendous battle' at Portobello Bridge.

With city transport at a standstill, they stayed out of town until the Rising was over. When they ventured back, Henry Street was a shambles and Samuels' Bazaar was gone. Replete with a year's stock of goods, newly delivered and paid for, the entire premises, like many others, had been looted and razed to the ground. Stolen items subsequently found in tenement houses or dumped in churches by looters afraid to take them home were piled into cells at various police stations. Ethel and her mother joined other shopkeepers in viewing the 'fur coats lying on bags of flour, silver tea-sets, jugs, pads of rings, a tangle of mixed jewellery, melodeons, bicycles, handbags, articles of clothing, a conglomeration of the loot from ruined premises.'

Ethel expresses the greatest admiration for her father. To support his wife and eight children he opened a wholesale business in Liffey Street, which prospered so well that he expanded into two nearby premises. He also operated what must have been among the earliest mail order businesses in Ireland, promoting his 'shopping by post' through a catalogue distributed throughout the country and weekly full-page advertisements in the popular magazine, *Ireland's Own*. The Government eventually paid compensation for the loss or destruction of property during the Easter Rising and he was able to resume trading in the rebuilt premises in Henry Street, described by Ethel as 'modern and attractive'.

Some immigrants acquired vocational training after they reached Ireland. Abraham Suslaw, born in Moscow, had been an overseer for the import and export of grain during a long sojourn in Antwerp. When he reached Ireland in 1918 he was sent to learn pressing at the Jewish-owned Abbey Clothing Company. 'What time do I work to?' he asked the boss, who jokingly replied, 'Work till the gas goes out,' and left him to it. He was still there the following morning. Others arrived with skills. Census returns for 1901 and 1911, as well as the Alien Register of 1914-22, list Jewish residents as frame manufacturers, glaziers, tailors, cabinetmakers, dressmakers, boot-makers, watchmakers, brush-makers, cap-makers, bakers, confectioners, photographers, cigarette-makers, engineer-fitters, clerks, milliners, wood carvers, upholsterers, auctioneers, diamond-cutters, furriers, hairdressers, pipe-makers, printers and skin-dressers. An eighteen-year-old Russian girl described herself as a bookkeeper and 'typewriter', the term then used for a typist.

In Lithuania, working conditions and pay had been so poor that a Jewish Labour Bund (union) was established towards the end of the nineteenth century. Ireland valued its skilled workers no more highly. In 1936, when fourteen-year-old Lena Curland was seeking her first job, she was offered 1*d* for sewing on a dozen buttons and finally settled for a wage of 7*s* 6*d* per week.

Manus O'Riordan has traced Irish-Jewish labour involvement back to 1908, when Yiddish-speaking immigrants formed the International Tailors', Machiners' and Pressers' Union, known for a time as 'The Jewish Union'. In 1909, the year it became a registered trade union, it organised its first strike, involving only Jewish employers. Philip Sayers, an active community member, negotiated some form of settlement. Three years later, when union membership included Christians, the union struck against exploitative bosses of all faiths. In 1912, it transferred its offices from 11 York Street to 52 Camden Street Lower, sharing premises with the Camden Street Synagogue, established there by Myer Joel Wigoder in 1892. A trustee of the union at that time was Isaac Baker, a Russian immigrant who represented it at the Irish Trade Union Congress of 1923. Other executive members were Abraham Sevitt and Harold Reeves, both tailors, and Harry Levitas, a presser. Jewish involvement declined, but the union survived as the Irish Garment Workers' Industrial Union. In 1926, it was one of a group of unions in dispute with the managements of Jewish-owned firms over closing for Jewish Holy days.

Manus O'Riordan names Philip Baigel as one of the activists in forming and constantly re-forming the Jewish Cabinetmakers' Trade Union, which did not survive. Frank Baigel, Philip's son, a dentist in Manchester, remembers his father's assertion that non-Jewish workers were afraid of being called socialists because socialism was condemned by the Catholic Church. Jewish interest in labour reform led to growing solidarity between the Irish Transport and General Workers' Union and the Tailors' and Pressers' Union; but craft unions continued to resent the intrusion of Jewish workers as competitors in their own trades.

Distinctions were drawn between 'the legitimate cabinetmakers of Ireland' and Jewish cabinetmakers, and complaints made about 'foreign workers and their practices'. The *Leader* in 1904 carried an advertisement from the Dublin Tailors Co-Partnership Ltd in Bachelor's Walk enjoining Irishmen to 'help us stamp out Sweated, Jewish labour, in the Tailoring Trade in Dublin.' Some blamed the Jews for the loss of jobs caused by mechanisation. Kevin C. Kearns in *Dublin's Vanishing Craftsmen* (1987) quotes one tailor as claiming that 'the machinery came in when the Jews came in' despite the fact that seventy-two Jewish tailors were listed in the 1901 census and few tailoring shops had machinery even into the 1930s.

Difficulty in finding work or the need to earn more than the job would pay forced many skilled early settlers into self-employment, often in back rooms or pokey premises. Later, ambition was the spur, with grown-up sons branching out or encouraging their skilled fathers to 'go it alone'. Either way, the successful emerged as wholesale manufacturers, master craftsmen or retailers able to offer employment to others.

Abraham Sabin left Russia as a boy of thirteen in the 1890s, intending to go to America. He was put ashore at Liverpool and remained there for some years. His daughter-in-law, Hilda Sabin, still has the notecase containing the *nedan* (dowry) his eighteen-year-old fiancée, Cecilia, brought with her when she came from Russia to be his wife. Wanting no more than the young woman herself, he refused the money which has been kept in the family, untouched, for best part of a century. They married in Liverpool. Abraham, a tailor, was employed by Burton's, then a household name in Britain for its good quality but inexpensive suits. The company transferred him to a Dublin branch in the 1920s, promising a directorship that never materialised.

In the 1930s, Abraham's adult daughter, Kitty, and his son, Carl, a master cutter, advised him to leave his dead-end job and open his own premises. From small beginnings in a house in New Street, the business expanded until A. Sabin Ltd was manufacturing in a three-storey building in Cecilia Street. The premises had previously been a medical school and Hilda Sabin, Carl's widow, remembers hearing that bones were found there after the students left. An ardent supporter of trade unions, Abraham considered it wrong for people to work all year round without a break. Maurice Snipper, who married Abraham's granddaughter, Mona White, believed he was the first Irish employer in the trade to offer his staff an annual week's holiday, originally at their own expense but later with pay. Workers employed by him tended to stay for 'years and years' and their number eventually grew to well over 200. Sabin's supplied suits and overcoats to Arnott's, Clery's, Switzer's and other big stores in Dublin and around the country. Kevin & Howlin, gents' outfitters in Nassau Street, bought Sabin's finest tweeds, exporting most of them to America.

Hilda remembers Mr Howlin calling at Sabin's factory daily at 11 a.m. until his death in the 1950s. Executing the same little dance each morning, he would ask, 'Are you ready, Abe?' whereupon Abraham, a diminutive figure beside the six-foot tall Howlin, left his brother Sam Sabin to supervise the tailoring, his son Carl to supervise the cutting and ample instructions for the morning's work, before accompanying his friend to their chosen venue for a drink. He was back in time for his driver to take him home for lunch at 1 p.m. and to chastise loudly anyone who had not fulfilled his set tasks. By 2 p.m. he was back from lunch and in full control. Sabin's prospered well enough to expand into retailing. C. and S. Ames in Henry Street and Weston's in Mary Street were two of the many outlets, each trading under a different name, that they opened around Dublin and in Dun Laoghaire.

Mona Snipper's father, Bernard (Barney) White, who married Anne Sabin, started a dress-hire business in the early 1930s from the small premises in Exchequer Street where he lived. Apart from one small shop in Capel Street, it was the only dress-hire firm in Dublin, and Mona can remember 'queues and queues' of people taking advantage of the service for weddings, staff functions and other special occasions. In the 1940s, Mr White opened his own clothing factory in Strand Street, where a staff of 120 made what some regarded as the best bespoke garments in Dublin. The firm also supplied suits to Kingston's, Best's, Siberry's, Byrne and Fitzgibbon's, Arnott's and retail outfitters all over Ireland. 'B. White Dress Suit Service' went from strength to strength, moving from Exchequer Street to Leinster Market, a laneway near the Gas Company in D'Olier Street, and finally to Hawkins Street. It remained in business for more than sixty years.

David Rivlin, who had twice escaped from his Russian barracks, was also a tailor. Agnes Gartland, in her nineties, remembered him well from Polikoff's, the tailoring firm in Kilmainham where she worked almost from its inception in 1933 until its closure, as Kilmain Clothing, in 1982. Employing 850 people, the factory was built to satisfy the insistence of Seán Lemass, Minister for Industry and Commerce, that all suits sold by Burton's in Ireland must be made in Ireland. Lemass performed the opening ceremony. The Jewish owner of the factory, originally from Poland, lived abroad and visited his enterprise once a year.

David Rivlin was appointed at Polikoff's in the 1940s as a temporary replacement for a foreman who had decided to enlist. Agnes Gartland described him as a 'very good foreman' and recalled his gracious apology, 'Me sorry, me sorry. I forgot!' when he upset her by complaining about her backlog of work before remembering she had been out for a week because of her father's death and funeral. When the man he had replaced was demobilised and claimed back his job, David protested, 'Me need the job,' but he had to go. Shortly afterwards he started his own business in rented premises in St Andrew's Street. Two of his daughters, Bertha and Connie, had worked with him in Polikoff's, and his two sons, Aaron and Eli, worked with him in St Andrew's Street. None of them had the worldliness that marks the successful businessman. Des Leech, a retired tailor, remembers that he failed to dupe David Rivlin only because he lost his own nerve. Looking for a vacancy where he could learn the trade, he called into Rivlin and Sons, where they required a skilled operator. Interviewed by David, he pretended a working knowledge of machinery he had no idea how to operate in the hope that he would glean enough information to bluff his way from the tailoring course he was due to start at the 'Tech' the following Monday night. When David said, 'OK, start on Monday morning,' he panicked and admitted that he could not even distinguish between the machines, let alone use them.

Eli Rivlin described his father as a carefree man who played the balalaika and squandered money with no thought of tomorrow on the rare occasions he had any. Often he came home penniless at the end of a working week, his earnings all spent on staff wages and expenses. He died a poor man. Years of thrift and hard work enabled his sons to buy premises in Dame Street in the 1960s, where they built up a clientele of private customers and made 'specials' for Kingston's, Gibson Price, Arnott's and a range of other outfitters who took orders for made-to-measure garments and sold them, Rivlin-made, under their own individual labels. Gentlemanly and soft-spoken, each brother was an expert in his own field. Aaron made the jackets, Eli made the trousers. Fanny Rivlin (*née* Cohen), Aaron's wife, finished and passed the finely tailored suits. The factory had been closed some years when Eli sat at a function beside Jack Steinberg who was wearing a Rivlin dinner suit. 'D'you see this, Eli?' said Jack, carefully fingering the lapel of his jacket. 'You and Aaron made it. I'm afraid to wear it in case I wear it out! Where would I ever replace it?'

Martin Sidney Rosenblatt, a bespoke tailor who traded as Martin Sidney, came to Dublin via London and Belfast. The Polish-born son of a tailor to the Russian Imperial Army, he established a bespoke tailoring business in 1948 in upstairs premises at 9 South King Street. The skills that won him ten *Tailor and Cutter* awards within nine years also drew a prestigious clientele that grew to include Patrick Hillery, President of Ireland, Donagh O'Malley, a cabinet minister, Jimmy Campbell, band-leader of the Theatre Royal, and numerous other political and theatrical luminaries. None of them would have disputed his advertised claim that 'there are no finer clothes than those tailored by Martin Sidney.'

Michael Walsh and Paddy Murphy worked for him at different times during the 1950s. Both describe him as 'top-class'. Paddy particularly remembers the constantly changing layout of the workshop, which 'could be one way when you came in the morning and another way when you came back after lunch.' Though he paid top wages, Martin Sidney's staff changed with almost equal regularity. Paddy noticed 'a restlessness about him' and a certain reservation towards highly trained employees who had learnt their skills elsewhere. Tailors resented it and quickly moved on. He did all his own cutting and the best tailors, in his opinion, were those he had trained himself. Within a month he could turn a country tailor, capable of only the roughest work, into a first-class craftsman.

When contemporary tailors were asking from £12 to £20 for a suit, he was charging £42 – which might explain his uncompromising attitude towards troublesome customers. His son, Stuart Rosenblatt, remembers suits being hung up and left on rails because his father refused to sell them to customers who displeased him. He dealt even more stringently with one person who repeatedly complained about the fit of a jacket. Based on his premise that 'craftsmanship is the secret of high-class tailoring' and his belief that 'if anything is worth doing, it's worth doing well,' Martin was a perfectionist. Garments leaving his workroom had to be perfect and he was the first to notice a flaw. In this case he considered the complaints spurious. The garment was altered, nevertheless, again and again, until the customer was finally satisfied. As it lay on the counter ready to be wrapped and paid for, Martin took a pair of shears, cut the jacket to pieces in front of the customer, and told him, 'Never come back!'

Not everyone could afford to be that independent. Maurice Bernstein, a master tailor before he arrived from Lithuania in the late 1890s, was glad to take whatever work he could get to support his wife and large family. Anderson and Anderson, a prestigious firm that catered to the nobility by royal appointment, admired his skill and gave out work to him. No one knew better than Maurice Bernstein the measurements of King Edward VII or how to accommodate the handicap that left Kaiser Wilhelm with one arm shorter than the other. Both customers might have been more than a little surprised had they known that the royal hunting jackets were made by an immigrant Jew in Dublin.

Jewish furriers arrived much later than the tailors, and mostly from Great Britain. Jack Bloom recalls that his father, Alfred Bloom, first came to Dublin in 1926 to open a branch for Kaufman's Successors, well-known London furriers. He was back in London in partnership with Nat Mendel when generous tariff concessions encouraged them both to settle in Dublin. In 1934, they began trading as Alfred Charles from 17 Dame Street, the same building that would house Jack Bloom Furmodes in the 1950s and was later acquired by Rivlin and Sons. Alfred Charles moved to Henry Street in the 1940s and continued trading until the partnership dissolved. Alfred Bloom Ltd opened soon afterwards at 18 Wicklow Street, later moving to North Lots.

Both Jack Bloom and his brother, Sidney, followed their father's calling and many other Jewish furriers appeared on the Irish scene. The Southern Fur Company in Grafton Street was owned by Walter White, originally from Glasgow. Two generations of the Vard family had fur businesses in Dublin, Cork and Belfast. A member of the Kahn family owned the Polar Fur Company at the top of Grafton Street, where a stuffed polar bear was displayed in the first-floor window. Several Jewish tailors specialised in remodelling furs. Some were chamber masters, the fur trade equivalent of the tailoring CMT (cut, make and trim). Almost all were manufacturers, some supplying the large department stores as well as private customers. Leon, the couture gown shop in Grafton Street, had its own fur room.

Knowledge and judgment of skins gleaned from his father, cutting skills learnt from Alf Solomons, manager at Alfred Bloom Ltd, and his natural flair for fashion and design equipped Jack Bloom to establish his own company. It later transferred to Abbey Street.

Fashion shows for modelling fur collections were well attended. The furs were placed on a rail in the dressing-room in the order in which the models would wear them and commentators described each one in turn from a script prepared by the furrier. Betty Wheelan was the commentator at one such show at the Shelbourne Hotel when she read a description completely at variance with the garment being modelled. Jack Bloom interrupted with, 'Betty, no! I'm sorry! The girls have mixed it up, and it's the wrong garment!' At Betty's suggestion he finished the commentary himself and henceforth presented his own fashion shows. A similar mix-up occurred later at a fashion show in aid of a Jewish charity at the Dr Leslie Golding Hall. On Jack Bloom's advice, the models were members of the community, not professionals, and one of them mistakenly put on a coat that belonged to a member of the audience. As she walked out onto the ramp, Jack delighted and amused everyone by announcing, 'And here is Barbara Cherrick wearing Mrs Morris's musquash coat, which was hanging at the end of the rail.'

Traditional fur-cutting and manufacturing is highly labour-intensive. To encourage young people to acquire the necessary skills, the Irish Fur Trade Association opened a fur school in the 1970s in the form of evening classes at the Technical College. Alf Solomons was the tutor. Most Jewish boys by then preferred to study for a profession but Jack Bloom never regretted his rejection of that alternative for himself. An accomplished painter into his eighties, he looked back with satisfaction on a career he had found artistically and financially rewarding.

Jewish cabinetmakers, like tailors, were often obliged to set up on their own. Baigel's, Caplin's, Lepler's and Milofsky's all became well-known furniture manufacturers and articles of furniture made by one or other of them can still be found in Irish homes.

Persecution drove Lewis Milofsky out of Poland in 1908, when he was eighteen years old. He was working in London as a skilled cabinetmaker when a friend in the trade introduced him to his sister, Chaya, visiting from Odessa. The young couple spent as much time as possible together, with Lewis walking Chaya home, Chaya walking Lewis back, and Lewis escorting her home a second time. They were married in London in 1910 and had ten children before they left in 1927. Two more were born in Dublin.

The London antique firm that employed Lewis Milofsky recommended him to Dublin colleagues for skilled restoration work, with no intention of making it a permanent arrangement, but he liked Dublin and decided to stay. Chaya and the family joined him three months later. In 1933, he opened the small workshop in Upper Jervis Lane, off Mary Street, that would become L. Milofsky and Sons, Ltd. As each Milofsky boy left school, all except one became apprenticed to the cabinetmaking trade, and one by one they joined their father's business. Daughters, Fanny Turk and Jean Solomons, worked in the office. Lewis spoke only broken English, so Fanny negotiated with customers. The business that began with a staff of two or three was employing about eighteen cabinetmakers, French-polishers and apprentices by the time Lewis died in 1967. More aware of current trends than his brothers, Ikey Milofsky suggested the firm should move away from labour-intensive manufacturing into over-the-counter DIY sales. The Woodwork and Hobby Supplies Centre was opened at Harold's Cross, run first by Ikey and then by his brother, Joe Milofsky. Their respective sons, Kenneth and Michael, now run the business from premises at Mount Tallant Avenue.

Abraham Noyek, one of the brothers who reputedly spent three years travelling to Ireland, arrived with a natural talent for wood-carving and cabinetmaking. In 1890, he set up home and began making high-quality reproduction furniture in a shed cum coach-house in the grounds of the Protestant Bishop's palace in Greenville Avenue. The bishop, Revd J.B. Wilson, took a liking to him and admired his work. When he left for England in 1904, he gave Abraham the use of the main house, large enough to accommodate his wife, Molly, the workshop and ultimately, their six children.

Abraham's reputation grew but his failure to exact payment for goods supplied left the family so poor that the boys had to sell logs after school. Molly already helped in the business by staining the furniture. When she decided to take responsibility for its financial affairs as well, she allocated Abraham 6d a week to spend on chocolate for the children and set about making the workshop pay. As demand for his fine workmanship grew at home and abroad, staff were employed to help manufacture Abraham's Chippendale, Adams and Sheraton reproductions. In years to come he would make the magnificent mahogany and glass cabinet ordered by the Bank of Ireland to display the Mace that had been used in the Irish House of Lords before its closure in 1800. Kept for generations in the family of the last Speaker, it was bought at auction by the Bank of Ireland when the Fosters finally decided to sell it.

In 1916, Abraham Noyek was living above a corner shop at 200 Parnell Street. Within a few years his son, Bernard (Barney), who began carving at the age of nine, was attracting the attention of passers-by by carving beautiful mahogany pieces in the shop window. The reproduction furniture was made in an adjoining factory in Granby Lane where a wood loft became a clandestine refuge for Jewish boys fleeing to Ireland to avoid conscription in Britain. In return for bed and board, they worked in the factory. Abraham's grandson, Aubrey Noyek, admits it was probably cheap labour but the 'fly boys' had the advantage of skilled apprenticeships in woodworking. When the war ended, some decided to stay in Ireland and start their own workshops, creating a demand for seasoned timber. Abraham's efforts to supply it changed the nature of the business. Teddy Noyek, Aubrey's father, had inherited his mother's business sense. In charge of sales from the age of twenty, he began sourcing the large amount of materials needed from abroad. By 1928 when the firm became A. Noyek and Sons, Teddy was flying to Paris for supplies. In 1929, he exhibited for the first time at the Royal Dublin Society in Ballsbridge where every piece of furniture he displayed belonged to his mother.

Abraham Noyek died in 1933 but the business continued under Molly and three of her five sons, Barney, Sam and Teddy Noyek, until 1939 when Teddy died and Barney went to Canada to help manufacture aircraft made from plywood. In 1946, sons Harry and Ivor Noyek returned from service in the American forces. They modernised the firm and Sam acquired the agency for Wareite, 'the plastic material beyond compare'. In the mid-1950s, he opened the first mill in Ireland to manufacture plywood. Using the slogan 'Noyeks for Plywood', A. Noyek and Sons prospered as an import/export company and wholesale supplier to the furniture and shop-fitting trade. The 50,000 square feet of premises they eventually occupied in Parnell Street and King's Inn Street was sold in 1963 to a multi-national company who retained both the family name and its expertise. In 1972, a devastating fire razed Noyek's Timber Merchants to the ground with the tragic loss of eight employees, still deeply mourned by their relatives and the Noyek family, who have never come to terms with the disaster. Aubrey, who had been its chief executive since 1969, opened Aubrey Noyek Ltd in 1980, a similar concern that continued in business for the next ten years until it, too, attracted multi-national ownership. In 1990, Aubrey moved with his family to Manchester where his sons, Theo and Jason Noyek, are the fourth generation to continue the family tradition of trading in wood.

Equally gifted with his hands was Sam Danker, who set up as a cabinetmaker in New Street in the early 1950s. Later his firm would move to 53 High Street, but it was in New Street that he began hand-carving the fine furniture bought by such prestigious customers as Seán T. O'Kelly, a founder member of Fianna Fáil and twice President of Ireland. Many of them became his friends and it was not unusual to find some prominent personage seated in his workshop enjoying a cup of coffee and a chat.

For a group that never totalled much above 5,000 souls, the Jews in Ireland were remarkably innovative. The Briscoe Brothers, Robert, Bert and Wolfe, opened the first cotton wool factory in Ireland. Converted from old tram sheds in Clonskeagh, Co. Dublin, into the Eircot Cotton Company in 1938, it manufactured cotton wool for hospital and domestic use from bales of imported raw cotton. Joe Briscoe describes it as a life-saver during the Second World War, when supplies were difficult to obtain. The factory exported cotton wool to Israel in times of need as gifts from the Irish Jewish community.

Tommy and Freda Noyek ran the only Doll's Hospital in Ireland. Dressed in white uniforms, with Freda sporting a matron's badge, they brought successive generations of children with 'sick' dolls into the back room 'surgery' of their shop in South Great George's Street. Cots for the dolls, displays of surgical instruments, a notice regarding surgery hours and a sprinkling of disinfectant added to the illusion of reality and helped to make children less apprehensive about real hospitalisation. Their retirement after forty years in business was marked by local newspapers as the end of an era.

The O'Connell Bridge School of Motoring at 1 Aston Quay was taken over by the Garb family in 1948. Using facilities and teaching methods unique at the time, they were the first school of motoring to teach lorry drivers and the first to replicate road conditions with an indoor simulator. Evening students attending their courses on car maintenance had the use of a car chassis for practical training. The school campaigned for the introduction of driving tests into Ireland. Theo Garb, who credited his sister, Lucy, with the concept of the school, had in his possession a photograph taken on 18 March 1964, the day test legislation came into force. It showed his mother with the Lord Mayor of Dublin and Nat Mendel, the owner of the building at Aston Quay, celebrating the event. By the time the school closed it had branches all over Ireland.

Bernard Spiro moved from Russia to England in the nineteenth century and then on to Ireland, where the family settled first in Cork and then in Dublin. His sons, Joseph, Louis, Harold and Campbell Spiro, opened the Invisible Mending Company (Imco) in Grafton Street in the 1920s using French invisible-menders. The dry-cleaning side of the business began small with garments being given out to larger firms for processing. By 1929 Imco had its own dry-cleaning factory in Merrion. It was sold in the 1960s as a chain of approximately fifty branches around the country, each still under the active management of the family. Its weekly sponsored radio programme, featuring Louis Spiro and presented by Éamonn Andrews, made Imco a household name.

Jack Segal, director of the Jewellery and Metal Manufacturing Company of Ireland, was Master of the Company of Goldsmiths in 1962 and again in 1976. His father, Reuben Segal, had held the same office in 1950. Deeply involved in community affairs and sometimes referred to as the Father of Greenville Hall, Jack walked to *Áras an Uachtaráin* and back again for the Saturday ceremony in 1966 when the Company of Goldsmiths presented President de Valera with a Jubilee-hallmarked silver salver to mark the fiftieth anniversary of the Easter Rising.

A manufacturer and wholesaler of silver- and tableware, Jack was well-known for the emblems, medals and trophies he supplied for schools, sports clubs and every kind of organisation and for his buttons for Garda Síochána uniforms. He made the badges for blood donors, designed a memorial plaque for the composers of the Irish national anthem, gold-plated the harp created by Oisín Kelly for presentation at the Golden Harp Singing Competition, and cast in bronze the papier mâché head of Brendan Behan made by Des McNamara for Séamus de Búrca. Doris Segal, Jack Segal's widow, clearly recalls the bronze head being in the Segal home before de Búrca and Jack presented it to the National Gallery of Ireland. When Jack Segal died in 1987, Seamus de Búrca, referred to him in a letter of condolence as 'a superb artist in metal'.

When Louis Solomon retired at the age of sixty-six as managing director of one of the country's biggest record wholesalers, he had been associated with the family firm for more than fifty years. Solomon and Peres, which grew to include a recording studio, was founded in Belfast in 1922 by his brother, Maurice Solomon, whose brother-in-law, Harold Peres, joined him later. Louis joined the business at the age of fourteen on an after-school salary of 4s per week. In 1947, when there were only five record dealers in Dublin, he joined the Dublin office at 21 Upper Liffey Street. In an article in the _Evening Herald_ in 1969, Louis Solomon recalled the old-style seventy-eights, records made from fragile shellac. He especially remembered the 5,000 singles of Bill Hayley's _Rock Around the Clock_ that arrived one year just before Christmas, all broken. Louis's nephew, Philip Solomon, discovered the Bachelors when they were still known in Dublin as the Harmonichords; his English company, Major Minor, put them into the British charts with around twenty hit singles.

Lionel Salem, a London photographer who settled in Belfast with his Irish wife, Joan Factor, opened Jaymar Studios at Carlisle Circus in the early 1950s. Innate skill and Lionel's tuition combined to bring Joan to world standard. She twice won the Ilford award for black-and-white photography in the 1970s and became an associate of the International Federation of European Photographers. Lionel, who lectured in photography all over Ireland, was the only photographer to serve as president of both the Professional Photographers of Northern Ireland and the amateur Northern Ireland Photographic Association. Linda Salem, their daughter, who now runs the studio, re-located since 1974, was the first wedding photographer in Northern Ireland to become an associate of the British Institute of Professional Photography. She is a past Northern Ireland chairman and United Kingdom chairman for International Photographic Awards.

The Lapedus family was making hand-made cigarettes at 49 Harcourt Street, Dublin, when prices per 100 ranged from 2s for standard quality to 8s 6d for the 'finest Turkish tobacco'. Simon Lapedus, a Lithuanian immigrant, was instrumental in extending insurance facilities to Irish Jews when he became an agent for the Guardian Insurance Company. Cork-born Louis Jackson, known to his friends as 'Bully', earned the additional nickname of 'Lavatory' when he invented El San toilets, and Maurice Cohen created a Mecca for the technologically-minded at 'Tomorrow's World' in Dublin's Grafton Arcade, the first computer shop in Ireland.

From the glass blowing of Mendel Waltzman at the Dublin Glass Bottle Company in Ringsend to the cutting and planing of wood at Factor's saw mills in Strand Street; from Raphael Silverman's 'Kitty's Stores' in Shantalla Road, hiring out 'ladders, garden equipment, Volumair spray equipment, mobile scaffolding towers' to his father's shop in Harcourt Street selling ballet shoes; from Gilbert and Sons' auctioneering to Alan and Gerry Benson's travel agency; from the Steinberg's Camac Transport to the tents made by Jeffrey Garber, there was hardly an occupation or business that was not represented in the Irish Jewish community.

For many it was not enough. Parents brought up in hardship, struggling for acceptance and independence, wanted status, earning potential, respect and recognition for their children. Gradually it came, as out of the rank and file there emerged a growing regiment of professional sons and daughters able and willing to make their mark on Irish society.

5

EDUCATION

Every Chief Rabbi of Ireland since Rabbi Jakobivits has conveyed a Jewish New Year message to Irish Jewry through the medium of the *Irish Jewish Year Book*. In the 1985-6 edition Rabbi Mirvis wrote, 'The key to the survival of the Jewish people is Jewish education.' It was a fundamental principle expressed by every Chief Rabbi before him; yet many in the community remained unconvinced. Jewish education may well have been paramount to their forefathers, among whom secular scholars were rare, but the hardships of an immigrant people had changed their own priorities.

Harold Mushatt, in an interview in 1990 with Niamh Brannigan and Susan Nolan for the archives of the Irish Jewish Museum, recalled that his mother reached Ireland in 1886 when she was only twelve. The grandmother who raised her in Russia had insisted she learn Latin because, 'one day you'll be going to Ireland, and if you know Latin you'll pick up the language very quickly.' Esther Hesselberg, *née* Birkhahn, born in Cork before the end of the nineteenth century, told Rose Hackett, Jenny Keely and Susan Nolan in a similar interview, that her father was English-speaking when he arrived in Ireland. May Gordon, born in Belfast in 1905, referred to the *gymnasium* (second-level school) her immigrant parents attended in the *heim*. May's daughter, Elaine Brown, remembers her grandfather as particularly well read and fluent in several languages.

Few arrived with such educational advantages, fewer still with a profession. Restricted Jewish entry into Russian second and third-level educational institutions kept numbers deliberately low and emigrating professionals may well have gone further afield, but tradition also played its part. Among Orthodox Eastern European Jews, material assets, family lineage and secular achievements counted for nothing in measuring the worth of a man: the only yardstick was the depth of his religious learning. Such unsophisticated values, combined with their quaint appearance and language, conveyed the impression that the newcomers were all ignorant peasants. It was an unjustified assessment.

The term 'rabbi' literally means 'teacher' and almost all the immigrant males were well-versed in *Torah* (Jewish Law), classical Hebrew and liturgical knowledge, imbibed from the age of three or four through local rabbis or religious laymen. Those who attended *yeshivas* familiarised themselves with the philosophical arguments, scientific views and legal opinions of the sages through studying the *Talmud* (rabbinic commentaries), *Mishna* (oral *Torah*) and *Gemarah* (commentaries on the *Mishna*). Some left *yeshiva* with rabbinical qualifications; others formed the nucleus of *chevra Gemarah* (study circles) wherever they settled. The rest received the kind of education that Ellis M. Sampson describes in 'Life in the *Stetl*' in the *Irish Jewish Year Book*, 1966-7 as typical of villages within the Pale of Settlement. Elementary *cheder* (Hebrew and religion classes) taught Hebrew reading and the rudiments of *Chumash* (the Five Books of Moses and sections from the Prophets) to boys and girls up to eight years old. Boys only, from eight to twelve, learnt Hebrew as a language and began studying *Tenach* (the entire Hebrew Testament including the Prophets). Older boys continued *Tenach* in greater depth and began the study of the *Talmud*. 'Unscientific but intense', the system provided a 'thorough knowledge of ancient Jewish history, the Bible and its language' for those who completed all three levels. Secular education, if required, was by private arrangement. Only a small minority benefited from the few well-organised and equipped Government schools.

Many who hoped to gain employment in Ireland as Hebrew teachers or cantors were disappointed to find others equally or better qualified for the few posts available, and much of the ardour for sustained religious learning fell away under the necessity of earning a living. No one mourned its passing more than Myer Joel Wigoder, who resented interruptions to his own studies even from the few customers who afforded him a meagre livelihood. Dogged religious scholars mostly remained poor; those who concentrated on business tended to prosper. Wigoder regretted the greater deference paid to the financial rather than the spiritual pillars of the synagogues and it grieved him that scholarship was not more respected in Ireland.

Even in the *heim*, religious instruction for girls had been basic. Most could learn how to keep a kosher home and all the prayers and blessings they needed, at their mother's knee. Boys required more intensive instruction. Preparation for *Bar Mitzvah* at thirteen implied familiarity with many of the 613 religious obligations expected of the adult male. Traditionally the ceremony presaged more detailed learning but religious education alone would not ensure success or even survival in the land of their adoption. At a time when newspapers in Ireland were estimating that chronic absenteeism from schools was leaving a third of Irish children without education, Jewish communities began making representations for Jewish schools that would combine secular and religious teaching.

Education in Ireland was overwhelmingly denominational, with the faith of individual ecclesiastical school managements determining the religious ethos of the school. The Commissioners of National Education were not averse to establishing schools under Jewish management. The South Terrace National Schools (Hebrew), next door to the South Terrace Synagogue in Cork, was the first to open, in 1891. Superintended by the Commissioners, it provided secular, Hebrew and religious instruction as part of its daily routine. In July 1892, the *Jewish Chronicle* reported that the district inspector found 'the different classes well up to requirements of their respective programmes' and their 'moral tone and discipline good'. In August the school's seventy-six pupils were taken to Crosshaven for an annual excursion. In December there was a prize distribution. Professor Hartog from Queen's College, Belfast, distributed the girls' prizes to Ada Solomon, Annie Cohen, the Lieberman sisters and Amelia Levy. The brothers G. and M. Goldfast were among the boy recipients.

There was little chance of Esther Hesselberg winning a prize. A 'dunce' in her own estimation, she did everything possible to avoid answering questions in class. Her constant requests to go to the toilet eventually led her teacher to suggest, 'Your mother should take you to the doctor, because you seem to be suffering from a floating kidney.' She left South Terrace National Schools at fifteen with no knowledge of Hebrew, which was taught only to boys, and only a basic understanding of other subjects. In later life she claimed, 'I only started learning at seventy'.

Absenteeism continued to draw general censure. The Catholic Archbishop of Dublin slated both 'neglectful parents', who kept their children at home, and employers who used them as cheap labour. In February 1892 the *Daily Independent* claimed that 26 per cent of the population was illiterate. In October the *Times* (London) deplored Irish educational law which set the minimum school attendance at four hours a day for only seventy-five days out of every six months. The *Jewish Chronicle*, by contrast, was reporting the opening of two more schools to meet the growing needs of Irish Jewry.

Regent Street National School in Belfast began secular and religious teaching in May 1892. At the 'conversaztione' held at 27 Fleetwood Avenue to mark its opening, tributes were paid to the president of the Belfast Jewish Community, Otto Jaffe, later knighted for his services, and to J. Freeman, its vice-president, as the prime movers in supplying 'a want long felt by the Jews in Belfast'. Adelaide Road National and Hebrew School in Dublin opened the following December. Designed to cater for 300 children, its classrooms were located in the basement of Adelaide Road Synagogue, where the congregation was urged to avail of its facilities. For a time they did. Many young immigrants learnt English there and in 1900 Maurice E. Solomons, its honorary manager, described it as 'the brightest portion of the work of the community.'

In 1906, at a prize distribution in Molesworth Hall, a 'handsome silver watch' was presented to best boy, Philip Bookman, and best girl, Esther Golding, 'as promised by Commissioner Sir John Nutting'. Revd A. Gudansky, headmaster of the Hebrew classes, thanked the Commissioners of National Education and the Dublin congregation for the school facilities provided. The district inspector's report that 'excellent work has been done in the school in the past year' and that 'Reading is clear and intelligent and Arithmetic really excellent', earned praise for the staff from Mr Solomons. He also praised his wife Rosa for her Sabbath morning classes. Founded by Mr and Mrs Solomons at the synagogue in Mary's Abbey, these classes were the only religious instruction available to girls. In 1895, Sir H. Cochrane, the Deputy Lord Lieutenant and a good friend to the Jewish community, had hosted a *Chanucah* treat for the children of the Sabbath School classes. At the 1906 prize distribution, his son, Sir Ernest Cochrane, expressed delight at 'the assemblage of so large a number of bright, intelligent children.'

Sir Maurice Dockrell, assisted by Mrs Rosa Solomons, distributed the prizes in March 1907 and on Sir Ernest Cochrane's behalf, presented silver watches to Louis Jackson (best boy), Ada Silverman (best girl) and Philip Gluckman and Bella Shillman (best singers). For the first time prizes were also awarded to Mrs Solomons' Sabbath classes. The district inspector reported the daily routine of the school 'well planned' and the children 'highly intelligent'. Good progress had been made. Pupils entertained with 'action songs, recitations, pianoforte performances'.

1907 was a good year for Jewish education. On 1 March, shortly before the Adelaide School prize distribution, the Marchioness of Dufferin and Ava officially opened the Jaffe National Schools in Cliftonville Road, Belfast. Bearing the family name of its main benefactor, Sir Otto Jaffe, the school would provide secular and religious instruction for boys and girls. A few months later in Dublin, Max Nurock, Joel Green and Meyer Scher took the first three prizes in a juvenile essay competition.

Through the early years of the twentieth century, all three Jewish schools in Ireland were regularly mentioned in the provincial section of the *Jewish Chronicle* in connection with pupils' progress, school activities and communal use of school premises. The Jewish Lads' Brigade was just one organisation that used the Adelaide Road schoolrooms as its headquarters. In January 1914, after an outing to the Princess Cinema Theatre sponsored by their former Staff Sergeant, Louis E. Wigoder, members met there to present him with an inscribed marble clock before his departure for Manchester. In February 1914, a party of 230 Adelaide Road pupils was taken to a pantomime at the Gaiety Theatre, where the best seats in the house were provided for them at 'nominal cost'. At a Jaffe School prize distribution the attendance was reported as 'well maintained' and progress as 'excellent'. Mrs Berwitz distributed the prizes. Each child received a gift and Cecil Levinson entertained with two violin solos.

In December 1920, the twenty-sixth annual report of the Dublin National and Jewish Schools showed the first signs of disquiet regarding Irish-Jewish education when the committee expressed 'keen disappointment at the lack of interest shown by the Jewish clergy in the welfare of the secular school.' Their appeal to spiritual and communal leaders to help 'make the school worthy of its place in the life of the community' went unheeded. An undated document in the archives of the Irish Jewish Museum refers to Mr Solomons presiding at a prize distribution at 'the National Secular School, Adelaide Road, and Hebrew and Religion Classes, Stamer Street.' Mr Solomons died within two years of the twenty-sixth report, so the split into separate entities must have occurred in 1921.

The establishment of the Irish Free State in 1922 placed Dublin and Cork beyond British provincial territory. By the 1930s, when the *Jewish Chronicle* carried a Republic of Ireland section, the secular Jewish schools in both places had ceased to function – the first victims of the insufficient funds and lack of support that would dog Jewish educational facilities in Ireland down the years. Both premises remained in communal use for many years. South Terrace National Schools was sold in the 1980s to help Cork's diminishing community finance the synagogue next door; the Adelaide Road schoolrooms became a communal hall.

The headmaster of the Religion classes at Stamer Street was Moishe Vilensky, born in Vilna (Vilnius) in the 1880s. The Russian authorities had put a price on his head some forty years later, for injuring a thug who was attacking Jewish women. 'Come to Belfast,' advised his friend from the *heim*, Isaac Herzog, then rabbi to the Belfast community. 'We need a headmaster for our *Cheder*.' Promising to send a ticket as soon as he settled, Moishe borrowed the fare from his brother, Isaac Vilensky, who had been saving for his own journey to freedom. Rabbi Herzog's call to Dublin encouraged his friend to transfer there too.

When Rabbi Herzog examined the Dublin children in 1922, he was 'highly gratified' and considered the schools could challenge comparison with any similar institution in Britain. The 124 boys in Stamer Street were making 'considerable progress', while the recently-formed girls' Hebrew and religion classes, with 122 pupils, were realising 'to the fullest extent the sacred purpose for which they have been established.' A past pupil, Chaim Herzog, the rabbi's son, was President of Israel when he described the standard of religious learning under Moishe Vilensky as 'outstanding'. A respected if somewhat absent-minded religious scholar, Moishe once gave a lecture wearing a shoe on one foot and a slipper on the other. Embarrassed when he realised the situation, he pretended he had a sore foot, and limped a little for effect. The vote of thanks included special gratitude for his kindness in giving the lecture 'even with a sore foot.'

In February 1925, 'in consequence of complaints of mismanagement', the committee of the *Talmud Torah* unanimously resigned. By that time, premises in Bloomfield Avenue were being used both for *Cheder* and various communal society meetings. Whether these overlapped the Stamer Street classes or replaced them is unclear. Three months later, when Bernard Shillman gave an interview to the *Jewish Chronicle*, he spoke of the Dublin Jewish community being 'still without a proper school building for our *Talmud Torah*' and described finances as chaotic. In commenting that 'the physical as well as the religious health of our children is being seriously endangered' he was almost certainly referring to the dilapidated condition of the *Talmud Torah* house in Bloomfield Avenue. He made no mention of secular education, but his comments might well have been the first move towards securing a new Jewish school for Dublin.

In 1925, the director of Jewish Studies in Britain noted the high level of spoken Hebrew and the 'very good work being done' at the Jaffe School but insufficient financial support gradually caused its standard to decline. An article in the *Jewish Gazette* of June 1933 referred to it as the 'permanent communal Cinderella' of the Belfast Jewish Community, which supported Jewish charities in Russia, Poland and Palestine but left its own *Talmud Torah* in constant debt.

In 1942, Harry and Dora Factor moved with their three young children from Dublin to Belfast. The local Jewish community advised that they send only their six-year-old son to the Jaffe School. Neither its Hebrew nor its secular teaching was rated highly, but it was the only *Talmud Torah* in the city. Their daughters' religious instruction could be adequately met by after-school classes at the Jaffe, and they would get better secular education elsewhere.

Most schools readily accepted Jewish children. In Dublin the Christian Brothers' School (Catholic) in Synge Street, St Catherine's School (Church of Ireland) in Donore Avenue, the Rathgar National School (Methodist) in Rathgar Avenue and the Damer School (Unitarian) in St Stephen's Green were representative of the many different faiths that educated them. It was a pattern replicated throughout Ireland wherever Jewish families settled.

Rathgar National School was only three years old when Lily Isaacs, from 34 Rathgar Road, was enrolled as its first Jewish pupil in 1899. The pattern of later enrolments mirrored the demographic changes in the Dublin Jewish community. Philip, Joseph, Abraham and Bertha Scher from 71 Leinster Road were among the seventeen Jewish children enrolled between 1900 and 1909. There were twenty-four more by 1919. Florrie, Mirell, Freda and Monty Toohey from 31 Westfield Road joined the school in 1925, bringing Jewish enrolment for the 1920s to seventy-nine. Though it reached its peak in the 1930s at 121, the admission of family groups, such as Rosalind, Shirley and Michael Jascourt from 35 Wasdale Park and Sylvia, Phyllis and Pauline Farbenbloom from 64 Lower Kimmage Road, raised the Jewish intake in the 1940s to 112. By the 1950s when the Baigel triplets were enrolled, it had fallen back to 100. In the 1960s it reached only 38; by the 1970s a mere 12. The last to enrol, in 1978, were Nichola and Tracy Eppel from 4 Greenlea Road.

Betty Ludlow, *née* Sproule, a pupil there from 1914 until 1920, recalls in the *History of Rathgar National School, 1896-1996* (1998) by David Kerr, that:

a white card ... was turned over each morning to RELIGIOUS INSTRUCTION. We had quite a few ... Jews with us and that was a signal for them to leave the room. If it was fine, they went to the playground, if not, to the cloakroom.

Other schools made similar arrangements. Harold Mushatt claimed he and other Jewish boys at the Christian Brothers' School in Westland Row 'got used to boys standing up each hour as the clock struck to bless themselves.' Jewish parents, uncomfortable with such practice, often supported the less demonstratively religious Protestant schools, including private institutions such as Miss Semple's School in Rathgar. A number sent their children to the nearest National School, irrespective of its denomination.

Arnold Herbert was a pupil at St Mary's Christian Brothers' School in Belfast when he came first in Irish in 1934. His parents refused the award of a holiday in the *Gaelteacht* (Irish speaking district) at the annual prize distribution, when the Archbishop of the diocese offered him a string of rosary beads, the headmaster explained Arnold was Jewish and had no use for them. The Archbishop apologised and promised him 'something else' but no alternative was presented. Sixty-three years later a *tallit* (prayer shawl), a *tallit* bag and a *yalmulka* (skullcap) arrived by post from Israel. The covering letter from Denis Gleeson, the headmaster, said he was 'putting things right' before he retired and had personally chosen the gifts in Jerusalem, 'spiritual homeland' to both of them.

Young Stephen Gaffson was less enthusiastic about learning the native tongue. His Irish teacher at Stratford National School was April Cronin, principal of St Catherine's since 1993. She recalls with amusement teaching the class that *féicim* meant 'I see' and *brea* meant 'fine'. When she tried to explain that *focal* meant 'word', it was all too much for Stephen. Pronouncing each Irish word correctly in the cultured accent he had inherited from his English mother, Joy, he politely declared, 'Miss Cronin, Irish is such a rude language! It's "feckim", "bra" and "fuckil!"'

Asher Siev's parents also found Irish a problem. In *To School in the City* (1997), a history of St Catherine's School by Irene Wilson Power, Asher recalls their shock when he began repeating at home the words he was learning in school. What they mistook for Christian prayers turned out to be only Irish songs. Asher still attributes his vocal ability to the singing lessons he had at St Catherine's.

Most Jewish children settled quickly into Gentile school life and made their own contribution to its environment. Doris Paisley and Doris McDonnell, both pupils at St Catherine's in the 1930s, recall their many Jewish friends there and the *matzo* they brought to school at Passover for teachers and fellow pupils. The Jewish girls were particularly good at organising end-of-term concerts. Lilian Harris, *née* Burnett, who attended from 1922 until 1931, asserts that 'they came into their own by performing ballet dances in wonderful dresses, which added to the colour and gaiety of the occasion.' Asher Siev remembers St Catherine's school outings when the rector, Revd Orr, provided suitable sandwiches for the Jewish children instead of the non-kosher sticky buns the rest were eating.

End of year celebration at Stratford kindergarten, June 1981. (From left to right) adults: Chookie Marcus, Marie Rifkin. Children, back row: John Simon, Daniel Marcus, -?-, Jason Rosenblatt, Aine ?, Richard Elliott. Next row: -?-, Judy ?, Lisa Harris, Susan Cohen, Dahlia Newmark, Louise ?. Seated: Fergus Byrne, Louise Carroll. Front row: Susie Simon, Emma Noyek, Barry Newman, Chana Adler.

Scholastically they enriched the school. Rolls of honour for female pupils dating from 1915 contain Jewish names for every year of their attendance. From Primary Certificate to Higher Certificate examinations with honours, in the Spring Show essay competition, the Band of Hope competitive examination in Temperance and Hygiene, Pitman certificates in Shorthand and examinations of the Royal Irish Academy of Music, they competed and succeeded. Many won scholarships to secondary schools. In 1921 the three Wesley College scholarships awarded to St Catherine's went to Jewish girls, Sarah Weiner, Posy Schrieder and Jessie Sayers. Among the boys, Reuben Crivon (1921), Cyril Weiner and Teddy Coleman (1924) and Cecil Mushatt (1925) won scholarships to Wesley College or St Andrew's. Cecil Mushatt's achievement of first place in all Ireland in Senior Grade French earned him the presentation of a leather-bound French history 'with gold edges' from the Government of France. Teddy Coleman scored the highest marks in mathematics of any candidate and passed the Higher Grade Certificate examination with 96.6 per cent. Of the ninety-nine boys who competed for places in Guinness in 1925, Harold Rosefield was placed first. Mr Griffin was headmaster at St Catherine's. Past pupil, Arnold Yodaiken, remembered his admonition to laggards to 'work as well as the Israelites'.

Some early immigrant families followed the local pattern of absenteeism. Of five Jewish boys aged between four and six enrolled at St Catherine's in 1906, none registered any attendance. In 1916, five-year-old Michael Isaacson from 51 South Circular Road, attended no more than eight days in the first term, nine in the second and eight in the third. Even the best attendees at St Catherine's, however, could not match the record of the Taylor family. At the annual children's tea party and prize distribution at the Damer School in 1916, a gold medal was presented to Louis Taylor for not missing a single day in his seven years at the school. His brother Daniel had won a similar award in 1915 for ten years' unbroken attendance and his brother Joseph held an equally unblemished record.

Max Bernstein was a pupil at the Damer School in the 1930s when 'more Jews attended than Christians'. He recollected it as a co-educational, mixed-faith school that catered to the poor of Martin Street, Warren Street and other working-class areas off the South Circular Road. All books and pencils were distributed free. By the time Alice Robinson attended, from 1949 to 1954, the school had no Jewish pupils, but she recalls a donation to the Unitarian Church from a Jewish past pupil. The gift was in gratitude that the schoolrooms had been preserved along with the church when some Unitarian land was sold.

By modern standards, discipline in all schools was strict and sometimes harsh. Pupils of St Peter's National School in Bride Street called it 'The Slaughter House'. Harold Mushatt, whose brother was one of its many Jewish pupils, referred to the headmaster, Joe Sleith, as 'a tough boyo'. The writer Leslie Daiken immortalized him in his book, *Out She Goes* (1963) with:

Auld Joe he is a bo,
He goes to church on Sunday
He prays to G-d to give him strength
To bash the kids on Monday.

In Louis Wigoder's time St Peter's had a class bully who made anti-Semitic remarks about 'sheenies'. The others encouraged Louis, already a good boxer, to set upon him. The bully lost the fight but Mr Sleith regarded the attack as a punishable offence. He chased Louis all round the school with a cane until he cornered him. Geoffrey Wigoder, Louis Wigoder's son, recorded his father's account of other chastisements practised at the school. One master punished boys by rubbing his unshaven face against their smooth cheeks; another would squeeze a boy's head between the top of his desk and a ledge.

For Jewish children, especially boys, schooldays were arduous. Most of them walked to and from school to save the tram fare. For some, like Harold Mushett, it was a considerable distance. Harold left home at 8.20 a.m. to walk through Blackpitts, Long Lane and Montague Street, past St Stephen's Green, into Lincoln Place and on through Kildare Street to the Christian Brothers' School in Westland

Row, a journey that had to be reversed at the end of the school day. George Smith recalls from his home in Texas that his mother, Eva Cristol, born in Cork in 1886, was let out of secular class in the afternoon to attend Hebrew classes 'as part of the school programme'. This was peculiar to Cork: elsewhere Jewish children had to face two hours of Hebrew tuition at the end of a long school day.

There was no shortage of Hebrew teachers. In addition to the classes held in Bloomfield Avenue, the Gavron sisters ran a Hebrew School of remarkably high standard at their home in St Alban's Road. Mr Slomovitch had a *Cheder* close by the Grand Canal and Rabbi Brown, remembered by Dr Harris Tomkin in a 1992 interview as 'a witty little man who stamped hand-delivered letters rather than defraud the Post Office', taught in Lombard Street. Rabbi Brown also taught pupils in their own homes, as did many another impoverished religious scholar desperate for a fee. The problem was the lateness of the classes. Tired even before *Cheder* began, children arrived late or missed lessons, a matter of grave concern even in families where religious observance was lax. It was particularly worrying when the children were spending every school day in a Christian environment outside Jewish control.

In 1924-5 both St Andrew's College and Synge Street Christian Brothers' School introduced Saturday schooling. A refusal to exempt Jewish pupils led to direct intervention from Chief Rabbi Herzog, who wrote to Mr Imrie, principal of St Andrew's, and the Catholic Archbishop of Dublin. Mr Imrie was not accommodating, and the *History of St. Andrew's College* by Georgina Fitzpatrick records the subsequent withdrawal of five Jewish pupils. That no new Jewish names appear on the Synge Street registers after that date suggests a similar response from the Archbishop. More worrying for community leaders was the flouting of Jewish religious practice by those families whose children continued in attendance. A new Jewish school, combining secular and religious teaching, was becoming an urgent necessity if Dublin was to maintain a Jewish way of life.

The fulfilment of that desire was the Zion Schools in Bloomfield Avenue. Five weeks before the official opening, an article in the *Jewish Chronicle* of 16 February 1934 hailed it as a school, 'the like of which does not exist in any other community in Great Britain or Ireland'. A community circular letter dated March 1934 detailing its 'lofty, spacious classrooms, Science Room, Cooking Room, Kindergarten and Hall for Physical Drill' promised a standard of secular education 'as can be obtained in the best national schools in the City of Dublin'.

Rabbi Herzog gave the project his full support but the person instrumental in achieving the new school was Arthur Newman, president of Dublin *Talmud Torah*. Early donations to a subscription list for a suitably inscribed oil painting of him to be hung in the school as a tribute, ranged from 10s 6d to 3 guineas. In an interview in the *Jewish Chronicle*, Mr Newman acknowledged that the magnitude of his task had been 'reduced by the sympathy received from the ministers of both Mr Cosgrave's and Mr de Valera's Governments.' Government sympathy took the practical form of approving the sum of £4,333 6s 8d to be paid out of funds provided by the State for the erection of national schools. The additional £8,000 needed for building and equipment had to be raised by the community.

The lease of Zion Schools, dated September 1933, was signed between Arthur Newman, David Cohen and Philip Baker for the Jewish community and the Commissioners of National Education. Among the objectives of national education stated in the lease was 'the fundamental principle that no attempt shall be made to interfere with the peculiar tenets of any description of Christian pupils'. As a school within the South Circular Road parish, Zion Schools would be open to all faiths.

Only two Christian pupils enrolled. One was Christy Collins, the son of Cecilia and Bill Collins, newly appointed caretakers to the school. Recently retired from the Royal Navy, Bill Collins was satisfied to accept the job even at a paltry £2 per week for both of them. To save the tram fare of 2d he often walked the long distance between the school and his home near Croke Park. A day that began at 7 a.m. might continue until 11 p.m. If the last tram or bus had left, the whole family walked home. In 1935, they moved to 43 Bloomfield Avenue, the former *Talmud Torah* house, where an upstairs room was still reserved for a small synagogue and Board of Guardian meetings. Christy's sister, Maura, could recall into her nineties all the residents of Bloomfield Avenue in the mid-1930s, often matching house numbers to names: the Woolfsons at number 32, the Robinsons at number 30, the Goldbergs at number 41. She also remembered her mother's first reaction to the hundreds of Jewish children she was expected to supervise. 'It's too many to manage,' she had wept. 'I'm going home.' 'Don't worry,' Bill had consoled her. 'We'll win the day.'

The pupils adored Bill from the time they saw him slide down the banisters and queued up for their turn to slide down in front of him. When war broke out on 3 September 1939, he was recalled to active naval service. Two weeks later he was among the crew of 1,200 lost when his ship, HMS *Courageous*, was sunk off the west coast of Ireland. He was only forty-eight. Cecilia Collins remained on as caretaker, helped now by her daughter, Maura.

The Collins family became part of Zion School life. Christy's pronunciation of Hebrew was good enough for him to stand in for a Jewish pupil who took ill before a *Purim* play; his knowledge of Hebrew melodies enabled him to correct a boy singing out of tune. When the Ladies' Committee organised school trips, he made sure the staff had tea by staying off work to help his mother load the kettle, the picnic table and a little stove into the lorry that bore them all away. When he died in 1977, pupils of Zion Schools lined the street as a mark of respect.

To Cecilia Collins, the children were her life. She always enquired whether their lunch was 'meat' or 'milk' so she could seat them at the appropriate table. She looked after cuts and bruises, wiped away tears, coped with toilet accidents and generally acted as mother during school hours. During one of her last illnesses she begged doctors, 'Give me a guarantee you won't let me die. I love the children.' Staff at the Adelaide Hospital thought she was referring to a few grandchildren and agreed to a visit. They were amazed at the crowd of pupils that trooped in bearing gifts. When she died in 1980, they honoured her as they had honoured Christy. 'A Tribute to a very special Lady' written by Rose Yodaiken, is displayed in the Irish Jewish Museum.

Maura Collins retired in 1980 when Zion Schools merged with the preparatory section of Stratford College in Rathgar. Though no longer official caretaker, she accompanied the school furniture to the new premises. Terry Samuels, helping to unload it, positioned a table and a chair and told her, 'That's your place, your corner.' Till illness intervened, she appeared every morning at 7 a.m. and spent the day voluntarily cleaning windows, floors and toilets just 'to have the company of the children'. She was invited to Jewish family celebrations and on one memorable occasion was presented with a bouquet at a function in Adelaide Road Synagogue. Till her final illness Maura acknowledged the good will and consideration of parents and staff, and declared, 'All the days of my life I'll never forget the kindness shown to me.'

Much of Zion's initial intake was from schools around the area. St Catherine's lost almost half its pupils and two teachers, Miss Barnett and Miss Sutton, a particularly strict disciplinarian. Others who taught in Zion Schools over the years were Frank Edwards, Joe Barron, headmaster, and the novelist Maeve Binchy, a part-time French teacher who wrote in the *Irish Times* of 20 April 1970 that she found the pupils 'brighter and more enthusiastic than any children I have ever taught'. She also recalled her *faux pas* in asking the class for their 'Christian' names and suggesting the boys take off their caps, unaware that covering their heads was obligatory in Orthodox Jewish practice.

Frank Edwards was a member of the Communist Party of Ireland. During the Spanish Civil War (1936-9) he took what he expected to be leave of absence from Mount Sion National School in Waterford to join the International Brigade, which defended Republicans against Franco. Instead, he was dismissed and barred from teaching in any Catholic school. Deprived of a livelihood until Rabbi Herzog offered him a post at Zion Schools, he taught there for thirty years. After his death his son expressed the family's gratitude to the Jewish community for employing his father when no one else would.

Joe Barron was a founder-member of Clan na Poblachta, a political party, and a member of Dáil Éireann. Cecilia and Maura Collins often had to deflect petitioners from interrupting his school day with constituency phone calls or visits.

Pupils at the new Zion Schools gained an immediate shorter school day. Infants were free to leave at noon. Older children attended secular school until 1 p.m. when they went home for what a circular letter of 1934 called 'a proper mid-day meal'. Classes resumed at 3 p.m. By 5 p.m., when *Cheder* would otherwise have just been starting, the school day was over. Any possibility that reduced secular teaching hours might hinder progress was discounted by the *Jewish Gazette*. Its edition of 3 February 1933 quixotically asserted that 'a Jewish child could well afford to miss an hour daily from lessons because the intelligence of the average Jewish child enables him to assimilate knowledge more rapidly than other children.' In fact their total teaching hours were re-arranged rather than reduced and it certainly had no detrimental effects. An inspector's report on Mr Cassidy's class in 1947 concluded, 'It is a real pleasure to examine these children whose school life is so pleasant, their comfort and their education so excellently provided for.'

Many past pupils of that era would challenge the inspector's opinion regarding the pleasantness and comfort of school life at Zion Schools. Harry Sternberg, now living in Australia, admits to being terrified by the discipline he encountered there. C.B. Kaye, from his home at Kibbutz Lavi, recalls that the beatings from one teacher 'sent kids back to their seats grasping the cold iron legs in a futile effort to ease the pain.' David Rivlin, son of Aaron and Fanny Rivlin, now living in Israel, remembers a little girl fainting and a boy soiling himself because 'naughty' babies and first years were not allowed out to the toilet.

Classroom discipline was very different when Jean Reuben, *née* Rivlin, David Rivlin's cousin, now an accountant in London, attended in the 1970s. She remembers an oral spelling test in which each child who missed a word had to stand against the wall. It ended with every child standing except Gitty Masar, whose broken leg entitled her to sit against the wall.

Childhood impressions of *Talmud Torah* teachers vary with memory and experience. Sandra Hesseg, *née* Cohen, now in Israel, remembers one teacher 'chasing pupils round the classroom with a strap'. Theo Garb, from his home in America, recalled the same teacher as 'strict but not unfair'. David Rivlin recollects him 'throwing chalk and dusters at the children' and reporting miscreants to the secular headmaster for caning next day, a punishment that absence deferred but never cancelled. To Eva Trungold, *née* Goldberg, who loved and respected him, he was 'a wonderful teacher who taught the class with kindness and humour and treated pupils with warmth and respect.' Michael Frohwein remembers Revd Bernstein from the BBC – Bernstein's *Bar Mitzvah* Class. At one stage Revd Bernstein tried bribing the younger children into greater attentiveness by offering sixpence for each correct answer. It was a regular if short-lived income for Doron Rivlin, Jean's youngest brother, now a solicitor in Australia. Bright and eager to learn, he sat at Revd Bernstein's table and listened intently while the rest chatted and misbehaved.

For Harry Sternberg and Frank Baigel in the 1940s the best Hebrew teacher was Menachem Mansoor from the Middle East, a Semitic scholar at Trinity College. A teacher in the Belfast *Talmud Torah* before moving to Dublin, he went on to a brilliant academic career in the United States. Harry Sternberg describes him as 'the only Hebrew teacher I can remember with a vocation for teaching' and Frank Baigel as 'an inspiration to the young of the community'. For David Rivlin in the 1960s it was Ellis Yodaiken, who settled in Israel; for Maerton Davis it was Cyril Rifkin, now living in London.

Lorraine Sieff-Shpall has 'fond memories' of Arnold Yodaiken, *Talmud Torah* headmaster from 1956 until he moved to Manchester in 1981 with his wife, Joan Yodaiken, *née* Dolovitz, also a *Talmud Torah* teacher. She still maintains she learnt more from Mr Yodaiken's kindness than from the severity of others. Also kindly remembered is Dr Teller, botanist and occasional lecturer to post-graduate education students at Trinity College. In addition to teaching Hebrew, he operated his own Dalton Tutorial School from 1935, first in Harcourt Street and later in Leinster Road, Rathmines. Inter-denominational, the DTS, deliberately misconstrued as Dr Teller's School, prepared pupils for examination or helped them catch up at their own pace on missed schoolwork.

Aspirations that had begun with national schooling quickly grew to encompass second-level education. By 1897 Wesley College and St Andrew's had seven Jewish pupils. Charles Spiro entered Trinity College in 1903 on a mathematical sizarship (scholarship) from High School. Even successful traders began to regard their income as 'scrambling for a living' and wanted something better for their sons or younger brothers. Myer Joel Wigoder records Harry Wigoder's determination to educate his siblings 'in a way that Europe understood education, master of some profession that would ensure … decency and comfort.' Ambitious Jewish parents wanted secondary education for their children long before Donogh O'Malley's education reforms made it free in 1967. Those who could not afford it depended on scholarships or deprived themselves to pay the fees.

Wesley College, Dublin, and the Royal Belfast Academical Institution taught generations of Jewish boys and girls. Dr Irwin, headmaster of Wesley College when Elaine Feldman, *née* Freeman, attended in the 1920s, told her he welcomed Jewish pupils because they 'brought honour to the school'. Then a boarding as well as a day school, Wesley reserved prefect status for its boarders until Elaine, at fourteen, complained to Dr Irwin about the lunch-time facilities for day girls. Unsupervised, they ate in the gymnasium where they played with the apparatus, raising dust during the meal and risking injury. When she suggested placing a prefect or teacher in charge, Dr Irwin asked her, 'Would you like to be a prefect?' Her appointment gave her full responsibility for lunch-time activities. Other popular secondary schools in Dublin were High School, St Andrews College and Sandford Park for boys and Alexandra College and Diocesan School for girls.

Both Catholic and Protestant secondary schools all over Ireland accepted Jewish children so long as applications were comparatively few. From time to time incidents occurred. When a teacher at the Presentation Brothers' College in Cork maliciously addressed a Jewish boy as 'Ikey' instead of using his given name, the whole class objected. For the next twenty-five years the teacher was himself called Ikey by a succession of boys, who applied the name with no inkling of how it originated. Allan Freedman recalls a teacher at High School in the 1940s boasting of the two sixth-year school trips he had organised to Nazi Germany, presumably with school sanction. More sensitive Jewish pupils felt some alienation and often suspected prejudice where none might have been intended. Others integrated well.

Secondary-school building was not a priority for early Free State Governments, and the availability of places was limited. As demand from the Jewish community rose, some school managements restricted Jewish entry by citing a policy of preferential admission for siblings and the children of past pupils. At the Presentation Brothers' College in Cork the unofficial annual quota was ten. In 1940 Fred Rosehill was the eleventh Jewish applicant. A 'little influence' from a Catholic canon, who happened to be a family friend, secured him a place but elsewhere quotas were more rigidly applied. The growing number of rejections, combined with the refusal to award a scholarship, won in open competition by a Jewish child, on the grounds that only Protestants were eligible, convinced Rabbi Jakobovits that the Dublin Jewish community needed its own secondary school. Only five people attended a public meeting called at his home to discuss the proposition. Four of them – Dr Harris Tomkin, Dr Teller, Elaine Feldman, whose mother had taught at the Adelaide Road School, and the rabbi himself – became the founders of Stratford College.

Afternoon *Cheder* classes for non-Zion pupils were held at the time in *Talmud Torah* premises on Terenure Road East. At the rabbi's request, the *Talmud Torah* agreed to the rent-free use of Stratford House for secondary teaching, but running costs would have to be met by the new school. Stratford College opened there in September 1952, taking its name from the house. A small senior sixth class already operating in Zion Schools was transferred with its teacher, Mr Shiel, to form the nucleus of first year, augmented by five fee-paying pupils. One of them was Elaine Feldman's son, Maurice.

The Department of Education paid capitation grants of approximately £15 per pupil and the incremental element of teachers' salaries. Though its only other source of funds was school fees, Stratford College never refused admission because of inability to pay and educated many children free of charge; some were additionally helped with uniforms and books from a private fund established by Elaine Feldman. Financial survival depended on employing staff who would waive their entitlement to a basic salary from the school and on enrolling new pupils for extra capitation payments. The 1950s had a surfeit of secondary teachers and many were satisfied to take interim, short-term posts at reduced wages. In one year Maurice Feldman had nine history teachers. Pupils were harder to find. Elaine Feldman, who lived into her nineties, admitted it took 'faith in a prayer' to entrust a child's education to the embryonic school. The surprising reaction of established colleges did not help. Previously 'full' schools suddenly found available places for every Jewish applicant, undermining the very *raison d'etre* of the project. Another unexpected obstacle was the unsuitability of Stratford House. From 1 p.m. children began arriving from other schools for *Cheder* classes, due to start at 3 p.m. Unsupervised, they shouted, bounced balls at the windows and played noisy games, distracting the Stratford College class, which continued until 4 p.m. If the school was going to succeed it needed its own premises.

Elaine Feldman agreed to buy 1 Zion Road, a beautiful multi-roomed house with conservatory and mimosatory for £4,250 with neither cash nor arranged funding. When she told Mr McCormack, manager of the Northern Bank on the South Circular Road, 'I've done a terrible thing,' he replied, 'On the contrary, you've done a wonderful thing,' and suggested that five people should each guarantee a loan of £1,000. Her husband, Jack Feldman, his brother, Karl Feldman, Hymie Green, Jack Segal and Arthur Herman obliged. A sympathetic brother superior sold them well-used school furniture and the nucleus of a science labouratory for £300. Alan Kutner, in the clothing trade, made uniforms.

The school year began with two classes: the now second-years from Stratford House and a small intake of new pupils, whose attendance became conditional on Stratford providing facilities for younger siblings, for the convenience of parents. No capitation or salary payment was available for preparatory pupils, so fees had to be charged. The teachers were mainly students, who expected no salary.

Dr Teller, described by Elaine Feldman as a genius, equipped the science laboratory and organised a Woodwork class by hiring a craftsman with teaching qualifications. By day he taught Carpentry; by evening he repaired the dilapidated desks which sometimes collapsed under the students.

Under the management of Dr Teller the school struggled on, supported by the Jewish Agency in London, which sent a succession of teachers on two-year contracts to teach Modern Hebrew and Religion at no cost to the school. Incredibly, it prospered. In 1968, pupils converted a school garage into a pocket theatre, where the Stratford Players could entertain an audience of fifty. *There was a Wall*, a play on the theme of the Warsaw Ghetto, was specially written for them by Mashey Bernstein and Estelle Feldman, Elaine Feldman's daughter. It was later performed in London where it received excellent reviews. Through the good offices of Dublin Corporation and Robert Briscoe, then Lord Mayor of Dublin, part of a newly filled adjacent quarry was secured as a playing-field: but the school was sorely in need of redevelopment.

Zion Schools also had problems. The *Talmud Torah* was mainly financed by a small percentage of the levy charged by synagogues for seat rental. In 1965 it had a deficit of £1,700. In addition to launching an emergency appeal, the *Talmud Torah* committee requested a serious rise in seat rentals and imposed charges for the hitherto free lessons given by *Talmud Torah* staff at Stratford College. Under the chairmanship of Monty Ross, 1970 finished in balance but two years later the levy had to be increased from 15 per cent to 45 per cent. It was still not enough. In 1975, the councils of Adelaide Road and Terenure Synagogues agreed to pay a flat contribution of £4,000 each, with other synagogues contributing according to their means. Lennox Street Synagogue paid £26.

Admission to Zion Schools declined steadily from the middle of the twentieth century and the proportion of non-Jewish pupils rose year by year. Jewish emigration caused inevitable depletion but many parents remaining in Dublin failed to support the *Talmud Torah*. As early as 1936 Revd Gudansky had described the bypassing of Zion Schools by parents living in the neighbourhood as a scandal. In 1959, when the school had an annually-rising debt of £16,000, Rabbi Jakobovits wrote, 'We never convinced the community of the need to pay for good education.' Rabbi Cohen later criticised parents who preferred 'the barest minimum of Hebrew education, a (private) lesson of one hour or two per week, haphazardly attended' to *Talmud Torah* teaching. For the convenience of families living in Mount Merrion and Foxrock, a small *Cheder* was opened at Blackrock Town Hall, but only drastic rationalisation was likely to attract the many Jewish children attending Gentile secular schools throughout the South Dublin suburbs.

A Commission of Inquiry was set up in 1965 to examine the feasibility of Zion Schools and Stratford College merging, preferably within the grounds of Maccabi, an extensive Jewish sports complex on Kimmage Road West. The grants that would follow Government approval, together with the sale of both school buildings, would make it financially viable. The more central site would hopefully attract a steady stream of pupils, who would pass as a matter of course from primary to second level education and make full use of the sports facility, also struggling to survive. In 1968, the Minister for Education, Donogh O'Malley, was guest of honour at a Stratford College prize distribution. Impressed by the school's achievements, despite its difficulties, he promised the bursar, Bernie Moss, a new school. Only Maccabi approval to build on its grounds was now required for the scheme to go ahead. In 1972, after a four-year debate, Maccabi decided against it. An alternative site on nearby Whitehall Road was considered but rejected as too expensive.

By 1977 Zion Schools had only seventy-six pupils. Of the twenty-nine four-year-olds enrolled that year, ten were Catholic and two Muslim. It was nevertheless a benchmark year for Zion Schools. After long negotiations to rationalise at least primary educational facilities within the community, Zion Schools and Stratford Preparatory Schools agreed to merge. A new Stratford National School would be built within Stratford College grounds with Department of Education approval and a subvention of 70 per cent of the building costs.

Barely three weeks after Stratford National School opened in September 1980, an arsonist set fire to a special school on the north side of the city and then attempted to burn down Stratford College. The new concrete building suffered no major structural damage, but tiled floors and ceilings melted in the intense heat and there was significant smoke and water damage to furniture and fittings.

Zion Schools was in the process of being sold but Stratford National School was able to make temporary use of the premises until repairs were carried out. The older secondary building was damaged beyond repair. A large detached house next door to Stratford College was bought and quickly converted into temporary classrooms until Donogh O'Malley's promise of a new school was finally fulfilled, under circumstances no one could ever have foreseen.

In the *Irish Jewish Year Book*, 1981-2, Rabbi Rosen was still looking forward to the construction of the new Stratford College Secondary School. By 1983 it was a reality, regarded by the rabbi as 'the most outstanding internal achievement of the past year.' Five hundred people attended the official opening by the Minister for Education, Gemma Hussey TD, 'to see for themselves [its] unique facilities and aesthetic surroundings.' In consultation with the heads of relevant university departments, Rabbi Rosen designed an approved syllabus that raised the standard of Hebrew and Religious education throughout Stratford Secondary School. In 1982, he spoke of Jewish educationalists regarding Dublin's schools as 'a model Jewish education system in Europe.' In 1989 the secondary school was unanimously awarded the Jerusalem Prize for *Torah* Education in the Diaspora by an adjudicating committee that considered it the most outstanding entry of the institutions for Hebrew education outside Israel.

Both schools have gained excellent reputations for their Hebrew and secular examination results. Secondary pupils generally proceed to third-level education and many have achieved academic success. When Danielle Collins sat her Leaving Certificate examination in 1999 she was able to offer the entire 600 points required for admission to the medical faculty at Trinity College, no isolated triumph in a school that always catered well for bright students. In 1968, 'The Irish Jews' written by Maeve Binchey for the *Irish Times*, claimed that the range of extra-curricular activities in the Jewish schools would 'gladden the heart of the most idealistic educational theorist'. Danielle Collins was only eight in 1990 when she started at Stratford National School and joined the already prize-winning chess club organised by April Cronin, then on their teaching staff. She proved a natural. In 1992, she represented Ireland in Poland in the under-ten section of the world championship; in 1996 she went to Moscow as one of the four Irish women chosen for the Irish Olympic team; and in 1998 she competed in Croatia in the European Women's Team Championship. She describes Stratford National School as 'really musical'. Tapes of Bach and Handel were played during art class, and Barry Murphy, one of the teachers, set *The Diary of Anne Frank* to music. Produced at the Rupert Guinness Theatre, it played to packed houses for three nights and featured every child in the school, from junior infants to sixth class. He also composed music for a record made by the children in support of the Chernobyl Disaster Fund. Alwyn Shulman, cantor at Terenure Synagogue since the early 1990s, sang with the children both on the disc and outside the HMV record store in Grafton Street, where the record was on sale. Adi Roche, chairperson of the Chernobyl Disaster Fund, gratefully accepted a cheque for several thousand pounds on its behalf.

Since the 1990s, Stratford National School has been mounting an even greater charitable project. Once every two years, during December school holidays, fifth and sixth class, ten to eleven-year-olds, sleep over for one night in a sponsored eighteen-hour fast for Concern. Classrooms become dormitories, each with its own supervisor, and a medical staff drawn from qualified parents is in constant attendance. The children are entertained with DVDs, games and music and allowed drinks. At the end of the fast the Parents' Association hosts a function traditionally presided over by the rabbi to the Dublin Jewish community, and the chief executive of Concern. The school has so far donated in excess of £80,000 and is Concern's most successful national school fund-raiser.

Thomas Hanley, headmaster at Stratford National School, joined the Zion Schools as a teacher in 1973. Within a few years its pupils were participating in the Dublin City Sports at Santry Stadium and winning both specific events and the title of overall individual athlete of the meeting. A founder-school in the Football Association of Irish Schools, Primary League, Stratford National School has won twice with a team comprising its own and St Catherine's pupils, re-establishing a link between Jewish children and the school that educated so many of them in the past. Stratford College makes no claim to be a 'sports school', but nearby facilities, such as Rathgar Tennis Club, Orwell Gym and the National Basketball Arena in Tallaght, are used to supplement its own two outdoor basketball courts, built on the reclaimed quarry.

The emphasis in Stratford College has always been on building initiative and self-confidence, rather than strict discipline, so liberties were frequently taken. Danielle Collins remembers a former pupil on a visit to her erstwhile classmates being mischievously dressed in Stratford College uniform and seated amongst them to participate in a class test. The teacher, seemingly unaware that she had left, amused the class next day by looking for her to explain corrections. Ian Rivlin, a total non-conformist, was at Stratford College in the 1980s. Already six feet tall, he steadfastly refused to wear school uniform trousers and left home every morning in jeans. When finally taken to task he innocently pleaded, 'But I can't get school trousers to fit me anywhere. I'm too tall!' The headmistress, Mrs O'Brion, sympathised and permitted him to wear the jeans, not realising his father was a master trousers-maker.

Stratford Schools became a small but thriving complex that incorporated Stratford Kindergarten (known as *Yavneh*), Stratford National School and Stratford College Secondary School. *Yavneh* was started in 1959 by the *Torah* Department of the Jewish Agency. In 1980, when it was revamped under the management of Chuckie Marcus, seventeen of its twenty-six children were Jewish. Each Friday the children of all faiths simulated the Sabbath table as 'mother' lit the candles and 'father' made *kiddush*. They all brought weekly *tzedakah* (charitable offering) which was donated to the Jewish Home of Ireland and they compared faiths. Muslim children went to the mosque on Friday, Jewish children went to synagogue on Saturday; Christian children went to church on Sunday. Their collective prayer was:

We thank G-d for all He has given us.
We ask Him to make us good people.

Jewish enrolment in 2002 was little Jessie Nelkin and even the addition of migrant children failed to raise it to viable numbers. In common with the rest of the complex, it never gained wholehearted support from the Jewish community and recently closed.

Jewish parents cite different reasons for educating their children elsewhere. Some preferred to maintain association with their *alma mater*, others wanted better sporting facilities and achievements, a wider range of subjects or even a form of special education that Stratford College could not provide. A few were averse to their children learning Hebrew, compulsory for all Jewish pupils. Almost all wanted the status attached to older, more prestigious educational institutions. In 1958, when Rabbi Jakobovits rejoiced that the aggregate attendance at Zion and Stratford was 220, it constituted only 40 per cent of the school-going population. Today, with the child population largely depleted by emigration, very few Jewish Stratford National school-leavers proceed to Stratford College where entry is predominantly non-Jewish.

Never as strong in Jewish ethos as exclusively Orthodox schools elsewhere, it still maintains a form of Jewish identity that is increasingly important as the community declines. Morning service is obligatory for all Jewish pupils and only kosher food is served on formal occasions. A *menorah* is lit in the entrance hall on *Chanucah*, a booth is erected outside the national school for *Succot*, the *Megillah* is read on Purim. In winter the school closes early for *Shabbat* and remains closed throughout all Jewish festivals. Stratford gives every Jewish pupil a sense of Jewish faith and tradition, affording for some a last opportunity to observe and participate in religious laws and customs no longer practised in their homes.

It took numerous well-meaning and dedicated people including rabbinic and lay school managers, enthusiastic Boards of Management, committed principals and staff, the Jewish Agency and active Parents' Associations to conceive, establish and maintain Ireland's Jewish schools. The fine men and women they produced might suggest that the schools served the Jewish community rather better over the years than the Jewish community served the schools.

6

CHARITY AND WELFARE

On Tuesday 7 November 1905 the *Evening Mail* reported a Dublin suicide. A nineteen-year-old Russian Jew named Smulowich, in Ireland for the past two years, had been found in his lodgings at 23 Warren Street 'hanging by a thick rope from the upper hinge of his bedroom door.' Recently arrived in Dublin from Tralee, his efforts at hawking goods in a basket had failed to relieve his poor financial circumstances, and he opted to end his life rather than accept help from co-religionists or others. No one had suspected he was suicidal.

Extreme poverty was commonplace among early Russian immigrants. A group of Russian and Polish Jews 'anxious to raise their educational status' were described as 'belonging to the poorest class' when they met in 1890 to establish reading and lecture rooms for immigrants. When Max Veitel, president of the Belfast congregation, appealed in 1891 for £400 to build a new synagogue, school and *mikvah* in a central location, the community could raise no more than £50 between them. Dublin encountered the same problem trying to finance Adelaide Road Synagogue. The published list of donations was simply 'not enough' and building could not be started without 'incurring the serious tax of mortgage'. By early March 1892, Dublin Jews were so desperate to finance their new synagogue that they took the unprecedented step of placing advertisements in daily newspapers asking Christian reciprocation for the Jewish contributions made to non-Jewish charities. *The Irish Times* of 3 March urged a 'generous response' to the appeal while the *Daily Express* told readers on the 4 March that it was the 'bounden duty of every Christian to assist the Jewish community in their pious work'. The response was indeed generous but it still left the Dublin Hebrew Congregation with a crippling debt that its members were in no position to meet.

The Russian immigrants promoted early marriage, often through matchmaking. Harold Mushatt recalled one *shadchen* (matchmaker) in his youth who 'walked around with a walking stick and bowler hat (with) photographs of a girl or a "fella" in his pocket'. He would knock at your door and ask to see your father about the 'nice match' he had on his books. Families tended to be large. Twins Hennie and Max Bernstein, born in 1921, were the youngest of twelve crammed into a small house in Rosedale Terrace, where they still found room for a homeless relative. Other large families managed for years in small houses in Warren Street or Martin Street, rented from the Artisans' Dwelling Company for 8s or 10s a week. Lena Curland's family paid 9s 6d per week, from a total income of £3. She spoke of constant hardship and of walking miles for cheaper groceries and vegetables.

Poor newly-weds might share a house or move in with parents until their circumstances improved. Much worse off were the complete families reduced to living in one room. Max and Sol Levitas remembered that experience vividly all their lives. Their Lithuanian father and Latvian mother had met in Dublin and married at Camden Street Synagogue in 1914. For a time they were sub-tenants at 8 Warren Street, officially let to Abraham (Ebber) Mirrelson. Max, the eldest child, his brothers, Maurice (Morry), Sol and Isaac (who died from a scalding accident at the age of one), and their sister, Celia, were all born there. A neighbour, Danny Devlin, training to be a priest, taught their father to read English. When Ebber Mirrelson died in 1925, the Levitas family was evicted. All six moved into one vacant room at 39 St Kevin's Parade, a house occupied by the Lewis family whose son would become a distinguished rabbi. One of Mrs Levitas's many hardships there was having to wait to use the stove in the shared kitchen until Mrs Lewis had finished cooking. They left for Glasgow in 1926.

Max and Sol Levitas brought their younger sister, Toby Middleboro, born in Glasgow, back to that house when the three visited Dublin in 2002. They reminisced with the then owners about how they used to jump through the low front window straight onto a couch rather than use the front door; but generally their childhood memories of six people sharing one room were less sanguine. Toby, who never lived there, had the most poignant recollection through her brother Morry Levitas, who confided to her, before he died, that the worst experience of his life was coming home from school as a nine-year-old the day of the eviction to find the house at Warren Street empty, his family gone.

Asher Siev, interviewed by Niamh Brannigan and Aiden Purcell in 1990 for the Archives of the Irish Jewish Museum, recalled that Ireland had many destitute Jews through illness, old age, ill luck, inexperience or lack of trade. In the early 1920s when his father's business declined, his maternal grandparents in Limerick sent boxes of butter, crates of eggs and other foodstuffs to help support the family. Dahna Davis, a native of Belfast, in a similar interview with Jennifer Kelly and Deborah Paget, recounted the hardships of her Lithuanian grandmother, Bassa Moiselle, *née* Hodes, who wrote home complaining that she had 'lost her tongue'. Her German, Latvian, Yiddish and Russian were all useless languages in Ireland. She eventually learned English from sitting repeatedly through the continuous performances of silent films at the De Luxe Cinema in Camden Street until she could understand the captions. Her daughter would later play the piano there to accompany the silent films. When Dahna's grandfather died prematurely in his own store, her grandmother was left with no means of livelihood and seven young children to support, one still an infant. She moved the family to a small house at 7 St Kevin's Road, where her little sons found her crying in the back yard and wanted to know why. They were too young to be told she grieved for her dead husband, the loss of her fine home in Stamer Street with its pony and trap and her desperate financial situation. 'Look', she said, 'there isn't a blade of grass,' making the lack of a garden her excuse. The oldest boy said, 'Don't cry. We'll make you a garden.' They did – out of wooden butter boxes formed into a large rectangle and filled with soil dug from around the Grand Canal. Near the outside toilet, they planted a lilac tree that grew to be a distinguishing feature of the little house. Dahna Davis also described how poverty could never be hidden, with front doors always open to neighbours and other unexpected visitors. Some walked straight into the kitchen and even lifted saucepan lids to see what was cooking.

The only saving grace of such public necessity was the assistance it brought, often from individuals little better off. Leah Calmonson remembers that everyone 'marched into a *simcha*', but everyone also 'mucked in to prepare it', and to pay for it too if need be. Revd Segal's widow, now living in Manchester, describes the community as 'like one family' in the way that everyone felt for everyone else's troubles. When a five-year-old in Clanbrassil Street died, the whole community mourned. Anyone passing a house with a light still showing late at night went in to find out what was wrong.

Most homes were secured with a Yale lock but the key to the Segal's front door was interchangeable with the key to the Yodaiken's. The Yodaikens were *kohenim* – descendants of priests forbidden to stay in the proximity of a dead body. When Mrs Fisher, Mrs Yodaiken's mother, died in the night, the Segals woke to find the Yodaikens in their home. They had used the duplicate key to let themselves in without disturbing anyone.

In Jewish philosophy the giving of charity is not a virtue: it is a duty that should be unsolicited and protective of the beneficiary's self-esteem. Synagogues collected charitable donations through *shnoddering*, offerings from worshippers called to the Reading of the Law and applied to the upkeep of the synagogue or other charitable purpose. It was the practice of honouring the most affluent to maximise income that upset Myer Joel Wigoder.

While immigration into Ireland was no more than a steady trickle, existing synagogues doubled as Friendly Societies to help those in need of immediate support. Representatives of the anglicised, affluent Jewish community or immigrants already established, such as Isaac Marcus, a native of Lithuania, frequently waited at ports of entry on the off-chance that Russian Jews might disembark. New arrivals were directed to lodgings in the homes of co-religionists and provided with a few items to begin peddling, or otherwise offered practical advice and assistance. Some were even married off.

By the end of the nineteenth century the trickle had become a stream. The census of 1891 shows that the Jewish population of Ireland had increased from 258 to 1,779 over the previous ten years, an increase of over 600 per cent. With *ad hoc* welfare arrangements swamped by the weight of numbers that could well double over the next ten years, the Dublin Jewish Board of Guardians was formed in 1889 to administer more structured relief. In 1924, Mr and Mrs A. Eliassoff presented the existing committee with their hand-written account of the Board of Guardians since its inception. *The Dublin Jewish Board of Guardians: An Outline of its History* was compiled at the suggestion of Jacob Hesselberg, who wanted to preserve the details for posterity. The intention was to update the account every year and print each new section with the corresponding current report and balance sheet. The updates were never written. More recent history of the Board of Guardians, like its origins, depends on what the Eliassoffs termed 'existing material and personal narrative'.

The Eliassoffs point out the close relationship between the size of a community and the number of its poor. Increasing demand made it 'necessary to systematise the giving of relief so that the deserving might be helped and any impostors descried.' Ten members of the Dublin Jewish community volunteered their services. Two of them, Jacob Hesselberg and Isaac Noyk, were still active in the organisation when the account was written. Both had become honorary life vice-presidents.

Initially the Board of Guardians was financed through permanent subscriptions which ranged upwards from 1*d* per week. The donor decided the amount and the method of payment which could be annual, quarterly, monthly or weekly. When the work became too onerous for volunteer collectors, a paid official was appointed for a time, and a successful concert and ball were held at the Round Room in the Rotunda as the first step in establishing a permanent fund. Part of the £100 raised was allocated to the founding of a second organisation, to be known as the Dublin Hebrew Philanthropic Loan Fund. Its object was 'to grant loans free of interest to Jews who reside in the city and county of Dublin'. Needy applicants who found it degrading to accept charity from the Board of Guardians could borrow from £5 to £35, with one surety for each £5 borrowed. In 'special cases' the committee could increase the loan to £50 maximum when seven sureties were required. Loans were repaid at not less than 6*d* per week for each £1 borrowed; sureties were expected to settle the debt after four consecutive weeks of non-payment and two weeks of ignoring reminders. According to the annual report for 1959, when loans totalling £845 were made to twenty-seven applicants, 'many guarantors failed to do so'.

To enable the Loan Fund to fulfil its obligations, community members generously 'lent sums of money gratis for protracted periods', bolstering the sum raised from the Rotunda function. In the opinion of the Eliassoffs, the Loan Fund was a 'signal success' which did an 'incalculable amount of good' and saved many a family from financial disaster. Until 1910 it functioned as a sub-committee of the Board of Guardians, and continued to submit all transactions for supervision by trustees even after it became a separate entity with elected office-holders. The Board of Guardians made good outstanding Loan Fund debts.

The first recorded president of the Board of Guardians was Joseph Greene, who served it 'with unparalleled zeal and devotion' for almost a quarter of a century from 1901, when its income was a modest £298, of which £293 was paid out in relief. By 1904 its financial transactions had grown to 'a magnitude that warranted the opening of an official banking account'. On his seventieth birthday, in 1915, Joseph Greene was made its first honorary life president in recognition of his services but ill health forced him to relinquish the presidency four years later. He was acting as treasurer in 1920 when the Board of Guardians decided to honour him with a presentation from all subscribers. At his request, the money collected was distributed among seven Jewish charities. Equally generous was Philip Sayers, honoured for his services to the Board of Guardians in 1922 on the occasion of his silver wedding anniversary. Realising a presentation was intended, he wrote to the Board of Guardians offering to match the sum raised and asking that the combined amount be allocated to a 'Mr and Mrs Philip Sayers Fund' to be used at the Board's discretion.

An early consideration of the Board of Guardians was the provision of coal for 'deserving families' during winter. In 1903, it acknowledged receipt of forty bags of coal from the Lord Mayor of Dublin for distribution amongst Jewish families. To avoid duplication of relief, the Coal Fund was amalgamated with the Board of Guardians in 1905 and administered by them through a sub-committee. Allocations of coal from the Lord Mayor had ceased by 1924, but the Board of Guardians continued to collect money and vote funds for its supply as long as the service was required.

The Shelter Fund was an independent body established in 1906 to provide temporary accommodation for Russian refugees of the 1905 pogroms. It quickly merged with the Coal Fund to become the Dublin Coal and Shelter Fund. No refugees were admitted into Ireland during the First World War, but appeals for general relief 'assumed unprecedented proportions' at a time when annual collections had to be suspended because of other community demands. The period was an enormous drain on Board of Guardians funds. Even in 1924 disbursements exceeded takings.

In 1933, the Irish Government imposed a tax of one ha'penny per pound weight on imported bread. It applied equally to imported *matzo*, causing additional hardship at Passover, a time of great expense. When Seán Lemass, TD became aware of the situation, he declared the tax was not intended to harm the Jewish people. Jewish poor could import *matzo* free of tax on production of a certificate from a rabbi.

Relieving hardship at Passover was an important aspect of the Board of Guardians' work, with a Passover Relief Fund ensuring that the needy were provided with basic necessities. The average collection in 1921-4 was £134, a sum that procured a prodigious amount of food 'in the hands of a wise and benevolent committee'. An annual contributor of 10 guineas was Samuel Lewis of London who had married Ada Davis of Dublin at Mary's Abbey Synagogue in 1867. A generous man in his lifetime, he died in 1901 leaving over £2 million, 90 per cent of which ultimately went to charity. Among his numerous bequests was £15,000 'to be invested and income for twenty years to be applied for the relief of the Jewish poor in Dublin'. It was mainly used in winter months for the provision of coal. In 1921, the capital sum passed into the hands of trustees, the bulk of the income going to the Board of Guardians, who regarded it as their first bequest. The capital remains intact, with the income still used to alleviate sickness, hardship, misfortune and the discomfort of old age combined with poverty. In 1966, the Board of Guardians supported Maurice Fridberg's suggestion of a 'happy holiday home' in Bray; it resulted in dozens of needy people enjoying a two-week holiday that July and August.

Not all the Board of Guardians' beneficiaries are Irish Jews. Non-Jewish charities are supported, as are Jewish people passing through Ireland who find themselves in difficulties. One such was a highly Orthodox man who reached Dublin in the 1980s accompanied by a young child he claimed as his. His appeal to the Board of Guardians was upheld by the then chairman, Ian Davis, who went to visit him at a caravan in Shankill. Complications arose when the Eastern Health Board brought an action against the man for abducting the child from a care home in England. Ian Davis and solicitor Lewis Citron, a vice-president of the Board of Guardians, went to court for the proceedings. They found the defendant outside the courtroom wearing a prayer shawl and phylacteries; he was still wearing them when he pleaded his case in court before the judge. The child was returned to care, and the Board of Guardians later discovered that the man had previously taken other children to the United States and South America in similar circumstances.

The generosity of Samuel Lewis marked a new era in the Board of Guardians' development and set an example that many others were to follow. Its most generous bequest came from John Currid, an Irish-born, non-Jewish donor, who died in London in 1983, leaving a fortune of £1.7 million derived from the sale of his amusement arcade in Talbot Lane, Dublin, and other property in Marlborough Street and Marlborough Place. Unsuccessful in his earliest business attempts, he had been helped through hard times by various members of the Jewish community. The Bank of Ireland Trust Department handling Mr Currid's affairs informed Dr Ellard Eppel that, in addition to family bequests, he had left considerable sums to a wide range of charities, including £500,000 to the

Archbishop of Dublin for distribution to the poor. The residue of his estate was bequeathed to the Dublin Jewish Board of Guardians because Jewish people had been kind to him in business. His request to be remembered in Jewish prayers is fulfilled on each anniversary of his death, when the synagogue hosts a *kiddush* in his memory. Currid's bequest accrued to approximately £600,000 and left the Board of Guardians in the happy position of being able to grant assistance to the needy until 2010 without recourse to special collections.

The Board of Guardians met in the 1950s at 43 Bloomfield Avenue. Young Bernard Baum went there every Sunday morning after his Hebrew class with Becky Gavron to meet his father, Maurice Baum, who served the Board of Guardians in every capacity for many years and gave its affairs priority over his own business. Bernard remembers seeing twenty-five to thirty men around a table and hearing voices raised in dissent. He also remembers the calming influence of his father's interventions and the compassion with which he and other members, such as Maurice Tolkin and Maurice Wine, dealt with matters of the utmost delicacy.

The Board of Guardians was only one of Maurice Baum's philanthropic interests. When Bernard married in 1966, he and his bride, Adele Seligman, received gifts from numerous non-Jewish charities supported by Bernard's father. In the 1980s, Adele and Bernard celebrated the *Bar Mitzvah* of their eldest son. Bloomie Sharpe, who succeeded her sister, Annie Danker, as authorised caterer, made a much more elaborate function than had been arranged. Offered additional payment, she told Bernard Baum, 'No, no! It's my way of showing appreciation for all the charitable work your father did over the years.'

In 1964 the Board of Guardians spent in the region of £3,000 on regular assistance to twenty-one families and emergency aid to thirteen transit cases. A report on its work that year claimed it continued to dispense special grants and weekly support 'with understanding and sympathy and in complete confidence'. Any less sensitive handling of its business stemmed from human frailty rather than any inherent fault in an organisation that has served the community well for more than a hundred years.

The poor were also assisted by two Friendly Societies, whose earliest preserved minutes date back to 1915; they may have been founded much earlier. The Ancient Order of Maccabeans Mount Carmel Beacon No. 10 and the Dr Max Nordeau Lodge No. 7 of the Grand Order of Israel and Shield of David Friendly Society had benefiting members who received modest relief in sickness or bereavement, and non-benefiting members. All were termed 'Brothers'. Each lodge had authorised pharmacists, who discounted medicines in favour of members, and at least one medical officer who was paid reduced fees to minister to members and their families at minimal rates or free of charge. In the 1930s they also paid members 15s per week sickness benefit, 7s 6d towards spectacles and 1 guinea for a specialist consultation or a surgical appliance. A Brother sitting *Shiva* received 2 guineas. Next of kin as named on each applicant's nomination form benefited by £50 when the Brother died.

Non-payment of the small subscription could result in loss of benefits or expulsion, and 'final' warnings were constantly being sent to defaulters by registered post, once, twice and even three times when long-standing arrears had accumulated to more than £1. They sometimes reached more than £3 before the member settled, making it difficult for the Dr Max Nordeau Lodge especially to meet its obligations. In 1956, it imposed a levy on members of 1s per quarter towards liquidating a deficiency of £4,000.

Not everyone was eligible to join the Maccabeans. In 1960, the age limit for membership was raised to fifty-five, with the proviso that death endowment be reduced to £30, or £12 10s in the case of a wife. Every prospective member had to submit a certificate of medical fitness, pay a proposition fee of 1s, and complete a proposition form that asked, in addition to personal details, whether the applicant was in sympathy with the Zionist cause and whether he was a suitable person to become a Maccabean. Applications had to be proposed, seconded and put to a vote. No surviving member can recall an applicant ever being refused, but claims for payment were denied when receipts were not countersigned by a Lodge Medical Officer. Brother White's application for a transfer from the Glasgow Lodge, when he moved to Ireland in the 1930s, was refused because he was over age. The Dublin Lodge agreed to 'supply him with medical attendance at the rate of 8s 6d per year and medicines as per prescription', but he had to retain membership of the Glasgow Lodge.

In 1937, the Ancient Order of Maccabeans bought Whorten Hall, near the canal bridge at Harold's Cross, for £350. The money was raised by transferring £300 from the 4 per cent Third National Loan to the Hibernian Bank until the overdraft was paid. Renamed Maccabean Hall, it served both as a meeting place for the Lodge and as a source of rental income. Fay (Fanny) Spiro from Dublin and Arthur Russell from England had their wedding reception there in 1941. Fanny's niece, Joan Finkel, then eight-year-old Joan Morris, remembers being the only bridesmaid and entertaining the company with a rendering of, 'I've got sixpence, a jolly, jolly sixpence'. Maccabean Hall charged the same rates as Greenville Hall. The Dr Max Nordau Lodge paid 6 guineas for eighteen to twenty meetings and the Jewish Debating Society half a guinea for a single booking, while the mission that wanted to hold gospel meetings five nights a week had to make do with three at a weekly cost of 1 guinea.

A variety of doctors and pharmacists, Jewish and non-Jewish, served both Friendly Societies with dedication. In 1940, Dr Lowe agreed to attend patients in need after 10 p.m. and on Saturdays and Sundays. In 1956, Dr Jacob (Jack) Robinson resigned after twenty-two years' service. With too many demands on his time, he resisted 'every inducement to remain'. Though both lodges expressed their inability to repay his 'kindness, skill and attention', they made presentations of a silver tray to him and silver candlesticks to his wife. He reciprocated by returning his final payment cheque, to 'be placed as a credit to the benevolent fund or otherwise as the committees wished'. Of the three candidates interviewed to replace him, Dr Irving Jackson was selected. McNally's, Brady's and Citron's, all in or around the South Circular Road, were three of the pharmacies that served the friendly societies over the years.

Though concentrating on social welfare rather than socialisation, the Ancient Order of Maccabeans presented a few successful functions every year, usually at *Purim* and *Chanucah*. An early 1960s *Purim* party at the Zion Schools advertised 'Cocktails, Tea, Cards, *Purim Spiel* (play), Hebrew and Yiddish songs by Cantor Gluck and choir' at admission charges of 3s 6p for Brothers, 5s for member couples and 5s for each visitor. The highlight of the year was their annual installation dinner. Held in December as a joint celebration of *Chanucah*, it was well supported by members and non-members, who enjoyed the guest speakers, the formal inauguration of office-bearers and an excellent meal. The dinner menu for 1963 was grapefruit, smoked salmon, chicken soup with *perogin* (meat pasties), roast stuffed turkey with roast potatoes, peas and celery, *Chanucah* pudding with sauce and fruit salad, coffee or Russian tea and petit-fours. The charge was £1 10s per couple for members and £1 10s per guest. By 1972 ticket prices had more than doubled to £4 per member couple and £5 per couple for guests.

The Ancient Order of Maccabeans closed in 1977. Maccabean Hall, badly deteriorated, was sold to its existing tenants and all assets distributed among the remaining Brothers. Retiring 'commanders' had always been allowed to keep their silver badge of office but the cast-metal circular emblems, bearing the outline of an eight-branched candelabra topped by a Star of David and worn around the necks of the rank and file, had traditionally been distributed at the beginning of each meeting and collected back at the end; they were now handed out as souvenirs.

In 1980 the Dr Max Nordeau Lodge also disbanded, as did the Dublin Jewish Hospital Aid Society, founded in 1924 to help the poor pay hospital bills. Its annual report and balance sheet for 1952 appealed for new subscribers and an increase in the subscription rate of 6s to 1 guinea per year. Collections no longer covered the cost of hospitalisation, recently raised to 5 guineas per person per week. The society also reminded subscribers that they had no personal entitlement to free hospitalisation; their contribution merely helped the less fortunate. That year the Medical Aid Society made grants on behalf of treated members to thirty-five hospitals and care centres, the largest amount of £35 going to the Meath Hospital, Dublin. A grant of 3 guineas was sent to the Irish Red Cross Society and 2 guineas to St John's Ambulance Brigade.

Growing affluence, a declining Jewish population and improved social welfare eventually rendered the Brotherhoods defunct, but they played an important role over many years in helping to mitigate hardship among Irish Jews.

Dublin *B'nai B'rith* (Children of the Covenant) was founded in 1954. The worldwide organisation began in New York in 1843, with twelve German Jews seeking to emulate Abraham's service to mankind through his covenant with G-d. Its benefits are non-sectarian. As one member expressed it in an article in the *Evening Herald* of 20 December 1971, 'I think as a Jew with fellow Jews to try to do something for my fellow man.' Dublin Women's Lodge No. 2,609 was formed in 1968. Well-supported in their early years, the two amalgamated into a Unity Lodge in 1978, when both were affected by declining interest and membership. By 1992 there was no Irish branch.

B'nai B'rith (Ireland) achieved much in its comparatively short lifetime. In 1961, the Men's Lodge endowed scholarships to the total value of £5,000 in seven Dublin secondary schools historically associated with the education of Jewish children. Stratford College, Wesley College, the Christian Brothers School in Synge Street, Sandford Park, High School, Alexandra College and St Andrews College all benefited. Stratford College was further endowed a year later when *B'nai B'rith* financed a new wing incorporating an assembly hall and additional classrooms. In 1965, during a prolonged bus strike, it delighted hundreds of patients and visitors by providing a voluntary transport service on Sundays from Burgh Quay to Blanchardstown Regional Hospital. In 1968, it adopted Louis Hyman's *History of the Jews of Ireland* as a project and helped sponsor its publication.

The Women's Lodge was equally active, interspersing good deeds with monthly meetings and social activities that included lectures, a cookery demonstration and visits to places of diverse interest, such as the Stock Exchange and the Guinness Brewery. In 1969, they equipped a sick bay at the Jewish Home, endowed a *B'nai B'rith* Nurse of the Year award at the Adelaide and Meath Hospitals, and arranged for the distribution of coal to a group of old people in the wider community. Each year from 1969 until 1971 the Men's Lodge collected funds and the Women's Lodge food and clothing to assist both Catholic and Protestant victims of the Northern conflict.

No social or philanthropic call went unheeded. They visited the sick, stocked hospital libraries, helped with street collections for Barnardo's Children's Homes, distributed their share of the 120 Meals on Wheels delivered three times a week to the needy of all faiths, and manned hospitals on Christmas Day to release non-essential staff. In 1971, they assisted the Irish Wheelchair Association with the two-week holiday they arranged annually for severely handicapped or underprivileged members. Arriving daily at St Benilda's College, Kilmacud Road, often with their children, the ladies served meals and took the generally housebound for walks or drives. At the end of the holiday *B'nai B'rith* organised a highly successful party at Castleknock College, providing food, entertainment and transport. The friendships formed that fortnight well outlasted the holiday, with many remaining on visiting terms. When the Women's Lodge was contacted by

Celia Gittleson baking for the Jewish Home, Pesach 1988.

the County Council in respect of a Jewish family with four or five children living as itinerants in a caravan on the north side of the city, they supplied their needs and were instrumental, with the Board of Guardians, in having them re-housed.

B'nai B'rith served the people of Dublin in many ways. It served the whole country when it raised money to buy letters written by Charles Stuart Parnell to Kitty O'Shea before their marriage. The correspondence, presented to the National Library, would otherwise have been sold abroad.

In July 1952 the American magazine *Commentary* published an article entitled 'The Old Days in Dublin: Some Girlhood Recollections of the 90s' by Mrs Jessie S. Bloom, *née* Spiro, which was reprinted in the *Irish Jewish Year Book*, 1952-3. Jessie was born in Dublin in 1887. In 1912, she married 'Irish Litvak' Robert Bloom and joined him in Fairbanks, Alaska, where he had been living since the days of the Gold Rush. In 1928, the couple returned to Dublin for nine years to give their four daughters 'a Jewish background' before finally settling in Seattle. Jessie's childhood home was in Windsor Terrace, opposite Portobello Barracks on the Grand Canal. She remembered it as open house to a constant stream of Russians, mostly refugees, who often came just to read and discuss the Yiddish newspapers her mother brought from abroad. The group eventually developed into the Jewish Literary and Social Club.

The organisations beginning to aid 'a community as poor as ours,' are described by Jessie Spiro as 'full of the milk of human kindness'. She dwells particularly on the Dublin Hebrew (later Jewish) Ladies' Charitable Society, known even in Jessie's day as the Ladies' Society. Though annual reports and balance sheets trace its foundation to 1894, Jessie claims it was established in 1898, when four charitable ladies enlisted the help of others to assist a young Jewish woman left stranded in Dublin when her husband continued on to America. He had made no contact with his wife two months later, when her baby was born. The Board of Guardians had no provision for dealing with such cases, so the women raised their own funds and started their own society. Bessie Gertrude Noyek and Rachel Leah Pushinsky (whose fowl made merry on Passover mead) are regarded as the founders. If two more ladies were involved, their names have not been recorded. Its first honorary secretary was Jessie Spiro's mother, who was presented with a Sheffield tea service and tray when she resigned from the office in 1908. Twenty members, 'drawn from the most prominent families in the community' formed the governing committee, and each elected president tended to serve 'almost for life', as did Molly Isaacson, who retired in 1965 after fifty-four years as honorary secretary.

The earliest meetings were held in the Spiro home once a month. Collections too were monthly, with two committee members calling at each household for subscriptions which ranged from 1s down to 4d or less, depending on ability to pay. Jessie recalled how 'we younger girls came in handy' as substitutes when a committee member was unavailable. In later years, as interest and membership declined, only one committee member did the rounds of outlying districts. Marleen Wynn, *née* Noyek, the granddaughter of Bessie Gertrude Noyek, remembers her aunt, Bessie Stein, collecting in the early 1950s. Bessie's husband, Abe Stein, placed his car and a driver at her disposal and she set off every Sunday morning, armed with a few flasks of tea and her receipt books, to collect around the suburbs. It was late afternoon before she returned, full of praise for the 'nice' people who told her, 'It's a pleasure!' as they paid their standard monthly 6d and for the considerate who gave 6s to cover the whole year, saving her further visits. The more affluent or generous paid up to 1 guinea per year.

Janie Davis, Isaac Fine's mother-in-law, was honorary treasurer of the Ladies' Society for many years and eventually an honorary life vice-president. During the 1960s, when Isaac Fine's three young sons were pupils at Zion Schools, they had lunch at her home in Emorville Avenue. Mordechai Fine still remembers the constant stream of poor women who came to her for help. 'Is your grandmother in?' they would ask and then add, apologetically, 'I won't keep her long.' When the boys returned after school to wait for a lift home from their father, the women were often still there, sitting along one wall of the kitchen, where they had all been fed. On Tuesday evenings the children stayed later. Sometimes a man called; Janie would take him into a private room and send him away with money in his pocket. The boys were grown-up before they realised they were witnesses to one of Janie's many secret acts of charity.

Deciding the relief justified by each set of circumstances was not easy and could lead to differences of opinion. Mordechai Fine recalls hearing of his grandmother's spirited defence at one committee meeting when she thought assistance was being unreasonably withheld. 'I'm telling you this lady needs shoes,' she kept insisting. When the committee still demurred, she lost patience and declared:

> I'm sick and tired of this discussion. If this lady comes to me again I'll give her my shoes if they fit her. And to prove that people need shoes in the street, I'm taking mine off and I'll go home without them.

A threat she immediately fulfilled. When she died in 1976, the Ladies' Society paid tribute to 'her wonderful goodness [and] remarkable devotion to those who needed a helping hand'.

The committee could also be misled into over-indulgence. Myra Gruson, the current president, remembers with good humour the poverty-stricken, unkempt, disreputable-looking immigrant who lived in a caravan at Spitalfields. The Board of Guardians gave him money and the Ladies' Society visited regularly to feed, clothe and generally look after him. When he suddenly took ill, Myra Gruson accompanied him to hospital in an ambulance. On the way he asked her to hold a sack he had brought with him. The 'dozens and dozens of £5 notes' found inside it after he died were more than enough to erect a headstone on his grave.

Over the years, the Ladies' Society provided a wide range of welfare services. In the 1960s they began a Jewish Meals on Wheels, cooked mainly by Penny Feldman, Joan Citron, Jill Woolfson and Myra Gruson. Hot soup poured from a flask on arrival and a main course were delivered to twelve or so needy people every Monday, Wednesday and Friday, when a double portion was left for *Shabbat*. Inspired by women like Hilda Woolfe, who continued the compassionate work of Janie Davis, and Hilda's ever-caring, ever-willing sister-in-law, Bessie Woolfe, they helped people wash and dress, washed their hair, cut their nails, took them to shops and entertainments, looked after their shoe repairs and dry cleaning and visited the sick in both general and mental hospitals, often bringing meals to patients who would not eat hospital food. Frequently they worked with other charitable organisations, Jewish and otherwise. Today, the Dublin Jewish Ladies' Charitable Society makes no communal collections. Its remaining funds are used to erect tombstones for those whose graves would otherwise remain unmarked, to make confidential donations to the needy with no family support and to help provide Passover fare for the aged.

In the early 1970s the Friendship Club was revived. Officially opened by the Lord Mayor of Dublin, Alderman J.J. O'Keefe, in 1963 at the Jewish Club in Harrington Street, it continued to meet there every Wednesday afternoon until the premises were sold a few years later. Activities continued at the Solomon Marcus Hall at Terenure Synagogue, with a membership of up to 150. Under the chairmanship of Doris Waterman, Florian Barron directed them in a production of *The Matchmakers* by Esther Morris, and they mounted an Arts and Crafts Exhibition whose forty-five entries earned the admiration of adjudicators from the Irish Countrywomen's Association. In 1968, the Lions Club of Ireland sponsored a free trip for them by jet plane to Shannon Airport and Bunratty Castle.

When poor response from volunteer drivers halted the Friendship Club's feverish activity at the turn of the decade, the Ladies' Society intervened and moved the meetings to Maccabi. One event Myra Gruson still recalls with amusement is the Chanucah Party that went somewhat awry. The organisers had prepared a traditional meal, the Chief Rabbi, Rabbi Alony and Revd Gittleson had accepted invitations and a women's group from Artane had volunteered to provide the entertainment for what they thought was a Christmas party. Using a manger as the central prop, they sang carols and filled the hall with Christmas cheer. Friendship Club members joined in, enjoying the novelty. Rabbi Alony walked out in disgust, with Revd Gittleson trying to placate him. The Chief Rabbi's reaction is not recorded.

Two extensions of the Ladies' Society were the Dublin Jewish Brides' Aid Society, now incorporated into the Ladies' Society, and the Ladies' Synagogue and Dorcas Society. With immigrant families and low-wage earners unable to finance their daughters' weddings, the Brides' Aid annual report of 1950 claimed 'the happiness of many … poorer co-religionists' depended on the Society's 'successful prosecution'. Founded in 1926 and again the brainchild of Rachel Leah Pushinsky and Bessie Gertrude Noyek, it provided grants for a wedding dress, basic trousseau and reception from accumulated small subscriptions and individual generosity. In 1931, when two applicants were each granted £20, the society's assets totalled only £30; a committee member immediately made up the difference. Lily Hardy, *née* Woolfson, now in her nineties, remembers her mother, Sarah Woolfson, being actively involved in the 1950s and '60s, when the amount usually given to each bride was £50. The balance sheet for 1961-3 shows a total grant to brides of £590. In the 1980s, when local families could support their own wedding expenses, Brides' Aid funds were re-directed towards Israel, where many an immigrant Russian bride was married in a wedding dress dispatched from Dublin, some previously worn under the *chuppah* (wedding canopy) in Terenure or Adelaide Road Synagogue.

The Ladies' Synagogue and Dorcas Society, founded by Rosa Solomons in 1902, convened regularly at her home in 26 Waterloo Road before moving to Adelaide Road Synagogue. Its purpose was to make women's and children's garments and distribute them to the poor and to look after the silverware and vestments of the synagogue. In 1916, members took on the additional task of completing 'over fifty articles for wounded (British) soldiers', a gesture gratefully acknowledged by the local committee of the Red Cross Society. Jane Gudansky served as its first president until her death in 1947.

In 1944, 'on account of material being too expensive', the women stopped sewing and began dispensing ready-made goods. The 'appalling poverty' in the community that year required the distribution of ninety-five garments, seventy-one pairs of shoes, four pairs of blankets and nine pairs of sheets, at a total cost of £120. They also spent £2 17s on having shoes repaired. The high demand for assistance made it necessary to increase subscriptions from 6s to 10s per year. Concentrating more and more on the provision of bedclothes and shoes, the Dorcas Society remained in operation as long as it was needed. It disbanded in 1968. Outstanding funds were used to endow a Ladies' Dorcas Society Ward at the Jewish Home of Ireland, the most ambitious of all Ireland's charitable institutions.

Jewish households traditionally looked after their own aged and infirm, but by the middle of the twentieth century families were starting to die out and emigration was isolating elderly parents, the single and the widowed, whose health was sometimes as poor as their circumstances. The Home for Aged and Infirm Jews of Ireland in Denmark Hill, later renamed The Jewish Home of Ireland, resulted from the generosity of Rifka and Zalman Potashnick, who lived in a large house in Castlewood Avenue, Rathmines. In business and locally they were known as Mr and Mrs Solomon, the name bestowed upon them on arrival in Britain by immigration officials who could not spell Potashnick and possibly misheard Zalman as Solomon. Their granddaughter, Cleo Morrison, *née* Wine, recalls her grandmother as a very charitable lady who befriended the highly Orthodox, scrupulously honest, but poorly-circumstanced Rabbi Brown, a widower largely dependent on community welfare. Wearing layers of coats to keep himself warm, he wandered from one Jewish household to another as much for the company as for one of the scanty meals he ate. Mrs Potashnick fed him regularly and went in search of him when he failed to appear for a few consecutive days. She found him in St Kevin's Hospital, his bed positioned just beneath a religious picture. He died there.

As much disturbed by the surroundings of his death as by the event itself, Mrs Potashnick summoned her husband home from business to hear the plan she had just conceived. With his approval she then phoned her son-in-law, Maurice Wine, who worked with the Board of Guardians, and told him to *nehm* (take) a piece of paper and *shreib* (write) what she dictated. It was a Deed of Gift. Removing themselves to a smaller house in Neville Road, Rathgar, the Potashnicks donated the family home in Castlewood Avenue to the Board of Guardians for use as a 'real Jewish home' for the aged and infirm 'not blessed with children or other relations who can lovingly care for them.' In practise the Home, supported by the Belfast and Cork communities, has always been open to any Jewish applicant, anywhere in Ireland, subject only to medical condition and the availability of a bed.

That it was established at Denmark Hill, Leinster Road, rather than Castlewood Avenue resulted from the unsuitability of the Potashnick house for communal living. That it was established at all may ultimately have been due to the persistence of Maurice Baum, who campaigned tirelessly for it and cajoled often reluctant businessmen into donating furniture, bedding and other essentials. Maurice Wine, Gerald Gilbert and Solomon Verby acted with Maurice Baum as joint trustees in buying the home of Hanchen and Louis Wine, Cleo Morrison's cousins. The Wine's American daughter-in-law, Claire Wine, had lived there for the first few years of her married life. When she later became a resident at the Jewish Home, she reminisced about the far-off days when she had entered the house as a young bride and played the piano in the conservatory.

The inspiration for the Home remained the Potashnicks'. In the brochure for the opening ceremony, Erwin Goldwater, chairman of the Home committee, gave them 'everlasting credit that never again will any of our poor and aged end their days in surroundings that are strange.' The proceeds from the sale of Castlewood Avenue in the 1970s, combined with 'a generous donation' from the Potashnick daughters, 'provided the magnificent sum of £10,000' towards extending the premises at Denmark Hill. Successive extensions and improvements, sometimes dictated by the Eastern Health Board, sometimes by fire regulations, dramatically changed its structure, its facilities and its capacity. Even its original synagogue, a replica of the one in Abraham Isaac Cohen's antique shop at Lower Ormond Quay, was eventually replaced elsewhere in the Home by a little jewel, dedicated to the memory of Revd Gittleson. Until his death in 1985, Louis Cohen, Abraham Cohen's son, took personal responsibility for that synagogue, which attracted a regular Shabbat *minyan* even from members of other *shuls*. He also hosted a *kiddush* at the Home every Sabbath and Festival.

Featured by Leo Walsh in the May 1968 edition of *Woman's View* under the heading 'A Shining Example', the Jewish Home maximised at forty-two beds. Though it offered 'the facilities of a geriatric hospital', residents traditionally paid only what they could afford; for some that meant no more than their State pension less spending money. To meet the high running cost, the contribution of the Eastern Health Board was augmented by straightforward donations, the purchase of 'Golden Bricks' as presentation certificates, the endowing of beds and wards in gratitude to or in memory of a loved one, the erection of memorial plaques and stained-glass window panels and a range of regular fund-raising activities. These included the Sportsman's Dinner at £100 per plate, garden parties, coffee mornings, auction suppers, annual bazaars, charity shops, raffles and fashion shows of which the most entertaining was the Tiny Tots held each year at the Gresham Hotel. With Betty Mirrelson describing each outfit, children from babes in arms to ten or twelve-year-olds traversed the catwalk to display current junior fashions. Even more imaginative was the Phantom Fashion Show, which never happened although tickets were sold for it.

Reduced support from a falling population, rising costs and growing deficits eventually demanded a change in policy. For a time new residents with property were obliged to meet maintenance costs by donating their vacated house, but failure to refund any residue after death was resented as unwarranted interference with family inheritance. New financial arrangements introduced a sliding scale of charges which rose to a set maximum with a negotiable added donation expected from the most affluent. Where a house was the only asset, it was still sold to defray expenses, but unused sums were refunded to the heirs. In line with what Myra Gruson calls its 'Robin Hood policy', no one was ever turned away for lack of means; it was a financial strategy that could not continue indefinitely. In 2003, the Jewish Representative Council called a communal meeting to discuss the 'crisis' at the Home. Treasurer, Maurice Cohen, outlined the stark position. The unexpected longevity of residents, depletion of income through falling interest rates, rising costs, reduction in financial support as the community declined and apathy had combined to reduce the Home to near-bankruptcy. Though many of its present residents required specialist nursing for dementia, strokes or Alzheimer's disease, Eastern Health Board subventions had fallen and several residents were paying in line with fixed arrangements that were no longer economically viable. Two were paying nothing at all. Its excess of expenditure over income plus the seven empty beds that the Home could no longer supplement for less well-off applicants had resulted in an annual deficit of €500,000. A further disadvantage was lack of space for modernisation into single, *en suite* units. Of the few alternatives to closure, the one most favoured by the management of the Home was moving, as a separate wing with its own synagogue and kosher kitchen, to an existing care institution, which would be responsible for its administration. In 1905, it amalgamated with Bloomfield Care Centre, a Quaker facility in Stocking Lane, near the scenic Dublin Mountains. The eighteen residents then at Denmark Hill were moved, two at a time, to their new surroundings which can accommodate up to twenty-seven Jewish people. Bloomfield Care Centre could not facilitate a synagogue but a 'prayer room' has been made available for regular Sabbath morning services and the Chief Rabbi supervised the purpose-built kosher kitchen daily until his retirement in 2008. It is still under *kashrut* supervision. The ultimate sale of the Denmark Hill property and other assets should expunge the accumulated debts that crippled the Jewish Home; it will hopefully also provide the wherewithal to provide current and future residents of Bloomfield Care Centre, who are in financial need, with the care, clothing and comforts they might otherwise lack. Dedicated workers like Myra Gruson are determined that, irrespective of location, the founding spirit of the original Home will never be forgotten.

The Jewish Home in Denmark Hill was blessed with some delightful ladies and gentlemen. Elisabeth Spain, whose grandfather settled and raised his family in Londonderry, was its youngest resident when she entered in her early thirties. The last of her immediate family in Ireland and frequently wheelchair bound from the rare condition of cerebral anoxia, she had a Masters degree in Hebrew and Oriental Studies from Trinity College, a teaching diploma in Speech and Drama and an Australian qualification in real estate. Fairly independent much of the time, she operated her own computer, actively supported Zionism and constantly involved herself in projects to aid the Home. Possibly her most successful were two community versions of 'Who Wants to be a Millionaire?' which between them raised more than €3,000.

Esther Hesselberg, who died twelve hours before her 104th birthday in February 2000, was a cricket fan since her youth and exulted in being '103 not out!' The *Irish Times* feature on the Jewish Home in October 1983 described her as 'a young eighty-seven-year-old' who played poker two or three times a week and went out to functions whenever she was asked. At ninety-three she featured in the appeal video made to raise $2 million for the Home's reconstruction and modernisation and appealed for it on *The Late, Late Show*. To celebrate her 100th birthday she wanted a buffet for 100 guests. When advised a standing function was inappropriate she exclaimed, 'I'm going to have chairs for my elderly friends,' clearly indicating she did not consider herself in that age group.

   In 1999, another resident, Albert Coss, was presented with the *Croix de Chevalier de la Legion d'Honneur*, France's most prestigious award. The only known Jew in the Republic to be so honoured, he earned the award for fighting on French soil in the First World War: he was fifteen. His service in the trenches with the King's Royal Rifle Corps ended abruptly a year later when his age was discovered and he was sent back to England, but he joined the Royal Artillery and saw further service in France and Belgium before the Armistice in 1918. His jocular reaction to the award, one of many he earned for specific campaigns and general service, was, 'They took their time!' Masking his blindness well, he enjoyed a joke and a laugh until his death in 2000. 'She's afraid I'm going to run off with a blonde,' he confided to Ronnie Appleton, a Belfast guest at his 100th birthday, to explain why he and his wife still held hands. Joe Briscoe, another guest, described ninety-three-year-old Millie as 'one of the sweetest ladies it is my privilege to know.' Three robberies within two months at their basement flat in Dublin had forced Millie and Albert Coss into the Home, completely changing their lifestyle. Nothing could change their temperament.

Apart from a few years in the late 1980s, when a paid administrator was employed, a dedicated volunteer committee and board of management administered the Home, with the invaluable assistance of honorary professionals such as medical officers and solicitors. From the early days, when Fanny Turk headed a vigorous ladies' committee, women were actively engaged in raising money and providing every kind of service and comfort for the residents. Nursing, therapy and catering have always been in the hands of paid professionals. One of them was Sarah Hyman, *née* Marks, in sole charge of the kitchens for over twenty years.

Sarah was only twelve when her snow-white soda bread was singled out from the yellow and even green efforts of her classmates at cookery classes in Zion Schools. The examiners who awarded her Gas Company certificates of competence advised her to take up catering. In the 1950s she opened a fish-and-chip restaurant next to the Apollo Cinema in Walkinstown with her husband, David Hyman, and her father, Harry Marks. They lived above the shop and converted a garage at the side into a lively snack bar, complete with jukebox. Serving only kosher fish cooked in permitted oil, they numbered several Jewish customers among their clientele. The business depended heavily on her father, who did the early-morning fish shopping as well as helping to cook and serve. When he became ill, David and Sarah, now with five young children, struggled on, but the premises closed in the 1960s when Harry Marks died.

The Jewish Club in Harrington Street served meals catered by Esther Green. Its management committee, seeking to retire her, offered the job to Sarah Hyman but she refused to deprive Mrs Green of a living. When Mrs Green left voluntarily in the 1960s, the Harrington Street premises were sold and the Jewish Club moved to rented rooms in Maccabi, where Sarah opened a little restaurant. Under the supervision of the *Kashrut* Commission, it was patronised by both Rabbi Rosen and Rabbi Mirvis, but falling Maccabi membership and increasing overheads made it unprofitable. Rabbi Alony begged Sarah, now a widow, to keep it open. 'The kids congregate here,' he told her. 'Otherwise they will go elsewhere.' Closures and re-openings followed in quick succession until 1991 when it closed for the last time. Other caterers found it equally unprofitable.

Sarah had meanwhile joined the staff at the Jewish Home. Her daughter, Lynn, who did all the baking, was her only Jewish assistant, but so vigilant was Sarah's supervision that Chief Rabbi Broder had no difficulty in continuing to certify the Home as strictly kosher. Sarah bought sensibly to save money, and the annual report for 1984/5 acknowledged her meals as of a 'particularly high standard, well prepared and attractively presented'. Successive annual reports paid 'special tribute to Mrs Sarah Hyman for the wonderful manner in which she provided for the residents'.

Demographic and social changes over the years irrevocably altered the philanthropic needs of Irish Jewry. In 1964, Gerald Gilbert, then president of the Board of Guardians, spoke of the 'unnecessary expense and overlapping of activities' in having five separate charities. He suggested that the Ladies' Society, the Jewish Home, the Philanthropic Loan Fund, The Hospital Aid Society and any other interested groups should amalgamate with the Board of Guardians to form a Jewish Welfare Board. It was a non-starter. Replicating the intransigence of the synagogue committees, no group would yield its independence even for the suggested trial period of two years. In 1974, when they were dispersing around £5,000 per year in casual and regular relief, the Board of Guardians considered renaming itself the Dublin Welfare Board, but nothing came of that suggestion either.

The generosity and compassion shown by Dublin Jewry to their own and the wider community was mirrored on a smaller scale in other Jewish centres in Ireland. Each looked after its own community and participated in general charitable work. In 1963, the Cork Jewish community, comprising only thirty families, was the first to respond to an appeal by Father Dominic Pire, winner of the Nobel Prize for Peace, on behalf of refugee children in Europe. In Belfast an appeal was made as early as 1899, when Revd B.H. Rosengard asked the Jewish community to contribute to the Royal Hospital, and they have been contributing ever since. In 1931, Barney Hurwitz presided at a meeting of the Sunshine Fund, newly established to give poor children a summer holiday in the country or by the sea; in 1936 Lord Justice Andrews expressed appreciation to Mr and Mrs Goorwitch for their support of the Samaritan and other hospitals in the city; in 1937 Mr Sergie presented two cheques for £125 each as the first instalment of the £500 each he had promised to the Royal Victoria and Mater Hospitals, while Mr Ross, chairman of the Belfast Hebrew Congregation, announced donations of £3,325 to congregational and other charities. Their 'generous support of the City Coal Fund' when they must also provide coal for their own poor was praised by the Lord Mayor, Sir Crawford McCullough. In 1953, the Jewish Ladies' Benevolent Fund presented a television set to the Thompson Memorial Home in Lisburn on the eve of Queen Elizabeth II's coronation.

Irish Jews were poor when Ireland was poor. Jackie Long, a retired pawnbroker, worked for Kilbride's in Clanbrassil Street Lower in the 1950s, when times were still hard and the pawnshop a convenient and popular source of ready cash. He remembers the Jewish traders in Clanbrassil Street and the poverty of Little Jerusalem. Philly Rubinstein was one of his customers for unredeemed pledges, but Jews pledging items was rare. One 'jolly' man accepted £5 for his violin every January and redeemed it every September, gladly paying the interest of 5d per £1 per month; another elderly gentleman made similar pragmatic use of an eighteen-carat gold Albert pocket watch 'as big as a turnip'. At a time when the vast majority of his customers were female, he never saw a Jewish woman in the shop, a remarkable tribute to the all-embracing compassion of a Jewish community that effectively looked after its own.

7

THE PROFESSIONALS

In the first decades of the twentieth century Sarah Woolfson was a young office worker in Cork, earning 5s per week. Her daughter, Lily Hardy, recalls being told that 4s of it was set aside 'to help make her brother a doctor'. Sarah's immigrant father, Solomon Clein, struggled as a peddler to support his wife and eight children but he was determined to have a doctor in the family. It was an ambition that developed into a top priority and even an obsession with many Jewish families. Most of them succeeded, even where it meant borrowing from the Loan Fund or making personal sacrifices to finance it. When a player was knocked out by a misdirected ball during a cricket match in 1937, there were seven doctors in the opposing Jewish team to rush to his aid.

The first Jewish doctor in Ireland was George Selig Wigoder, a brother of Myer Joel Wigoder who always referred to him as Selig. Driven from his Russian homeland, he studied and qualified in Leipzig, only to find he would have to move on if he wanted a medical post that did not infringe his Sabbath. His brother persuaded him that Ireland would welcome an Observant doctor and Selig set himself the task of learning English, determined to practise immediately on arrival. He passed the examination for British registration in Edinburgh and three days later affixed his brass plate bearing the name G.S. Wigoder, MD to the door of his Dublin home.

In his book, *My Life* (1933), Myer Joel Wigoder records that his brother, known to patients as Dr George, 'speedily gained the esteem of the community'. Distinguished by his top hat, he made visits in 'a big open black coach' pulled by a grey horse and driven by a coachman. The saving of life overrides the Jewish Sabbath but to avoid the infringements of carrying and riding, he dealt with Sabbath emergencies by having his bag driven in the coach while he walked behind it, a custom he maintained even after his conveyance became a motor-car. One of the earliest doctors to substitute tablets for liquid medicine, his panacea for every ill was, 'I vill give you a pink peel and a vite peel and you vill be all a-right.'

Dr George was followed by a succession of able GPs. Dr Robinson, born in 1899, qualified in 1931 at the Medical School of the Royal College of Surgeons of Ireland (RCSI). An accomplished musician, he paid his tuition fees by playing till 11 p.m. every night as leading violinist in the Gaiety Theatre orchestra, after which he went home to study. In an obituary in the *Irish Times* on 27 March 1980, Professor Jacob (Jack) Weingreen described him as the 'ideal family doctor', who attended patients any hour of the day or night and, whatever his work load, always found time to chat. His very presence made them feel better. As well as serving the Friendly Societies, he was honorary physician to the Board of Guardians and the Jewish Home, which he helped establish. Anne Lapedus Brest, from her home in South Africa, recalls how he regaled patients with a chorus of 'Pop Goes the Weasel' while Dr Sam Davis remembered him exercising in front of patients, placing hands on hips, bending forward, straightening up. Children idolised him as he stood by their beds and pretended to play his violin. When the Diploma in Child Health was introduced, he was its first recipient and gave years of service to the Children's Hospital in Harcourt Street. As doctor to generations of the same family, he guarded confidences 'like a father confessor'. He was preparing for afternoon surgery when he died, aged eighty-one, within minutes of feeling weak, 'a man so special that his place can never be filled.'

Dr Irving (Irvie) Jackson, who qualified at the RCSI in the 1950s, was another who gave patients round-the-clock service for almost fifty years from practices in Chapelizod and his home at 97 South Circular Road. His obituary in the *Jewish Telegraph*, written by his cousin, Ernest Shapero, refers to his humble, Lithuanian background. His father, who had journeyed to Ireland to escape pogroms, was killed in a road accident in Dublin, leaving his mother, Annie Jackson, *née* Isaacson, to rear the family of four children alone. Only her many sacrifices made it possible for him to study. A bachelor all his life, he lived with his mother who supervised afternoon surgeries in her living-room, which functioned as his waiting-room. A framed photograph of the youthful Irvie as a champion boxer adorned the sideboard, but in adult life he was more interested in greyhound-racing. He owned several dogs and his favourite haunts of an evening, before surgery from 10 to 11 p.m., were the greyhound stadiums at Harold's Cross and Shelbourne Park. A man who showed 'love, compassion and kindness', he was an excellent raconteur with an exquisite sense of timing 'that left listeners in tears of laughter'.

Dr Manne Berber, a native of Glasgow, graduated at Trinity College in 1952. Three years later he opened a private practice in Churchtown, where he quickly established himself as an able and caring physician. The poor were often treated free of charge, and he might even leave a donation when he visited a home in obvious need. 'What's the good giving them antibiotics? They need food,' he once exclaimed after leaving 10s with a mother who could not afford milk for her sick baby.

Most Irish doctors of the time were members or associate members of the Royal College of General Practitioners (London) (RCGP) Manne Berber was at the forefront in campaigning for an Irish College. Soon after joining the East of Ireland Faculty of the RCGP in 1965, he was appointed its only tutor. His duties took him around the country lecturing to the different faculties. When the Irish College of General Practitioners (ICGP) was established in the 1980s, he became Director of Training for its Dublin region.

Dr Berber served on numerous committees. His ability and reputation earned him many honours and he became provost of the East of Ireland Faculty of the RCGP, chairman of the Irish Council and a ministerial appointee to both the Medical Council and the Postgraduate Medical and Dental Board. His service to the RCGP was regarded as 'incalculable' and his tireless efforts did much to improve the image of the general practitioner. At the age of fifty-nine he became the first Jewish vice-president elect of the ICGP, which ensured automatic presidency the following year. Two weeks later death deprived him of the honour. The scheme that began with him alone later required four doctors to manage it.

Active in the Jewish community as president of *B'nei B'rith* and the Dublin Jewish Students' Union, Dr Berber also served as an executive member of the Co-ordination Committee of the Northern Relief Fund and chairman of the Churchtown Community Care Committee. At the mass held for him in a local church, the officiating priest told congrgants, 'You've just lost your best friend.'

Dr Ellard Eppel, who married Professor Abrahamson's daughter, Beth, was associated with the Jewish Medical Society for many years. A meeting ground for medical and ancillary professionals, it took on the additional function of Jewish Medical Benevolent Society when Maurice Mirrelson, then president of the Board of Guardians, asked if they could assist a Jewish medical student whose father had died without leaving him the means to complete his studies. In strictest confidence, it afterwards provided for any final year medical students unable to meet their fees.

Dr Eppel became the first Jewish president of the ICPG and Beth the first president's wife to receive a president's wife's badge. Demand for the same token of esteem in succeeding years resulted in its automatic presentation to all presidents' wives and to past presidents' wives who had not yet received one. As a mark of their respect for Dr Berber, the ICGP presented his widow, Marie Berber, *née* Waltzman, with the badge she would have received had he survived to fill the presidential post.

Dr Malka (Millie) Luxenberg, *née* Vilensky, who settled in Israel, planned to become an engineer until she realised she would be the only female student on the course. With two aunts still practising medicine in Russia and her brother

Joe studying to become a doctor, she decided to do the same. Graduation from Trinity College in 1950 made her one of a number of Jewish lady doctors in Ireland, but in 1952 she took her skills to Israel. Two years later she returned to resume her studies in Dublin, accompanied by her first husband, Joseph Fraenkel, a native of Yugoslavia, and their first child. In 1955, she became a Licentiate of Apothecaries' Hall, which qualified her as a pharmacist. The pharmacy she opened with a partner in Walkinstown had a surgery behind it, where she saw patients only by appointment. Jack Segal, a philanthropist to many individuals and organisations, helped her financially, and she is proud of the fact that she repaid him every penny. Strict compliance with Orthodox Jewish custom prohibits the earning of money on the Sabbath; Millie complied by giving Saturday profits to her non-Jewish partner, who attended to all pharmacy customers on that day.

Many Jewish doctors chose to specialise. Dr Harris Tomkin, whose son, Professor Gerald Tomkin, is a consultant physician specialising in diabetes, worked for sixty years as an ophthalmologist at the Royal Victoria Eye and Ear Hospital in Adelaide Road. His son, Dr Alex Tomkin, joined him there and was honorary secretary to its Medical Board until his untimely death at the age of forty-seven. A consultant to several Dublin hospitals, Alex was a pioneer of contact lenses. In 1977, he discovered *Toxocara canis* (dog's roundworm) in an eleven-year-old who would otherwise have gone blind; testimonials from other patients laud the 'miracles' he performed in giving their children 'the gift of sight'. His son Richard Tomkin was a joint founder and Health Service Manager of the Centre for the Care of Survivors of Torture, the only agency in Ireland dealing with such immigrants.

Dr Nafti Jaswon, one-time president of the Pathological Section of the Royal Academy of Medicine in Ireland, lectured in Pathology at Trinity College and was a consultant pathologist and governor at Dr Steevens' Hospital, where Dr Joe Lewis was a general physician and cardiologist and Dr Norman Jackson a dermatologist. Dr Cecil Mushatt (schoolboy recipient of the French Government's leather-bound history book) researched blood diseases with bacteriologist Professor Joseph Bigger, and bovine TB in children with Dr Robert Collis; a laboratory was specially equipped for him at Trinity College. After he left for America in the 1940s he studied Psychoanalysis with Dr Hanzachs, an associate of Sigmund Freud. Dr Geoffrey Keye was surgeon in charge of out-patients at the Meath Hospital when it amalgamated in 1998 with other Dublin hospitals to form the new Tallaght Hospital, where he was appointed to the same post but has since retired.

The life of Professor Leonard Abrahamson, familiarly known as 'the Abe', has been documented by his eldest son, Mervyn (Muff) Abrahamson, in his book, *Leonard Abrahamson, 1896-1961*. Born in Russia, Leonard was brought as a child to Newry, Co. Down, where he was the first Jewish pupil to attend the Abbey, a Catholic school. The bond that developed between him and the principal, Father Dempsey, lasted until the latter's death. Unusually gifted, he received the highest marks in Ireland in Irish and German when he sat the Intermediate Examination at the age of fourteen. It was the start of a meteoric academic career. In 1960, when the Abbey formed a past pupils' union, Frank Aiken, TD, then Minister for Foreign Affairs, was elected one of its presidents; the other was Leonard Abrahamson, chosen as the school's most gifted pupil. He graduated in Medicine at Trinity College in 1919 with first-class honours and was awarded the Banks Medal and the Fitzpatrick Travelling Scholarship, which he used for postgraduate studies in Paris, accompanied by his new wife, Tillie, *née* Nurock. His first appointment was at Mercers Hospital at a time when coronary thrombosis could be diagnosed only at post-mortem and mortality rates were high. The artist Jack Yeats was one of many patients whose death was made more peaceful by Dr Abrahamson's 'wisdom and compassion'. Disapproving of specialisation in medicine, he described himself as 'a general physician with a special interest in diseases of the heart' but many already regarded him as an outstanding cardiologist. When a grateful patient presented the hospital with the first electrocardiograph machine in Ireland, Dr Abrahamson was the first to diagnose coronary thrombosis in a living patient. Though he welcomed medical innovations, prevention was better and he campaigned for the purity of Dublin's milk supply to help reduce the incidence of tuberculosis.

In 1926, Dr Abrahmson was appointed Professor of Pharmacology at the RCSI, where the standard of teaching was considered comparatively low. Though his own lectures were described as 'second to none' and his bedside teaching as 'outstanding', he could do little to raise the general standard until he also became Professor of Medicine in 1934. Within his twenty-seven further years of leadership and example the RCSI came to be recognised as the medical college 'offering the best training to be found in the country'. He financially aided students in need and continued to care for patients even after they left hospital. From 1930 he was president of the Dublin University Biological Society, and he held the same position at the RCSI from 1933. In 1949, he became president of the RCSI and examiner in Medicine both for Trinity College and membership to the Royal College of Physicians in Ireland (RCPI).

An excellent public speaker, he could always be relied upon for a witty riposte. At one meeting of the prestigious Clinical Club, where membership was limited to thirty doctors, he sat beside his friend, Joe Lewis. The speaker was discoursing on the various techniques of performing circumcision when Dr Abrahamson interrupted. 'Forget all that,' he advised. 'Consider instead the ritual Jewish method, which produces a completely functional and aesthetic result. Show them, Joe!' On another occasion, when he was delivering the first medical report on the use of gold salts in the treatment of rheumatoid arthritis, one of the assembled doctors, J.C. Flood, remarked, 'I wonder if the professor has found any way to recover the gold from the urine for re-use.' Interpreting the remark as an anti-

Semitic reference to alleged Jewish meanness, Dr Abrahamson replied, 'Dr Flood is qualified in Medicine and Law and is also a Doctor of Divinity. He could be said to have more degrees than a thermometer, but without the same capacity for registering warmth.'

From the 1920s to the '60s Dr Abrahamson was regarded as the natural leader of the Jewish community. He was president of the Jewish Representative Council and the Jewish National Fund (JNF) and involved himself with Victor Waddington in preparing a report on the plight of German Jews affected by the war. His death in October 1961, ironically from coronary thrombosis, was announced on Radio Éireann and widely reported in medical journals and the Irish and English press. 'I remember your father well. He once saved my life,' was an oft-repeated expression of condolence and appreciation to members of the family. Messages from the President of Ireland, Church leaders of all faiths, the judiciary, the medical fraternity, friends and patients paid tribute to 'his kindness, his skill, his charm, his friendliness'. L.S. Grogan, a friend from university, recalled him as 'one of a courageous group who formed the backbone of (Trinity's) *Cumann Gaelach*' (Gaelic Society). His friend Dr Geoffrey Marshall wrote, 'I never had … a more generous and trusted colleague … I loved and admired him.' The Jewish community paid tribute to him by endowing a Leonard Abrahamson Memorial Lecture at the RCSI and planting trees in Israel in his name.

Muff Abrahamson was born in 1926. A graduate of Trinity College, he became Professor of Pharmacology at the College of Surgeons and assistant visiting physician to the Richmond and Associated hospitals. In 1973, he settled in Israel. His twin brothers David and Max were born in 1932 in Portobello Nursing Home, a private hospital near the Grand Canal originally built as a hotel for barge passengers. The drama that followed their birth when Portobello went on fire, is recorded by another brother, Maurice (Mossy) Abrahamson in 'Over Sixty Years Ago', as a glimpse of Irish childhood in *Between You and Me*, edited by Don Briggs. The Fire Brigade was still bringing the blaze under control when Dr Abrahamson arrived to visit his wife and infant sons. With 'flames leaping out of the windows' and everyone else brought to safety, he was appalled to discover that his wife and sons were still inside the building. Tillie would not let the firemen risk the lives of the premature infants by taking them down the fire escape in the cold night air and she refused to leave without them. The nurse on duty stayed with her. Told to extinguish lights because there was a gas leak, they waited in darkness until the firemen could lead them to safety by way of the staircase. They had just left the building when the ceiling of Tillie's room collapsed.

David Abrahamson became a veterinary surgeon in London but returned to Dublin to study Medicine at Trinity College and eventually became a psychiatrist. Mindful of their father's views on specialisation, his family greeted the news with, 'He has disgraced us all but it might have been worse. He could have become a surgeon!' David shares the family sense of humour. One April Fool's Day he told a ward sister, 'You know I used to be a vet. I'm very concerned about a gorilla. I think he's schizophrenic and I want to admit him.' Ignoring both the strangeness of the request and the date, she replied in all seriousness, 'But, doctor, I have no beds!' In 2002, he was invested with an MBE for his services to Psychiatry in Britain, an honour that earned him a Christmas card from 10 Downing Street.

Dr Bethel Solomons was born in Dublin in 1885. His mother, Rosa Solomons, *née* Jacobs, who chose the site for the Adelaide Road Synagogue, was English. Educated to the same high standard as her ten brothers and sisters, she spoke fluent French and German, taught at the Adelaide Road School, performed public piano duets with Bethel in his teenage years and wrote poetry. Bethel's father would have been English, too, had his grandmother not been visiting Dublin at the time of the birth. When he married Rosa, he extended his practice as an optician to a consulting room in Dublin, scorning to open a shop. In 1902, he became Dublin's honorary consul to the Austro-Hungarian Empire and was leader of the Dublin Jewish community for many years.

Bethel entered Trinity College in 1902. The third Jew to qualify there in Medicine, he was the first in Ireland to specialise, choosing gynaecology possibly through his esteem and affection for Sir Arthur Macan, then master of the Rotunda Hospital. In 1911, when he was already a consultant gynaecologist at Mercer's Hospital, Bethel became an assistant master at the Rotunda. Though the mastership was supposedly open to all faiths, Dr Hastings Tweedy had already warned him, 'They will never appoint a Jew.' Dr Tweedy was wrong. Dr Solomons was elected master in 1926. His seven-year period of office was marked by innovations. In 1927, he introduced a paediatric specialist into the Rotunda and opened its first Radiology Department. A new wing containing what was then 'a modern operating theatre suite' was built in 1930. In 1933, he created the post of theatre sister. His busy schedule encompassed Rotunda work, home visits, private practice and attendance at nursing homes, such as Hatch Street and Portobello. His patients ranged across the entire social stratum. To ensure that Dr Solomons received notice of his wife's first confinement, Viscount Brookborough, then head of the Royal Ulster Special Constabulary (RUC), summoned him by telephone, by telegram and by military radio. A bodyguard of RUC personnel met him at the border and escorted him to Co. Fermanagh for the birth. He attended the wife of playwright Dennis Johnston for both her confinements and was rewarded with a copy of Johnston's plays inscribed, *To B.S. because of the part he took in my greatest work.* Another pregnant patient asked by Bethel, 'How can I help you?' she replied, 'I have come to be confirmed,' upon which her accompanying friend advised her, 'Tell him you're stagnant.'

Dr Solomons travelled as far as London for confinements and encountered all kinds of maternity and gynaecological problems. He invented the placenta forceps and was the first to employ an assistant gynaecologist (hitherto avoided lest they poach patients), the first to suggest that sterility might stem from the male and among the first in Ireland to perform caesarean operations. Towards the end of his mastership he was awarded an honorary fellowship of the American College of Surgeons. In 1946, he was elected president of the RCPI, another Jewish first. The General Medical Council appointed him inspector of examinations in Midwifery and Gynaecology to the Medical Schools of Great Britain and Ireland as well as watchdog for teaching methods, equipment and the general organisation of hospitals. In addition to his autobiography, *One Man in his Time* (1956), he wrote standard textbooks on gynaecology, midwifery and obstetrical diagnosis and treatment.

Married to a former concert pianist, he was a supporter of the arts and had a wide range of interests, including sports, contract bridge, and membership of the Royal Zoological Society of Ireland where he lit cigarettes for a companionable chimp who smoked while they strolled the grounds together. He favoured votes for women and their admission as fellows to the College of Physicians.

Both his sons became fellows of the RCPI. Michael, described by his father as 'a born midwife', also became a fellow of the Royal College of Obstetricians and Gynaecologists. He was assistant master at the Rotunda and later served Mercers and the Royal City of Dublin (Baggot Street) Hospitals. Bethel junior was a dermatologist at Dr Steevens' Hospital and Baggot Street.

It was once a requirement of the Rotunda Hospital that even doctors with their own cars make home visits by private brougham or jaunting car; the dress code for the occasion was a frock coat and silk hat, whatever the weather. Dr Solomons became a familiar sight in Dublin as he set out to attend patients, frequently accompanied by Nurse Ada Shillman, in 'her long black nurse's cape and cap with streamers'.

Ada Shillman and her husband had settled in Cork in 1882. In 1888, she obtained a Diploma in Midwifery after attending a course of instruction at the Cork Lying-in Hospital. In 1892 the Shillmans moved to Dublin, where Ada practised her calling until her death in 1933. Julie Lapedus, a granddaughter living in South Africa, describes her as 'a household name in Dublin Jewry'. Ada's son, Bernard Shillman, in *A Short History of the Jews in Ireland*, recalls that she acted as 'arbitrator and mediator in many a family squabble' as well as attending confinements. Her cash book for 5 April 1895 to 5 April 1905, now in the Irish Jewish Museum, records the hundreds of transactions made over that period and the variation in her fees that reflected the patient's ability to pay. Average confinement charges were around 7s 6d, but in 1897 a baby was delivered for 2s and though 'treatment' as a procedure is always unspecified, the Tomkin family paid £3 for it in 1895, compared with the Levy's 7s 6d in 1897 and only 6s in 1898. Though in poor circumstances herself, with eight children and an ailing husband unable to work, she provided the poverty-stricken with 'food and raiment, milk and swaddling clothes', in addition to free treatment.

It was customary at that time for midwives to register births. To avoid constant journeys to the General Register Office, Ada Shillman registered clusters of newborns on the same day, without necessarily specifying each one's date of birth. She registered Millie Vilensky as 'Female Vilensky'. Millie's mother had to swear before a magistrate that she had never given birth to another girl before Wesley College would accept her as eligible for the scholarship she had won. Dora Factor, one of Ada's many deliveries who had an 'official' as well as an actual birthday, discovered that registration derelictions were not peculiar to Ada Shillman. When she applied for a ration book in Belfast in the 1940s for her young son, Stanley, born in Dublin in 1936, she was told that he did not officially exist; the Jewish midwife attendant at that birth had not registered him at all.

Apart from collecting for the Jewish Ladies' Charitable Society, Ada Shillman is identified by her son as the 'Jewish nurse' who 'canvassed her co-religionists' to raise enough money to equip the first floor of St Ultan's Hospital for Children when it was founded by Dr Kathleen Lynn in 1919. She also assisted Bethel Solomons in establishing a free dispensary for Jewish women at 43 Bloomfield Avenue, never missing one of the twice-weekly clinics held there over many years. When she died, Bethel Solomons wrote of the personal loss he felt in losing a friend and acknowledged her as 'one of the best midwives I have ever met … quite impossible to replace.' That was not the view of little Becky Moiselle, later Isaacson, whose mother was Ada Shillman's friend. Associating Ada's visits with the arrival of yet another baby, she always cut them short by surreptitiously miaowing like a cat. Ada had a fear of cats and left in a hurry. Despite her childhood attempts at family planning, Becky Moiselle also became a midwife. Ellard Eppel, her nephew, recalled that she was obliged to stop attending poor people privately when she ended up 'giving them more than she was earning.' Her son, Elijah Isaacson, who became an anaesthetist, was one of the few Jews in the 1930s to study at University College Dublin. A third Jewish midwife was Nurse Smith, originally Shultz.

Still practising as a nurse is Anna Adler, *née* Witztum. Born in Dublin and educated at Alexandra College, Dublin, and Methodist College, Belfast, her mind was set on nursing even as she began a course in Physiotherapy at Queen's University and the Royal Victoria Hospital in 1965. She abandoned it for nursing within two years, but St Vincent's, the Mater and the Adelaide Hospitals all refused to take a Jewish trainee; each hospital had its own religious ethos and would consider no application until she was qualified. Baggot Street Hospital was more accommodating. When Anna asked at her interview, 'Does religion matter here?' the reply was, 'Certainly not!' She found the Rotunda, where she did Midwifery, to be pro-Jewish, the matron even phoning to enquire what she would like to eat. Posts as theatre nurse in St Ultan's, Temple Street Children's Hospital and St Vincent's Private Hospital followed. She is now on the staff of Mount Carmel Private Hospital.

Anna was still at Baggot Street Hospital, working in casualty, when Mrs Masar was knocked down at a pedestrian crossing in Morehampton Road. Admitted by ambulance, she was too shocked even to give her name. Seeking identification, Anna opened her handbag and out fell a *sheitel*, the wig traditionally worn after marriage by highly Orthodox Jewish women. Anna explained that she was Jewish, too, and during the three months that Mrs Masar stayed in hospital, she invited Anna to her room every Friday night to participate in the Sabbath ceremonies she normally performed at home and to share the kosher food brought in by her daughter, Eva.

Susan Cohen's interest in nursing began in the early 1980s when her 'dollies were always sick'. For a period of eighteen months, as a teenager, she worked voluntarily at Our Lady's Hospital for Sick Children, Crumlin, spending Christmas and weekends in the playroom or helping to feed, change or just cuddle the babies. In her transition year at Stratford College she did work experience at the Adelaide Hospital. Not allowed to help make beds 'in case creases were in the wrong place', she filled flower vases, tidied linen cupboards, cleaned dentures and helped serve meals. None of it helped secure her a trainee position in Dublin's Catholic or Protestant hospitals, which were continuing to admit only students of their own faith. Susan obtained her qualification as a registered sick children's nurse at John Moores University, attached to Alder Hey Hospital, Liverpool. In 1999, though it had no official vacancy, a position was created for her at Eaton House, the hospital's respite unit for children with profound multiple disabilities. A year later, when Our Lady's Hospital for Sick Children offered posts at one of its intensive care units, she was interviewed successfully and returned to Dublin, where she spent sixteen months. She saved several lives through resuscitation and has a collection of children's photographs from grateful parents who told her, 'We owe our child's life to you.'

Ireland had Jewish dentists before the beginning of the twentieth century. Academic qualifications were still optional when Susan's grandfather, Maurice (Modgie) Davy, began practising. His brother, David, served the requisite alternative of a four-year apprenticeship before going to America for further experience. He returned to Dublin in 1914 with the latest techniques and his practice in Sackville Street was soon thriving. Modgie joined him as an apprentice after leaving St Andrew's College. In 1981, when he wrote 'Long in the Tooth, Dentistry – the Early Years (1921-9)' for the *Dublin Jewish News*, Vol 7, No.2, he remembered earning 2s 6d for his first extraction.

The Dental Act (1921) changed the situation. Only existing 'dental operatives' with a minimum of five years' experience could register; the rest had to study dentistry. Modgie Davy had just begun a university entrance course as a preliminary to taking dental qualifications when the establishment of the Irish Free State rendered the Act null and void. David had gone to London, so Modgie abandoned academic study and took charge of the surgery. In 1928, the Irish Free

State passed its own Dental Act, accepting for registration only those already on the British Registry or entitled to be. That left Modgie and several other officially unrecognised Jewish dentists among the 300 'special category practitioners' who fulfilled neither criterion. He took his problem to Robert Briscoe, his local TD, and was in the visitors' gallery when Dáil Éireann debated the issue. It was decided that a qualifying examination would suffice for registration. Modgie took a year off work to prepare for it. Of the 100 who presented themselves at the Royal College of Surgeons, only 30 per cent passed. Modgie Davy was among them. He opened a surgery at 75 Thomas Street, where he practised for fifty years until his retirement in 1980. For twenty-five of those years he also attended patients at St Patrick's Hospital and was proud of the many letters of commendation he received.

Nathan Gross experienced difficulty of a different kind when he tried to set up practice in Harrington Street in the early 1940s. The premises were owned by Mrs Schlegel, a Catholic, who shared them with the leaseholder, a dentist named Corcoran. Mr Corcoran agreed to sell the practice and assign his interest to Mr Gross, subject only to the 'technicality' of Mrs Schlegel's consent. She refused it on the grounds that Mr Gross was a Jew. He challenged her decision in court as an infringement of Article 44.2.3 of the Constitution of Ireland, which forbids the State to 'impose any disabilities or make any discrimination on the ground of religious profession, belief or status'. Mr Justice George Gavan Duffy upheld Mrs Schlegel's right as a citizen to object to sharing the amenities of the premises with someone she found distasteful, whatever her reason. Referring throughout the case to Mrs Schlegel as Irish and Catholic and to Mr Gross – also an Irish citizen – merely as a Jew, he considered that anti-Semitism was 'notoriously shared by a number of other citizens' and was 'too prevalent' to be considered 'as the eccentric extravagance of a bigot'. G. M. Golding, reviewing the case in his book, *George Gavan Duffy, 1882-1951* (1982) considered the judgement sound but felt that the language in which it was dressed 'marred badly' Gavan Duffy's generally liberal approach. His remarks carried an inference that Catholic citizens had more rights than citizens of any other faith. Mr Gross set up his dental surgery elsewhere; his son, Howard Gross, continues to practise in Dublin.

Family involvement in dentistry was not unusual. Louis Wigoder claimed to be the first Jewish dentist to qualify at Trinity College but his older brother, Philip, had graduated in dentistry from the Royal College of Surgeons ten years earlier, in 1903. Seton Menton is the dentist son of a dentist father, and Hymie Woolf – who once replaced all his instruments to perform a Passover extraction for a highly Orthodox cousin – is succeeded in the profession by two sons and three nephews; but no Jewish family can rival the contribution made to dentistry by the Birkhahns and Schers of Cork.

Ben Birkhahn qualified as a dentist in 1916. His nephew, David, followed suit in 1951. Seven years later, David's sister, Shirley, became the only Jewish dentist to qualify at University College, Cork. Two other siblings, Sandy and Claire, became doctors. Their father, Joe Birkhahn, Esther Hesselberg's brother, had a dental practice in Bantry, Co. Cork, with branches in several neighbouring towns. Asked once what his qualification, BDSI (Bachelor of Dental Surgery Ireland) stood for, he replied, 'Best Dentist in South of Ireland,' a description that fitted him perfectly in the eyes of one little girl who afterwards worked for him. Invited in Religion class to name the most famous Jew, instead of answering, 'Jesus', as expected, she replied, 'Mr Birkhahn, the dentist from Bantry.'

Joe's patients included the nuns in all the convents in West Cork. A second dentist in the area complained of Joe's monopoly to the Bishop of Cork, who replied that the Reverend Mother was capable of looking after her own affairs. He also attended the playwright, George Bernard Shaw, who required dental treatment while visiting Glengariff in 1916. When Joe realised after four or five visits that he had been treating *the* George Bernard Shaw, he refused payment. In *Back to Methuselah*, which he wrote in 1921, Shaw refers to Joe as 'a West Cork dentist' and sent him a signed copy of the play, inscribed, 'A friend in need is a friend indeed.'

Israel (Isa) Scher was a founder-member and Dean of the Cork Dental School, then an annex of the North Infirmary in Mulgrave Road. His four sons, Gerald, Leslie, Eric and Ivor all became dentists. Three of them taught with him at the Dental School and all five Schers were in practice at the same time. Ivor, Leslie and Eric were fellows of both the Royal College of Surgeons of England and the Royal College of Surgeons of Edinburgh, while Leslie and Eric became Professors of Prosthetics, Leslie in Cork and Eric in Belfast.

Abe Cowan whose sister, Stella, married Isa Scher and produced the fine family of Cork dentists, practised in Dublin, where his distinguished patients included Dr Douglas Hyde, first President of Ireland. One of the first dentists to use an X-ray machine, he died of leukaemia before the danger of excessive X-ray exposure was realised. His son, Adrian – known to family and friends as Eddie – qualified in Dentistry in 1941 and in Medicine in 1943. An expert oral surgeon, he worked with his father at 19 Harcourt Street before establishing a surgery in Merrion Road where his own son continues to practise. Despite commitments at home that precluded his attendance at course lectures held in England, Adrian Cowan was the first Irish practitioner to pass the examination for fellowship of the Royal College of Surgeons of England. He taught at the Dental Hospital, Dublin, and was both teacher and examiner at the College of Surgeons in the dental faculty he helped to found with Rodney Dockrell. After three years of service as vice-dean, he was appointed dean of the faculty.

From the middle of the twentieth century, Adrian Cowan became more and more involved with the *Federation Dentaire Internationale* (FDI), the international body that brings dentists together for joint research and information. As chairman of its Educational Committee he travelled the world twice with his wife, Phyllis, *née* Boland, who recalled a visit to the Vatican when the FDI group was to be presented to the Pope. The Cowans, the only Jews among them, phoned in advance to discuss protocol. Though the temperature was 95°F (35°C), Phyllis was instructed to wear a black dress with long sleeves and a black mantilla. She sweltered during the hour's delay while the rest of the female participants, in light summer attire, enjoyed the sunshine.

Following awards from the American College of Dentists in 1966 and the American Dental Society in 1975, the FDI honoured Adrian Cowan in 1979 by electing him to their List of Honour, 'in recognition of his distinguished services to the dental profession', a distinction reserved for only twelve people worldwide. His research work on the use of Xylocaine successfully reduced the amount of anaesthetic used in dental treatment. Known as Cowan's Minimum Dosage, its demonstration by him on film was used extensively for teaching. In 1989, he was elected to honorary membership of the International Association for Dental Research. Rodney Dockrell, in his obituary of Adrian Cowan in the *Irish Times* in 1996, wrote of the 'patients who worshipped and a large body of medical colleagues who respected him'.

Dr Peter Cowan obtained fellowships in oral surgery and restorative dentistry from the Royal College of Surgeons in Ireland and the Royal College of Surgeons of Edinburgh. Like his father before him, he was vice-Dean of the Faculty of Dentistry at the RCSI and later dean. His sister Pamela married Dr David Harris, a world-wide expert on implant dentistry; his sister, Gillian, married Dr Derek Freedman, a specialist in sexually transmitted diseases including HIV and AIDS.

The Irish Jewish community also produced several opticians, a few physiotherapists and a number of pharmacists, one of whom, Arthur Elyan of Cork, was also a chiropodist. Of the many Jewish-owned pharmacies, the best known in its time was Mushatt's, at 3 Francis Street, Dublin, where Rabbi Alony ordered powdered aspirin for the Passover. Éamonn McThomáis mentions Mushatt's in his book *The Liberties of Dublin* and always pointed out the shop during his guided tours of the Liberties, with the commentary, 'Mr Mushatt, he cured every corn and bunion from Lamb Lane to Howth Head and every pimple, wart, cough and skin disease from Swift's Alley right out to Clondalkin Round Tower. G-d bless you, Mr Mushatt, 'cos you were of great service to Dublin and the people of the Liberties.' Other writers agreed. In *Around the Banks of Pimlico* (1985), Máirín Johnston wrote:

Mushatt's, that's the shop! Everything branded KK. Asked what KK stood for, Mr Mushatt laughed and said, 'King of Kures.'

In *Jaysus Wept*, a play by Pete St John set in a Dublin public house during Holy Hour, the character Anyway Keogh, a chain smoker who finishes buttonholes for a Jewish tailor, exclaims:

A chemist is a chemist but the Mushatt brothers were the proof of Dublin genius.

The Mushatt brothers were Louis and Harold. Louis was a qualified pharmacist who had trained in Misstear's at Leonard's Corner on the South Circular Road. When he decided to open his own shop, the landlord of 3 Francis Street asked permission of the established pharmacist around the corner before letting him have the premises. 'Give it to him,' the established pharmacist replied. 'He won't last three months.' When Mushatt's closed in 1967 it had been in business forty-three years.

Harold Mushatt was only fifteen when he joined his brother in 1924. He had a fund of stories about customers, such as the one about the bald man who wanted something to make his hair grow. Louis, bald himself, recommended a specific hair tonic and shampoo that should be applied together. 'I'll tell you what, Mr Mushatt,' said the customer, 'you use it on *your* scalp and I'll come in next week. If your scalp is improved I'll buy it!' Customers making anti-Semitic remarks were forced to back out of the shop as Harold or Louis faced them, moving closer and closer. After one such incident Harold confided his annoyance to his non-Jewish friend, Harry Rantz, a porter at the Bank of Ireland. Harry consoled him with, 'Nobody has anything against a Jew, only those that owe them something and don't want to give it back.' Harold never qualified. He carried on the business after his brother died by employing a pharmacist and reputedly sold the rights to manufacture their unique KK Bronchial Emulsion for coughs, their KK Corn Ointment and their KK soap.

Equally popular remedies in some quarters were Rosenthal's Cough Balsam and Rosenthal's Corn Cure, dispensed and dispatched from The Modern Pharmacy at 6 Merrion Row from 1923 until 1964 and then from the Harcourt Street Pharmacy until its closure in 1969. Sam Rosenthal, born in Cork in 1894 and later a peace commissioner, was employed as a pharmacist by Hayes, Cunningham and Robinson when he fell in love with twenty-year-old Rosie Isaacson on seeing her photograph. They were married in 1923.

His daughters, Audrey Sless and Sonia Patt, describe their father as 'a man of great integrity'. The poor of the area regarded him as their doctor as well as their pharmacist, expecting his diagnosis of their complaint as well as a cure. They were never disappointed. Audrey clearly recalls him opening tubes of expensive ointments to apply a little to some rash or sore and discarding the rest as unsaleable. 'Put tuppence in the Poor Box on your way out,' was his only request for payment. The playwright Hugh Leonard recalled somewhat different curative skills in a radio interview with Marian Finnucan. Asked for his best tip to cure a hangover, he replied, 'When I was a civil servant many years ago, we used to go around the corner to Mr Rosenthal, the chemist in Merrion Row, mostly because he had two beautiful daughters.' After a 'telling off' he was given a pink mixture which tasted 'like drinking sand' but 'did the trick'.

After Medicine, the chosen profession for ambitious Jews in Ireland was the Law. Prominent among the solicitors was Herman Good, one of the country's best-known legal figures. The son of Revd Gudansky, a Russian immigrant who was minister at Adelaide Road Synagogue for more than forty years, he was born in 1906 and attended St Catherine's School and Wesley College before studying Law at Trinity College. He specialised in criminal work. A gifted speaker and actor who appeared at the Abbey Theatre and the Queen's, he was auditor of the Solicitors' Apprentice Debating Society and won all three medals awarded by the Law Society for oratory, legal debate and impromptu speaking. The first Jew to join the Labour Party, he contested the Dublin Townships constituency in the 1944 election against the political heavyweights Seán MacEntee and John A. Costello. His street canvassing met with insults and anti-Jewish heckling, and he reckoned himself lucky not to lose his deposit.

Dublin solicitor Don Buchalter was apprenticed to Herman Good and both he and solicitor Mervyn Taylor worked for him at the start of their careers in the 1950s. They left to start the law firm of Taylor and Buchalter in 1954 when he refused to increase their weekly salary of £5 to £6. Don Buchalter recalled the 'prostitutes and likely murderers' that filled the office at 22-3 Dawson Street, constantly stealing the electric heater from the waiting room. A court appearance at the time merited a fee of £3. Herman Good generally insisted on payment in advance, and many of his files were marked FP (fee paid). When a regular client, a prostitute, objected, he told her, 'I'm sorry. You and I belong to the two oldest professions in the world, and they both have the same rules: money in advance.'

Don Buchalter's son, Richard, and a grandson watch Rabbi Schreibhand from Manchester finish the last few letters of a newly-written Sefer Torah about to be dedicated at Terenure Synagogue in memory of his late father (April 2008).

Though many families with potential malefactors put money aside weekly to ensure his services in an emergency, Herman played a leading role in the Labour Defence League, set up to defend the poor in court, and handled cases free when occasion demanded. An article in the *Evening Standard* (London) of 3 June 1967 described him as 'the definitive Dublin Jew ... a kind of hero among the poor whom he has made a specialty of helping.' His cases ranged from the comparatively insignificant to the sensational. He was defending solicitor when protesters on an unemployment march were charged with breaking windows, when Paul Singer was acquitted on charges of conspiracy and fraudulent conversion connected with Shanahan's Stamp Auction Ltd, and when the Shan Mohangi murder trial was heard.

The Minister for Justice, Brian Lenihan, TD, paid tribute to his 'outstanding ability' at a testimonial banquet in his honour when he was made a temporary judge of the District Court in 1966. That he was over sixty engendered doubts about the wisdom of a permanent appointment, but he was such a popular figure that political and legal pressure was brought to bear. Within months he was confirmed as permanent. Opposed to both corporal and capital punishment and an advocate of prison reform, he quickly established a reputation for humane decisions, sometimes presaging his judgement with, 'What am I going to do with you?' Many defendants specifically requested that he judge their case. The excellence of his work on the bench led to further promotion in 1977 when he became a judge of the Special Criminal Court. When he retired from the bench he was honoured with membership of the Special Criminal Court, a voluntary post. In the court tribute to him after his death, Mr Justice Doyle described him as a man who 'leaned naturally towards clemency, based on a life-long experience of and sympathy with human frailty.' Tall of stature, charismatic and a committed Zionist, his involvement in Jewish community life was total. He was president of the Dublin Hebrew Congregation and honorary life president of Dublin Maccabi Association. The Jewish Representative Council, which he served for ten years as chairman, honoured him in 1970 by naming a room for him at the University of Jerusalem. The seventy friends who travelled from Dublin for the dedication ceremony heard him tell the audience it was the happiest moment of his life.

Another Dublin solicitor honoured in Israel is Judge Hubert Wine, whose career mirrored Herman Good's in many ways. Born in Dublin in 1922, he was apprenticed to Herman Good and spent his first year of qualified practice with him. At twenty-three, undaunted by the sixteen Jewish firms already practising law in Dublin, he started on his own, specialising in criminal, property and accident cases. In 1974, the Minister for Justice, Michael Noonan, TD, informed him that his name had been put forward for a judgeship. He declined the honour. With a list 'a mile long', he had no time for it and Saturday court sittings would impinge on Sabbath observance and affront his extremely Orthodox mother. 'I respect you for that,' the Minister replied, and persuaded him to accept the post on the understanding that he would attend Sunday court instead whenever necessary.

His first appointment was to Rathfarnham District Court, a building so small that litigants queuing outside on the street could be heard discussing the details of their cases while another was in progress. Its worst feature was a repellent smell every Monday morning, which eventually caused Judge Wine to adjourn the court. It took the lifting of floorboards to reveal a dump just below the judge's seat, where traders were throwing unsold fish every week-end. At one time Judge Wine sat in the criminal section of Dublin District Court, where Herman Good had sat fifteen years before. He appreciated the honour but deprecated the title of District Justice that accompanied it. Barristers supported his objection and the Department of Justice changed the appellation to Judge of the District Court.

In 1989, he moved voluntarily to the District Court at Dun Laoghaire. Though it doubled his workload and working hours, he never carried a scheduled case forward, no matter how late the court sat. Nor would he allow a defendant to be brought into court in handcuffs, the normal practice for those with a previous conviction. Once, in severe pain, Judge Wine had to be carried into court. While recovering in Blackrock Clinic from a subsequent hip operation, he exercised his right to constitute any premises within the district a court and heard cases in his room for a period of three weeks. In 1990, he opposed the express wishes of the Director of Public Prosecutions and the combined Departments of Justice, Education and Health in the matter of a fifteen-year-old girl whose case was heard at Dun Laoghaire court. Remanded in custody to Mountjoy Prison, 'the poor unfortunate child', as he termed her, 'the victim of terrible sufferings and traumatic experiences since the age of ten' had allegedly injured another child. The authorities, having no suitable rehabilitative placement available, wanted the charges withdrawn, an option that would have left the girl 'out in the streets to fend for herself'. In Judge Wine's view, and according to medical and psychological reports, she needed help, love and care. He rejected official directives and a commitment was finally made by the Minister for Education, Mary O'Rourke, TD, to open a suitable centre within two months. The *Sunday Tribune* of 21 January 1990, echoing the opinion of every newspaper in the country, described him as 'a man of principle, courage and determination'.

Two days before his obligatory retirement at the age of seventy, Gardaí in Dundrum escorted Judge Wine to the Garda Station in Upper Georges Street, Dun Laoghaire, which they were about to vacate for the badly-needed new premises and courthouse he had secured for them in Corrig Avenue. Before an assembly of 250 gardaí from six different stations the Chief Superintendent presented him with a Waterford crystal vase. Other testimonials and presentations followed. Garret FitzGerald, one time *Taoiseach* and leader of Fine Gael, expressed 'admiration for [his] compassionate administration of justice.' Mary Robinson, President of Ireland, referred to 'the dedicated contribution Hubert Wine has made during his time as a solicitor and as a judge.' With money collected from non-Jews in Ireland and America as well as from co-religionists, the Irish Friends of the Hebrew University in Jerusalem endowed a lecture room in his name at its Law Library.

A congregant in Adelaide Road Synagogue from the age of four, Hubert Wine was only twenty-seven when he began working on its council; he was an honorary life president when the synagogue closed. In 1973, he became Adelaide Road Synagogue's representative on the Jewish Representative Council, where he afterwards served as chairman for two seven-year periods. He remained actively involved in communal affairs into his eighties.

Though Ireland under British rule had many Jewish barristers, Bernard Shillman claimed to be the first in the Irish Free State when he was called to the Bar in 1926. Born in Dublin in 1893, he attended Westland Row Christian Brothers' School, where he was taught mathematics so effectively that he was admitted as a Government student in Mathematics to the Royal College of Science for Ireland, an opportunity not previously afforded to a Jew. Two of his classmates at Westland Row were Peter Judge, better known by his stage name of F.J. McCormack, and the actor, Paul Farrell. Both of them appeared in the film *Odd Man Out*. When Bernard Shillman told his children he had been on the set, they asked, 'What part did you play, Daddy?' He replied, 'The titular part. I was the odd man out.'

In 1948, he was called to the Inner Bar, the first Jew in the twenty-six counties to receive the appointment. Though he never practised at the English Bar, he became an honorary Queen's Counsel at Gray's Inn, London, at the invitation of Sir Hartley Shawcross, a prominent English barrister. Already a civil servant in the Department of Agriculture, he was engaged in law only part-time when he wrote *The Law Relating to Workmen's Compensation in Ireland* (1934). It was the first of a series of legal works that encompassed Irish licencing laws, factory registration, trade unionism and trade disputes, yet he found time for other interests. Dame Sybil Thorndike, the celebrated English actress, initiated a long correspondence with him regarding a pamphlet he wrote on '*Macbeth' and its Qualities of Tragedy* and Dr Hertz, Chief Rabbi of the British Empire, dubbed him 'the historian of Irish Jewry' when his book, *A Short History of the Jews in Ireland*, was published in 1945; it was the only title he valued in a lifetime of academic achievement.

His obituary in the *Irish Jewish Year Book*, 1966-7 refers to Bernard Shillman as a fervent Zionist and energetic communal worker who served as honorary secretary to Zion Schools, the Dublin *Talmud Torah* and the Dublin Hebrew Congregation. He was writing a book on probate law when he died in 1965.

Dr Joshua (Joe) Baker and Samuel Crivon, both born in 1906, were friends and contemporaries of Herman Good. Dr Baker, a native of Dublin, was a senior counsel and an outstanding legal expert. His academic career encompassed a double first at Trinity College in Hebrew and Oriental Studies and Legal Science, which earned him a gold medal and a scholarship to the United States, where he gained his doctorate. Despite a heavy legal practice, he lectured at Trinity College for thirty years in Hebrew and as Reid Professor of Criminal Law. When he died in 1979, another contemporary and friend, Professor Weingreen, referred in an obituary in the *Jewish Chronicle* to his 'lucid, analytical mind, genial personality, special sense of humour and many acts of friendship.'

Samuel Crivon, born in London, was only a few years old when his family settled in Dublin in Longwood Avenue, next door to the Gudansky family. Working by day at the Northern Bank, he studied Law at night and was called to the bar in 1931. He remained in practice for more than fifty years. In 1965, he became a senior counsel. A sound general practitioner with particular expertise in conveyancing, he could handle every type of legal work and acted as standing counsel for Herman Good throughout their professional lives. He helped to draw up the constitution of the Jewish Representative Council and gave free legal advice to practically every organisation within the Jewish community. He was honorary secretary of the Dublin Hebrew Congregation for eighteen years and a life president of Adelaide Road Synagogue.

Henry Barron was born in Dublin in 1928 to Irish parents of Lithuanian descent. His father, a railway engineer, worked in India, and Henry had been there and back three times by the age of five. With his parents continuing to live abroad until 1939, he was sent first to Castle Park, Dalky, and then to St Columba's College, Rathfarnham, Co. Dublin, both Protestant boarding-schools, before he began studying for the bar. He qualified in 1950. One of his cases, concerning the setting aside of an adoption order in respect of a six-year-old child, led to an amendment of the Constitution of the Irish Free State to clarify beyond doubt the validity of adoption orders made by the Adoption Board rather than by a court.

In 1982, he was appointed a Judge of the High Court where one of his decisions led to an alteration in the procedure for the issue of proceedings in criminal matters in the District Court; another concerned an application by residents of Carlow seeking to prevent the bishop from making alterations to Carlow Cathedral. High Court decisions can be referred to the Supreme Court, where judges sit in groups of three or five. Judge Baron's referrals were not always upheld, but he himself became one of the final arbiters as a member of the Supreme Court from 1997 until his retirement in 2000 when he was appointed the sole member of an Independent Commission of Inquiry into the Dublin and Monaghan bomb explosions of 17 May 1974, which claimed thirty-three lives and injured 137 people. In Dublin the bombs exploded in Talbot Street, Parnell Street and South Leinster Street as throngs of commuters, already inconvenienced by a bus-strike, were making their way home from work. Among the dead was Simone Chetrit, a Jewish *au pair* from France. The explosions were attributed to Ulster extremists with persistent suggestions of British military involvement;

Chief Rabbi Isaac Cohen, visiting the injured in hospital, spoke of terrorism as 'today's greatest destroyer of justice'. The formal inquiry, which began twenty-six years after the event, followed pressure by investigative television programmes, led by Yorkshire Television in 1993, and a campaign by bereaved relatives. From 1983 until 2002 Henry Barron was visitor to the University of Dublin (Trinity College), where he sat with the chancellor as a court of final appeal relating to internal matters.

Raphael Siev served the State in a legal capacity for more than thirty years. Born in Dublin to Edith Arnovitz of Limerick and her husband, Albert Siev, the infant brought to Manchester when his Russian mother died in childbirth, Raphael attended Dublin schools and Gateshead *Yeshiva* before becoming a barrister in 1960. In 1968, he became legal assistant in the Land Registry. Two years later, he was appointed to one of three vacancies in the Department of Foreign Affairs and began work on the legal documents connected with Ireland's membership of the Common Market. He was appointed an Irish delegate in 1972 to legal committees of the Council of Europe in Strasburg and his work took him to numerous destinations on diverse missions. In New York he attended the General Assembly of the United Nations; in Montreal he dealt with Civil Aviation Law; in Vienna he worked on Diplomatic Law; in Washington he negotiated Diplomatic Privileges; in Brussels and Jamaica he attended meetings of the International Sea-bed Authority. As Deputy Head of Mission in the Irish Embassy in Copenhagen, he was accredited to Denmark, Norway and Iceland. At Strasbourg he represented Ireland before the Board of Human Rights and spoke at the United Nations in New York from the rostrum of the General Assembly Hall. Involvement in International Law gave Raphael Siev a sense of fulfilment he could never have derived from practice as a barrister. After his retirement, he continued to advise, on a voluntary basis, anyone who could benefit from his wealth of legal experience and remined actively engaged until his sudden, tragic death in 2009. His brother, Asher Siev, a solicitor, was appointed Ireland's first Jewish public notary.

On 12 December 1977, the *Belfast Telegraph* recorded the death of His Honour, Judge Bernard Fox, former Recorder of Belfast and second citizen to the Lord Mayor from 1945 until 1960. Born in 1885, he attended the Belfast Royal Academical Institution and won first place in the bar examinations of 1919. In the early 1930s, he unsuccessfully defended Eddie Cullen, the only Jew ever hanged in Crumlin Road Prison. His son, Jackie, on becoming a Resident Magistrate, formally addressed as 'Your Worship', quipped at a bar dinner, 'For years you have honoured my father but by G-d, you'll worship me!' On one occasion Jackie and his brother, Lennie, both appeared before their father, one acting for the plaintiff and one for the defendant. Sibling rivalry overcame legal niceties when Lennie lifted one of Jackie's documents. 'Your Honour,' protested Jackie, 'he took my paper!' transposing the formal title for the 'Daddy' he would otherwise have used.

Judge Fox was legal advisor to the Northern Ireland Ministry of Home Affairs and chairman of numerous Government enquiries ranging from teachers' salaries to the decasualisation of the Belfast docks. He was a trustee of the Belfast Hebrew Congregation and chairman of the Belfast Jewish Institute.

Ronnie Appleton was a pupil at Belfast High School. Called to the bar in 1950, he became a Queen's Counsel in 1969 and Northern Ireland's senior prosecutor in 1974. The post involved him in all principal terrorist cases and in the Scarman Tribunal, which investigated the specific events of 1969. When he had occasion to address the House of Lords in the Moses Room, where a mural depicts Moses descending to the Israelites with the Ten Commandments, the joke that quickly circulated was, 'On the wall was the Lord handing down the Law to the Jews and on the floor was a Jew handing up the law to the Lords.'

The number of Jews who proceeded to third level education in Ireland has always been disproportionately high for the size of the community. Their contribution to academic life has been equally remarkable. In 1965, Norman Adler was on the editorial board of *Awake*, a student weekly at Trinity College, Dublin; Stanley Waterman was chairman of Trinity's Geographical Society; Alec Feldman was business manager of *Miscellany*, another Trinity College weekly, and Laurence Jacobson was vice-president of the most influential student body in the country, the Union of Students in Ireland.

The *Jewish Chronicle* has been recording the academic and professional successes of Irish Jews since before the end of the nineteenth century. In 1887, Walter W. Harris graduated in Arts from the University of Dublin with very high marks in all subjects. In 1891, Asher Leventon, son of the minister at Adelaide Road Synagogue, passed the professional examination in Pharmacy and won a prize in Practical Pharmacy. In 1907, David S. Clarke, BA, a fourth year medical student, won a first-class prize in Pathology at the Faculty of Medicine in Queen's College, Belfast.

Jessie F. Sayers entered Trinity College in 1922 as the first woman student to be admitted on a sizarship. While still at school she had gained first place in Honours Mathematics three years running in an all-Ireland competition and won two Intermediate scholarships. She graduated with first-class honours, a gold medal, a research scholarship and the Wall Biblical scholarship. When she left Ireland for Holland in 1933, her post as a journalist with the *Irish Times* was filled by her sister, Edie Levin, also a graduate of Trinity College.

A.J. Leventhal, known as Conty or Con, became a Trinity College lecturer, essayist and man of letters. As a young graduate in 1921 he visited James Joyce, who played and sang 'Hatikvah', the Jewish national anthem, for him; Joyce also revealed some of his sources for the Jewish characters in *Ulysses* but claimed they had all left Dublin. Under the pseudonym of L.K. Emery, Con Leventhal wrote what was described as 'one of the first and most appreciative reviews of *Ulysses*'.

With Joyce's work generally regarded as blasphemous, no one would print it, so Leventhal produced the one and only issue of a magazine he called the *Klaxon* in which he printed the review himself. In the *Irish Times* of 29 February 1984, Fergus Pyle described him as a man with a rare talent for friendship who was part of the Dublin literary scene from the 1920s until he moved to Paris in the 1960s. His friend, playwright Samuel Beckett, initiated what Con Leventhal's widow called 'a most extraordinary expression of affection for a most extraordinary man.' It took the form of donations of pictures, books and memorabilia that were sold off at Trinity College to raise funds for a postgraduate travelling scholarship in English or modern languages in Leventhal's name. Beckett's contribution was signed copies of limited editions of his plays and some manuscript pages.

Dublin-born Maurice Jaswon, a brother of the pathologist, Nafti Jaswon, was the son of an Irish mother and Lithuanian father. Both his parents had lost their fathers at an early age and were raised by family members in Switzerland, where they met. The romance continued by correspondence after his mother returned to Dublin and his father to Lithuania, but no marriage was permitted until rabbis in Kovno received letters from Rabbi Herzog and Rabbi Gavron vouching for the bride and testifying to her virginity. Maurice Jaswon was a pupil at Wesley College when he won a sizarship in Mathematics to Trinity College in 1940. In 1942, he was named a scholar in Mathematics, an honour reserved for the best student in each academic year in each faculty. He recalls Hyman Tarlo, who subsequently became dean of the Faculty of Law in the Australian National University in Canberra, as another Jewish scholar in his year. Maurice graduated in 1944 with a double first in Mathematics and Physics and became Professor of Mathematics at the City University in London after serving for three years as visiting professor at a number of American universities.

Cornelius Lanczos, brilliant mathematician, talented pianist, lecturer and writer, was born in Hungary. In the period 1928-9 he worked in Germany with Albert Einstein and during the Second World War contributed unwittingly to research for the atomic bomb. He was a world expert in numerical analysis and his studies were among those that paved the way for the modern computer. Brought to Ireland in 1953 by the *Taoiseach*, Éamon deValera, as Professor of Mathematics at the Dublin Institute for Advanced Studies, he held the post for twenty-one years and completely integrated himself into Irish-Jewish life. He was a member of the Royal Irish Academy and his many academic distinctions were enhanced by the award of honorary degrees for his 'magnificent contribution to international mathematics'. When he died in 1974 the Irish Academy of Sciences paid him a memorial tribute at the International Conference on Numerical Analysis being held at University College, Dublin.

Equally outstanding among the academics of his time was Jacob Weingreen, professor of Hebrew at Trinity College, Dublin, for forty-one years. Born in Manchester in 1908, he was brought to Belfast as a six-year-old and moved with his family to Dublin in 1921. His career at Trinity College began in 1926 when he was awarded a sizarship in Hebrew; he went on to win a gold medal and the Wall Scholarship in Hebrew. By 1930 his first-class honours degree in Hebrew and Semitic Languages had gained him the post of Hebrew lecturer. A year later he became an assistant to the Professor of Hebrew, succeeding to the chair in 1937 when the incumbent, R.M. Gwynn, a clergyman of the Church of Ireland who was also Professor of Ancient Semitic Languages, acknowledged that Mr Weingreen would be more suitable for the post and should become Professor of Hebrew in his stead. A gifted teacher, Professor Weingreen numbered many prominent academics and clerics among his divinity students, who referred to him as 'the finest Christian in Ireland'. One, also a scholar in Maurice Jaswon's year, subsequently became a canon and in retirement continued to send Maurice New Year greetings, quoting Hebrew texts he had learnt from Professor Weingreen.

Professor Weingreen's *Practical Grammar for Classical Hebrew* earned him world acclaim. A standard textbook for both Jewish schools and Church of Ireland seminaries, it sold so many copies since its first publication in 1939 that the Oxford University Press celebrated its Golden Jubilee. Used at the Hebrew University, it has been translated into many languages, as well as appearing in a Braille edition. It continues to be the definitive grammar for Hebrew scholars throughout the world. In addition to writing three other books of Judaic interest and numerous studies on Old Testament and general Jewish themes, Professor Weingreen devoted much of his time to biblical archaeology. His collection of archaeological artifacts from excavations in Samaria and elsewhere in Palestine formed the basis of the Museum of Biblical Antiquities, opened in 1957 at Trinity College. In 1977, it was renamed the Weingreen Museum, in recognition of his contribution in establishing and maintaining it.

From accountancy to zoology, there is hardly a facet of Irish professional life that the Jewish community has not served with distinction. The 'brain drain' of the many skilled professionals who emigrated has been as much a loss to Irish society as it has been to the Jewish community.

8

ARTS AND CULTURE

Despite the strong emphasis placed by parents on the study of Medicine and Law, Jews in Ireland, including doctors and solicitors, displayed an early interest in arts and culture. *Facts and Fancies*, a book of poems written by Rosa Solomons while she rested to avoid a miscarriage before the birth of her daughter, Estella, was published by Williamson McGee of Nassau Street Dublin, as early as 1883. The first of two books by Dr George Wigoder on complex religious themes appeared in 1905, followed in 1914 by the first of four books on sacred texts and prayers written by his brother, Myer Joel Wigoder. Tania Vilensky, the Russian-born mother of Dr Millie Luxenberg, was a published writer of poetry in Russian, Yiddish and English, and delighted friends with readings of her work. In 1968, Mercier Press published *Jonathan Swift and Contemporary Cork* by Gerald Goldberg, then a practising solicitor. His investigation into Swift's refusal to accept the freedom of the city of Cork was praised as a fine piece of original research. Dr Alex Tomkin played the cello in a regular weekly quartet and practised daily with his children. Barrister David Goldberg, Gerald Goldberg's son, began exhibiting in 1975 when he became a full-time painter and print maker. Shown in Cork and Dublin at venues that included the Royal Hibernian Academy (RHA) and the Oireachtas (house of parliament), his work has also been exhibited in England, Sweden, Holland and the United States. Bernadette Greevy, the renowned contralto, fittingly opened one of his exhibitions at which paintings of orchestras and musicians showed the skilful combination of his interest in art and music. Though still painting and exhibiting, he became a senior counsel in 1999 and returned to legal work.

Estella Solomons, the revolutionary sympathiser born to Rosa in 1882, was the first Jewish Associate of the Royal Hibernian Academy and remained a contributor for sixty years. 'A Georgian Doorway' and her other images of decaying Dublin, together with her etchings, 'have left a wonderful record of an Ireland lost to development'. As well as being shown generally, she had a solo exhibition of her landscapes in 1926 and a second in 1931 of various places she had visited. Her marriage to Séamus O'Sullivan, poet, essayist and editor of *Dublin* magazine, long deferred because of her parents' objections to intermarriage, placed her at the centre of cultural life in the Dublin of her day. In an article in the *Irish Times* on 3 December 1982 celebrating her centenary, Brian Fallon described some of the portraits she left of a whole generation as 'inspired.' His contention that she was less popular than she deserved was vindicated some years ago when a large exhibition of her work at the Frederick Gallery sold out. In 2003, a one-hour documentary, Estella, made by RTÉ, engendered renewed interest in her life and work.

One of Irish Jewry's best known artists was Aaron (Harry) Kernoff. Born in London in 1900, he had a Russian father and a Spanish mother descended from the Chancellor of Spain who enabled Queen Isabella and King Ferdinand to finance the explorations of Christopher Columbus. In 1914, the family moved to Dublin, where he became a night student under Harry Clarke, Patrick Tuohy and Seán Keating at the Metropolitan School of Art. In 1923, when Jack Yeats judged the entries, the Taylor Art Scholarship in watercolour and oil painting was awarded to Kernoff, the first night student and the first Jew to receive it. Between 1926 and 1958 he held sixteen one-man exhibitions in Dublin. By the time he died on Christmas Day 1974, his work had been shown in Britain, mainland Europe, the United States and Canada. An article in the *Irish Post* of 11 January 1975 listed his typical subjects as 'dockers, street musicians, turf cutters, tinkers, islanders of Dún Chaoin and the Blaskets' but he also portrayed contemporary personalities. Poets William Butler Yeats and Patrick Kavanagh, and writers James Joyce, Oliver St John Gogarty, Brendan Behan and Flann O'Brien (who wrote his *Irish Times* column as Myles na gCopaleen) were among the many who sat for him at his attic studio in Stamer Street. Playwright Seán O'Casey reputedly disliked his portrait so much that he threatened to sue if it was hung. He never did. Kernoff also painted the Dublin character, The Toucher Doyle, said to have acquired his name when he 'touched' King Edward VII for a fiver at Leopardstown Race Course. Kernoff was 'touched for ten bob' during the sittings.

A familiar figure by day in a corner of Mc Daid's pub in Henry Street, where he sipped and observed from beneath his wide black hat, Kernoff spent his evenings in Neary's in Chatham Row. He still found time to write satirical verse, to design stage settings and costumes, and to publish three books of woodcuts, many on Jewish themes. In 1976, when his work formed part of the National Gallery's display in Texas, he was celebrated at home in a memorial exhibition at the Hugh Lane Municipal Gallery of Modern Art. Fellow artist Gerald Davis described him in the exhibition brochure as a much-loved character, while the *Irish Post* article referred to him as one who loved Ireland and Dublin and 'projected our lives and

times in simple, clear and straightforward terms'. After his death, it considered 'all
... terribly empty and quiet now that Harry is gone'.

Less influential in artistic life but also an acknowledged and talented artist was
Stella Steyn. Her Russian father and German mother were both brought up in
Limerick, where they married in 1890 before moving to Dublin. After leaving
Alexandra College, she spent a short time in Germany studying art before
enrolling at the Metropolitan School of Art in Dublin. Her teacher, Patrick Tuohy,
a family friend, influenced her in favour of French painting. In an article in the
Irish Times of 16 November 1983, fellow student Hilda van Stockum wrote, 'Stella
Steyn awed me with her elegance ... artistic colour combinations and fashionable
get-ups. She was very talented.'

In 1926, she made the first of several visits to Paris. Years later, in a memoir
published in *Stella Steyn (1907-1987): A Retrospective View with an Autobiographical
Memoir*, she recalled that her mother, who was to accompany her, told Arthur
Griffith's wife that Tuohy had given Stella a letter of introduction to James Joyce.
Mrs Griffith said she had heard plenty about 'that fellow Joyce' from her husband,
who thought him 'a thorough ruffian who had written a book no decent person
would read' – an opinion Mrs Steyn confided to Joyce as Dublin's impression of
him. He did not hold it against her and invited Stella to illustrate *Finnegan's Wake*,
then being printed in instalments as work in progress. The Steyn's first impression
of Joyce was of 'a tall slender man ... wearing a shade over one eye – a little
languid and fragile.' Stella's mother felt immediate sympathy for him. Despite his
apparent indifference, he was not insensitive to Irish opinion. When Stella heard
him singing melancholy Irish songs to his own piano accompaniment she asked,
'Would you not like to go back?' 'No,' he replied. 'They jeer too much.'

Stella Steyn's work was exhibited in Britain and the United States as well as in
Ireland, where she had a solo exhibition at the Dublin Painters' Gallery in 1928. In
1930, when an article in *Paris Montparnasse* referred to her as 'un nom a retinir: Stella
Steyn', St George's Gallery in London held a solo exhibition of her drawings, etchings
and lithographs. She enjoyed a second solo exhibition in Dublin before she left again
for Germany to become the first Irish artist to study at the Bauhaus in Dessau, then
regarded as the leading art school in Europe. She found Dessau dominated by Nazis,
and the cover she produced for a German magazine 'caught precisely the exhilaration
and threat of the early Nazi rallies'. She is credited with being the only Irish artist of
that decade to take an interest in German contemporary art. When the Nazis forced
the Bauhaus to close in 1933, she left Germany on a one-way ticket sent by her
mother, who feared for her safety. On the way home she met her future husband and
spent the rest of her life in France and England, where she died in 1978.

Another Jewish artist with Joycean associations was Gerald Davis, born in Dublin
in 1938. Described in the winter 1997/8 edition of the *Jewish Quarterly* as 'a

painter, performer, broadcaster and gallery owner', he also presented the best of Irish jazz, spoken arts and comedy under his Livia Records label. A regular contributor to cultural publications, he was a long-standing member of the International Association of Art Critics and lectured extensively in Ireland and abroad. His interest in the work of Joyce and Beckett dated from his teens and both writers influenced his painting. His patron and friend, Wolf Mankowitz, the distinguished English writer who made his home in Ireland, encouraged him to create an exhibition based on *Ulysses*. In 1977, the resultant eighteen canvases, one for each episode of the book, were exhibited under the title Paintings for Bloomsday at the Barrenhill Gallery on Howth Head on 16 June, the date celebrated as Bloomsday. Davis, dressed in a bowler hat and Edwardian suit made for the occasion by master tailor Louis Copeland, masqueraded as Leopold Bloom for the opening. He played the part every year since, to popular acclaim, in Ireland and around the world, until his death in 2005. Though he described himself as more of an enthusiast than an authority on Joyce, his interest brought him into contact with such experts as Brendan Kennelly, Senator David Norris and Joyce's biographer, Richard Ellman.

It was Christopher Ryan, his teacher at St Andrew's College, who developed Davis's interest in art. When he left school at sixteen to join his father's stationery business in Capel Street, he continued to paint, studying at night in the National College of Art and Design. He had his first solo exhibition in 1962. In 1970, when part of the business premises became the Davis Gallery, Cearbhall Ó'Dálaigh, Chief Justice and future President of Ireland, officially opened the display area, then housed on the first floor. Its Silver Jubilee exhibition was opened twenty-five years later on the ground floor by the then President of Ireland, Mary Robinson.

Interest in the theatre prompted him to found the Stratford Players and he performed at the Pike Theatre and the Gate. His interest in jazz led to his promotion of concerts at the National Concert Hall and Kilkenny Arts Week and his appearance with A Brush with Jazz at the Cork Jazz Festival. In 1977, the Arts Council awarded him the Douglas Hyde Gold Medal for Historical Paintings. In 1980, he co-ordinated an Irish Arts Festival for the Irish Government in the United States and was cultural advisor on several committees as well as informal cultural go-between for Ireland and Israel. His 165th one-man show took place in his own gallery in 2002.

Ruth Romney is Ireland's only Jewish female sculptor. Born in Dublin in 1932, she was only thirteen when her drawings were exhibited at the Guildhall, London. Her first professional work after training at the National College of Art was connected with dress design. Working as a freelance, she made illustrations of designer Sibyl Connolly's seasonal collections and went on to devise a two-year course in fashion design — as distinct from practical tailoring — for the Grafton Academy of Dress Design where she lectured. With her son, Chaim Factor, and

Eric Dineen she became involved in the late 1970s in sub-editing and publishing *Art about Ireland*, a magazine designed to promote public awareness of Irish Art.

By the time Ruth stopped lecturing in 1978, Chaim was pursuing an art career from the garage of the family home. Passing through the kitchen one day with a lump of clay, he handed it to his mother and said, 'Sit down there and model something!' She did. The tiny head was cast and still sits on the family sideboard. The ease with which she could translate experience into something three-dimensional delighted Ruth Romney, and she began making figurative pieces that capture movement and action. At thirteen she had declined an invitation to study ballet with the Sadler's Wells Company, but she now merged her continued interest in ballet with her skill in sculpting to produce models of ballet dancers in motion. In 1986, and again in 1989, when the Bolshoi Ballet performed in Dublin, she was invited to mount corresponding exhibitions of her ballet bronzes. She recalls the pleasure of meeting members of the company and watching their performance 'from a privileged vantage point'.

Two other highlights of her artistic career were the unveiling in 1990 of her portrait bust of William Dargan (1799-1867), the man responsible for most of Ireland's railway network and the opening of the National Gallery, and her participation with eleven other Irish artists in a cultural exchange tour of Israel in 1999. The Dargan bust was commissioned by Wicklow County Council for the Wicklow Heritage Centre, with a second edition commissioned by the Ulster Transport Museum; the tour was a prelude to an exhibition at Dublin Castle of the artists' impressions of Israel. One of her pieces, incorporating Hebrew lettering in polished bronze, was bought by the Jewish National Fund for its head office in Israel.

Ruth Romney at work on the model for the bronze bust of William Dargan, unveiled 1990.

Gerald Davis (right) with tour guide during cultural exchange
visit to Israel in May 1999.

Over the last two decades Ruth Romney's work has been shown fourteen
times at the Royal Hibernian Academy. She has exhibited in group exhibitions
in Britain and France as well as throughout Ireland, and her bronzes and
commissioned portraits are in private collections around the world.

Chaim Factor's career developed rather differently. An article by Andrea
Morton in the summer 1986 edition of *An Droichead*, described him as 'a
distinguished young Irish sculptor'. Though his painting and sculpture are
represented extensively in collections at home and abroad, he first displayed his
artistry through the medium of wood. Steeped in the smell of sawdust and the
texture of timber from his grandfather's sawmills in Strand Street and his father's
wood-turning business, he was trained by craftsmen and began carving three-
dimensional shapes from blocks of wood. Night classes in drawing were followed
by full-time attendance at the Dun Laoghaire College of Art. With sculpture seen
as a natural progression of his talent, he continued to design and make wooden
objects, concentrating on miniature Georgian doorways and traditional rural
shop-fronts before turning to custom-made furniture and the renovation of
objects and buildings of national importance. Trinity College Dining Hall and the
Seanad chamber at Leinster House are two that have benefited from his expertise.
He created the mouldings and panelling for the organ case of the National
Concert Hall as well as advising on organ cases in the English university town of
Cambridge and in Salt Lake City in America.

In October 2002, while walking near his studio in Co. Wicklow, Chaim's
attention was drawn to a tree whose bark had been curiously damaged. Leaving
the road to investigate, he discovered that a car had hit the tree, veered off the

road and landed upside down in a deep ditch full of water, where it lay almost submerged and quite hidden from the casual passer-by. A neighbour, quickly alerted, arrived with his digger, and together they pulled out the car. Inside they found the trapped driver sitting on the steering wheel, her head touching the brake pedal. Only her mouth and nose were still above water. Her amazing stamina had kept her alive in an air pocket for thirty-six hours, but she could not have survived much longer. The Gardaí arrived soon after, followed by an ambulance, but it was Chaim Factor's interest in wood that had saved Lisa Landau's life. His timely intervention and resourcefulness were rewarded by Irish Water Safety on 6 February 2003 in the National Concert Hall. Together with twelve others who had rescued people from imminent watery graves, he was presented by the Minister for the Environment with a 'Just in Time' award.

An experienced lecturer in drawing for sculpture and all aspects of furniture design, including model-making and three-dimensional studies, Chaim has produced newsletters specific to sculptors and potters, illustrated *Family Planning Irish Style* by Alan Shatter and completed two books of poetry.

Irish Jewry has always been interested in theatre. In June 1890, following her professional debut in England, Sarah de Groot, daughter of the president of the Dublin Hebrew Congregation, appeared in Dublin as Desdemona. In December 1890, she performed with other artists at Dublin Castle 'by command of their Excellencies, the Lord Lieutenant and Countess of Zetland, before a large number of the elite of Dublin'. Two years later she appeared before them again at a charity performance at the Gaiety Theatre, 'crowded from floor to ceiling' with an audience that included the Lord Mayor of Dublin and the Chief Secretary for Ireland. In 1908, Gertie Buchalter, *née* Shillman, appeared in a Yiddish play at the Abbey Theatre. Six years later, Mr de Groot's fourteen-year-old granddaughter, Eileen Cohen, was invited by the Lord Lieutenant to appear at Dublin Castle at a ball, which she 'complimented by her graceful dancing'.

Several community groups, such as the Jewish Debating Society, became involved in staging amateur dramatics. In 1922 the Jewish Dramatic Circle was revived, with meetings and rehearsals held at the Adelaide schoolrooms. That same year three short plays, one in Yiddish by Shalom Aleichem, were performed at the Empire Theatre in aid of the Ukranian Relief Fund. Regular performances from the formalised Dublin Jewish Dramatic Society, founded by Larry Elyan, became a feature of Jewish cultural life from the mid-1920s to the mid-50s, when productions became more spasmodic before petering out. Its presentations were always well received. In 1948, a review signed 'RMF' (presumably R.M. Fox) considered that its cast of sixty in David Pinski's *The Treasure* at the Gaiety Theatre had given 'one of the most enjoyable shows in its history'. A fashion and gossip columnist rated it 'one of the best amateur dramatic societies in the city' after its 1954 production of *Spring Song* by Bella and Samuel Spewack; the article further

Gaiety Theater programme for *The Treasure*, a play in three acts by David Pinski, performed by the Dublin Jewish Dramatic Society on Sunday, 18 April 1948.

praised its generosity in always giving the proceeds to deserving charities, which included the Catholic Stage Guild Benevolent Fund.

Surviving programmemes show some of the regular performers and production team as Bob Lepler, Joseph Elliman, Dahna Davies, Sidney Lazarus, Bernard Moss, Helen Marcus, Jerry Alexander, Florian Barron and Sam Lynn. Some became involved with prestigious amateur dramatic societies in the wider community, such as Pilgrim Productions, founded by Mollie Griffin from among fellow-pupils at Sion Hill Dominican Convent. When Sam Lynn and Bernard Moss appeared in Pilgrim Productions' 1952 presentation of *Colombe* by Jean Anouilh at the theatre of the Royal Irish Academy of Music, Val Murkerns claimed their performances 'would have been remarkable even among professionals'. Sam Lynn was also in the 1953 cast of Pilgrim Productions' *Happy as Larry* by Donagh MacDonagh, when Zally Barnett and Bernard Moss were two of the stage managers.

Sam was born in 1922 to a Lithuanian mother who reached Ireland as a young child in 1896 and a Polish father, originally named Lipschitz, who fled conscription. He was one of a small group of Jewish performers who turned professional or semi-professional. In 1954, he appeared at The Gate in *Not for Children* by Elmer Rice, with Christopher Casson, Milo O'Shea, Maureen Toal and Coralie Carmichael. Though the play proved unpopular in Belfast, where it was withdrawn at the Royal Opera House, a Belfast review referred to Sam Lynn's performance as 'magnificent'. Another claimed 'the honours of the night must go to Maureen Toal and even more perhaps to Sam Lynn, who really held the whole thing together'. Dublin audiences enjoyed the play. Sam Lynn was described by the *Evening Standard* of 26 November as 'an evening's entertainment in himself'.

Despite regular appearances with the Dublin Globe Theatre Company and Dublin Gate Theatre Productions, where he worked with Michael McLiammoir and Hilton Edwards, Sam found professional theatre financially unrewarding. In the early 1960s he left the stage for a career in accountancy.

Harold Goldblatt remained a professional. Born in 1901, he was a member of the Belfast Jewish Institute Dramatic Society in 1929 when its performance of Israel Zangwill's *The Melting Pot* won the President's Cup at the Northern Drama Festival. Shortly afterwards, with a small number of fellow members that included the talented Beatrice Hurwitz, he transferred to another amateur group, the Ulster Theatre. In 1939, at his instigation, the two dramatic societies amalgamated with a third, the Northern Irish Players, to form the Group Theatre, renamed the Ulster Group Theatre in 1940. Described by the *Northern Whig* of 18 June 1957 as 'the most successful experiment ever launched in Northern Ireland','it netted the actors the unprecedented profit of £40 in its first twelve weeks. Normally popular with playgoers as a theatre workshop that introduced new writers to the stage, its audience after a night of heavy bombing on 14 April 1941 consisted of a seventy-year-old woman and her two daughters, who were sent home when the police discovered an unexploded bomb behind the theatre.

In 1959, Harold Goldblatt resigned as managing director of the Ulster Group Theatre because of an internal dispute, but he subsequently became one of the most familiar faces on television. A role as technical advisor on Jewish custom and ritual to Franco Zefferelli's television epic *Jesus of Nazareth* was greatly assisted by the knowledge gained as a youthful honorary secretary to the Belfast Hebrew Society. Harold made forty-one films, alongside what the *Newsletter* of 10 July 1976 referred to as 'a roll-call of world-renowned artists'. Remembered as the actor-producer-director who introduced professionalism into Northern Ireland's amateur theatre, he had just recorded a radio play for the BBC and was working on a film with Barbra Streisand when he died in London at the age of eighty-one.

To offset the difficulty of finding plays with suitable Jewish themes, Esther Morris wrote her own. Her three plays, *The Conscript*, *The Matchmakers* and *The Story of Purim* were published by Erskine Macdonald of London in 1928 under the collective title *Tears of Laughter*. A note to the edition claims the plays reflected 'the indirect outcome of the author's personal experience'. How wide an audience they reached is not clear, but local Jewish drama groups certainly staged them with success.

Many Jewish girls found an outlet in dancing. Anne Lapedus Brest still remembers the canary costume she wore for the dancing display given by pupils of Christine

Kane and Ada Elliman at the Olympia Theatre, Dublin, on 21 May 1950. Little Minnie Turk was a regular child participant in Noel Purcell's pantomimes at the Theatre Royal. Joan Davis, *née* Citron, became a professional. A child pupil of Evelyn Burchill for ballroom and tap-dancing, her adult forte was contemporary dance. For two years she travelled to London at weekends to study with the London School of Contemporary Dance before jointly establishing the Dublin Contemporary Dance Studio. In 1979, she founded the Dublin Contemporary Dance Theatre.

Dancing saved the life of Helen Lewis, a native of Czechoslovakia. Ill and starving during her incarceration at the Nazi concentration camp at Stutthof (Sztutowo) in Poland, she was suddenly nursed back to health at the whim of the camp commandant so that she could choreograph the Valse from *Coppelia* for a Christmas show. Deprivation returned after Christmas, but she survived every hardship, including a death march, and eventually reached Belfast, where she married, raised a family, founded the Belfast Modern Dance Group and became a celebrated choreographer for theatre and opera.

In 1914, Rachel Levin from Portobello Road, Dublin, came first among the twenty entrants for the annual Vandeleur Scholarship for Senior Pianoforte at the Royal Irish Academy of Music (RIAM). With a score of 98 per cent, the fifteen-year-old was the youngest winner in the history of the Academy. Ray Levinson from Brookvale Avenue, Belfast, also a pianist, gained her first musical degree at the age of fourteen and in 1920 was the only Jewish girl in Belfast to become a licentiate of the Royal Academy of Music (London). Gloria Joy Gordon, also from Belfast, became a fellow of the London College of Music at the age of twenty-one. A frequent broadcaster, she had gained her teacher's diploma at the age of fifteen; in 1953 she was awarded the London Poetry Society's highest award, the Shakespeare Plaque.

Dina Copeman, born in Dublin at the turn of the century to Lithuanian parents who came to Ireland in the 1890s, was the eldest of nine children. Less poverty-stricken than most immigrants, her father was able to provide her with the musical education her talent merited. She studied piano with Michele Esposito, an Italian composer and teacher resident in Ireland, who established her as the country's foremost young musician. She was a teenage concert performer when the Hallé Orchestra engaged her as their pianist.

Her father's untimely death left Dina Copeman providing for the whole family. She accepted the teaching post offered by the RIAM as a weekday commitment and travelled to Liverpool every weekend for Hallé concerts. As guest pianist she played with the Royal Philharmonic Orchestra and gave the first radio transmission for 2RN in 1926, the first of many broadcast performances. As teacher, examiner and performer she devoted her public life to music and her private life to her family, educating all eight of her siblings. Five became doctors and three dentists.

Elaine Brown, *neé* Goldwater, also a talented piano teacher and former pupil of Dina Copeman, describes her as 'very beautiful with lustrous black hair swept up on top of her head and a rich sense of humour.' She accepted only gifted students and summarily dismissed at the end of the year any scholarship-holder not up to standard. Best efforts were often torn apart and even satisfactory performance never praised. Girls found her particularly severe and tried to sandwich their lessons between two boys, when they might find her less of a martinet. Elaine remembers being one of six prize-winning students chosen to perform for Prince Ranier and Princess Grace of Monaco, patrons of the Academy, during their State visit to Ireland. Both her own dress for the occasion and Dina Copeman's had been made by Elaine Brown's mother, May Goldwater, *née* Gordon, also a gifted musician as well as a talented dressmaker. Trained in cutting and design by Robinson and Cleaver in Belfast, May Goldwater made all Miss Copeman's performance gowns, dressed theatrical wives of all faiths, and counted almost every Jewish woman of distinction among her customers. She also provided many a poor bride with a free wedding dress and trousseau. When Elaine, herself a skilled needlewoman, arrived early for a final practise on the day of the Rainier performance, she found her teacher trying on her chiffon gown. Its copious skirt had been hand-finished to the length required for high-heel shoes, but the distinguished pianist had suddenly decided to wear low heels and the dress was too long. She demanded that Elaine shorten it. 'But I came in to practise,' protested Elaine. 'You're not going to get any better,' she was informed, 'so just shorten my hem!'

Dina Copeman was equally forthright when the Rippon Piano Company of Holland attempted to set up an Irish branch in the 1950s. As senior professor at the RIAM, she was invited to bring six boys and six girls to Shannon, where they would be filmed in evening dress playing twelve Rippon pianos for a publicity campaign. Asked on film what she thought of the Rippon piano, she replied, 'It was once a very fine tree,' killing both the advertisement and the prospects of the firm.

She died in 1978. Her funeral was attended by President Hillery, members of the Judiciary, the entire staff of the RIAM, the music department of Trinity College and Colman Pearse, her Shabbos goy and conductor of the RTÉ Symphony Orchestra (now the National Symphony Orchestra). As a tribute to her memory, a Dina Copeman Commemorative Committee at the Academy arranges sponsorship for young musicians to appear at the National Concert Hall. It gives a Dina Copeman award at the International Piano Competition held there every two years, and a Dina Copeman Cup at the Feis Cheoil. Many of her talented students went on to musical careers, and almost all the Academy's present teachers are past pupils.

Elaine Brown, who uses Dina Copeman techniques (without her censorious attitude), dates her interest in music from the day when she and her older brother, Maurice, sprang open the lid of their locked piano by jumping off it once too often. She was seven. Sitting at the keyboard, she played familiar tunes by ear. The locked piano was symptomatic of a tragedy in her mother's life. Classically trained as a pianist by Professor Bass (born Leopold Schultz), a German Jewish immigrant to Belfast who became its foremost piano teacher, she was gripped by the new craze for jazz. She was still in her teens when she formed May Gordon Orchestra Jazz in 1924, with Dave Glover on violin, Bert Wheedon on guitar, her brother, Barney Gordon, who doubled as vocalist, on drums and Eddie Pearl, alternating with May on piano and also playing the banjo. By day she perfected her dressmaking skills, by night she entertained, playing one-night dances and seasonal bookings all over Northern Ireland. In 1934 she married. When her first child, born a year later, died at the age of three, May's musical career was over; she locked the piano and never played again. Eddie Pearl became a broadcaster and pianist on Cunard liners, Bert Wheedon joined the BBC as a guitarist and Barney Gordon went on to play drums with the Oscar Rabin and Ted Heath bands. When he visited his sister in Dublin with his drum-kit, little Elaine Brown, now reading sheet music, accompanied him on the piano. Barney was horrified to hear her playing the music as it was written.

'What have you done to her?' he exclaimed. 'She has no sense of rhythm!'

Elaine began formal music lessons at the age of nine, the first pupil of Ethel Levy, who built up a large body of students on the strength of Elaine's progress. By the time she was twelve she had reached grade 8 in the RIAM examinations and was awarded a scholarship. She became a teacher and performer. Marriage to Leslie Brown, an engineer who plays classical guitar, raising a family and brief sojourns in Britain and the United States, left her early career somewhat checkered, but in 1969 she returned to Dublin and began teaching extensively. Some of her best pupils were RIAM students sent by Dina Copeman, who found them too timid for her own aggressive approach. Others came through an unusual barter arrangement she had with Judith Segal, *née* Shreider, another distinguished Jewish pianist and teacher at the Academy. Judith sent good but non-competitive students to Elaine Brown who sent exceptional students to Judith Segal. Around 1980, when she returned to the Music Department of Trinity College as a post-graduate student, Brian Boydell, Professor of Music, suggested she teach in the College of Education, the teacher training department of Trinity College. She remained on the staff until her retirement in 2008.

Elaine's younger daughter inherited the family's musical talent. Older siblings, Fiona and David, both attended the RIAM and David taught his little sister, Melanie, to read music when she was six, a skill she immediately put into practise by playing a difficult piece of music in key, without the benefit of instruction. Within a year or two she was giving recitals at the College of Music; by eighteen she was qualified to teach at the RIAM and won a sizarship at Trinity College, graduating in music in 1993. An exponent of the violin and viola as well as the piano, she concentrates on composing and was composer in residence to The National Chamber Choir, Ireland's only professional choral group, until 2000. One of her commissioned Hebrew pieces, *Behold the Miraculous Light*, a celebration of *Chanucah*, was performed at Dublin Castle and the National Gallery, with eight singers holding the *Menorah* lights, and was broadcast on both RTÉ and Lyric FM. The entire choir sang in Hebrew when her *Three Blessings*, commissioned by Trinity College as a major piece for choir and orchestra, was performed at the National Concert Hall. A short work on the Holocaust commissioned by the Wexford Musical Festival was so successful that it was subsequently performed at the Cork Festival and televised. For the inauguration of the Ark Children's Centre in Temple Bar, Dublin, she was commissioned to set to music the art and poems of the children of Tereisenstadt (Terezín) in Czechoslovakia, the show-piece concentration camp kept by the Nazis as proof to the Red Cross of their good faith, before they sent the children, clandestinely, to die in the gas chambers. Based on the theme, 'I have not seen a butterfly round here', her chilling piece for piano, cello and flute begins with the laughter and singing of children, then changes key threateningly as the laughter dies, to be replaced by a baby's cry, and silence. It was performed at the Academy and made available to all third-level colleges.

Melanie is an examiner at the RIAM, both locally and around the country, and her music has formed part of their examination syllabus. She is currently completing her doctorate in liturgical Jewish music in Ireland at the Irish Academy of World Music and Dance at Limerick University, where she sometimes lectures. Another successful academic muscian is Rachel Factor who has a master's degree in Music Performance and Musicology from the National University of Ireland (Maynooth). Playing both the piano and the harpsichord, she has performed with Ireland's leading orchestras, recorded lunch-time concerts for Lyric FM, Ireland's classical music radio station, and participated in chamber music festivals. She recently completed a Vivaldi concert tour.

In 1925, the *Jewish Chronicle* reported the decision to form a Jewish orchestra in Ireland, to be called the Cecilian. J. Rubenstein was appointed provisional musical director, and prospective members were asked to apply in writing. Whether it materialised is not certain, but a report in the *Irish Times*, 15 January 1985 refers to a Jewish orchestra in Dublin in 1918. There was certainly no shortage of musical talent. Louis Hyman claims in *The Jews of Ireland* that Philip Michael Levenston became an orchestral leader at the old Theatre Royal when he was only twelve. Awarded a scholarship for violin at the RIAM, he became a professor there and led the Viceregal orchestra and the Dublin Philharmonic as well as conducting at the Queen's Theatre in Pearse Street. Spreading his talents among all denominations and social groups, he provided bands for military and hunt balls while leading a choir at Adelaide Road Synagogue and giving free violin lessons at the Marlborough Street Training College. Other Levenstons were equally gifted in music; the family's dancing academy at 35 Frederick Street is mentioned in *Ulysses*.

There were twelve children in the Rosenberg family, all musically inclined. Four became professional. Their father, a native of Lithuania, settled first in Edinburgh and then moved to Dublin in 1878, when his son, Max (Marks), was nearly two. A brilliant violinist, Max Rosenberg studied at the Royal Academy under Professor Guido Papini. He was leader of the Gaiety Theatre orchestra from the age of seventeen until he retired sixty-two years later. In 1943 he told the Evening Herald that the fifty years since he first took his place in the orchestra pit 'went like a flash'. Gaslight in theatres was just giving way to electricity when he started, and he remembered the performance given by oil lamps and 'thousands of candles all over the place' when an industrial dispute left the theatre in darkness.

Max Rosenberg played in concerts and musical shows in Leinster Hall, Hawkins Street, later the site of the Theatre Royal, and in the Gaiety Theatre for performances by nineteenth-century and early twentieth-century thespians such as Sir Henry Irving, Ellen Terry, Sarah Bernhardt and Sir Herbert Beerbohm Tree. His opinion in 1943 was that 'present day actors cannot compare with the old ones'. He was first violinist when Sir Arthur Sullivan, of Gilbert and Sullivan fame, conducted in Dublin in the 1890s and when Sir Charles Stanford conducted his own opera, Shemus O'Brien. He was principal viola for Dr Esposito's 'celebrated Dublin performance'.

Failing eyesight forced him to relinquish the leadership of the Gaiety Theatre orchestra eight years before he retired, but he continued to perform as one of its viola players. When he died at the age of ninety-two, Dr John F. Larchet, president of the Dublin Grand Opera Society, paid tribute to him as 'a fine musician and a most reliable orchestral player' who during his career played in practically every orchestral concert in Dublin. His brothers, Harris and Gabriel Rosenberg, both violinists, and Solly, a cellist, were also members of the Gaiety Theatre orchestra. The Rosenberg Brothers' Band, a string quartet, gave afternoon tea concerts at the DBC Café on St Stephen's Green, as well as playing for special functions at Dublin Castle. Max's son, David, became a cellist at the Olympia Theatre and then at the Theatre Royal, where he frequently conducted in the absence of Jimmy Campbell, its resident conductor. David's nieces, Thelma Woolfson, Arleen Millea and Gloria Frankel, all remember enjoying free performances at the Gaiety Theatre and wandering freely, as children, into the orchestra pit.

In May 1953, the Dublin Jewish Musical Society gave a recital of classical and folk music at the Royal Hibernian Hotel as the Jewish community's contribution to An Tóstal, the national Festival founded that year. Artists included Dina Copeman, Malcolm Burack, Dave Green and Beulah Cowan with Philip Modell conducting the Musical Society choir. Madame Van Alst had a string quartet that played light classical pieces on regular afternoons in Roberts' Café at the top of Grafton Street. Loretta Wine, a native of Dublin who studied piano in Paris and London, was director of the Irish National Youth Orchestra for seventeen years and one of the directors of Irish National Ballet.

Danish-born Lief Reck escaped by fishing boat from Nazi-occupied Denmark in the Second World War to join the Free Danish Forces in Sweden. He arrived in Ireland in 1951 at the invitation of Sadie Elkinson, who had met him while working in Copenhagen. Within four days he was engaged to be married to her sister, Rhoda.

'I don't like rushing into things!' he told Rhoda, facetiously, to explain his 'delay' in proposing.

To remain in Ireland legally for more than six months he had to be married to an Irish citizen. Their marriage of convenience in the register office was followed a year later by a religious ceremony under the obligatory *chuppah* in the Nissan hut that served Terenure Hebrew Congregation before the synagogue was built.

Lief began playing the violin at the age of six. At seventeen he abandoned classical music to form a semi-professional jazz group that played at nightclubs, restaurants and private functions in Copenhagen. Even as Denmark's leading jazz violinist he knew his music would not support him in marriage, so jazz in Ireland was relegated to evenings and weekends. To earn a living he and his wife designed and made children's clothes. From four machinists the number of their employees grew to eighty-five, and they eventually had half a dozen branches of 'The Young Ones', their retail shops, in Dublin, Dun Laoghaire and Blackrock.

Lief found a fellow jazz enthusiast in Gay Byrne, the radio and television presenter. They met when Lief was performing and Gay was master of ceremonies at jazz concerts in Dublin and other venues. When Gay Byrne created the *The Late Late Show*, Lief was a frequent guest. Often regarded as Ireland's answer to Stephane Grapelli, he entertained at the Cork Jazz Festival twelve times. When he played at the Gorey Arts Festival in August 1980, Niall Tobin had appeared the night before and Éamonn Kelly, the Horslips, Mackem and Clancy and U2 were all to follow later in the month. As well as performing in Britain, Europe and the United States, his extensive Irish venues included the National Concert Hall and Christmas luncheons hosted by the Danish Government for diplomats. The *Irish Times* review of a concert he gave at the Theatre Royal in 1968 stated that 'jazz fans almost tore the ceilings down with applause' after one performance by 'the Fiddling Viking' with the Ian Henry Quintet. Ian Henry was the stage name of Jewish Dubliner, Henry Garber, a classical pianist who turned successfully to jazz under Lief Reck's influence; he later became a doctor. When Reck's own jazz quintet gave a concert at the Town Hall, Cavan, in 1979, they were referred to as 'five of the finest and most highly acclaimed jazz musicians in Ireland'.

Two Jewish Dubliners who provided unlimited entertainment for the Irish public were Maurice and Louis Elliman. A document on Maurice Elliman's life compiled by two of his twelve children, Geoffrey and Hymie Elliman, describes him as 'a penniless but pious Jewish immigrant who came from Russia in 1894 and founded both a family and an entertainment industry'. The sixteen-year-old arrived via Liverpool after months of walking, begging rides, sleeping in barns and working for his food. Unable to spell his name for immigration officials, he pointed to a nearby poster advertising Elliman's embrocation, and Moishe Hellman became Maurice Elliman.

Travelling for a paltry living was not new to him. In Russia he had moved weekly from village to village with a travelling choir that sang in return for lodgings and a few kopeks. In Ireland he peddled. Two years after his arrival he married sixteen-year-old Leah Smullen, the daughter of the house where he first lodged. Children came quickly, precipitating a need for extra income. His venture into a restaurant and swimming pool in Dalkey failed, but by 1910 he had a fruit shop in Aungier Street and a horse and cart for deliveries. He lived in a flat above the shop. At Samuels' Wax Works he quickly recognised the potential in early moving pictures that his friend Joshua Samuels had overlooked. With travelling shows a popular form of entertainment, Maurice Elliman took his own version to country halls and canvas tents. Using a hand-operated projector, he showed whatever few films were available and augmented the entertainment with a boxing booth, where a prize of 10s was offered to anyone who could beat the resident boxer in a three-minute round.

Assisted by his older children, he opened his first cinema in 1911 in a rented disused garage in Pearse Street. Renovated with bench seating, it became the foundation stone of a cinema empire. A year later he opened Dublin's first modern cinema in Redmond's Hill. Its destruction by fire put him temporarily out of business but did nothing to stop his long-term progress. With the support of other businessmen he formed a company to build the De Luxe Cinema in Camden Street. Its auditorium, confectionery stall, 400 upholstered seats and projection room for continuous screening made it Ireland's first luxury cinema.

One of the many buildings to suffer irreparable damage in the Easter Rising was the Metropole Hotel in Sackville Street. Metropole and Allied Cinemas Ltd, with Maurice Elliman as its managing director, bought the site and developed it into the Metropole complex, with a cinema on the ground floor, a restaurant overhead and a ballroom on the top floor. Its opening in 1921 made, 'Meet me at the Metroplole' the popular prelude to many a Dublin rendezvous. The Corinthian Cinema on Eden Quay, nicknamed 'The Ranch' because it showed so many cowboy films, opened in 1932. Two years later he acquired the Queen's Theatre in Pearse Street, where films were combined with a live stage show featuring a resident chorus; the character actor Noel Purcell started his stage career there. Ownership of the Gaiety Theatre followed, then the Savoy group of cinemas in Dublin, Cork and Limerick and the Theatre Royal, capable of seating 4,000 people and regarded by many as a 'white elephant' that would never be filled. This gloomy forecast might have proved correct had it not been for Maurice's second son, Louis Elliman.

Philip B. Ryan in *The Lost Theatres of Dublin* (1998) describes 'Mr Louis', a qualified pharmacist, as the greatest impressario Ireland ever produced. During the Second World War, when only Irish talent was available, he promoted recruitment by featuring 200 soldiers in the variety show 'Roll of the Drum', the proceeds of which went to the Army Benevolent Fund. The shows he produced under the name of T.R. Royle made Noel Purcell, Cecil Sheridan and Jack Cruise household names. The quizmasters Eddie Byrne and Éamonn Andrews both won acclaim on the stage of the Theatre Royal with the popular quiz game 'Double or Nothing'. Jimmy O'Dea, the Gate Theatre Company and semi-professionals such as the Rathmines and Rathgar Musical Society made regular seasonal appearances there, as well as in the Gaiety Theatre. They continued to entertain when the war was over, sandwiched between international stars such as Judy Garland and Danny Kaye and the leading opera, ballet and theatrical companies of the day, until television and rising overheads took their toll. The Royal's last show, 'Royale Finale', was performed on 30 June 1962.

The Ellimans were businessmen as well as entertainers. For Maurice a word or promise was more binding than a contract and Louis was known for his many acts of generosity. In 1941, he gave the Dublin Grand Opera Society rehearsal facilities at the Royal. In 1942, when fire destroyed the Abbey Theatre, he offered the Queen's in Pearse Street as a temporary home. He brought the Variety Club, a charity for under-privileged children, to Ireland and formed the Cinema and Theatre Benevolent Society of Ireland. Several times he rescued Michael Mac Liammoir and Hilton Edwards from what Philip B. Ryan calls 'sticky financial situations', and Ryan claims Orson Welles left Ireland 'owing Louis a considerable amount of money.' Fr Cormac Daly, chaplain to the Catholic Stage Guild, said he knew of one priest who would not have been ordained without Maurice Elliman's help.

Managing director of Odeon (Ireland) Ltd, chairman of Amalgamated Cinemas Ltd and joint founder of Ardmore Studios in Bray, which brought the film-making industry to Ireland, Louis Elliman died in 1965 at the age of sixty-two. Maurice Elliman's funeral to Dolphin's Barn in 1952 had required a Garda escort and the switching off of traffic lights to accommodate the crowds. Louis was similarly honoured. Those attending his funeral included representatives of the State, amateur and professional theatre, the cinema industry, the Jewish community and his many business and charitable interests. Mícheál Mac Liammóir and Hilton Edwards spoke of his death as 'a profound loss' and said, 'Louis was like a brother to us both.' Ernest Blythe, managing director of the Abbey Theatre, referred to him as 'a friend in need'. Maureen Potter called him 'a great and lovable man' and suggested the Gaiety Theatre be renamed the Louis Elliman Theatre.

A pioneer of Irish film-making was Isaac (Jack) Eppel, a doctor and pharmacist who had a chemist shop in Mary Street and brought acts to Rathmines Town

Hall as a part-time impressario. With no knowledge of film production, he ruined himself financially and wrecked his marriage to make *Irish Destiny*, the first fictionalised account of the War of Independence. The last silent film made in Ireland, it combined newsreel footage of 1920-1 with dramatic sequences shot in 1925. Partially colour-tinted by hand, it was enthusiastically received during its two-week run at the Corinthian Cinema in Dublin in April 1926 and in cinemas around Ireland. In 1927, Irish-Americans approved it at Daly's Theatre, New York. The British banned it in its original form.

The director and photographer of *Irish Destiny* were almost the only professionals connected with it; Abbey Theatre actress Sarah Allgood sued because she was promised a part that did not materialise. Among the amateur cast was sixteen-year-old Evelyn Henchy, later Lady Evelyn Grace. Spotted and hired by producers while at a funfair in Bray, she was considered too young to watch the love scenes and had to avert her gaze while on set. In October 1984, she wrote to the *Irish Times* praising Dr Eppel and wondering why his effort had received no real recognition. A reply from Liam O'Leary, then associated with the Irish Film Archive, informed readers that the film was preserved in the Library of Congress, Washington, together with the historical data and memorabilia connected with its production. O'Leary considered Eppel 'one of the enterprising filmmakers of the 20s' and the film itself 'historically important'. Harry Browne, reviewing it for the *Irish Times* almost seventy years after its production, agreed. 'Isaac Eppel,' he wrote, 'merits a place of honour in Irish history.' The occasion was a special showing at the National Concert Hall in December 1993 with President Mary Robinson as guest of honour. Mícheál Ó'Súilleabháin composed an orchestral score especially for the occasion. *Irish Destiny* was presented at the National Concert Hall again in March 2006. On both occasions what the audience saw was 'an absolutely true reproduction'. The original remains in Washington but the Irish Film Archive has a relevant original of its own – a poster from 1926 advertising *Irish Destiny*, found in 1988 beneath the linoleum of a Dublin tenement.

Journalist Carolyn Swift, also Jewish, paid tribute in the *Irish Times* to another Irish-Jewish film-maker in 1983 after the sudden death of Norman Cohen in Los Angeles. He was only forty-seven and had just signed a contract to direct a feature film. Norman's career began at the cutting table of his father's factory in Dublin but he wanted to cut film, not cloth for children's clothes. In 1955, he became a trainee in the right sort of cutting room in London. His progress over the next four years enabled him to edit films for RTÉ before going to Ardmore Studios to work on *The Blue Max*. Involvement with the Film Unit of the Irish Film Society gave him the urge to direct, and he made his first short film in 1961. *Down Boy!* starred Milo O'Shea and a cast of dogs. It was followed by *Brendan Behan's Dublin*, with the voices of Ray McNally and the Dubliners, and *The London Nobody Knows*, produced in England with James Mason. His production of Spike Milligan's comedy autobiography *Adolf Hitler: My Part in his Downfall* won acclaim, while his *Importance of Being Dublin*, starring Mícheál

Mac Liammóir, was compared by one reviewer to the work of James Joyce for its presentation of the city and its population, 'warts and all'. He was engaged in two productions for Warner Brothers when he died.

Norman Cohen was held in affection and esteem by everyone who worked with him, and Carolyn Swift particularly praised his 'absolute integrity, patent honesty, generosity and consideration for others.' She considered his death 'a considerable loss' to the film industry in general and to the Irish film industry in particular. To mark their esteem, the Variety Club of Great Britain set up an appeal for £6,500 for a Norman Cohen Memorial Sunshine Coach for handicapped and underprivileged children.

The man described in the *Irish Times* of 18 November 1979 as 'the most consistent of Irish film-makers' is Louis Marcus, born in Cork in 1936 to parents of Lithuanian descent. His father's family originally settled in Cork but moved on to Dublin, where his father was born. His mother's family went first to Limerick and then on to Cork, where his parents married and settled. The Marcus household encouraged music, literature and the arts. Louis trained as a violinist and played with the Cork Symphony Orchestra but his ultimate career was shaped around his interest in films and his commitment to the Irish language. He left Cork in 1959 with a degree in French and English. Even before graduation he was active in the Cork branch of the Irish Film Society and worked in Dublin as assistant editor on the *Gael-Linn* films *Mise Éire* (I am Ireland) and *Saoirse?* (Freedom). The first documentary he directed was *The Silent Art*, highlighting the work of sculptor Séamus Murphy. It was a project made possible only by financial help from his mother and the use of free equipment and assistance from his friends and colleagues in the Irish Film Society. In 1967 the Irish Film Society published *The Irish Film Industry*, originally written by Louis Marcus for the *Irish Times* as a series of articles. It concluded that Ardmore Studios was designed to encourage the production of foreign films in Ireland rather than to develop an Irish film industry and led to the establishment of a Government-sponsored Film Industry committee, under the chairmanship of John Huston.

Twenty of the more than eighty documentaries Louis Marcus made on the life, legends, history and culture of Ireland won international awards and Festival prizes at Berlin, Moscow, London, Chicago and Oberhausen. For thirteen years he was a freelance film-maker for *Gael-Linn* and subsequently worked for other organizations and television stations, including *Radio Telefís Éireann* (RTÉ), TG4, Ulster Television, Channel Four and Thames Television. For Waterford Crystal he produced *Conquest of Light*, described by the *Irish Times* of 18 June 1988 as 'superbly crafted'. A past member of the cultural relations committee of the Department of Foreign Affairs, the Arts Council, the Board of the Abbey Theatre and the Irish Film Board, he was designated a permanent member of the Academy of Motion Picture Arts and Sciences and of *Aosdána*, as well as being an honorary member of the Royal Hibernian Academy.

Louis Lentin, a native of Limerick, had the distinction of inaugurating two television services, RTÉ in 1961 and Israeli Television in 1968. His interest in theatre began when his parents encouraged him to join the Jewish Dramatic Society, in an attempt to overcome his shyness. Louis became a medical student but his experience with the Trinity Players and the Studio Theatre Club whetted his appetite for directing, and in 1958 he abandoned medicine to form his own professional theatre company, Art Theatre Productions. Among its many Irish premières were Samuel Beckett's *End Game* and *Krapp's Last Tape* and Edward Albee's *Zoo Story*. He was one year into a scholarship at the Carnegie Institute of Drama in Pittsburg, studying for a degree in theatre direction and lighting, when his father's death in 1960 brought him back to Dublin. He continued to direct for Art Theatre Productions and Phyllis Ryan's Gemini Company and achieved a noted success at the 1961 Dublin Theatre Festival with *The Voice of Shem*, Mary Manning's adaptation of *Finnnegan's Wake*. It went on to represent Ireland at a theatrical festival in Paris and had a season in London.

Invited because of his television studies to join the infant RTÉ, Louis Lentin was floor manager for its first production, a benediction led by Archbishop McQuaid. He went on to direct a multitude of programmemes, including the news and *Monica's Kitchen* with Monica Sheridan, before joining the Drama Department, then headed by Hilton Edwards. One of his many drama productions was *Insurrection* in 1966, Hugh Leonard's dramatic reconstruction of the Easter Rising that formed part of the Golden Jubilee commemorations. When the Six-Day War broke out in the Middle East in 1967, RTÉ gave him leave of absence to join volunteers in Israel offering three months' service, but his seat on the plane was allocated to someone else. Louis picked up a passenger in London in his two-seater Spitfire Triumph, and drove to Israel. By the time he arrived the war was over, but he stayed on as European advisor to the Foreign Office Film Department. He was almost due to leave when he was persuaded, as the only professional television director then in the country, to assist the embryonic Israel Experimental Television. What he describes as 'one of the most marvellous and emotional moments of my life' occurred when he directed Israeli Television's very first production, a live broadcast of the 1968 Independence Day military parade.

The following year he returned to Ireland with his Israeli wife, Ronit, *née* Saltzberger, whose own experience at Israeli Television enabled her to join him at RTÉ as a production assistant. In 1979, he became Head of Drama. His decision to end *The Riordans*, a popular television serial for more than sixteen years, was controversial, but he compensated viewers with *Thursday Play Date* and *The Sunday Series* which featured plays mostly by new writers, such as Maeve Binchey and Eugene McCabe. He also brought viewers his innovative television production of Handel's *Messiah*, featuring the shofar as the last trumpet.

In 1990, Louis Lentin left RTÉ to establish the award-winning Crescendo Concepts, one of Ireland's most highly regarded production companies. *Dear*

Daughter, shown in 1996, an account of Christine Buckley's search for her parents, became a catalyst for the inquiries that followed his exposé of the suffering and abuse of children in industrial schools. His next project, *Grandpa, Speak to Me in Russian*, is more personal. He describes it as a complex examination of his feelings that he is Irish but not of Ireland; here because his paternal grandfather, Kalman Lentin, found his way to Ireland with a wave of immigrant Jews.

Ronit Lentin, who now holds a doctorate in Sociology, is director of Ethnic and Racial Studies at Trinity College. Already a published author in Israel, her output since has been impressive. In addition to academic articles and works of fiction, she has drawn specific attention to the way in which political circumstances affect women, especially those caught up in the Holocaust and the Palestinian-Israeli conflict. *Racism and Anti-Racism in Ireland* (2002), jointly edited with Robbie McVeigh, is dedicated to two victims of racism, Ettie Steinberg 'murdered in Auschwitz', and Zhao Lui Tao, a Chinese immigrant, 'murdered in Dublin, January 24, 2002'.

Jewish Ireland has contributed much to the field of literature. Hannah Berman, who came to Ireland as a youngster, wrote her first novel, Melutovno, in 1914 and her second novel, Anthills, in 1926. They both depict Jewish life in her native Lithuania. Her third novel, *Joseph Drawbridge*, portrays life among English Jewry of her time. A contributor to many British periodicals, she also translated Yiddish writers, including *Shalom Aleichem*, into English. She settled in England, where her services to literature were rewarded with a Government pension.

David Marcus, brother of Louis Marcus, gave up law for literature. A somewhat reluctant student when reading for the bar in the company of former *Taoiseach* Jack Lynch, his boyhood passion for Irish verse crystallised in early manhood into an even greater interest in the short story. The *Dublin* magazine and the *Bell* were the only outlets in the early 1940s for that particular genre, and their coverage was limited. With family support as his only asset, he launched *Irish Writing*, a quarterly magazine dedicated to the best of short-story writing and the promotion of new talent. The first issue appeared in 1946, the last in 1954. Doomed financially by a trade embargo that limited its sales in Britain, it was a huge literary success. In his autobiography, typically named *Oughterbiography* (2001), David listed Liam O'Flaherty, Frank O'Connor, Sean O'Faolain, James Stephens, Louis McNiece, Lord Dunsany, Patrick Kavanagh and Somerville and Ross among its early contributors. His approach to George Bernard Shaw for a contribution resulted in the one word 'No' written large on a postcard but most writers, including Samuel Becket, were happy to be listed in its contents. David's next venture followed much the same path. Nineteen issues of *Poetry Ireland* yielded a total profit of only £15, but it became a showcase for new poets and brought the work of Thomas Kinsella, Anthony Cronin and other newcomers to public attention.

Incorporating *Poetry Ireland* in *Irish Writing* as a poetry supplement, David Marcus struggled on until common sense dictated that he put his livelihood above his love of literature. In 1958, he left for London, where he became an associate and then a fellow of the Chartered Insurance Institute, but life as an insurance claims manager held no allure. The notion of editing short stories for a national newspaper occurred to him soon after his return in 1967. He was on his way to suggest it to the editor of the *Irish Times* when he met Tim Pat Coogan, editor of the *Irish Press*, who seized on the idea. David became both literary editor of the *Irish Press* and editor of *New Irish Writing*, the page in the *Irish Press* devoted to the presentation of stories and poems. Among the many new writers featured over the years, he particularly remembered Neil Jordan, who, apart from achieving acclamation as a film actor, has since written three successful novels. Until his retirement in 1986, David Marcus's *New Irish Writing* introduced readers to seventy-five or eighty new short stories every year. A modest man, he discounted any praise for his efforts and insisted that 'it's the writers that have been marvelous. They made my life for me.' He died in 2009. His own published works include three novels and a collection of short stories.

Leslie Daiken, a member of the Yodaiken family, familiarly addressed as 'Yod', was born in Dublin in 1912. Educated at St Andrew's College and Wesley College, he studied languages at Trinity College, where he won the vice-chancellor's prize for English in 1931. Though his academic expertise was in linguistics, with particular emphasis on the speech and development of children, his interests and research made him an authority on subjects ranging from politics to pub games, from tourism to trams, from street games and ballads to the social ramifications of inter-racial education in an African school. A member of the Connolly Association, the London branch of *Tuairim* (Ideas) and the London Dublinmen's Association, he was a frequent contributor to journals and wrote extensively about his experiences and knowledge of Dublin, London and Israeli life through poems, plays, films and books. He was broadcast on BBC, Radio Éireann and the Israeli Broadcasting Service; his documentary on Trinity College Library was televised.

The Leslie Daiken Collection in the National Library contains documents in English, Hebrew, Irish, French, German, Italian and Dutch and includes letters to him from Austin Clarke, Cyril Cusack, Hilton Edwards, Con Leventhal and his Dublin Jewish fellow-writer, Milisande Zlotover. His study of children's games and toys made him a welcome guest at children's parties, where he participated with delight; *Children's Games Throughout the Year*, *Let us Play in Israel*, *Teaching Through Play* and *Children's Toys Throughout the Ages* all reflect his interest in the subject. The personal collection of children's toys he established in a London basement in 1951 developed into the renowned National Toy Museum in Brighton. An authority on James Joyce and a friend of Connor Cruise O'Brien, Samuel Beckett and other eminent writers, Leslie Daiken was on leave from his post as lecturer in Education at the University of Ghana when he died in 1964.

Another writer interested in young people is London-born Marilyn Taylor, daughter of Lord Fisher, a former Labour peer and one-time president of the Board of Deputies of British Jews. A graduate of University College, London, she came to Dublin in 1960 when she married Mervyn Taylor. She was the librarian at St Louis's School in Rathmines when her responsibility for ordering books led her to discover a niche in the market. 'Lively, readable, teenage novels with Irish setting and a bit of substance' – the kind of book that might encourage reluctant teenagers to read – were non-existent. She decided to write her own. For three consecutive years from 1994, O'Brien Press published what became the Jackie and Kev trilogy. Only the second book, *Could I Love a Stranger?* (1995) had any Jewish connection; its sub-plot of refugee children fleeing Nazi Europe by Kindertransport captured the interest of senior primary and junior secondary readers and their teachers. As a successful children's writer, she was invited to speak in schools and libraries and at teachers' and librarians' conferences. Always she was asked, 'What happened next?' Pressure from readers to experience beyond the Kindertransport led to *Faraway Home* (1999). Though a work of fiction, it was firmly based on the factual Millisle Refugee Farm in Co. Down. Winner of the Bisto Irish Children's Book of the Year Award, a recommendation from the American Jewish Library Association and a Blue Peter award, *Faraway Home* is widely used in schools as 'the only Irish instrument of holocaust information there is'. Her most recent book, *16 Martin Street*, touches on the same subject as she traces the efforts of Jewish and Gentile neighbours to prevent the discovery and deportation of a Jewish refugee from Nazi Europe.

The earliest known of the many newssheets and magazines produced by the Irish Jewish community over the years was the *Jewish Record*, believed to have been edited by Dr Teller in 1935. From 1936 to 1937 the *Glasgow Jewish Echo* included an Irish supplement. *Nachlath Dublin*, sub-titled 'the official organ of the Dublin JNF Commission', followed in 1943, first as a monthly, then as a quarterly, now as an annual. Its first editors were Jack Weingreen, Manny Brown and Asher Benson, followed by Maurice Fridberg, a gifted amateur photographer and publisher who widely exhibited his abstract photographic studies of trees, roots and stumps and produced high-quality Hourglass Library editions of Irish poems and short stories. Its present editor is John White. From 1951 to 1952 Bernard Shillman edited Halapid ('jewel'). The *Jewish Leader*, assembled by a Mr Benjamin who retired to Ireland from England, appeared in 1954, to be succeeded by the student magazine, Chadashot, from 1959 to 1971.

An initiative of the 1970s, the *Dublin Jewish News* (DJN) was the responsibility of an editorial committee that eventually comprised Asher Benson, Marilyn Taylor, Joan Finkel, Louise Crivon, Carol Golding, Hilary Gross and Ronit Lentin. More successful than its predecessors, it continued into the 1990s, when a member of the community claimed to have been misrepresented and issued writs to each person involved in the offending issue. Personal financial loss, combined with a wariness of continuing their previously untrammelled style, dampened the enthusiasm of the voluntary workers, and publication ceased. *The Scribe*, 'Organ of Dublin Jewry', appeared in the 1980s. The 1990s' effort was the *Jewish Voice*, largely the work of two students, Natalie Wynn and Barry Robinson.

In Belfast the *Jewish Gazette* and the *Kibbitzer* were replaced in the early 1950s by the highly successful *Belfast Jewish Record*. Its original ten issues a year have been reduced to four, but it still has a circulation of 350, mostly among expatriates. A veteran of its editorial board is Norma Simon, *née* Cravitz, a native of Scotland, who moved from Dublin to Belfast in 1957 when she married Harold Simon. Employed at one time as secretary to both Rabbi Carlebach and a Presbyterian minister, she and Gail Taylor, *née* Bloom, were the first two women elected to the council of the Belfast Hebrew Congregation. Norma Simon became its first female secretary. Now into her eighties, she still supervises the kosher kitchen, orders kosher food direct from Manchester and keeps a check on the communal diary to make sure proposed functions do not coincide.

A display case at the Irish Jewish Museum for books written by the Jews of Ireland is too small to contain them all. It does not include David Feldman's definitive work on Irish Postage Stamps or *Wrap It Up* (1988), the comprehensive guide to gift-wrapping by Arona Khan, who has seemingly been making parcels since she wrapped her grandmother's knickers into individual pairs at the age of three. Also missing are Michael Sayers' play, *Kathleen*, which had its world premiere at the Olympia Theatre, and the book he jointly wrote on the Soviet Union, hailed by one critic as 'fact that read like choicest fiction'. There are many other omissions; but the books, plays and poetry prominently displayed, together with other cultural achievements, are more than enough to justify the claim made by Ruari Quinn in 1987 that the Jews as Irish people have made an 'enormous contribution to the development and richness of our nation.'

9

POLITICS AND WAR

The first Jew to be elected to Dublin Corporation was Lewis Harris, who became alderman for South Dock Ward in 1874. His death two years later, on the eve of his appointment, deprived him of becoming Ireland's first Jewish Lord Mayor. Some years later, that honour passed to Sir Otto Jaffe whose grandfather had founded the Belfast Jewish community when his extensive mercantile interests brought him there from Hambourg in 1845. Otto's father had paid for the synagogue, Hebrew school and minister's residence in Great Victoria Street built in 1871 to serve Belfast's fifty-five Jews. In 1894 Otto became a councillor. He was a member of the Belfast Harbour Board, a governor of the Royal Hospital and consul to the German Embassy when he was elected Lord Mayor of Belfast in 1899 and again in 1904.

Another politically minded Belfast immigrant from Hamburg was Gustav Wilhelm Wolff, judged by the *Evening Herald* of 1 September 1893 to be worthy of 'the highest esteem, almost veneration' as one of the founders of Harland & Wolff, the Belfast shipbuilding company. He was parliamentary representative for East Belfast for eighteen years.

The example set by such civic-minded, established Jews was not lost on the Russian immigrants. Long before 1963 when Barney Hurwitz, president of the Belfast Jewish Community, was rewarded for his services with an OBE in the New Year Honours List, they were serving Ireland, north and south of the border, in local and central Government.

One of the first four peace commissioners appointed by the Irish Free State to the city of Dublin was Jacob Elyan, whose father ministered to the Cork Jewish community. John Redmond hoped to scotch Ulster's insistence that Home Rule was Rome Rule by sending Elyan to Westminster as an elected representative of the Irish Parliamentary Party, but ill-health prevented him from standing. Louis Hyman claims he later refused a seat in the Senate.

Though the tendency of early settlers was to keep a low public profile, a small politically-minded group established the Judæo-Irish Home Rule Association at a public meeting in Dublin's Mansion House in 1908. Its honorary secretary was Joseph Edelstein whose immaculate dress is described in a document in the Irish Jewish Museum, handwritten by his friend Harry Kernoff, as comprising 'Edwardian coat, butterfly collar, cravat, velvet collar plus bowler hat and stick'. His propensity to wait patiently for arrest after breaking the glass of public fire alarms frequently landed him in trouble. When the mental hospital in Grangegorman, Dublin, certified him as sane, he took great pleasure in brandishing his certificate of mental competence and boasting he was the only man in Ireland who could prove his sanity. In fact Edelstein, a member of the Moisel family mentioned in *Ulysses*, was a highly intelligent linguist and writer who reputedly wrote political speeches for Robert Briscoe.

How he came to be in Portobello Barracks after the unlawful shooting of Francis Sheehy-Skeffington, Thomas Dickson and Patrick J. McIntyre remains a mystery. In his *Echo of Irish Rebellion 1916, a Vindication of Mr Joseph Edelstein*, he details the insinuations made against him at the Royal Commission of Inquiry that followed the executions effected by order of Captain Bowen-Colthurst. T.M. Healy, representing the families of two of the victims, accepted the assertion made by the *Evening Mail* that Edelstein was a 'spotter' for the British. It was Edelstein's information, he alleged, that had led to the arrest of Dickson and McIntyre and went on to imply that Edelstein 'knew something' about the British Army bomb that shattered the windows of Alderman Kelly's shop, where both men were arrested. Again and again Edelstein interrupted the proceedings to protest his innocence and object to being used as bait because he was a Jew. 'The malicious and false statements made by Mr Healy,' he declared, were 'beyond nature to endure'. At the end of the hearing Mr Healy admitted his information regarding Edelstein was 'absolutely and entirely wrong', and he apologised with repeated exclamations of, 'I am sorry, extremely sorry.'

Joseph Edelstein was not the only Jew affected by the political turmoil of Ireland's struggle for independence. Gertie Shatter, *née* Samuels, recollected in an interview in 1990 with Susan Nolan and Damien Walker for the archives of the Irish Jewish Museum that her grandfather died at his home in Aungier Street the week of the Easter Rising. With no firm willing to drive a hearse through the gunfire, the elderly Jewish owner of a mineral-water factory offered the use of his horse and dray to move the coffin to Dolphin's Barn Cemetery. At Harold's Cross the dray was stopped by British soldiers, who opened the coffin to search for ammunition. The Samuels' family home was within range of the firing that emanated from Mount Argus, but its walls were so thick that no bullets penetrated, and relatives from more vulnerable houses sought shelter there. One wall of the Nurock's house at 79A South Circular Road bore the evidence of sprayed bullets long after the fighting was over. Norman Reeve's tailoring shop in Harcourt Street was destroyed by fire.

'A dangerous expedition accompanied by the stutter and snap of machine-gunning,' was Leslie Daiken's description of a journey to Clanbrassil Street for brown bread, a few pickled herrings and saveloys during the Civil War, as cross-sniping between the Volunteers and the British echoed from the roof-tops along the route. Esther Hesselberg remembered running 'faster than Ronnie Delaney' with her four-month-old baby after she witnessed the Irish Republican Army (IRA) attack two policemen emerging from the railway station at Bantry and the indiscriminate retaliatory firing of the one who survived. Speaking of 'the terrible times we had during the Troubles', she also recalled her brother losing all his hair from shock when he was held up in 1919 on his way to Castletown Berehaven, Co. Cork, by two gunmen who forced him to drive to a boreen strategically chosen for holding up a mail van.

For one whole season in the 1920s, Greenville Hall held 'Cinderella dances' when everyone had to leave before curfew began at 9 p.m. The streets were deemed even more unsafe when Jews became the target of a spate of shootings in and around Little Jerusalem. Though Kevin O'Higgins, TD, then Minister for Justice, insisted the incidents were not sectarian, armed guards were drafted in to patrol the Jewish quarter. In 1923, Emanuel Kahan (Nouky Kahn) was shot dead and his companion, David Miller, wounded when they were accosted on leaving the Jewish Literary and Debating Club in Harrington Street. Shots were fired after both were questioned and admitted to being Jewish. A man positively identified by the survivor was charged with Nouky's murder but acquitted when he pleaded mistaken identity. The guilty party, he claimed, was his brother, who looked remarkably like him but had since left the country. Nouky's sister, Esther Kahn, maintained Nouky was the victim of regular soldiers, a view denied at the time but substantiated by newly released Department of Justice files. The case for compensation was lost when the official inquiry found he was 'not killed in connection with State business and there was no proof that the murderers were servants of the State'.

Mervyn Abrahamson, an infant, had been fortunate to escape the same fate two years earlier. His young nurse, Evelyn Lowe, was pushing his pram through St Stephen's Green in 1921 when a gunman took refuge behind it. Pursuers shooting at him missed their quarry, the baby and the nursemaid. St Stephen's Green was the site of another vicious attack in 1925 when brothers Bernard and Samuel Goldberg, meandering through the park on a visit to Ireland from Manchester, were stopped, asked their names and fired upon. Samuel suffered a head wound; Bernard was killed.

Many Irish Jews, like Myer Joel Wigoder, 'felt a deep obligation and gratitude to England for its role in protecting persecuted Jews from Tsarist Russia'. Geoffrey Wigoder, his grandson, recalled his own childhood waving of a Union Jack when Queen Victoria made a State visit to Dublin, but he also remembered hearing the popular ditty:

Ireland was Ireland when England was a pup
And Ireland will be Ireland when England's buggered up.

A yearning for their own independent homeland encouraged many Jews in the
Southern counties to empathise with Irish Nationalism. The *Irish Worker* of 3 May
1924, edited by Jim Larkin, lists A. Weeks, a Jewish Volunteer, among those killed
in action in the GPO on 14 April 1916, the first day of the Easter Rising; he had
laid the foundation stone for Adelaide Road Synagogue the day before his death.
Respectable Jewish women such as Fanny Goldberg in Cork joined *Cumann na
mBan*, the women's auxiliary of the Irish Volunteers, which 'nursed the wounded,
carried dispatches, transported ammunition and did everything but actually
shoot'. Jewish peddlers trading within British Army barracks were sometimes
persuaded to conceal weapons for the Volunteers inside their packs, and fugitives
were sheltered in Jewish homes. When General Richard Mulcahy tried to evade
capture by hiding in the back garden of Dr Miller's house in Longwood Avenue,
he was brought in to spend the night underneath a bed and left the following
morning dressed in one of Dr Miller's suits. The IRA underground newspaper,
An tÓglach, was secretly printed by Abraham Spiro at the family printing firm,
which continued to employ Oscar Traynor, then officer commanding the Dublin
Brigade of the Irish Volunteers and later Minister for Justice.

Another sympathiser was Philip Sayers, who drove leading Republicans,
including Arthur Griffith and Mrs McGuinness, the Nationalist candidate's wife,
to the 1917 Co. Longford election and reputedly helped many people in trouble,
including Joe McGrath, later associated with the Irish Hospitals Sweepstake.
Estella Solomons, the accomplished artist who painted herself in uniform, was
a member of the *Cumann na mBan* group trained by Phyllis Ryan, wife of Sean
T. O'Kelly, one of the early leaders of *Sinn Féin* and later President of Ireland.
In *Portraits of Patriots* (1966) Hilary Pyle reveals that the artist's sudden interest in
growing 'superb heads of lettuce' at her home in Waterloo Road had little to do
with feeding her surprised family. They were cultivated to conceal ammunition
hidden in the garden until she could deliver it to a butterman in Baggot Street,
who taught her how to use a revolver before he was arrested for watering his
milk. Her studio at 17 Great Brunswick Street (Pearse Street) became 'a place
of refuge for many whose political and national activities had brought them a
very undesirable amount of notice'. Ostensibly helping with heavy studio work,
the fugitives sat for portraits, most of which had to be destroyed to protect their
whereabouts. After the Easter Rising, Estella Solomons served as a committee
member for the Prisoners' Dependants' Fund.

In the opinion of W.M. Goldblatt, such activities placed Northern Ireland
Jews in an 'unenviable' position, and he criticised as 'extremely unfortunate' E.E.
Burgess's statement in a supplement of the *Jewish Chronicle* of 31 March 1922 that
'the Jews of Dublin and other centres under the new regime have always been

in hearty sympathy with Young Ireland in its struggle for political and national independence'. He pointed out that 'Northern Ireland Jews had to carry on their daily business often in contentious areas where they were roughly questioned as to their own political opinions' and that 'murders are hourly committed in the names of Unionism and Sinn Féin' with men being shot in the main thoroughfares 'for the mere expression of their opinion'. As to Burgess's assertion that 'two young Jews were high in the councils of the Irish Republican Party, 'Mr Goldblatt contended that while the Jewish cause remained 'in the throes' it was 'no source of pride to Jews in general that this or that individual was prominently associated with this or that struggle for emancipation.'

The two individuals referred to were undoubtedly Michael Noyk and Robert Briscoe. According to Piaras Béaslaí, biographer of Michael Collins, one of the leaders of the IRA campaign and Minister for Finance in the Republican Government, Michael Noyk was 'the one Dublin solicitor implicitly trusted by Collins' and 'the principal agent in the purchase of houses and offices for Dáil and IRA work'. Noyk's own statement, now in the National Library, claims most of the premises he acquired were rented under false names. One had a secret room built into the wall for papers; another had a compartment for hiding gold. 'Come over, Michael, they are here again,' was the telephone message Noyk regularly received during raids on the premises of the *Gaelic Press* in Upper Liffey Street.

Even more important to the Nationalist movement was Noyk's defence of IRA prisoners. From securing the acquittal in 1914-15 of James Mallins, charged with the larceny of a soldier's gun left in a corner of his barber's shop while the owner was having a haircut and shave, Noyk went on to defend *Cumann na mBan* women caught with guns in their homes, IRA men arrested for illegal drilling and six on murder charges connected with Bloody Sunday, 21 November 1920, when the IRA killed eleven British intelligence agents in their hotel bedrooms. Newly-arrived English police recruits, dubbed the 'Black and Tans' because of their parti-coloured uniforms, opened fire in reprisal at Croke Park, Dublin, during a football match, killing one player and eleven supporters and injuring sixty spectators. Noyk described the trials, held in the Council Chamber of the City Hall, as 'protected by sentries with machine guns and rifles' in a room 'filled with Secret Service men'.

Some of the cases Noyk sought to win were indefensible. For Seán MacEoin, who had caused numerous deaths and injuries as commandant of the Longford Brigade, the only chance of evading the death penalty was escape. Noyk thought the escape plan devised by Collins was 'futile', but he was fully prepared to play his part by smuggling a gun into Dublin Castle had Collins not taken his advice and aborted the project. MacEoin's life was eventually spared as a *quid pro quo* for Collin's signature to a ceasefire.

In 1918, Noyk became election agent for Seán T. O'Kelly and Countess Markievicz, the staunch republican activist. Both remained in prison during the campaign and both were returned with 'overwhelming majorities'. From 1920 he was constantly involved in tracing the whereabouts of suspects held without trial in secret locations and in attending hearings at *Sinn Féin* courts all over Ireland. When his own offices at 65 Lower Leeson Street and 12 College Green were raided, he claimed 'there was hardly a scrap of paper or a document that had not been turned inside out, but they got no information.' On the night he was arrested in a curfew round-up and ordered at gunpoint into a lorry, he had an incriminatory letter from Countess Markievicz in his pocket. He managed to pass it to a friend, who tore it up and scattered the pieces surreptitiously onto the roadway. The first of his next day's clients was dealt with at the Bridewell, in the cell he had occupied overnight.

Michael Noyk was at the graveside for the oration by Padraig Pearce at Donovan O'Rossa's funeral and at Dun Laoghaire harbour when Éamon deValera and other nationalists were welcomed home from British jails with a chorus of 'God Save Ireland' as their boat touched the pier. Arthur Griffith was 'a close friend' and Peadar Kearney, who wrote the words of the 'The Soldier's Song', later Ireland's national anthem, referred to Noyk as his friend and solicitor in letters to his wife from Ballykinlar Camp, Co. Down, in 1921. He was buried in 1966 with honours accorded by The Dublin Brigade of the Old IRA. On 13 September 1976 Candida (Eileen O'Brien), reminiscing about Michael Noyk in 'An Irishman's Diary' in the *Irish Times*, wrote, 'My youth was filled with tales of Michael Noyk's amazing courage when he was prominent in the National Movement and of his amazing generosity at all times.' She marveled that Noyk, 'gentle … like a lovely teddy bear,' had done such heroic deeds.

Robert Briscoe became a legend in his own lifetime. His father, 'Poppa' Briscoe, staunchly patriotic since his arrival from Lithuania at the age of fourteen, was a pacifist. Though he named one of his sons Wolfe Tone in honour of the hero of the 1798 Rebellion, the patriot he most revered was Charles Stewart Parnell, who promoted change without bloodshed, and he begged Robert not to join the *Sinn Féin* 'fanatics'. That his father's disapproval upset him is clear from Robert Briscoe's autobiography, but he still took the Oath of Allegiance to the Irish Republic, a prerequisite to joining Countess Markievitcz's Fianna Éireann, the revolutionary youth movement inspired by Baden Powell's Boy Scouts.

After the Easter Rising, 'Poppa' Briscoe sent his son to America on the White Star liner, *Baltic*. The journey, intended to carry him away from a theatre of war, initiated him instead into a mesh of intrigue and daring far more hazardous than any front line. Norah Connolly, daughter of James Connolly, the revolutionary Labour leader, was a fellow-passenger, and he willingly agreed to take care of a sealed envelope 'in case she lost it'. She had retrieved it ashore before he realised he had been used as a courier for dispatches to the German ambassador regarding the 'German Plot' to import arms and men into Ireland to fight Britain. By the time he returned in 1917, he had attended *Clan na Gael* meetings and fallen under the influence of young revolutionaries such as Liam Mellows. He shared a cabin on the journey home with Éamonn Martin, for whom he created a diversion at immigration control to draw attention away from Martin's false passport.

Briscoe became a messenger for the IRA, collecting and transporting arms so successfully that Collins promoted him to General Headquarters. Acting ostensibly as a small Jewish merchant, he adopted the name Captain Swift for his clandestine work and graduated from buying arms and dumping them in Britain, Belgium and Holland to the importing of large-scale consignments by sea. The *Amita* was loaded and ready to sail from the free port of Hamburg when it was raided. Briscoe, considered an innocent bystander, had better luck with the *Karl Marx* which brought in arms, with the *City of Dortmund* which carried IRA personnel and with the *Hannah* which landed successfully with '500 pistols, 200 rifles, a few machine guns and a million rounds of ammunition'. During the Civil War, which followed acceptance of the Anglo-Irish Treaty, Robert took the Republican (anti-Treaty) side, aided at times by his wife, Lily, who once ensured the safe delivery of a dispatch from Collins to the Galway Brigade commander by placing it in their baby Joan's nappy.

Wanted during the Civil War by the Free State Government as 'a dangerous character', Briscoe had many hair's-breadth escapes. On one occasion he emerged from a hotel room in Cobh to 'pistols poked in his belly' by Free State soldiers, who had entered the town overnight. Knowing he might be shot without trial if recognised, he claimed to be a wool merchant. One soldier asked, 'Are you a Jewman?' 'Yes,' replied Briscoe, whereupon a second declared, 'We'd be wasting our bloody time with him!' and kicked him down the stairs and out into the street.

His 'wanted' status ended with the cessation of fighting in 1924. Having found employment for as many former IRA men as possible, he concentrated on providing for his wife and family, who had depended for years on the IRA maximum allowance of £7 per week and been subjected to constant harassment from the authorities. A founder-member of *Fianna Fáil*, he stood as a *Dáil* candidate three times before he was elected in 1927, one of the fifty-seven *Fianna Fáil* deputies advised by de Valera to take the Oath of Allegiance to the British sovereign under protest. By the time he retired in 1967, he had been returned in eleven consecutive elections.

Robert Briscoe had been a member of Dublin Corporation almost continuously for thirty-five years when he put his name forward in 1955 for election as Lord Mayor of Dublin, an annual political appointment made by the councillors from among their own ranks. He withdrew to leave Denis Larkin an uncontested Labour Party candidate but in 1956, when Larkin sought a second term, Briscoe opposed him. Each contestant gained nineteen votes. Following tradition, their names were placed in a hat. Robert Briscoe became the first

Jewish Lord Mayor of Dublin when his was the name drawn, 'an example to the world,' he claimed, 'of tolerance in my country.'

Unlike his Catholic predecessors, forbidden at that time to attend any church service outside their own faith, he attended services of all denominations. His year of office was a triumph for Irish Jewry and the country at large. To Americans, Irish Jews were still something of a rarity, and an Irish Jew of Briscoe's prominence was unique. John Hynes, Mayor of Boston, introduced him at the Boston St Patrick's Day parade with, 'Once there was an Irishman and a Jew – here he is!' His two months' good-will visit to America encompassed 2,000 invitations, many from groups that were neither Irish nor Jewish. Briscoe described the experience as 'hectic, exhausting, inspiring, humbling and the happiest two months of my life.' Under pressure from de Valera, who thought it 'for the good of Ireland', he stood for Lord Mayor again the following year. The result was another draw, but this time his opponent's name was drawn. Robert was elected to a second term of office in 1961. In 1988/9, when Dublin councillors again elected a Jewish mayor, it was Ben Briscoe, Robert Briscoe's son, who entered the Mansion House.

Ben Briscoe was born in Dublin in 1934 and educated at St Andrew's College. His interest in politics developed early, and from the age of eleven he watched *Dáil* debates from the public gallery. In 1964, he was persuaded by *Fianna Fáil* to stand for his father's seat. Elected for Dublin South Central in 1967, he went on, as his father had done, to win eleven consecutive elections, retiring in 1999. Together they gave more than seventy years of unbroken service to the State, the longest of any father and son.

Ben believes that the role of a public representative is to act as buffer between the people and the bureaucrats. Constituency work became his prime concern, with the dignity of the person inviolate at every intervention. A man who mistook his clinic (advice centre) for a medical clinic and complained, 'It's my ears, doctor: there's wax in them,' was never apprised of his error; instead he received a letter addressed to the Eye and Ear Hospital asking that they look after him.

As Lord Mayor, he was equally considerate of the people. When he realised that the only tributes available to him for rewarding the special achievement of citizens were a civic reception, afforded to victorious sports teams and visiting dignitaries, or the Freedom of the City, reserved for luminaries such as the Pope, Nelson Mandela and Mother Theresa, he instituted the Lord Mayor's Awards. The first recipients were Frank Feeley, the city manager, Margaret Dunne who started the 'People in Need' fund-raiser, Ronnie Delaney, 1956 Olympic gold medalist in the 1,500 metres, and Éamonn Coughlan who created a new record for the indoor 1,500 metres. Lord Mayor's Awards have been continued ever since. During his official tour of America to boost tourism and investment, he visited twenty-one cities in thirty-five days and marched in five St Patrick's Day parades. At one function in 1989 a guest, confusing him with his father, asked,

Ben Briscoe, Lord Mayor of Dublin, samples the millennium cake watched by Taoiseach Bertie Ahern and members of the public, Dublin 2000.

'Is that guy still Lord Mayor?' Ben, overhearing the comment, turned to him and asked, 'How do I look for ninety-nine?'

Ben earned the accolade of 'most generous of all Lord Mayors' in the *Dublin Historical Record* of September 1989 when he donated to the Civic Museum all the gifts presented to him and his wife, Carol, during his mayoralty. From the cut-glass plaque incised with an Arabian eagle, the gift of His Highness Prince Abdullah Bin Faisel Bin Turki al Saud, to the small coloured drawing presented 'To the Lord Mayor, 23/9/88 from all the Cubs of Navan Road,' every gift made to the citizens of Dublin during his year of office, his to keep by tradition, were handed back to the City. They included a magnificent Waterford crystal bowl of 1,000 cuts, a richly embellished eighteen-carat gold ornamental sword and so many items of beauty, rarity and value that the Civic Museum could not house them all; overflow items went to the Civic Library, the Municipal Library and the Hugh Lane Art Gallery.

Gerald Goldberg and Herman Good were named by a law lecturer in Trinity College as the two best orators in Ireland. Both distinguished criminal lawyers, they had much in common and enjoyed their friendly rivalry with what Gerald's son, David Goldberg, describes as 'terrific humour and rapport between them.' Gerald was born in Cork in 1912 to Lithuanian parents. He qualified as a solicitor in 1933 and practised in Cork for almost seventy years, championing the working class and a variety of unpopular causes. David, who sometimes acted as counsel in his father's cases, remembers him defending Jehovah's Witnesses in Limerick, street women in Cork, and suspected IRA activists charged with importing guns into Waterford on the ship *Claudia*. His lifelong defence against anti-Jewish bigotry began as a student at University College, Cork, when he was refused the right as an 'alien' to speak at the Philosophical and Literary Debating Society.

The first Jewish member of the council of the Incorporated Law Society, Gerald served Cork Corporation as an Independent from 1967 to 1975, when he joined *Fianna Fáil*. In 1977, on the nomination of John O'Malley, a senior counsel, he became Cork's only Jewish Lord Mayor. Trinity Bridge, the footbridge he declared open across a water channel off Union Quay, became known to locals as the Goldberg Bridge; humourists called it the Passover Bridge.

An historian, voracious reader and expert in Hebrew texts, he was awarded an honorary doctorate of Laws in 1993 by University College, Cork. Its president, Dr Michael Mortell, referred to his contribution to the cultural life of Cork and the nation and to the hardship and prejudice he had overcome to emerge as 'one of the best-known and respected Irishmen, Corkmen and Jews.' Cork's Jewish citizens in general were honoured in 1989 when Pat Dineen, chairman of Cork Gas Company, presented land to the city and named it Páirc (Park) Shalom, in recognition of his pleasant childhood, while growing up around the 'Jewtown' area.

Another Jewish solicitor involved in local politics was Quentin Crivon, who rejected invitations to stand for election to Dáil Éireann. The son of Samuel Crivon, he is a practising solicitor who was in partnership with Richie Ryan until Ryan was appointed Minister for Finance in the *Fine Gael*/Labour Coalition Government of 1973-7. In 1966, he was elected to the committee of his local residents' association; a year later he was representing the organisation at the Association of Combined Residents' Associations (ACRA). As chairman of ACRA from 1970 to 1975 he campaigned for the abolition of rates and ground rents and a reduction in mortgage rates, then exorbitantly high. During the general election of 1973 ACRA's demands became a political football, with *Fine Gael* promising abolition if successful at the polls and *Fianna Fáil* following suit to prevent loss of votes. Quentin admits that other factors influenced the electorate in denying *Fianna Fáil* an overall majority, but he has no doubt the ACRA campaign played its part. Ground rents were less easy to remove than rates, for constitutional reasons, but amending legislation was introduced in 1977, both through ACRA's lobbying and Crivon's legal contribution, which provided the Government with a blueprint for simplifying the procedure. When the Building Societies Association proved obdurate in unilaterally reducing interest rates, the Government placated ACRA by subsidising mortgages, which reduced them from 16 per cent to 10 per cent. His threat to put the weight of ACRA behind the abolition of estate duty, which could often be discharged only by the sale of inherited property, led to its replacement by a more lenient gift and inheritance tax.

Alan Shatter, a Dublin solicitor, had no political ambitions in the 1970s, but his awareness of the deficiencies in Irish Family Law was honed by his active involvement with the Free Legal Advice Centres and social groups such as AIM (supporting battered wives), Children First (dealing with adoption law) and CARE (promoting the rights of deprived children). To this day he believes the extent of child abuse would have been recognised much sooner if CARE had been taken more seriously at the time.

Irish Family Law had been unchanged for more than a century when Shatter first advocated reforms in a report by the Free Legal Advice Centres in 1972.

He reiterated his proposals in 1977 in *Family Law in the Republic of Ireland*, which went into four editions. In 1978 he satirised Charles Haughey's Family Planning Act of that year in *Family Planning, Irish Style*. Launched by barrister Mary Robinson, later President of Ireland, it became a best-seller. Its title may have influenced Haughey in defining his banning of condoms, except on medical prescription, as 'an Irish solution for an Irish problem'.

As an acknowledged expert on Irish family law, Shatter had been dealing regularly on *The Gay Byrne Hour* with the legal problems of radio listeners when Garret FitzGerald, leader of *Fine Gael*, imposed him as a local Government candidate in 1979. He topped the poll for election to Dublin County Council. In the 1981 general election he was elected to Dáil Éireann for the Dublin South constituency. He held the seat for more than twenty years, during which time he published more private members' bills from the opposition side of the *Dáil* than any other deputy in the history of the State. Covering social reform, criminal, environmental, international and property law, health, justice and sport, they included the Judicial Separation and Family Law Reform Bill, brought before the *Dáil* in 1987. Based on a Joint *Oireachtas* report that had considerable input from Shatter, it recommended much the same measures he had promoted in 1972; it was passed into law in 1989 to 'almost universal agreement across the religious, social and political spectrum'.

The Judicial Separation and Family Law Reform Act (1989) revolutionised Irish Family Law. It was the first legislation in Ireland or the United Kingdom to require courts to evaluate a wife's home-making skills as equal to her husband's provision of income, and introduced the 'breakdown of marriage' as grounds for separation. A range of new financial and property orders were instituted to help alleviate the consequences of marital breakdown, and solicitors were required to advise couples of the availability of counselling and mediation services that could facilitate the resolving of their difficulties without unnecessary contention. Family law courts were held apart from all others, and court procedure made less intimidating by dispensing with gowns and wigs. Overall, the act laid the political and legal foundations for the constitutional change in 1996 that resulted in the introduction of divorce. Shatter's third book, *Laura*, was launched in 1989. A fictionalised account of the pitfalls of Irish adoption law, it was another manifestation of the combined literary ambitions and reforming zeal he had demonstrated early in life.

Alan Shatter was still a student when he and his friend, Alan Eppel, together with Carol Danker and Trish Tolkin, the girls they would respectively marry, founded, wrote, printed and distributed a Jewish community newssheet called *Ruach*, in circulation from 1969 to 1973. The same group, together with Eddie Segal and Alan Benson, formed the Irish Soviet Jewry Committee. Aided by a sympathetic retired army officer who spoke Russian, they regularly phoned Jews in Moscow and Leningrad and drew public attention to the refusal of the Soviet

Government to allow Jews to emigrate, and its persecution of Jews who applied for exit visas. Refusniks, as denied applicants came to be called, were dismissed from their posts, deprived of their rights, harassed and even imprisoned. The 35s, an all-female society in support of refusniks, was formed in the 1970s by the women among a party of British tourists in the Soviet Union who noticed a thirty-five-year-old Jewish woman holding a banner bearing the words 'Let my people go'. Branches spread throughout Britain and mainland Europe. Lynn Jackson, *née* Taylor, chaired Ireland's 35s for eighteen years, during which time she co-founded 35s in Luxembourg and co-ordinated the activities of all the groups into one massive campaign. In 1984, in co-operation with Mervyn Taylor and Ben Briscoe, then fellow members of Dáil Éireann, Alan Shatter obtained Government backing for an all-party motion in the *Dáil* in support of the right of Soviet Jews to emigrate, the first of its kind to be passed by a member state of the European Parliament. A similar motion was put through the *Seanad* by Senators David Norris and Mary Robinson.

Shatter visited the Soviet Union in 1985 with Senator Seán O'Leary, later a circuit court judge. Evading constant KGB surveillance, they met refusniks in the underground at outlandish hours, contacted them from a network of phone boxes and held banal conversations for the benefit of hidden microphones while communicating through exchanged notes. Through the pretext of discussing traffic violations, they presented an official of the Justice Department with a written protest against the Soviet Union's violation of the Helsinki Accords, the right to family re-unification. More than twenty years later, several Irish Jews who had made similar trips to Russia to offer comfort and to smuggle in articles that ranged from prayer books to computers, related their sometimes humorous but always frightening experiences to an audience in the Samuel Taca Hall. In Ireland demonstrations were peaceful. One tactic was presenting members of the audience at Russian ballets, concerts and circuses with a rose, to which was attached a message reading, 'Enjoy the performance but please remember the hundreds of thousands of Jewish refusniks in the Soviet Union who are not free.' The campaign ended only after Soviet repression had been swept away by Mikhail Gorbachev's *glasnost* and *perestroika*. Today, the Irish National Council for Soviet Jewry helps Russian immigrants settle in Israel.

Alan Shatter lost his seat in the *Fine Gael* debacle of the 2002 election but continued to practise law in Dublin from 4 Upper Ely Place, former home of Sarah Curran, the fiancée of Robert Emmet, hanged in 1803 for revolutionary activities, and George Moore, celebrated Irish poet and writer. He was re-elected in 2007 and nominated Minister for Justice, Equality and Defence in the *Fine Gael*/Labour government formed in 2011.

Marriage to the daughter of a British Labour Party politician and work as a solicitor with Herman Good gave Mervyn Taylor an early insight into social issues. Regular political discussions with three neighbouring couples sharpened his awareness. In 1968, all eight joined the Labour Party on the same night; by 1969 Taylor was chairman of the local constituency council. He became Labour Party candidate for Dublin South-West in the 1973 election by default. The chosen candidate was Brendan Halligan, general secretary of the Labour Party for many years. When Halligan was re-assigned as director of elections, no one was willing to replace him as a candidate. Mervyn Taylor, as chairman, felt obliged to step into the breach. He received 3,000 first-preference votes, but failed to gain a seat.

In 1974, and again in 1979, he was elected a member of Dublin County Council for Tallaght and Rathcoole where he demonstrated his concern for the residents, opposing both irresponsible land zoning and the local siting of a toxic dump, and promoting the development of open spaces, playing fields and community centres. A specialist in planning law, he gave free planning advice to individuals as well as to local residents' and tenants' associations. In 1977, he was elected chairman of Dublin County Council but failed again to win a *Dáil* seat. His third attempt, in 1981, succeeded, and he topped the poll in 1989 and 1993. From serving as vice-chairman under Michael D. Higgins, he defeated Ruarí Quinn to become chairman of the Labour Party, 1982-7. As an opposition backbencher he became spokesman for Education and Finance. With Dick Spring leading the Labour Party in the *Fianna Fáil*/Labour coalition Government of 1993 to 1994, Taylor, already Labour Party whip, was invited to join the cabinet as Minister for Equality and Law Reform, the first Jew in Ireland to rise to Cabinet rank.

The department for Equality and Law Reform was an entirely new concept. Mervyn Taylor's brief as its First Minister was to institute major reforms in family law that would ultimately include divorce legislation, forbidden under the constitution of Ireland. A successful referendum to amend the constitution was pivotal to success and Taylor was at the centre of promoting it. That no anti-Semitic backlash resulted from a Jewish minister effecting legislation at variance with Catholic dogma says much for the common sense and tolerance of the Irish people. As part of the Labour Party's promotion for the referendum, Taylor addressed public disquiet through local radio stations. During one phone-in programmeme a listener asked how a member of the Jewish faith and a follower of the Old Testament could advocate divorce when the Lord abominates it. He replied, 'The Lord does abominate divorce. We all abominate it, but it is very necessary for a small number of people in unusual circumstances.' Generally, he found that his religion was not an issue and the referendum was passed. The resultant Family Law (Divorce) Act (1996) allows divorce by consent to couples who have been living apart for at least four years, the best compromise obtainable from a population forced to choose between religious and social ethics.

In 1983, when 155 members of Dáil Éireann voted in favour of a referendum on abortion, Mervyn Taylor was one of the eleven who voted against.

He considered it would be 'sectarian against minority religions' and potentially 'an uncertain constitutional enactment.' In an oblique reference to his Jewish faith, he told the other ten dissidents, 'Now you know what it's like to be a minority!'

During the five years of Taylor's ministry, twenty-two pieces of legislation were passed. They included the registration of still-born babies and the Enduring Powers of Attorney Act, which makes it possible for elderly persons still in possession of their faculties to plan ahead by legally appointing someone to act on their behalf should the need arise. Other issues dealt with were the greater protection of persons suffering domestic violence, the Council of Europe's Convention on the Exercise of Children's Rights and enhanced civil legal aid. An Equality Authority was established to deal with alleged inequalities on grounds of race, religion, colour or nationality through an Equality Tribunal.

Mervyn Taylor's period as minister was considered unusually productive and beneficial to the electorate. One Labour Party member describes him as 'completely honest and upright', another as possessing 'that special quality some of the great socialist European leaders have, vision and deep compassion for the poor and oppressed'. Yet a third characterised him as 'the king-maker in the party' who, without question, would have made the best party leader. He still practises law and continues to take an interest in Jewish affairs.

Other Irish Jews became active in public life through different channels. Rabbi Leventon's son, Asher Leventon, despite the misery associated with military service in Russia, joined the Indian Medical Service in 1895 as a surgeon-lieutenant. Though he rose to the rank of lieutenant-colonel in the British Army and became a Commander of the Order of the Indian Empire, he never forgot the Irish Jewish community and hosted an annual *Chanucah* treat for the Hebrew classes he once taught at the Sabbath School in the synagogue at Mary's Abbey.

The British Jewry Book of Honour, edited by Revd Michael Adler and organised by Max R.G. Freeman, is a list of the Jewish servicemen who died in the First World War. It includes the names of seven Irishmen: Lieutenant L. Barron, Second Lieutenant S.J. Dundon, Private E. Camrass and Private H. Marcus from Dublin, Lieut. I. Gorfunkle and Private I.M. Freedman from Belfast and Private H. Smith from Cork. A memorial plaque in Belfast bears the additional names of Private B. Goldie and Able Seaman B. Sergie.

In 1987, on the fiftieth anniversary of the Spanish Civil War, Manus O'Riordan paid tribute at the Irish Jewish Museum to both the Irish and the Jews who fought in Spain with the anti-fascist International Brigade. Maurice Levitas was both Irish and Jewish. Influenced by the poverty that drove his family to Britain from their one-roomed flat in the Lewis home when he was only ten, and by the 'left wing' attitude of his father, Harry Levitas, an ardent trade unionist, he joined the British Communist Party in 1933; in 1938 he went to Spain as a member of the British battalion. He was fortunate to survive. Captured three months later with others termed 'Communists, Socialists, Jews and machine-gunners', he had to dig what he expected to be his own grave. Mussolini's sudden decision to exchange captive internationalists for fascist prisoners saved his life, but he spent a year in a concentration camp.

Sergeant Pilot A. Goldstone, Captain L. Herbert MC, Pilot Officer L. Sharpe and Able Seaman A. Taylor were four Belfast Jews who lost their lives in the Second World War. Beside the plaque that bears their names in the foyer of Somerton Road Synagogue is another expressing gratitude from 'the Jewish members of HM forces stationed in Northern Ireland to the Belfast Jewish Hospitality Committee and the Belfast Jewish Institute'. One of those welcomed was Harold Smith, a South African lawyer commissioned in the Royal Navy. He met his future wife, Rada Hyman, while on shore-leave in Belfast, settled there and became both a councillor and president of the Belfast Jewish Community. In addition to chairing numerous committees dealing with civic affairs, he was chairman of the Belfast branch of AJEX, the Jewish ex-servicemen's association, as well as captain of the Ulster Division of the Royal Naval Voluntary Reserve and of the *Caroline*, a British training ship permanently anchored in Belfast Harbour.

In 1940, after the fall of Dunkirk, Herman Good and Lionel Jackson chaired a special meeting at Zion Schools. Robert Briscoe brought a Government representative, and together they urged members of the community to help repel an expected German invasion. The Irish army, the Local Defence Force (LDF), the ARP and the Local Security Force (LSF), who were auxiliary police, all needed volunteers. Emile Zlotover, who went on to become an actor and playwright, was then a student at Trinity College and already a member of the Regiment of Pearce, the student cadet corps, which should have qualified him for a commission. When he was later denied officer status because he was Jewish, he spent the war entertaining troops in France and Belgium with the Entertainment Corps (ENSA), but at the time he assured Maurice Factor that he met with no anti-Semitism, and Jews could safely volunteer.

Maurice Factor was one of nine Jewish young men who went as a group to the *Garda* Station in Terenure to offer their services. The three doctors among them were refused, possibly because their profession justified a military rank that the State was not then prepared to accord. Maurice joined for a period of seven years, the rest for the duration of the Emergency. Most left long before on one pretext or other, mostly to join the British forces, as did one of the rejected doctors, Ronnie Brass. Louis Davis saw active service with British paratroopers; Harold Vard was at the D-Day landing. Captain Leslie Joseph Samuels, a doctor in the Royal Army Medical Corps, was awarded the Military Cross for tending the wounded 'under heavy gunfire for five hours' at the River Trigno, when 'his cheerfulness, courage and bravery under the worst conditions were an inspiration and example to everyone.'

Maurice Factor served in the Irish army for three years as a non-comissioned officer with the Searchlight Section of the Anti-Aircraft Division and became a qualified instructor in chemical warfare. The adjutant at St Bricin's Military Hospital wanted to sponsor him for a commission as a quartermaster in the Medical Corps, but he refused. With the exception of one officer, whose extreme bigotry made Maurice's life 'a misery', he encountered no racial prejudice and still recalls with pleasure the ten or more Christmas Eves he spent with his wife, Ruth Romney, at the home of his former commanding officer.

Uccy Fine, a pharmacist, left his shop to volunteer. Refused a commission, he went to Macroom Hospital as a dispenser. Sam Danker and Billy Cornick served with the Anti-Aircraft Section at Sandycove. Both obtained early release, but Billy remained a reservist which restricted him from leaving the country and obliged him to attend a training session every year at the Glen of Ihmal. Asher and Hymie Seligman served with the LSF. Myer Lipsitz was one of several awarded medals for LDF service from 1939 to 1946.

Michael Coleman's military career began at the age of fifteen when he told recruiting officers at Kevin Street Barracks he was eighteen. At sixteen he was a sergeant in the LDF, teaching other recruits how to use arms and ammunition. Each week he marched his company of 120 men through Washington Street into Griffith Barracks on the South Circular Road, to the amusement of local Jews and the Jewish men under his command, all of whom knew his true age. In June 1944, six days after D-Day, he went to Belfast to join the Royal Air Force, hoping to become a flight engineer or wireless operator; instead he was offered the job of rear gunner, which he would have accepted had an RAF sergeant not advised him to take something else or go home. 'Paddy,' he told him, 'I've just come back from operations, and how we get the rear gunner out of the rear turret is by hosing out what's left of him.' Michael went into the Motor Transport Division and served in Italy and Austria before his demobilisation in 1947.

Ikey Milofsky left home in 1939, ostensibly to meet a friend at the Corinthian Cinema on the Quays. Next day his family received a letter saying he had joined the Royal Engineers as a sapper. A few months later his brother, Sidney Milofsky, went to Belfast 'to see a customer', who turned out to be a recruiting officer for the RAF. He was wounded during action in India but remained in the Royal Air Force until the end of the war.

Joe Briscoe joined the ARP in 1941, when he was only thirteen. Two years later he became a private in the LDF with the 11th Field Ambulance Company, explaining away his youthful appearance with, 'I was always young-looking for my age.' When the FCA replaced the LDF as the second-line reserve, Joe began to progress through the ranks in what he describes as the best years of his life. Marriage, family commitments and his dental practice were no impediment to obligatory parades three times a week, and he scheduled his annual holidays to coincide with summer training camp. His wife, Debbie, always 'a camp follower', would stay in a rented cottage nearby. Joe was commissioned in 1957 and reached the rank of commandant before he stood down in 1993, the last officer to wear the Emergency Service Medal. His stand-down parade in Cathal Brugha Barracks was reported *in An Cosantóir*, July–August 1993 as 'a milestone' in the history of the defence forces.

Dermot Keogh, in *Jews of Twentieth-Century Ireland*, draws attention to a *Garda* report of 7 May 1940 that suggests the influx of Jews into the armed forces 'put others off joining'. No one would have been deterred by the wartime service of Robert Khan, brother of the murdered Nouky Khan and a senior civil servant in the Office of Public Works. Fluent in Yiddish, as well as English, French and Hebrew, he censored all letters in Yiddish sent into or out of Ireland during the Second World War. With family affairs their main topic, the only subversion he found was the occasional plotted *shidduch*, as parents in one country looked to another to find an eligible spouse for their offspring. He also acted as secretary of the refugee settlement at Millisle, Co. Down. His sister, Esther, took over his role as Irish correspondent for the *Jewish Chronicle* when he died in 1951.

In 1942, when tentative stories about Nazi atrocities were beginning to circulate, it was clear to Bertha Weingreen that survivors would be greatly in need of succour once the war was over. A lecturer in English and Drama who opted to work with coloured students in her native South Africa, it is thought she met her husband, Professor Jack Weingreen, on one of his archaeological expeditions. After their marriage in 1934, she taught elocution in Dublin and involved herself in communal affairs with robust unconventionality, even arriving it is said at one function with a highly-coloured tea cosy on her head instead of a hat.

To prepare herself to offer relief and rehabilitation, she studied for diplomas in Social Science and Public Administration and trained as an auxiliary nurse in Dublin hospitals. In 1944, the Jewish Relief Unit, formed by like-minded British Jews, accepted her as a volunteer member. When the war ended, survivors of concentration camps were classified as 'displaced persons' (DPs). The Jewish Relief Unit was one of only three groups validated by the British Government for service in liberated zones under British jurisdiction. To enable her to serve where civilians were barred, Bertha, in common with all other volunteers, was incorporated into the British army with the rank of lieutenant; on her appointment in 1946 as chief welfare officer for all Jewish DPs in the British zone of Germany, she was promoted to lieutenant-colonel. Her role as commanding officer at Bergen-Belsen made her senior to her husband, also a lieutenant-colonel, who was there as Director of Education. At Lübeck, even more than at Belsen, Bertha Weingreen was stricken to find sick children whose 'faces resembled the faces of mummified Egyptians' and whose arms and legs were 'sticks at the end of which were claws'. The kindergarten she opened in Berlin was stocked with toys sent by the Dublin Jewish community, while tailors among the survivors were set to work making new clothes from Irish cloth. Forty-eight years later Jack Weingreen described the scenes that drove her to tears as still coming back to haunt her. She told the *Irish Times* in 1985, 'I had more anger than sorrow that people all over the world allowed it. The world knew.'

Six million deaths had decimated European Jewry. Traumatised, destitute and unwanted, the most pressing need for survivors was a country of their own. The distant dream had become urgent necessity, and Zionists everywhere demanded the return of the homeland they considered theirs by Divine right since biblical times. The Jews had nowhere else to go. With neither the British administrators of Palestine nor its largely Arab inhabitants willing to yield it peacefully, Jews around the world prepared to fight for it.

One of them was Michael Coleman, who volunteered in Glasgow. In a cloak-and-dagger-type operation, he was instructed to meet other volunteers at Euston Station in London 'under the clock at 4 p.m.' carrying a copy of the *News of the World* in one hand and the *Glasgow Herald* in the other. The assembled group were introduced to each other but forbidden to communicate during the boat and rail journey to Marseilles, where their passports were taken for safe keeping, rendering them technically stateless. At a DP camp they waited with holocaust survivors and other volunteers, not all of them Jewish, until the then sympathetic French arranged sea or air transport to Palestine.

Michael was posted to Airfield Ground Defence to help safeguard the three Second World War flying fortresses that constituted the heavy bomber base of what would become the Israeli Air Force. Ostensibly bought for a film location in America, they were diverted from their flight path to land in Palestine. Their crews later established the first training school in Israel for aircrew. Michael, at twenty-three, was too old for admission.

Irish-born Louis Harris and Solly Cantor served in the Israeli army. Monty Harris, who later founded the National Wholesale Grocers' Alliance in Ireland, was a dedicated fighter in the *Irgun Z'vai L'umi*, a pre-State underground movement. When Menachem Begin visited Britain in 1979 as Prime Minister of Israel, he decorated Monty with the *Irgun* medal. In 1981, Victor Waddington died; obituaries in the *Irish Times* and *Jewish Chronicle* referred to him as a Scarlet Pimpernel. Narrowly escaping arrest on more than one occasion, he had masterminded 'brilliant coups' that 'whisked' desperately needed aircraft and other supplies out of their home country and into Palestine without the formality of an export licence. The historian, Louis Hyman, fought with another underground movement, the *Haganah*.

The establishment of the State of Israel in 1948 had important repercussions for Irish Jewry. Pioneers, ardent Zionists and the religious all wanted to play their part in building the embryonic state into the 'milk and honey' land of their dreams. One after another, individuals and families left Ireland to settle there. A few returned, unable to face the hardships; the majority stayed, influencing Israel's development from the kibbutzim to the Knesset. In *Ireland's Other Diaspora: Jewish-Irish Within, Irish-Jewish Without* (2002), Ronit Lentin estimates the number of Irish-born Jews in Israel at approximately 300. Chaim Herzog became its sixth President and his brother, Yaakov, Director-General of the Prime Minister's office in Jerusalem.

With Israel surrounded by hostile nations, the political situation after the Declaration of the State remained taut. In May 1967, the President of Egypt called for 'total war' and the Syrian Defence Minister for 'a battle of annihilation'. The Iraqi President described the existence of Israel as 'an error' they must 'wipe off the map'. The process began on 22 May, when Egypt requested the withdrawal of the UN Emergency Force on the Sinai-Israel border and blocked the Straits of Tiran to Israeli shipping. The cutting off of Israel's oil supply and its trade with Asia and East Africa was an act of aggression by international law, and the first shots were fired on 5 June.

Irish Jewry observed the day as a fast for peace in Israel, but they also offered political, financial and social help through an Israel Emergency Committee, formed by the Jewish Representative Council. A deputation called on the Minister for External Affairs, Frank Aiken TD, to ask for Ireland's support of Israel at the United Nations, while fund-raising began on an unprecedented scale. The Variety Club of Ireland hosted a film premiere, sympathisers donated silverware and jewellery for a sale, and local wholesalers and manufacturers stocked a thrift shop free of charge. Each organisation mounted its own individual event, families even curtailing wedding and *Bar Mitzvah* celebrations in favour of the appeal. Support flooded in from Irish people of other faiths, whom Rabbi Cohen would later thank for their 'expressions of sympathy, admiration and goodwill.' The Cork community's separate collection, described as 'magnificent' in the *Irish Jewish Year Book* 1967-8, brought the total raised to £56,000.

To replace some of the Israeli men and women obliged to leave civilian duties for active service, twenty-one volunteers, chosen from the 100 who applied, were organised rapidly for interview and medical examination through the secretarial efficiency of Joan Finkel. By the time they left for Israel, on 12 June, the Six Day War was over. Left without cover when the small Israeli Air Force destroyed 300 Egyptian aircraft, mostly still on the ground, the Egyptian army was routed and the Jordanians driven back. The divided city of Jerusalem had fallen entirely into Israeli hands. When Frank Aiken, during a *Dáil* debate on the Middle East urged Israel to withdraw from the conquered territory, both the leader of the Opposition, Liam Cosgrave, and *Fine Gael* member, Richie Ryan, objected to his anti-Israeli stance. Newspaper editorials suggested that 'sympathy for the Israeli cause [was] widespread throughout Ireland'.

Shrugging off as wry humour any attempt to classify them as 'Catholic Jews' or 'Protestant Jews', the Northern Ireland community has tried to remain aloof from local political and racial tensions, but it has not gone unscathed. Though not necessarily specific targets, Jewish shops and homes have been damaged in terrorist activity. Leonard Steinberg, warden of the Belfast Hebrew Congregation, was wounded and Abraham Herbert fortunate to escape unhurt when both their houses came under attack. Hundreds of Jews left the Province for mainland

Britain or further afield. That comparatively few travelled south could be due to Dublin Jewry's own declining numbers but Gerald Goldberg, in a Thomas Davis Lecture on RTÉ Radio in May 1973, attributed it to the political settlement of 1922, which, in his view, prevented Irish Jews from developing into one united community. With no common council, religious leadership, educational policy or sharing of problems, he feels the Jews of Northern Ireland grew apart from their southern brethren, until they had more affinity with the Jews of Britain.

The internal politics of the Irish Jewish Community and its relationship to the community at large is the province of the Jewish Representative Council. Formalised in 1938, the advisory body was conceived a few years earlier when Rabbi Herzog sought guidance from respected community leaders on extra-congregational matters. Estelle Menton, *née* Miller, is so far the only woman to have chaired it and she became its first female president. Over the years the 'Rep Council', as it is familiarly called, has changed its constitution many times, but it broadly comprises at least one representative from each Dublin organisation, including the Orthodox synagogues, and a small number of freely elected independents. Essentially a debating forum and facilitator, the Rep Council, an entirely voluntary organisation, has no power to impose its views and has often been challenged. It still remains an active force within the community.

Much of the Rep Council's work is in countering anti-Semitism through its Public Affairs Committee. Minutes from 1948 show some of its interventions in that year. Protests at the publication on 15 March of a statement by a Mr Donnellan urging no one to sell land to Jews resulted in a printed apology from the *Irish Times*. When Ernest Woods was challenged about anti-Semitic remarks reported in the *Irish Independent* of 30 October, he claimed he had been misquoted. Anti-Semitic occurrences at the Gresham Hotel on New Year's Eve brought a visit to its management from Professor Abrahamson and Herman Good.

Even after the opening in Ireland of an Israeli Embassy in 1996, twenty-one years after negotiations began, the Rep Council applied a low-key attitude to suspected racism and discouraged members of the community from writing letters to newspapers or otherwise becoming personally involved. In 1998, the first Israeli ambassador to Ireland, Zvi Gabay, at a symposium in Trinity College, underlined the many factors Ireland and Israel have in common; but he also commented on the 'disproportionate' and 'in most cases, distorted and one-sided' media coverage of the Arab-Israeli conflict. The next incumbent, Mark Sofer, advised by his predecessor to develop a taste for Guinness 'which has a way of solving difficulties', was more outspoken and for the first time urged individual community responses.

Generations of prejudice, mistrust and frequent maltreatment have made Jews sensitive to opinion, and they cannot easily distinguish between anti-Israeli and anti-Semitic sentiments. Neither was evident in the Irish Christians who joined

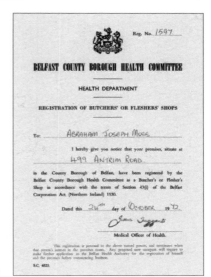

Reg. No. 1597

BELFAST COUNTY BOROUGH HEALTH COMMITTEE

HEALTH DEPARTMENT

REGISTRATION OF BUTCHERS' OR FLESHERS' SHOPS

To: ABRAHAM JOSEPH MOSS

I hereby give you notice that your premises, situate at

499 ANTRIM ROAD

in the County Borough of Belfast, have been registered by the Belfast County Borough Health Committee as a Butcher's or Flesher's Shop in accordance with the terms of Section 43(i) of the Belfast Corporation Act (Northern Ireland) 1930.

Dated this 24th day of OCTOBER 19 72.

Medical Officer of Health.

Registration certificate issued to Abe Moss, who took over the kosher butcher shop in Antrim Road, Belfast, previously owned by Mot Nemtzov.

the seven-day Israel Solidarity Trip that left Ireland in November 2002. Sporting green caps with tricolour emblems, seventy-five people, fewer than half of them Jewish, spent what many regard as the most rewarding week of their lives touring sites of religious, historical, and cultural interest. Among the many charismatic, influential and interesting personalities they met were former chief rabbis and Israeli ambassadors to Ireland, the serving incumbent, Patrick Hennessy, the mayor of Jerusalem, Ehud Olmert, who accepted messages of goodwill from the mayors of Dublin and Belfast, David Horowitz, the Jerusalem correspondent of the *Irish Times*, and Irish Jewish expatriates. A second solidarity trip took place in 2004. That Jew and Gentile could share the experience in fellowship and mutual respect is a testament to the tolerance of both. It also serves to underline the impact made by Irish Jews on Irish society.

10

SPORTS AND ENTERTAINMENT

On 26 May 1971, 9,000 supporters turned out in Waterford to watch a Senior League of Ireland soccer match between their home county and the Dublin club, Shamrock Rovers. Among them were the four Woolfson brothers, Max, Solly and 'Duffy' who had travelled from their homes in Boston, and Simon who had come from Dublin. At half time they watched their nephew, Bryan Woolfson, also from Dublin, present a cup for Waterford Under-Fifteen Football Championships in the local Schoolboys' Football League. In memory of his father, it was inscribed:

> The Maurice Woolfson Perpetual Challenge Cup,
> presented by the Woolfson family 1971.

The *Irish Times* described the cup as a trophy 'that must rank among the finest in Irish soccer'.

Maurice Woolfson was a pioneer of Waterford football in the 1920s and '30s. Born in Waterford in 1910 to parents who left Riga in 1888, he lived with his family in a house in Manor Street where the top floor was Waterford's synagogue. When Bryan revisited at the end of the 1990s he found it converted to a Muslim centre.

Under Maurice Woolfson's chairmanship the Evergreen Club became one of the best in Ireland. From 1938, when they won the Football Association of Ireland (FAI) Minor Cup, he had their unswerving devotion. 'There will never be another Maurice Woolfson,' they lamented when he left in 1940 for Dublin, where he made a point of attending every game with a Waterford player on the team. Regarded as one of the best judges of soccer in the country, his death in 1969 'saddened the hearts of all who had the privilege to know him'. His brother,

David, nicknamed 'Duffy' in Waterford (from *Duvid*, the Yiddish form of his name), was honorary secretary to Evergreen when he led them to the 'fabulous double' in 1953 of both the FAI and Munster Junior Cups.

Despite the traditional tendency of Orthodox Jewry to regard sporting pursuits as a waste of learning time, Irish Jewish interest in sport goes back to 1895, when the first Jewish sports club was formed in St Kevin's Parade, Dublin. In *Summing Up* (*1895-1954*) written as part of the souvenir brochure for the opening of Maccabi Sports Grounds in 1954, Harold Davis names the captain as Max Hool and one of the players as L. Landau, later mayor of Bulawayo. Two others were probably M. Jacobson and B. Eppel, elsewhere described as Ireland's first Jewish cricketers from play recorded in 1899.

'Dublin Jewish Sports Clubs of the Past', written in 1943 by 'Oldtimer' for the commemoration magazine that celebrated Carlisle Cricket Club's twenty-fifth anniversary in its own grounds, records the first Jewish association football club as Adelaide, formed in 1900 and named for the newly opened synagogue. Disbanded after just a few seasons in the 'general despondency' that set in when Michael Noyk broke a leg during play, it was replaced by the less aggressive Adelaide Cricket Club. In a match against Skerries in 1903, Ely Buchalter was the only player to wear 'whites' and was the talk of the village in his 'strange gear'. That same year Max Hool scored a seven in Phoenix Park, 'the biggest single stroke ever hit there'. The ball soared out of the public cricket ground, down the steps and past the iron gate.

Michael Noyk, happily recovered, was among the players who won the Sunday League in 1905. So exciting was the finish, with G. Hool and N. Sigman still in and only twenty more runs needed for victory, that 'all the other matches in the same park ceased play to watch'. Many members of the Adelaide Cricket Club were medical students who left Ireland on graduation; when several qualified in 1912, the club disbanded. Younger members continued playing for their schools; older ones joined the Railway and Steam Packet Union, now the Railway Union, where they successfully participated in the Senior League.

In 1906, the Adelaide Football Club was revived. They finished their first season of Sunday football as runners-up in the Oaklands League and came third in the Junior Alliance of 1907/08. Competing in the Leinster Minor Cup, they 'created a sensation by the number of replays in the semi-final against G.S. and W. Railways'. The second replay was occasioned by supporters invading the pitch in the excitement of Adelaide leading 3-2. The fifth, at Dalymount Park, gave Adelaide the decisive victory of 2-1.

In 1907, a Jewish football club was established in Belfast in connection with the Jaffe National School. A Zionist rugby club formed in Dublin to play friendly matches, and the newly formed Dublin Company of the Jewish Lads' Brigade began earning 'high respect' for their standard on the sports field. The Jewish Lads'

Brigade brimmed with all-round enthusiasm, even forming a bugle band, but it, too, was short-lived, disbanding soon after its leader, Dr Wigoder, left Dublin.

'Oldtimer' claims that the Vernon Club, formed by under-fourteens in 1921, had 'a glorious career'. Runners-up in the Sunday School League, they won every competition they entered. For four consecutive years from 1922 they won the fourth division of the Leinster League. Success continued into 1924 and 1925, when they won the Minor Cup, but with no grounds of their own they were unable to enter a higher league and disbanded.

The cycle of enthusiastic beginnings followed by closure in the face of obstacles seems to have dogged many an early Jewish sports club. The one exception was Carlisle.

Interviewed by Cormac Behan and Raymond Farrell in December 1990 for the archives of the Irish Jewish Museum, Dr Gerry Tolkin traced the origin of Carlisle as a Jewish cricket club to the inventiveness of four Jewish boys forbidden by their parents to play games on the Sabbath. One of them was Willie Wiener. In 'March of Time' in the silver anniversary magazine he recalls how a few non-Jewish friends from Carlisle Street, part of the South Circular Road Jewish enclave, formed their own cricket club in 1908, with 'two bats, one set of stumps, one pair of pads and one ball', a birthday gift to the lad who would become Captain Ramsey, honorary treasurer of the Irish Rugby Football Union. On Saturday afternoons the eight to thirteen-year-olds set off for the public cricket grounds in the Phoenix Park, joined by Wiener, 'Nemo' Levison, 'Tarrant' Green and 'Acky' (Henry) Hesselberg. Forbidden to carry on the Sabbath, the Jewish boys had to leave home ostensibly empty-handed. They set off for a fictional walk wearing 'a tennis shirt outside, white flannels under the ordinary trousers and a white shoe secreted in each outside pocket of an overcoat'. Their Christian opponents had to be equally devious later on when Carlisle played on home ground. To avoid the consequences of infringing their own Sabbath, the team that played on Sunday morning was always listed as A.N. Other.

By 1910, the non-Jewish members of Carlisle had all dropped out, selling on their cricket assets 'for the sum of £2.10.0 on credit'. The all-Jewish team continued to trek to the Phoenix Park, 'where twelve different matches were in progress at the same time with balls flying in all directions and fielders from different games knocking each other over'. To settle their cricket debt and supply themselves with 'necessary accoutrements', all members agreed to a weekly subscription of 6d, a noble sacrifice that deprived them of 'strap liquorice ... gur cake ... hard gums ... and the occasional visit to the Tivoli or Empire'.

In *Carlisle Rugby Football Club*, a writer posing as 'Scrum Half' attributes the formation of the Carlisle Rugby Players to a determination to maintain members' interest outside the cricket season. In 1910, they beat Rathmines XV 9-0, with Dr H. Levison as their captain. The following year, playing Merrion, 'Lizzie' Hool intercepted a pass near his own line, cut through, beat the full back, ran the full length of the field and collapsed five yards from the line crying, 'Oi, ich ken nit gain vi-ter!' (I can't go any further!). A later injury smashed his front teeth.

Their complement of fifteen players was depleted in 1912 when H. Jackson, J. Sacks and A. Hofferman all emigrated to South Africa and five others defected to soccer. The seven remaining regular players were augmented by eight soldiers from the West Riding regiment stationed in Dublin; when they were recalled in 1914 at the outbreak of the First World War, the rugby club disbanded with H. Hesselberg as its last captain.

The Jewish rugby player *par excellence* of that era was Dr Bethel Solomons, whose parents intended him to leave St Andrew's College to be educated in France, where his sisters were already at school. When his headmaster, W. W. Haslett, protested, 'You can't send him to France. We want him for the rugby team!' Bethel was allowed to stay, and describes rugby in his autobiography as 'one of the outstanding features of my early life.' Nominated for all eleven of Ireland's International games, he played in ten and became a member of the selection committee for International Rugby teams. After one victory in Scotland, *The Pink Un* initiated the story of a Dublin tippler who responded to the general praise for the 'grand Irish team that won today', with, 'Call that an Irish team with fourteen Protestants and one bloody Jew!' The story still goes the rounds with many variations in the setting, but the punch line remains the same.

Cricket practise continued illicitly over the next few years in Goodbody's fields at the rear of Dufferin Avenue, where two street railings were always bent back before a match so players could squeeze through if the law appeared. The notion of having their own grounds came with rising membership and the enthusiastic example set by many of the non-Jewish clubs to which Carlisle members belonged. Cinema shows, concerts and raffles eventually yielded enough to pay the rental for one year on the National Bank grounds in Green Lanes, Kimmage (Greenlea Road). With no possibility of employing a grounds man, half the members marked out, wired off and prepared the tennis courts; the rest cut out a cricket pitch and the surrounding grass with their own lawnmowers, brought to the grounds each evening. A steam-roller to flatten the ground was hired from Dublin Corporation and at one stage a horse was acquired to pull it.

To coincide with the opening of the 'spick and span' Carlisle Cricket Grounds on 'a glorious summer day' in 1918, the club changed its name to Carlisle Athletic Union. A 'keen Ladies' Committee' catered for all. The limitations of Carlisle's facilities were no drawback to the fifty members who built their social life around it. Dr Jimmy Tolkin, Gerry Tolkin's uncle, described the 20 by 10-foot pavilion without water or electricity as 'a thing of beauty and perfection'. Making tea by candlelight on a primus stove with water carried from neighbouring fields added to the attraction, while the 'splendid condition' in which they kept the grounds raised the standard of their play. The camaraderie of away games was equally enjoyable. Their silver anniversary magazine records Barney Wigoder winning first prize of a live pig in 1924, when Carlisle played a match in Grange Con, Co. Wicklow, and all the players bought local raffle tickets. Another happy memory was of Jimmie Harris transporting the entire team together with equipment in his 'famous Lincoln car' to fixtures within the city and beyond.

When the lease ran out three years later, Carlisle functioned for several years from the College of Surgeons' grounds in Bird Avenue, Clonskeagh. The grounds they eventually occupied in Parkmore Drive were offered for sale before the war at £4,000. It was an impossible sum for the impoverished Club to raise, and they settled for a rental lease that would expire in 1946.

Carlisle's policy of operating solely on membership fees left the club dependent on community support. It was not forthcoming, despite the introduction of rugby and table tennis sections, and the placing of a second-hand piano and gramophone in the clubhouse for a lively dance or sing-song at the end of every fixture. In 1943, when its president, Herman Good, reviewed the future of Carlisle, he wrote, 'I can think of no Jewish institution in this city which has received so little support and encouragement from the members of their own community.' The same year, 1943, also saw the death of Louis Bookman, a member of the Buchalter family. An outstanding sportsman who made his mark with Belfast Celtic, he played for Bradford City in 1912 before moving to West Bromwich Albion in 1914 for what the *Footballer*, June-July 1994, called 'a substantial fee'. In 1919, he joined Luton. He won his first cap against Wales in 1914, represented Ireland at association football and cricket on many occasions, and was a recipient of one of the gold watches presented to each member of the Irish soccer team that won the Triple Crown. Carlisle instituted a Louis Bookman Memorial Cup as a league trophy in his memory.

Another milestone that year was Carlisle's affiliation to the Maccabi World Union, defined by M. Mansoor in 'The Jew as Sportsman' as 'the supreme Jewish Sports authority'. The Maccabi World Union was established after the First World War by the German-Jewish sports association, Judische Turnerschaft, to consolidate the many Maccabi Associations that had sprung up worldwide since 1895, when the first Maccabi Club was formed in Constantinople (now Istanbul). Its motto was 'a healthy soul in a healthy body'. In 1932, and again in 1935 it hosted the Maccabiah, the Jewish world games on the style of the Olympics, in Tel Aviv. The third, originally scheduled for 1938, was postponed by political events until 1950, when it became the first to be held in the state of Israel. The team Ireland sent that year was small but it included Ernie Cantor, an international wrestling champion.

In the mid-1940s, despite financial straits, the committee decided to exercise the indefinite option they had been holding for years on Dublin Corporation grounds at Kimmage Road West. Jack Roberts, a veteran Irish-Jewish sportsman who lived into his eighties, was still a newcomer to Dublin when Noel Jameson, a solicitor member of Carlisle, negotiated the terms on Carlisle's behalf in the 1930s. Jack clearly remembered Carlisle's instruction to Noel to cancel the option when the advent of the Second World War made it impossible to finance the move, and Noel's foresight in ignoring the instruction. In *Dublin Maccabi Association, Incorporating Carlisle*, the magazine produced in 1979 for Maccabi's silver anniversary, Noel Jameson, then president of Maccabi, recalled the 'lengthy representations followed by a cliff-hanging delay' when Dublin Corporation unexpectedly tried to cancel the option by issuing a compulsory purchase order. He also paid tribute to their 'understanding of our problems and their assistance in enabling us to attain our longed-for and long-awaited goal.' While negotiations dragged on, Carlisle continued at Parkmore Drive on annual leases and moved for a short while to rented grounds in Shelton Park. It was 1952 before Billy Cornick, whose death in 2009 ended a long association with Irish-Jewish sport, became chairman of the building committee whose members he acknowledged as 'the finest bunch of men I ever worked with.'

The new clubhouse and grounds opened in 1954 as Dublin Maccabi. Lord Nathan, chairman of the European Maccabi committee, travelled to Ireland to open the Aaron Hool entrance gates, sponsored by the Hool family as a memorial to Aaron's long involvement in Irish sport. The official blessing of the grounds by Rabbi Jakobovits was conditional on the gates never being opened to admit cars on the Sabbath or Holy Days: play proceeded on those days, but members entered on foot through a side gate, later providing a potential bonanza for traffic wardens by parking outside. Non-Jewish players and supporters adhered to the stipulation more faithfully than members of the community. Dr John Simon, a grandson of the nineteenth-century cricketer Mick Jacobson and now a trustee of Maccabi, recalls infringements, but he also remembers that cars were never parked within sight of the entrance, out of deference to Revd Gittleson, who lived across the road.

Though the use of the 8½ acres was restricted to sporting activities, its 150-year lease was renewable for another 150 years, and rent was fixed at £124 per year with no reviews. When Ben Dunne bought over the lease in 1999, it cost him approximately £4 million

Within a short time Maccabi had 1,000 members, including a large number of children from the age of seven. It continued to offer the wide range of sports initiated by Carlisle. Their rugby XV had been formed in 1937 by Maurice Stein. Though eight of the team were able boxers, almost all were novice rugby-players. To offset the possibility of last minute defections, Maurice, the team captain, and his brother Stanley, always arrived with at least half a dozen spare sets of togs, so that spectators could be pressed into service in emergency. Louis Verby had formed the soccer club in 1948.

The introduction of new sports, together with social activities, enabled the *Irish Jewish Year Book*, 1956-7 to list Maccabi sections as soccer, rugby, cricket, tennis, cycling, wrestling, boxing, table tennis, bridge, athletics, dramatics and debating. In later years there would be badminton, judo and a gym that offered weight-lifting. It would also boast a snack bar or restaurant and even its own magazine,

The Shofar, in addition to acting as unofficial marriage bureau. Many a Jewish couple met at Maccabi, where social events also included dances, record sessions, lectures, musical evenings and art exhibitions.

Not all the incorporated sections were legacies from Carlisle. The Dublin Jewish Boxing Club had been formed in 1934 by Victor Newman and Lionel Jackson, both boxing enthusiasts rather than boxers. Established in a warehouse 'somewhere off Parliament Street', it became a popular means of learning self-defence in an Ireland where Jews and other faiths still operated an 'us' and 'them' policy.

The Jewish Boxing Club started with a full team representing all eight categories from flyweight to heavyweight. When they faced their first opponents, Dublin University Boxing Club, at the Trinity College gym in September 1934, a large contingent of Jewish followers cheered them on. Many other 'grand nights' followed at Arbour Hill, Collins Barracks, Cathal Brugha Barracks and even at Greenville Hall. Their large following made the Jewish Boxing Club popular opponents in a sport where friendly fights otherwise attracted few supporters. Several club members went on to tournament boxing and quite a few collected Novice League titles. Chaim Herzog, the Chief Rabbi's son and a boxing enthusiast from schooldays, became an Ireland bantamweight champion. By 1943 when 'Ringside' wrote 'The Dublin Jewish Boxing Club' for Carlisle's

Dublin Jewish Boxing Club, 1937/8. From left to right, back row: Dr N. Jackson, I. Green, P. Levene, J. Woolfe, S. Levene, I. Sevitt. Middle row: J. Resnick, H. Woolfe, LDSI, M. Cohen, N. Harris, S. Isaacson, B. Citron, T. Glasser, D.M. Robinson LDSI, Dr L.H. Robinson. Front row: W. Briscoe, F. Isaacson, V. Newman (chairman), M. Hayes (trainer), J. Briscoe, R. Briscoe TD.

silver anniversary magazine, the club had about forty members, from twelve to thirty years old. Practise was held in the basement of Adelaide Road Synagogue where a gym had been established with 'splendid facilities' that were otherwise little used.

Billy Cornick was one of several Jewish boxers who widened their experience by joining non-Jewish clubs and he believed participation in sport was pivotal in establishing amicable relations between Jew and Gentile. For many it was their first close encounter with members of another faith, and friendships were formed where no contact had previously existed. Spectators could be more reactionary. Leslie Silverstone remembers the wartime heckling of 'Hey, Jewman! Hitler'll get you!' He also recalls the female spectator who hit him on the head with an umbrella and called him a 'bloody Jewman' when he saved a goal during a soccer match in Drogheda.

Though wrestling within the Jewish community had fewer enthusiasts than boxing, and Jewish wrestlers never aspired to their own club, four of them – brothers Roy and Henry Alkin, Jackie Vard and Ernie Cantor – founded the Irish Amateur Wrestling Association in 1947, later affiliated to the World Amateur Wrestling Association. Jeffrey Garber, a semi-professional jazz drummer, was an early participant. He began weight-lifting and keep-fit exercises at the Apollo Club, Mendel Stein's gym in Mercer Street, in 1949 Though facilities were basic with after-training showers dependent on enough rain water having collected in the tank, Jeffrey went almost every night. Several others put in a brief appearance before losing interest. A few reached championship standard. Ernie Cantor and Jackie Vard were consistently excellent. Ernie won for Ireland in three consecutive years in the International Triangular against England and Scotland and represented Ireland at the Maccabiah of 1950. An injury ended his own wrestling career but he still regards Jackie Vard – a member of the Irish team at the 1952 Olympics in Helsinki and Irish lightweight champion – as among the best lightweight champions in Europe.

To improve his style, Jeffrey Garber switched from Mendel's gym, where there was no one to coach him, to sessions with Dick Vekins, the trainer in wrestling and keep-fit who started the Vulcan Club. In 1952, weighing 8st 2lb, he became Irish flyweight champion; in 1956 he won two silver medals at the fifth Maccabiah. There was another Jewish success in 1958 when Norman Cohen, representing Maccabi, won the Irish Wrestling Featherweight Championship.

When wrestling events moved from the Apollo Club to the basement of Adelaide Road Synagogue or to Carlisle Grounds in Parkmore Drive, association meetings took place in the ladies' clothing factory owned by Jackie Vard's family. Jackie later established the Spartan Wrestling Club in Werburgh Street, which Michael Coleman recalls as producing 'many fine wrestlers and honours for Ireland'. Michael, a regular participant, remembers some of the other active Jewish members as the Lewis brothers, Cecil Wiener and Philly Weinberg. Dick Vekins continued to train the few remaining Jewish proponents when the wrestling venue changed to Maccabi. Mendel Stein transferred his gym there in 1976.

Over the years Michael Coleman has served the Irish Amateur Wrestling Association as secretary, chairman and president. In 1965, he participated in the World Wrestling Championships in Belle Vue, Manchester as Ireland's only international judge and referee.

Good administration and talented players gave Maccabi many moments of glory. Australian-born Julien Weiner, who later played against England as the first Jewish sportsman to be capped by Australia for a test match, was brought in as cricket coach for the summer of 1978. He helped mould the talent of Mark Cohen, born in Cork in 1961 and a cricket player at Carlisle from the age of seven. Mark's talent blossomed in the late 1970s. In 1979, he had an exceptional season, scoring six successive centuries within a fortnight in various Representative and Senior League matches. Tipped by the *Sunday Independent* on 19 August 1979 to become 'a rare phenomenon (with) little to stop him making it to the top of the profession', he attributed his batting success to Weiner's special coaching. In 1980, with his heart set on 'sampling first-class cricket', he went for a week's trial to Middlesex and Glamorgan. He scored an unbeaten century for Glamorgan, playing alongside Ritchie Richardson who went on to captain the West Indian team, while his performance at Middlesex earned him a three-month contract. He made his first appearance for Ireland at the age of nineteen against Wales. Over the next decade he became a leading player for the Irish cricket team, gaining sixty-nine caps and being listed among the top ten Irish batsmen of all time.

Pragmatism demanded a more secure future, and Mark opted for a career in Business Studies; but to Alf Solomons, one-time president of the Leinster Table Tennis Association, he was a 'prodigy' who developed into a fine batsman and a captain of distinction. Tribute was paid to Alf's own skills in the *Irish Times* of 1 June 1976, when the sports editor wrote, 'Were one to list the eleven legislators who have done most ... for Irish cricket, the genial Alf Solomons could well qualify to open the innings.' Associated with Carlisle Cricket Club from 1932, he was remembered by Billy Cornick as its 'backbone'. He served on the field and in committee for continuous decades and together with Willy Samuels made what is remembered as 'a feared open bowling partnership'. In 1988, eighteen years after they entered the senior league, Ger Siggins wrote in the *Sunday Tribune* of Maccabi's incredible cricket success. Listing some outstanding players, he mentioned Mark Cohen who had finished the season little short of 1,000 runs, and Stephen Mollins, who would be appointed an international selector for Ireland. Stephen's nephew, Jason Mollins, who has captained the Irish cricket team, and his brother, Greg Mollins, are the only Jewish brothers ever selected to represent Ireland. Their cousin, Lara Mollins, was a member of the Irish Ladies' International Cricket team and the only Jewish girl to play cricket for Ireland.

Spectators at the Old Pavilion, Carlisle Cricket Grounds,
Parkmore Drive *c.* 1945. Adults facing camera (left to right):
Hymie Feldman, Dave Barling, Billy Cornick, Herman Good,
Siva Solomons *née* Millar, Leah Goldberg *née* Baker.

Other sections did equally well but neither national nor international
recognition was enough to keep Maccabi buoyant. Declining membership due
to emigration was exacerbated by ageing, death and general lack of interest.
As John Simon puts it, 'the nursery had gone.' In the 1950s, most Jewish children
of secondary-school age attended schools where sports were either compulsory
or recommended. Stratford College had no such ethos. Campaigns for new
Maccabi members invariably failed. One person approached to join while dining
at the Maccabi restaurant replied, 'When my kids are older.' He was told, 'I hope
it'll be here when your kids are older.'

Disappearing with the all-Jewish teams was Maccabi's Jewish identity. When
a fixture prevented a player from going to synagogue on the anniversary of a
death to recite the memorial prayers that required a minyan, the Jewish team had
formed one on the grounds, wherever they were playing. John Simon remembers
Kaddish being said after a match in Clontarf, while one bemused opponent
observing the ritual after a home victory at Maccabi was heard to ask, 'Do they
always do that when they win?'

Maccabi was never 100 per cent Jewish, but from the late 1960s onwards the
small minority of non-Jews grew to a majority. By 1997 membership was down
to 100, and Maccabi's overdraft, already standing at £125,000, was rising at a rate
of £30,000 per year. The management council decided it was time to close.

Maccabi's substantial funds are now administered by nine trustees. Originally limited to the sponsorship of sport or education, the funds are now additionally available by Court Order to assist the youth, relieve the elderly, advance social, cultural and religious projects and support former Maccabi members who have suffered serious injury. All individual and corporate beneficiaries must be Irish Jews. At present the trustees make grants to Stratford College, the Jewish Home of Ireland, the Dublin Jewish Youth Leaders' Council and the Jewish Representative Council, whose allocation is applied specifically towards the youth services now organised by Rabbi Lent.

Still active is Edmondstown Golf Club. The publication issued in 1994 to mark its golden jubilee records how Dublin Jewish golfers were once obliged to travel to Greystones, Delgany or even the Isle of Man to find a course that would accept them. Golf clubs in other cities were equally exclusive. Dr Ivor Scher recalls from his home in Israel that he and his brother, Leslie, were reduced to playing in what was then an 'up-and down-hill poor nine-hole course' in Kinsale because 'other Jews before us failed on any pretext to get into prestigious Cork golf clubs.' When a professor colleague asked, 'Why Kinsale?' the brothers replied, 'Anti-Semitism.' Without their knowledge, the professor approached the Cork Golf Club committee. Rumour had it that he threatened to resign his own membership and disclose the reason to the press if Jews were not admitted. Whatever he said was effective: the Shers, invited to submit applications, were elected members. When Ivor was adding his name to the club board for his first competition, one member remarked loudly, 'I suppose you will sign your name in Hebrew!' He signed in Irish. Over the years he played there, he came to feel fully accepted and won many trophies, including the 1908 Cup, the club's annual competition.

In 1933, Dublin golfers formed the Dublin Maccabean Golfing Society, with a limited membership of thirty. David Cantor was its first president, and early meetings were held above a shop at Kelly's Corner. When the club proved unexpectedly popular, membership was increased to fifty but there was still a waiting list.

Thoughts turned to a Jewish-owned golf club when wartime travel restrictions made journeys to 'outlying places' difficult or impossible. Harrie Barron, later Edmondstown's first captain, dressed in old tweeds and gum boots, negotiated the purchase of land and buildings at Edmondstown Park Farm in the hills of south Co. Dublin, on the recommendation of Philly Rubenstein, the Clanbrassil Street butcher. Philly knew the site was for sale through buying cattle from its owner. At the first formal meeting of Edmondstown Golf Club at the Zion Schools on 5 April 1944, the Dublin Maccabean Golfing Society handed over all its trophies and funds, contributing £120 towards the £2,892 15s 6d paid for the seventy-five acres, two roods and nine perches. The membership fee was set at 5 guineas.

Regulations introduced during the Emergency left twenty-four statute acres still under tillage, so the original course was only nine holes. A horse bought for £25 (plus £15 extra for the harness) to pull the roller over the extensive grounds, even with the assistance of a mare, proved inadequate to the task. In 1947, a different kind of horse power was introduced in the form of a jeep. Victor Newman's gift of adjacent fields bought specially for the club, in addition to its own purchase of 12.5 acres in 1966, enabled the course to be extended over the years to thirteen, then fifteen, then eighteen holes.

The original farmhouse became the clubhouse. The cowsheds served as locker-rooms, a place for caddies and a professionals' shop. There was no electricity. In the late 1940s, Edmondstown paid £800 for the Arcadia Ballroom's Nissen hut, the structure that had inspired the Terenure Synagogue committee to erect a Nissen hut of its own in the grounds of Leoville when they needed temporary accommodation. When refurbishment at the Metropole Ballroom made its maple flooring surplus to requirements, Geoff Elliman was instrumental in obtaining it for the clubhouse, which was entirely replaced a decade later under his stewardship. The present facility, constructed in the late 1980s when Selwyn Davies was captain, was officially opened in 1990 by Frank Fahey TD, then Minister for Sport.

Veteran Jewish golfers remember workmen in 1950 uncovering Edmondstown's unsuspected Bronze Age site while levelling a slight hump near one of the holes. The artifacts found were donated to the National Museum of Ireland, which dated them at 1000 BCE. They also remember the two-seater plane that landed on the fairway when the pilot lost either his control or his direction. He and his girlfriend were revived at the clubhouse bar, often no more than a few crates of stout and ale consumed at the sing-song to piano accompaniment that followed the day's play. Each member had his own repertoire: for Dr Joe Lewis it was 'Trees'; for Harold Mushatt and 'Rusty' Ross it was 'The Dublin Fusiliers'. The anonymous writer of 'The Members' in the golden jubilee souvenir brochure recalls the bleak period of a few weeks when the piano seemed to have broken down until the senior piano-tuner from McCullough Pigott discovered three pickled meat sandwiches entangled in the strings!

A highlight of every year was the Captain's Dinner. Guests at the first one, held at Greenville Hall in 1945, paid £5 per ticket, which included free drink. Though Mrs Danker's catering charge was only 2 guineas per head, and a 'half-one' could be bought for 10d, so much was imbibed that night that no profit was made. 'Wonderfully entertaining after-dinner speakers', 'the best entertainers of the theatrical profession' and 'Mrs Danker's scrumptious kosher meal' combined to make Captains' Dinners eagerly awaited and well-supported occasions.

By the end of the 1950s founder-members were yielding their positions to younger players who took the game more seriously. A few, like Don Buchalter and Henry Barron, had learned their skills at university and played 'to or just above single handicap golf'. As play and management improved, members became involved in inter-club competitions.

Two of Edmondstown's brightest stars were Joe Bryan, son of Gerry Bryan, the green-keeper, and Mark Bloom, who also reflected his father, Jack Bloom's interest in the sport. Joe at eighteen had beaten Irish international Jackie Harrington in the first round of the Irish Amateur Close Championship in Cork and went on to win both Junior Inter-provincial and Senior International caps. Mark, capped three times as an inter-provincial rugby player, won the Ulster Boys' Championship in 1966; Junior International, Senior and Inter-provincial caps followed in 1970.

The depletion of the community has reduced Jewish membership to a small minority, but Edmondstown Golf Club continues to thrive.

Golf clubs were not alone in rejecting Jewish members: equally selective and expensive until past the mid-twentieth century were the yacht clubs. In 1963, Joe Briscoe became the founder-commodoree of the Dun Laoghaire Motor Yacht Club, where fees were realistically set. Never intended as a Jewish club, its articles of association specifically state that 'nobody shall be refused membership on the grounds of race, colour or creed', a unique ruling for its time; in deference to the founder-commodoree it was agreed that annual general meetings would never be held on Friday nights. In the 1970s, Malcolm Alexander experienced no difficulty in joining the Howth Yacht Club. Election to the prestigious Royal Irish Yacht Club remained selective, but rejection was not always on religious grounds. A high level of support, especially from members of the club who belonged to the Judiciary, helped Malcolm to become its first Jewish member. In the early 1990s, he was appointed house chairman, and he became chairman of the club's Ten-Year Development Committee before he left Ireland in 1998. In 1994, he participated in the Irish National Sailing Championship for nine-metre Shipman class yachts. He won the two-day Wicklow event over four races by a margin of eight seconds.

Early Irish motor clubs also excluded Jews, until Nathan Lepler, affectionately known as Lep, changed the situation so dramatically that a picture of him wearing the presidential chain of office of the Royal Irish Automobile Club (RIAC) once graced their offices in Dawson Street. To Ann Stephens, secretary of the Leinster Motor Club, he was 'a seriously lovely man'; his long-time friend and associate, Dominic Murphy, described him as 'a gem of a person' and 'historic in motor sport in Ireland'. In 1986, a few years before his death at the age of eighty-nine, Lep told Dominic in recorded reminiscences that he was born in Russia and had come to Ireland during the First World War to visit an aunt and uncle. The outbreak of the Russian Revolution in 1917, the anti-Semitic situation he had left behind and pressure from his uncle all decided him to stay, and he became 'more Irish than the Irish themselves'. When his uncle died in 1918, Lep was only twenty-one, but he assumed full responsibility for his aunt and her family of three

Malcolm Alexander (Royal Irish Yacht club), Irish National Sailing Champion 1994, aboard his racing yacht in Dun Laoghaire harbour.

children under the age of ten. By 1919 he was participating in motor sport, but early victory in a motorcycle trial brought him no reward: the prize was withheld because he was a Jew. Determined to open motor sport to all faiths, he founded the Leinster Motor Cycle and Light Car Club, in conjunction with Sir Hugh Massey, in 1921. Though Saturday motor competitions were the norm, the Leinster Club held events on Sundays, with no detriment to its success. Now affiliated to the RIAC, it has become, in Dominic Murphy's opinion, 'the leading motor club in Ireland.'

Lep was a committee member continuously from its inception, serving as president on several occasions, including its fiftieth anniversary year, when he was awarded the club's Gold Insignia. In 1934, he introduced the Leinster Trophy Race for cars on the circuit of the Leinster 200 motorcycle race he had initiated in 1923. Now run at Mondello Park, Nass, it attracts drivers of international status such as world champions Mike Hawthorne from Britain, Ayrton Senna from Brazil and Mika Hakkinen from Finland, who have all been winners. A keen competitor into the 1950s when he contested the Monte Carlo Rally in a Jaguar, Lep officiated at every Leinster 200 and Trophy Race, even running a shuttle service in Killarney one Easter Sunday from the Circuit of Ireland offices to the cathedral so that competitors could attend early Mass. Accompanied over the years by a succession of poodles, each one named Swazie for its predecessor, he acted as club steward, started races, judged competitions and attended every meeting, always with 'something nice' in his car for general distribution. For Ann Stephens he brought bananas, because he mistakenly thought she liked them. During the Second World War he crossed the road to Griffith Barracks from his home on the South Circular Road to teach recruits to ride motorcycles.

In his eightieth year Lep was awarded the Ivan Webb Memorial Prize in recognition of his 'massive contribution to motor sport'. Other tributes, tangible and verbal, abounded. As far as Dominic Murphy is concerned, Lep *was* the Leinster Motor Club; but no one thinks more highly of him than Fanny Jackson, one of the Lepler cousins he helped to rear. Five years old when her father died, she remembers Lep taking her as a teenager to Wesley College in the sidecar of his Montgomery and the loving care he bestowed on all the family 'till the day he died'. When *Motorsport* printed an obituary, Michael O'Carroll summed up the general opinion of Nathan Lepler when he wrote, 'Motor sport has lost one of its endearing gentlemen.'

It was Nathan who introduced Jack Toohey to motor sport. In 1935/6, he won the Leinster Trophy on a 933cc Ford, scoring what *Motorsport* of 7 May 2002 referred to as 'his double winning success in the Leinster Trophy events over the Tallaght circuit'. Jack's reaction into his ninetieth year was, 'I enjoyed that!' In 1954, Jack founded the Trial Drivers' Club. Dominic Murphy, whose uncle's firm, Smithfield Motor Company, built Jack Toohey a 933cc Smithfield Special after his Leinster Trophy success, enjoyed many visits to Jack Toohey's Galway home, which had been designed by 'the man who built the *Titanic*'.

Another Jewish motor enthusiast was Cecil Vard, described by Dominic Murphy as 'a fabulous driver' and by his brother, Leslie Vard, as 'the finest in Ireland at that time.' He was still in his twenties when he entered the Monte Carlo Rally in 1951, its first Irish Jewish competitor. Driving his mother-in-law's new Mark V Jaguar, which Leslie ran in for him, and in competition with the 400 best drivers throughout Europe, he was placed overall third. Leslie was invited to be Cecil's co-driver, but he lacked the £100 necessary for travel expenses. In 1953, Cecil was placed fifth. Talented though he was, he never regarded motor sport as more than an enjoyable hobby and stopped competing at that level when the expenses of participation rose to thousands of pounds. In 1955, he became a founder-member and first president of Dublin Lions, the first of the Lions Clubs International to be established in Ireland. To celebrate the 25th anniversary of the charitable organization which caters for the elderly, Cecil suggested treating some of the old folks to a week's holiday at Butlin's Holiday Camp. The scheme proved so popular that it became a district project and about 1,200 old folk are still treated each year to a week's holiday. Leslie Vard, already an inter-provincial table-tennis champion, was also a car driver and won the all-Ireland Test Driver's Championship in 1969.

Jewish people interested in equestrian sports encountered no discrimination. Vicky Rose, *née* Cherrick, remembers riding her pony, Gentle June, as a youngster in the 1950s, alongside her sister Diana, the cousins Joan and Valerie Citron and Bernice Rivlin, the 'outstanding talent' among them, who later took a qualification to teach horse riding. The many senior riders included Vicky's parents, Gay Golding and Dr Bethel Solomons, who sometimes surprised patients by appearing at their bedside in hunting costume and was jocularly referred to as master of the Rotunda Harriers. Equestrianism was an expensive hobby. Stabling charges for horse-owners was £2 to £3 per week, and riders had to be correctly dressed. Callaghan's in Dame Street was a popular outfitter, but many patronised the Jewish tailor, Harry Bridburg, who made cavalry twill jodhpurs 'beautifully'.

Popular riding schools among the Jewish community were Iris Kellet's in Mespil Road and Colonel Dudgeon's in Stillorgan. The youngsters who rode every day in summer competed in gymkhanas at venues that included the Royal Dublin Society grounds, during the Spring and Horse Shows. Victories earned them rosettes and minor trophies; participation gave them the opportunity of seeing Ireland's best riders such as Iris Kellet on Rusty, Tommy Wade on Dundrum and rising stars like Paul Darragh and Eddie Macken. For Vicky Rose it was 'a great period of life'. She shared lessons with Charles Haughey, a future *Taoiseach*, went to a pony-club camp with Lady Nesta Fitzgerald, daughter of the Marquis of Kildare, and participated in a one-day event at the country estate of Lord and Lady Carew and their daughter, the Honourable Diana.

An introduction to hunting was usually affected through the South County Dublin Harriers, but some preferred a more stimulating quarry than the sack doused in aniseed used in drag-hunting or even a live hare. Michael Noyk's son, Billy, a solicitor and accomplished artist whose favourite subjects were women and horses, hunted with the best-known packs in the country, including Ward Union, Meath, South Co. Dublin, Bray Harriers and East Galway. Active in the All-Ireland Polo Club, he was a founder-member of the Goldburn Beagles and their chairman and master for twenty years. His role in the film, *Knights of the Round Table*, which demonstrated his excellent horsemanship, was perfect casting for the intrepid man who once suffered injury defending three ladies under attack from 'a group of bag-snatching thugs'.

Racing fascinated Professor Leonard Abrahamson. His son Muff recalled him as a careful gambler who studied form but still managed to back the wrong horse in the face of conflicting advice. He also owned racehorses. Vincent O'Brien trained his horse 'Oriental Way' and Fred Winter was the jockey when it rode in the Aintree Grand National in 1955. On the morning of the race the professor was unusually slow in dressing. When Mossy, who accompanied him to Aintree, asked, 'What's wrong?' his father, ever the optimist, replied, 'I can't decide what tie to wear in case I'm presented to the Queen when my horse wins.' David Vard, who spent his weekdays in Dublin as a furrier and his weekends at Loughtown Stud in Co. Meath, owned 'Archive', the sire of 'Arkle', the steeplechaser that made Irish racing history. His friend, the Aga Khan, visited him regularly at his Grafton Street premises.

Ian Vard, David's grandson, recalls the occasion when he came with his then wife, film star Rita Hayworth, and treated her to a voluminous mink coat. Vicky Rose's father, Wolfe Cherrick, trained racehorses and bred brood mares. He gave Pat Taffe, who rode Arkle to glory, his first professional ride and sold off in foal the brood mare that produced Team Spirit, another Grand National winner.

The *Jewish Chronicle* of 27 August 1920 names Harry Wigoder, founder of the Adelaide Football Club, as 'one of the best known figures in Irish Athletic circles'. He was in his shop one day when a group of local boys asked for a contribution to the door-to-door collection they were making to buy football jerseys for their team. He asked them to leave their collection box and return next day. When they called back, the box was gone, together with its contents of 1s 1½d; in its place were twelve new football jerseys and Harry readily accepted the boys' invitation to become president of their club. It was no isolated act of generosity. Some of the many players he encouraged became what Harry's father called 'first class', and Harry made sure they had 'good clothes and boots' when they played a big match in England. On one occasion he even took off his overcoat and put it round the shoulders of a newsboy who had 'no coat and no waistcoat'. The lad was trying to sell evening papers at Nelson's Pillar after ten o'clock at night. 'Comfort yourself in that,' Harry told him as he boarded his tram home.

Over the years Harry Wigoder became chairman of the Shelbourne Football Club, president of the Leinster Senior and Junior Football Associations and a member of the Irish Football Association, where he had the reputation of being a fine judge of a player. Always an athlete, he enjoyed early success by winning the Leinster Open Cycling Championship over the quarter mile and took a keen interest in golf and cricket. Known as 'a steady opening bat and a useful slow bowler', he captained both the Clontarf Cricket Club and the Railway and Steam Packet Union Cricket Club and helped to organise the *Tailtean* Games.

Two other veteran all-round sportsmen were Dr Louis Jacobson and Judge Hubert Wine. Dr Jacobson, entitled to wear the coveted 'pink' at Trinity College in the 1940s for his double colours for cricket and rugby, played cricket for Ireland more than a dozen times. In 1952, he played at Lord's cricket ground, London, and he was still in form more than forty years later when he became probably the oldest winner of the Captain's Prize at Edmondstown Golf Club. Hubert Wine, now in his late eighties, recalls with pride his participation in a wide variety of sports. In 1939, having successfully played for Ireland against England, he was selected as the first player to represent Ireland in a Table-tennis World Championship. His letter to the World Association explaining that he could not play on the Sabbath resulted in official permission to stop play before dusk on Friday and resume when the Sabbath was over. He had reached the fifth set of the Wembley quarter-finals with a score of 20-all when he tripped over one of the iron bars supporting the net. Its fall broke his leg, making further play impossible. When his Swedish opponent absolutely refused to take a walkover, Hubert instructed two men to assist him to the table so he could give him the two points needed for victory. He yielded one point by placing his hand on the table, a recognised foul, and the second by deliberate poor batting as two assistants held him upright. Honour was served and a Swedish victory declared.

In 1987, in a first for Ireland and possibly for world Jewry, Hubert Wine was unexpectedly approached with a request to hold the thirty-eighth annual ecumenical Gift of Sport service, traditionally held at St Patrick's Cathedral, Dublin, within the Jewish community. The event, which he organised jointly with Chief Rabbi Mirvis at Adelaide Road Synagogue, was televised by RTÉ, and he still remembers the thrill of being invited to deliver the main speech, 'The Gift of Sport', before the President of Ireland, the leaders of Church and State and a capacity congregation that overflowed into the street.

Ethel Elliman, Leslie Spivack and Martin Simmons, all fencing champions in their own class, represented Ireland at the 1961 Maccabiah; Pat Newman *née* Ruben, had successes in junior championship netball in the 1970s. Jonathan Kron, whose many other triumphs include the European Indoors Championship of 1995, set long-jump records for every age group, from under-thirteens to senior men's, and won the long-jump national title for five consecutive years from 1990, when he became World Junior Champion. Karen Eppel, a swimming teacher, became a Federation of International Hockey (FIH) umpire and officiated at fifty internationals representing Ireland and Europe in field hockey. She also officiated at two World Maccabia Games.

Appointed an International Umpires Manager by the European Hockey Federation (EHF), she also serves the (FIH) as a trainee FIH Umpires Manager; her duties include attendance at International Hockey Tournaments to appoint officiating umpires to matches, to assess and grade accordingly and to ensure they have uniform interpretation of the rules. Karen is also training to be an Automated External Defibrillator (AED) and a Cardiopulmonary Resuscitation (CPR) instructor.

Impressive results on the sports field did not preclude other leisure activities. One popular alternative was card playing. Aimed at sociability rather than gambling, games of poker, solo, whist, pontoon, bridge and rummy took place in almost every home. One pensioner has childhood memories from the 1940s of weekday rummy being played for ha'pennies at the family flat in Harrington Street. Ladies, all cousins, arrived immediately after lunch, and play continued until there was barely enough time to get home and prepare the evening meal they called 'tea'. The discarded packs of cards became playthings for the children. Within the more formal setting of the all-male Jewish Club in Harrington Street and the Jewish Institute in Belfast, as well as in privately arranged poker schools, stakes could be somewhat higher and serious money lost or won.

Bridge was also taken seriously by players north and south of the border. Many reached championship standard. Prominent among them are Don Seligman who played in the Olympiads and European championships and his wife, Barbara, a World Bridge Master who is mentioned in the *Encyclopaedia of Bridge*. Among the other gifted players were Dr Marcus Shrage, originally from Belfast, whom Don Seligman's mother, Esther, refused to consult professionally because his surgery was in Killester, and Monty Rosenberg, also from Belfast, who was once called to give evidence in court. When the judge, a keen bridge player, heard Monty describe himself as 'an antique dealer and bridge player', he set aside the legal enquiry to ask, 'What system do you play, Mr Rosenberg?' Dave Rivlin was also an antique dealer and bridge player. On one occasion he gave a book on bridge to his friend, Harry Fine, who played for Ireland at International level. Asked a few weeks later if he had found the book useful, Harry replied, 'Yes, it was. I've a table with a short leg and it's propping it up.'

The *Jewish Chronicle* of early to mid-February 1922 gives a cross-section of the many other social and cultural activities that would expand over the years. Weekly meetings of the Dublin Jewish Students' Union included a lecture on 'Jews in Modern Times' and a concert and tea at the Celtic Café two weeks later, for which Mr B. Lapedus kindly lent his gramophone. A musical programmeme presented to the Girls' Club by Mrs Schreider, together with the Misses Rubenstein, Gurevitch and Baigel, followed the reading of a paper on Heine by Mrs I. Briscoe. The Literary and Social Club debated with the Jewish Students' Union 'that the preservation of Yiddish is necessary'; Joshua Baker read a paper in Hebrew to *Pirchei Yehudah* on Josephus and advance notice was given of a *Talmud Torah* dance. In Belfast the Jewish Literary Society heard Mr L. Wigoder read a paper on wit and Cork announced the opening of its own Literary Society.

There was also the start of an extensive range of Zionist activities. The Women's Zionist Organisation in Ireland, believed to be the first WIZO in the British Isles, dates back to 1900 when, to quote Daphne Sieff of the Federation of Women Zionists in London, 'Zionism was unpopular, labourious and fraught with many disappointments.' A diamond jubilee brochure of 1960 claims its founders as Esther Barron, Dora Ginsburg and Rachel Nurock. Sheelagh Boland's *Short History of the Women's Zionist Movement in Ireland* attributes its foundation to Esther Morris and Tilly Berman. Either way, it was floundering when Rose Leventhal was elected its first president-cum-chairman in 1904. Described by Sheelagh Boland as 'a great Zionist who wrote verses and songs about returning to Zion,' she held the office for forty-four years, increasing the membership from a handful to hundreds and establishing a pattern of fund-raising for the welfare of women and children in Palestine. A letter of congratulations from Sarah Herzog, widow of the former Chief Rabbi, on the occasion of the diamond jubilee refers to Rose Leventhal as 'that grand old lady' and marvels at her 'vision that we would have our own State'. Her successor, Ethel Freedman, equally eulogised for her sustained efforts, inaugurated the annual WIZO concerts at the Gaiety Theatre, courtesy of Louis Elliman, who donated his theatre, equipment and staff for the occasion. Much if not all of the 'considerable sums' raised went to the Jerusalem Baby Home, founded in 1955. A favourite project with Dublin women Zionists, it incorporates a hospital and nurses' training school for Jews and Arabs.

Belfast WIZO began in 1902 with Rebecca Cohen collecting subscriptions of 1*d* per week door to door. Marriage to Pincus Eban and a sojourn in Edinburgh left her fledgling society in the hands of Edith Bogan, but the Ebans returned to Belfast. Rebecca 'devoted her life to Zionism', continuing to collect pennies, despite ailing health, 'in fair weather or foul, undaunted'. Her husband, equally ardent, was thoroughly displeased when her successor as president, Alice Samuels, chose to attend her own engagement party instead of chairing a Zionist meeting scheduled for the same night.

Bertha Weingreen's arrival in 1934 added a new dimension to Zionism in Ireland. A member of the Young Israel Society in South Africa, she started Ziona groups north and south of the border to capture the interest of the adult daughters of the aging Daughters of Zion. The Belfast group declined when the Jewish Community dispersed after the Blitz of 1940 but once people began drifting back, she travelled from Dublin to re-establish Belfast Ziona, which continued successfully as a fund-raising activity. Dublin Ziona, with Bertha Weingreen in the chair until 1941, was cultural as well as fund-raising and continued to prosper. Three of its most successful fund-raisers were an annual dance held jointly with the Jewish Medical Society, an annual all-day fair and the Ziona Follies, a 'mirth-raising parody' organised by Lily Fine. In recent years Dublin Ziona was chaired by the dedicated and able Beth Eppel, who proved to be irreplaceable. While she fought in 1998 to recover from an illness that later claimed her life, Ziona closed. Over the years, branches of other Zionist groups such as Young WIZO, *Huldah* and *Hadassah*, flourished in Ireland until membership fell away through ageing, apathy and emigration.

Male Zionist fund-raising was concentrated in the Jewish National Fund (JNF), a worldwide organisation that encouraged every Jewish household to contribute to a 'Blue Box' bearing the slogan 'A penny a day is the JNF way'. Emptied regularly by volunteer collectors, the Blue Boxes netted substantial amounts from regular offerings, *simcha* donations and a percentage of the kitty when card games were played. From 1948 its biggest fund-raiser and social event was the Blue and White Ball, held for the first time at the Metropole and afterwards either there or at the Shelbourne Hotel. Comprising dinner, cabaret and dancing, it featured the most popular stage and radio entertainers of the day and crowned a Blue and White Queen, chosen from young representatives of the different Jewish societies. Esther Kahan was JNF secretary for thirty years until her retirement in 1985.

Both Cork and Belfast had Jewish youth groups in the 1950s, and Dublin abounded with youth organisations. *Torah V'Avodah* (1927), *Habonim* (1929), *Tifereth Bachurim* (1937), a Youth Section of the JNF (1941) and *Bnei Akivah* (1945) all promoted greater Jewish awareness through education and social activity. *Hechalutz* founded in 1954 and somewhat short-lived, prepared young pioneers for settlement in Israel. There was also a flourishing Scout and Guide movement.

The Scout Troop registered in 1925 as the 16th Dublin (Jewish) Troop began life as the 1st City (Commissioner's Own) Troop in the garage of 6 Leinster Road, home of Harry and Millie Marks, whose sons, Nathan and Benny, were founder-members. Formed at the suggestion of Norman Jackson and Henry Simons on the arrival of a warranted Jewish scoutmaster from London, it was nicknamed Jackson's Troop. The scoutmaster, George Morris, gave it the London troop colours of blue and gold to avoid the expense of buying a second scarf. Meetings were moved from the garage to the kitchen on the excellent behavior of the boys and from there to the Adelaide Road schoolrooms. From 1934 they were held at Zion Schools.

In 1929, George Morris and the two Marks boys attended their first jamboree, the only three Jewish scouts among the more than 200 who assembled that year at Birkenhead, Cheshire. In 1938, the troop enjoyed a two-week summer camp in Jersey, at a cost of £5 per head, which included the journey by sea. A Jewish resident who took the opportunity of praying with them to recite memorial prayers expressed his gratitude by treating the boys to a aeroplane flight, then a rare and exciting experience. There would be later jamborees and scouting trips to the Channel Islands, the Isle of Man, Britain, Holland, France, Greece and Hungary; but Powerscourt Demesne in Co. Wicklow became the regular camping site by kind permission of Lord Powerscourt. A newly formed Rovers' Crew heaved rocks out of the river to provide clean water and erected a serviceable hut out of logs cut from blown-down trees and dragged to the site. They raised the £14 10s needed for the wooden roof by subscribing 6d each per week. Much of the donkey work was supervised by Joseph Levy (Joe Jay) who became a national commissioner of Boy Scouts. In 1975, he was awarded the Order of the Silver Shamrock for his 'outstanding efforts' on behalf of the Scouting movement in Ireland.

The guiding force behind Dublin's Scouting success was Maurie Gordon, who arrived in Dublin from the United States in 1930. He quickly became assistant scoutmaster and then scoutmaster in 1936 when George Morris was promoted to group scoutmaster. Maurie's American Scouting experience, combined with a natural talent for leadership, spurred the boys into 'their highest level ever of proficiency'. A keen promoter of sport in general and swimming in particular, he set his troop an excellent example when he rescued a drowning woman from the River Liffey in 1944. The Scouting Association awarded him a silver medal for gallantry. In 1961, he received a second medal 'in recognition of his long and outstanding service to Scouting', and in 1973 a bronze medal marked his fiftieth year in scouting. Believed to be the longest serving Jewish scout in the world, he was group scoutmaster of the 16th Troop when he retired in 1989. They held a special Sabbath service for him at Adelaide Road Synagogue, and Eoghan Lavelle, Chief Scout of Ireland, presented him with the Silver Elk, the highest award in Irish Scouting, at a tribute dinner. His sixty-five years of service were further marked by the dedication of a woodland area of Tymon Park in the South Dublin Scout District and a plantation of trees in Israel.

In 1932, a Cub Pack was formed in the Assembly Rooms of Adelaide Road Synagogue under a Mrs Douglas, assisted by Hymie Danker. The first two cubs enrolled were Ralph Morris and Barney Stein. The 23rd Dublin (1st Jewish) Girl

Guide Company started in 1925 under Bertha Good, Herman Good's sister. The 24th Dublin (2nd Jewish) followed in 1932. Amalgamated in 1973 into Terenure Company, it closed in 1986. Myrna Elliott, *née* Winton, reopened it a year later and remained its captain until, grouped with Highfield and Rathgar, it disbanded in 1996. Brownies followed a similar path. The 23rd (1st Jewish) and 24th (2nd Jewish), originally under Ruth Glass and Golda Gruson, amalgamated in 1966 and closed in 1968. Barbara Cantor, *née* Milofsky, revived them as Terenure Pack in 1972 and was Brown Owl until its closure in 2001. Bertha Weingreen, a girl guide in South Africa, became guide commissioner of the Jewish Rangers she formed in 1940.

In 1973, Estelle Feldman was one of two Irish girls chosen to represent Ireland at an international 'round up' of guides in Idaho, USA. Her mother, Elaine Feldman, responded so efficiently to the request of the then guide commissioner, Mrs Beatty, for new summer uniforms that she was invited to join as a district commissioner. Long after she retired as controller of the distribution centre at Guide Headquarters, her continued help once or twice a week qualified her as one of the oldest active guides in the world.

There was no Jewish Guide movement in Dublin in the early 1920s when young Jennie Rubenstein, later known to everyone as Jennie Z., tried unsuccessfully to join the all-Protestant St Ann's Company. She settled perforce for the Woodcrafter League of Chivalry, an American youth group that attracted many other Jewish youngsters of the time. Born in Dublin to immigrant parents, Jennie Z. left Wesley College to become a professional violinist under the tutelage of her brother, Dr Jack Robinson. She played in the Phoenix Cinema on the quays, at 'hops' in Greenville Hall, and at formal dances, concerts and *céilithe*. She was still young and single when she gave up professional music to work for her solicitor brother-in-law. 'Study law,' he advised her and eventually she did. In 1969, already distinguished as Irish Jewry's first woman peace commissioner, she became the first grandmother to be called to the Irish bar.

Even among the erudite, committed women in Ireland who immersed themselves in communal and Zionist affairs, Jennie Z. was noticeably active. Early training in the Jewish Debating Society, modelled on the Solicitors' Apprentices' Debating Society, earned her gold medals for both oratory and impromptu speaking; she proposed, seconded or participated in almost every debate. In 1936, on the recommendation of Rabbi Herzog, she was selected from women all over Ireland and Britain for the award of an *Aishit Chayil* (Woman of Worth) Scholarship, which financed her first trip to Palestine. The telegram informing her of the award misprinted the English translation as 'Woman of Work', an unintentionally apt description for this very busy lady. As well as travelling to promote Zionism, she was president, vice-president or active committee member of a range of organisations including Young *Mizrachi*, the Jewish Debating Society, the Ancient Order of Maccabeans, the Hebrew Speaking Circle, *B'nei B'rith*, the Jewish National Fund, the Jewish Home of Ireland and the Irish-Israel Friendship

League. She was the first woman president of the Jewish Students' Union, a member of the international committee of the Irish Housewives' Association, an invited observer at the assembly of the World Council of Churches in York and the founder of the Child Resettlement Fund aimed at helping displaced or disadvantaged children who had made their home in Israel. A popular lecturer and sometime contributor to the magazine *Young Zionist*, the one thing she never found time to do was practise law.

Until affluence and tour companies directed holidaymakers towards Benidorm and Majorca, the favourite holiday venue of Irish Jews was Bray, Co. Wicklow. The poorest of Jewish families managed day trips by train from Harcourt Street station; the better off stayed for all or part of the summer season, with husbands and sometimes older schoolchildren commuting each weekday. Doris Waterman remembered Clanbrassil Street urchins putting their heads around the shop door to shout, 'Give us back Bray and we'll give you back Jerusalem!' – a message repeated as graffiti on the railway bridge as the train entered Bray.

Joseph Vilensky, Dr Millie Luxenberg's brother, was staying at Rubinstein's Kosher Hotel in Bray when American guests heard him sing. Enthralled by the youngster's fine tenor voice, they offered his family 'money for life' if he would accompany them to Hollywood for a singing career. 'I don't sell my child,' his mother told them. Joseph, who loved singing, was disappointed. When he became a doctor he sang between patients as well as for charity and on RTÉ.

Some families stayed in a kosher guesthouse, where a 7 a.m. *minyan* finished in good time for men to catch the 7.55 train to Harcourt Street. Gerry Tolkin from his home in Canada remembered the morning when they were one man short, and three of the group raced across the promenade to bring back a regular early-morning swimmer as the tenth man. Misconstruing their shouts and gestures as a form of greeting, their friend waved back from the sea. A resident out walking his dog misinterpreted the entire situation. Thinking the swimmer was drowning and his friends trying to raise the alarm, he jumped into the water fully clothed to rescue the man who frantically fought the 'madman' he thought was attacking him.

Minyan facilities were also available at the home of Jennie Z. and her husband, auctioneer Gerald Gilbert, at 5 Newgrange Park, Meath Road. Their daughter Ruth Bernstein, who went to live in London, remembered playing with the Abrahamson children 'right across the street'. She also remembered going to the station every week to collect the *Shabbat* chicken, sent by train from Clanbrassil Street in a brown paper parcel. Bessel Cohen, *née* Deitch, also recalls the family meat supplies arriving by train but theirs came in the suitcase her grandmother took empty to Dublin and brought back full.

Those staying in rented seaside houses loaded utensils, food and even furniture into vehicles as if, remembers Jeanne Silver in San Diego, 'they were going to Siberia instead of twelve miles away.' Her father, Eddie Barron, used to fill the lorry belonging to Toohey's, the family furniture business on Bachelor's Walk. Syd Barnett, when he managed Clein's bakery, took the back seats out of his car to make extra room for all the *challahs*, *bagels* and other products he was bringing out to Bray.

A favourite treat of Bray holidays were knickerbocker glories, luscious confections of ice cream, fruit and fresh cream served in every ice-cream parlour. Allan Freedman now in Canada, considered himself lucky if an indulgent aunt or uncle bought him one knickerbocker glory per year. Another Bray delight was Dawson's Arcade, with its dodgem cars, slot machines and other gambling devices. Though Frank Baigel remembers 'the joy of getting two strawberries in a row and getting 2*d* back,' most punters came out poorer than they went in. The exceptions were eight-year-old Bessel Deitch and her twelve-year-old sister, Marlene, whose penny stakes, rolling down a slot towards losing lines, were often pushed to winning numbers by Cathy Dawson, the arcade-owner's daughter. Other Bray pleasures came free as Dublin visitors stood to watch the afternoon open-air entertainment, ignoring both the deckchairs offered at 3*d* each and the basket passed around for voluntary contributions. The Coons sang, juggled, told jokes and made magic; an amateur talent spot offered audience participation. It was Bessel's and Marlene's enthusiastic applause when Cathy Dawson appeared that earned them their bonanza in the arcade.

Most Jewish communities in Ireland were too small to be self-sustaining in recreational pursuits. Dublin, because of its wider range, could have been, had the activities been fully supported, but many preferred to sample the pleasures of the wider community. Even active participants could find Irish-Jewish recreational life stifling, and some longed for the privacy and anonymity in personal relationships available only in wider environments. Others look back with nostalgia at the vibrant, active lifestyle they once enjoyed within a community so close-knit that friends were often indistinguishable from family.

11

PRESENT AND FUTURE

Anyone wishing to meet a microcosm of Irish Jewry in the first decade of the twenty-first century would still turn to Dublin but they would find no Jews in Clanbrassil Street and few enough at the two remaining Orthodox synagogues. Sabbath services at Terenure Synagogue might average about 100 people; at *Machzikei Hadass* there might barely be the ten required for a *minyan*. The best place to discover Irish Jewry now is at the Irish Jewish Museum in Walworth Road although even that experience has been diminished by the untimely death in 2008 of its curator, Raphael Siev, the 'retired' international lawyer whose guided tours and encyclopedic knowledge provided a fascinating insight into Irish–Jewish history.

Raphael Siev's association with Walworth Road was lifelong, dating back to when the building was a synagogue. His father, Albert Siev, the last of his generation to be associated with it, was central to the disagreement that arose regarding its assets when Walworth Road Synagogue closed in 1970 and passed into the hands of trustees. The Rep Council wanted the building sold to defray some of the community's debts, as had happened when Lombard Street Synagogue closed; Albert Siev wanted the proceeds used for another community asset, preferably a new *mikvah*, though he had no objection to Raphael's alternative suggestion of an Irish Jewish Museum.

Asher Benson had been thinking of such an establishment since 1978. Born in London, he was at an *Habonim* camp in Bedford before the outbreak of war in 1939 when he met Ida Silverman from Drogheda, one of the contingent of Irish *Habonim*. The correspondence they began lasted throughout his military service and culminated with their marriage in 1946. The couple settled in Dublin where Asher immediately involved himself in community affairs by sub-editing *Nachlat Dublin* with Maurice Fridberg and helping Asher Green reconstitute

Dublin *Habonim*. From 1979 to 1997 he was also Irish correspondent of the *Jewish Chronicle*. In 1978, he accepted a challenge to prove his hypothesis that the community had enough historical material for an exhibition. A few months later, '100 Years of Irish-Jewish Life' opened in the Dr Leslie Golding Hall to such enthusiasm that Asher went on collecting exhibits, storing his growing collection in a room above the vestry of Adelaide Road Synagogue and in other diverse places.

When Albert Siev died in 1982, the future of Walworth Road Synagogue was still unresolved; no *mikvah* had been built, and Asher Benson's collection still had no permanent home. Rabbi Rosen brought a Rabbi Posen from England to advise on the feasibility of erecting a *mikvah* and museum in a joint building in the grounds of Terenure Synagogue. The visiting rabbi suggested putting the ritual baths on the ground floor and the museum above it. Keeping a straight face, Asher asked if it would be possible to make the floor of glass. With equal sobriety, Rabbi Posen replied, 'I don't think that would be practical.' The plan was never implemented.

In 1984, a Museum Committee was formed, with Dr Gerry Tolkin as chairman and Asher Siev as vice-chairman. The trustees offered the committee a licence to use Walworth Road Synagogue for an Irish Jewish museum. Little more than a dilapidated shell, the building needed refurbishment from the roof down, plus the installation of masking lights and a burglar alarm. Through the good offices of Ruairí Quinn TD, then Minister for Labour, young people from AnCO (now *FÁS*), the Government training scheme, worked on it free of charge as part of their work experience. They painted the area, catalogued the material and even restored the Hebrew script around the Ark. Restoration was still in progress when journalists in Europe, Israel and the United States started taking an interest and unusual artifacts and information began trickling in. Declan McSweeney wrote of two Jewish families in Tullamore in the 1930s; Jimmy Dalton sent the business cards and pictures he had found in an old shoe-box relating to the taxi service Joe Mirrelson had operated from the 1920s at the rear of his home at 25 Dufferin Avenue. Sir Alfred Beit from his home at Russborough, Co. Wicklow, sent a donation, claiming his paternal grandparents were Jewish, and expressing 'the greatest respect for Jewry and admiration for its remarkable achievements.' The official opening of the museum by Chaim Herzog, President of Israel, was marked by the Irish Philatelic Service of *An Post* with a commemorative handstamp. Featuring a harp within a Star of David, it bore the words 'Irish Jewish Museum, Baile Átha Cliath, 20 June 1985', and was applied to all letters placed in the special post-box sited there for that day. In 1986, Jack Resten fitted its first showcases, with the help of a grant from *Bord Fáilte* (the Tourist Board).

With Asher Benson as its first curator and staffed entirely by volunteers, the museum, which incorporates an historic kosher kitchen, attracted 1,800 visitors from twenty-five countries in its first year. By 1988 it had become what *Bord Failte* described as a 'great attraction for foreign tourists', thanks to the generous intervention of an American philanthropist. Harold Smerling, who grew up in Brooklyn 'among the Irish', had already planted lines of trees outside St Patrick's Cathedral in New York. He now donated $21,000 dollars to the Irish-American Fund for the development of the Ladies' Gallery in the former Walworth Road Synagogue. His private gift to the museum was a portrait of Chaim Herzog by the French artist René Bouchara.

An excellent cultural venue for small gatherings, the museum has hosted many functions of Jewish and general interest, encompassing musical evenings, debates, receptions, lectures and even weddings, as well as special exhibitions. On-going internal improvements have made the displays increasingly attractive, and a growing number of visitors of all faiths, from home and abroad, regard it as essential viewing. 8,500 signed the visitors' book in 2002. Some are meeting Jews for the first time; some are expatriates in search of their forefathers; a few, including a South African writer, are descendents of the families that once resided on the museum premises or officiated at Walworth Road Synagogue services.

A Japanese professor and expert on James Joyce regards his regular trips as a kind of pilgrimage; many, like the Nobel Laureate who ended his visit by putting on *tefillin* for the first time since his *Bar Mitzvah*, find it an incredibly rewarding experience.

Other than the nominal charge made to groups for an informative guided tour, there is no entrance fee, but voluntary contributions are welcome; donations, letters of appreciation and artifacts frequently arrive after visitors have returned home. Gentile contributions have included documents detailing the British apprehension of migrant ships carrying Jews to Palestine in 1946-7 and a jar of fat, verified as human, that the donor claimed he was forced to melt down in a Nazi labour camp. Limited in display area and sorely in need of improved archival facilities, the museum could be greatly enhanced by expansion and plans to extend it are in progress. At an estimated cost that has already risen from €5 million to €10 million three adjoining houses could be incorporated to transform it into a complex with more exhibition space, a research room, library, sales area, restaurant and audio-visual facilities. Raphael Siev was confident the money would be raised once planning permission was granted.

The Irish Jewish Museum is now run by a management committee. Yvonne Altman O'Connor is one of the ten committed people, Jewish and Gentile, who organise volunteers, schedule school visits, help with research, escort visitors and generally maintain the facility at the high standard set by its late curator. Though proud of her own Jewish ancestry, Yvonne first learned about Judaism while attending college in the United States. Teaching in a Jewish school enhanced her knowledge and her association with Raphael Siev encouraged her to take an active part in preserving the history of Irish Jewry. Under the chairmanship of Moti Neuman and with Debbie Briscoe and Asher Siev as life presidents, the

Irish Jewish Museum remains one of Jewish Ireland's greatest assets and well entitled to its description in the *Jewish Chronicle* in 1988 as an 'oasis of growth in a declining community'.

That the community was declining was irrefutable. Irish Census figures show reductions of 16.7 per cent from 1946 to 1961, 19.1 per cent from 1961 to 1971, 19.2 per cent from 1971 to 1981 and 25.7 per cent from 1981 to 1991. By 2002, when returns showed fewer than 1,800 Jews in Ireland, Judaism on the Census form had become a faith to be entered under 'other religious minorities'. The fall in Jewish population after the Second World War was not unique to Ireland, but so steep a rate of decline from the mid-1940s in a land free from overt anti-Semitism gives rise to some speculation regarding the catalyst.

Rathnait Long in an essay, 'A Question of Survival: The Jewish Community in Cork,' attributes Cork's decline to over-assimilation, a charge that could equally apply elsewhere in Ireland as a growing number of Jews strove to emulate their Christian neighbours. Larry Tye in *Homelands* (2001) points to conflicting loyalties between Ireland and Israel, with Ireland often the loser. Ronit Lentin's study for *Ireland's Other Diaspora: Jewish-Irish Within, Irish-Jewish Without* yielded other possible causes. Fay Meltzer in America saw Ireland as nothing more than an 'accidental landing point' for Russian emigrants, a 'way station' for families making a home elsewhere. Another considered that 'diasporicity was programmemed into young Irish Jews since childhood'. Michael Roddy in a Reuters article of 6 March 2003 suggested 'muted anti-Semitism' as the root cause, citing a spin-off from Ireland's dismal response to Jewish immigration in the Nazi era and the difficulty some Jewish doctors experienced in obtaining bed allocations in Catholic or state-owned hospitals.

Many Jews left Ireland to secure their Jewish identity in larger or more Observant communities; others simply followed the traditional Irish pattern of seeking their fortune elsewhere. Successive local newssheets blamed the accelerating exodus on the mismanagement of community affairs, pointing specifically to the general lack of consensus on every issue of communal importance and the cavalier attitude of ruling elders towards the youth of the community. As early as 7 December 1968, community inaction spurred *Chadashot* to protest, 'Had the leaders embarked on a deliberate policy of extinction of the Dublin Jewish community, they could not have been more effective.' The *DJN* of June 1984 headlined its issue 'Community in Crisis' and described the initial process of selecting a successor to Rabbi Rosen as 'inept'. The spring 1996 edition of the *Jewish Voice* spoke of 'lost opportunities' and 'a community that buried its head in the sand and allowed fundamentalists to have their way'. Its last issue, in spring 1997, noted no change through its five years of publication in the attitude of the Representative Council towards the youth, the unification of Adelaide Road and Terenure Synagogues, or their own accountability.

Depletion of the Jewish populations in Belfast and Cork had left spiritual
guidance in the hands of reverends or lay leaders. To avoid a similar situation
developing in Dublin after Rabbi Mirvis left in 1992, Rabbi V. Silverman visited
periodically from London, pending the appointment of a new Chief Rabbi,
whose main challenge, in the opinion of the *Jewish Chronicle* of 8 May 1992,
would be maintaining an 'infrastructure that would make considerably larger
communities envious'. Carol Golding, *née* Elliot, a member of a sub-committee
of the Rep Council, placed the emphasis elsewhere: for her it was 'absolutely
essential that the appointee ... make life so Jewishly attractive that people will
want to stay on after college.'

Rabbi Simon Harris was appointed in 1993. In his Jewish New Year broadcast
two months after his arrival in Ireland he said he was 'struck by its natural
beauty and by the open-heartedness, friendliness and warmth of its citizens.'
In an interview with Natalie Wynn for *The Jewish Voice* he described the Jewish
community as 'very warm, good, solid, traditional' and said he had never before
felt 'so invigorated and fulfilled.' He told Fiona Kelly in an interview in the *Irish
Press* on 5 December 1993 that his exhaustion at the end of an eighteen-hour
working day was 'a testament to the vitality of the community'.

Now living in Britain, Rabbi Harris prefers not to discuss the reasons why he
left Ireland inside a year, even before his induction. An independent and forward
thinker, he went against British rabbinical trend when he agreed to meet the
Palestinian president, Yasser Arrafat, on a visit to Britain and Ireland. Accompanied
by Martin Simmons, Alan Benson and Joe Briscoe, then respectively chairman,
secretary and head of the Public Affairs committee of the Rep Council, the rabbi
shook hands with Arafat and referred to the historic meeting as one 'between
brothers ... Jews and Arabs.'

More controversial in Dublin was his attitude to religious practice. Denying
he was a diehard conservative, he nonetheless considered 'the raising of higher
moral principles to be the job of the clergy' and advocated a return to strict
Orthodoxy, a prospect as unpalatable to some non-conformist members of
Orthodox synagogues as to the Progressives, whom he vainly advised to 'rejoin
their co-religionists in common prayer.' Favouring 'a thorough investigation of
every aspect of organised religious life in Ireland,' he instigated an examination
by the London *Beth Din* of all basic products regarded in Ireland as kosher. When
Dublin's ritual slaughter methods were declared unsatisfactory, Irish Jewry was
left with no supply of fresh kosher meat. It would lose its supply of fresh kosher
fowl when Ireland had neither *shochet* nor kosher butcher shop. The unused hen
house, opened with such pride in the 1950s, fell into total disrepair.

The rabbi's views on the future of the Dublin community were equally
unpopular. He advised the sale of both large synagogues, along with every other
saleable community asset, to finance 'an American-style community centre' and
the visits of 'leading Jewish thinkers and personalities' from throughout Europe,

who would attract a following to our shores. With smallness the current trend in the establishment of Modern-Orthodox communities in Britain and America, Dublin's depletion was not an obstacle. 'The action could be here,' he concluded. 'Let's do it while we can reap the benefits.' Nothing was done.

Rabbi Silverman returned to fill the breach until 1996, when Rabbi Gavin Broder was inducted as the next Chief Rabbi of Ireland. His wife, Daniella Broder, *née* Frankelstein, had Irish connections through great-grandparents who are buried in Dublin, grandparents who had lived in Lombard Street, and a Dublin-born mother who had graduated from Trinity College. Rabbi Broder was born in South Africa in 1963 and educated in Johannesburg and New Zealand, where his father held rabbinical posts. When a call brought his father to England, Gavin attended Gateshead Yeshiva and Jews' College. He was rabbi at Newbury Park in Ilford, Essex, when he received the call to Ireland. 'How did you get to be Chief Rabbi of Ireland?' Gay Byrne asked in an interview on *The Late Late Show* soon after his arrival. He jokingly replied, 'I was the only candidate.' In fact, his interest in the post began with an approach from the Rep Council. He knew before he came that it encompassed multi-faceted communal duties as well as a diplomatic role, but he was not prepared for what he describes as 'the force of the disagreements between individuals.' Despite agreeing with Rabbi Mirvis's contention that communal discord was limited to synagogue closure, he still found the community 'polarised within its own *shuls*,' with little or no inter-congregational contact.

A major setback to the community was the rabbi's declaration in 1997 that cakes supplied by Bretzel, Dublin's only supplier of supervised bread and patisserie since 1964, contained certain non-permitted ingredients and could no longer be regarded as kosher. When permitted substitutes suggested by the rabbi were tried and rejected by the bakery, Bretzel bread was also proscribed, and it was mutually agreed that an alternative kosher supplier should be found. Connolly's was a smaller bakery with no retail outlet of its own. Its chief baker had made *challahs*, bagels and doughnuts in a kosher bakery in London and willingly complied with Jewish requirements, but the new arrangement had little community appeal. Connolly's bread was of a different texture and its selection of cakes limited. Unless someone brought supplies from London or Manchester, kosher households requiring greater variety had to bake or do without. 'Sorry I've no cake,' became a common apology to the unexpected visitor, and many blamed the rabbi. Some still blame him for encouraging the departure of the many families with young children who emigrated during his rabbinate. Rabbi Broder concedes that he told one couple they were doing the right thing in leaving but feels their decision had been made before he was consulted. He denies giving unsolicited advice or ever influencing anyone's judgment.

Powerless to stem the tide of emigration, he suggested the establishment in Dublin of a community *kollel*, a centre for possibly ten religious couples who would study *Torah* by day and pass on their learning to the general community through social and cultural programmemes. Such a scheme had helped revitalise other dying communities, and a sub-committee of the Rep Council was formed 'to evaluate the relative merits of establishing a *kollel* in Dublin'. Carl Nelkin's report of May 1999 rejected the viability of such a scheme. Expensive both to implement and maintain, even its long-term benefits would be uncertain. In the short-term its only result might be a new antagonism within the community between the non-Observant locals and the ultra-Orthodox members of the *kollel*. The suggestion might be 'revisited' at a later date but a 'professional communal worker' was seen as the best immediate strategy.

One of Rabbi Broder's achievements was bringing Irish kosher certification of supervised products to standards of international acceptability through closer links with the London *Beth Din*. Coca-Cola was one of many firms that began exporting Irish-made kosher products worldwide. The caramel for Coca-Cola was brought from America to Ireland, mixed locally with concentrates, shipped on to Israel for bottling, and re-exported back to Europe, certified 'Kosher for Passover'. *Kashering* plants and supervising production became a growing part of the rabbi's work.

To improve the standard of religious teaching in Stratford Schools, Rabbi Broder began discussions with the Department of Education towards updating the syllabus and introduced the first formalised curriculum into Stratford National School. For a time he brought youth leaders from England once a fortnight to take morning service and provide an afternoon social programmeme for children on *Shabbat*, even offering to find half the funds when the Rep Council demurred about the cost. He brought the youth leaders again for *Simchat Torah* to engender the traditional spirit of liveliness into the occasion, but he could not provide the sustained educational and social environment needed for the strict Orthodox upbringing of his own four sons.

In addition to holding a ladies' study group at her home and preparing eligible girls for *Bat Chayil*, Daniella Broder spent much of her time advising women who consulted her; many of her confidantes remain good friends and some still phone for advice. The Broders enjoyed their time in Ireland and regard their stay as 'fruitful', but despite its diplomatic functions, scenic beauty and the warmth of the Irish people, Danielle, especially, became anxious to leave. For the sake of their children, they moved to London in 2000, a year before the rabbi's contract became subject to renewal. The local priest who had greeted him on arrival with letters read aloud in church, brought a parting gift and the Broders took away many fond memories. Asked now what he misses most about Ireland, Rabbi Broder smiles wistfully and answers, 'I can tell you in one word. Everything!'

In May 2001, Baila Erhlich's shop in Clanbrassil Street closed for the last time. Administered by the Rep Council and run by the staff that had worked for Baile, trading continued after her death, but the substantial losses incurred could not be sustained indefinitely. Following approaches from the Rep Council, David Brown, proprietor of the Big Cheese Company, agreed to stock kosher products in his Trinity Street shop. With foot-and-mouth disease prohibiting the importation of fresh or frozen meat products from Britain, David imported meat and fowl from France and a small variety of kosher grocery items from Paris or Manchester, but the arrangement was highly criticised. The prices, the limited range of goods and the quality or size of the French imports all became subject to comment; but the real crux was location. No one wanted to shop in the city centre for everyday commodities: the community wanted a specifically kosher shop in Terenure. So did David Brown, but his suggestion of a kosher coffee shop cum grocery in the Terenure area was rejected by the Rep Council as impossible to supervise in the absence of a Chief Rabbi. In a gesture of compromise, he arranged for SuperValu, a supermarket in Churchtown, to carry some kosher products, directly imported from Manchester and London under the aegis of a sub-committee of the Rep Council. Its location was acceptably convenient, but the prices were higher again than in town, and the range even more limited. Filling the larder with kosher food had become an obstacle course that those on the periphery of Orthodox practice were not prepared to negotiate.

The feeling of apathy and resignation permeating the 1,000 or so Jews who still remained in Dublin, many too elderly to care, made almost believable Geoffrey D. Paul's prophecy in 'Jews in the Emerald Isle' in the colour supplement of the *Jewish Chronicle*, 9 June 1979 that 'all will be in the cemetery within two or three decades'. Paul Gallaher's portent in 'The New Exodus – Irish Style' in the *Irish Times* of 16 June 1994 was equally defeatist. He wrote, 'Ireland's once vibrant Jewish community now appears to be in irredeemable decline.' Young people he interviewed agreed with him. Daniel Miller, president of the Jewish Students' Union in Ireland, reduced to only twenty members, spoke of an 'atrophied future'. The *Jewish Voice* in its closing issue criticised 'the lack of motivation among the young members of the community who have the ability but not the interest to keep our voice alive.'

The twentieth century closed with the situation unchanged. Friends and relatives were still departing; communal assets were being sold off; long-established organisations were defunct. Dublin had no rabbi, no satisfactory kosher shopping facilities and no universally accepted plan for its future.

Though scarcely recognised as such at the time, the arrival in 2000 of Rabbi Zalman Lent and his wife, Rifky Lent, *née* Loewenthal, was the first chink of light in the 'doom and gloom' that Howard Gross acknowledged as 'the norm within the Dublin Jewish community' in his editorial for the *Irish Jewish Year Book* 2000-1. Born in 1974 in Reading where his father was teaching at Carmel College, a Jewish boarding-school, Rabbi Lent grew up and was educated in Manchester. *Yeshiva* training brought him to Montreal, Melbourne and New York, where he and Ricky were living with their baby daughter when he heard that the Dublin

Jewish community was seeking a community programmemer, primarily for its youth.

Rabbi Lent is part of the *Chabad-Lubavitch* movement, begun in Eastern Europe two centuries ago. Founded with the goal of communicating Jewish spiritualism and values, it has 2,500 centres worldwide and is the largest Jewish outreach and educational organisation in the world. As its official representative in Ireland, Rabbi Lent combines his youth programmeming and communal responsibilities with outreach work to the unaffiliated members of the wider Jewish community – the key, he firmly believes, to its sustained growth. Another aspect of his work entails welcoming and frequently entertaining Jewish visitors to Dublin, irrespective of their nationality, degree of Orthodoxy or length of stay. A Sabbath table laid for twelve or more guests is commonplace in the Lent household. He has been instrumental in having the now defunct Jewish Home of Ireland converted into two student houses, one male, one female, to help newcomers adjust more quickly to both Jewish student and Jewish community life. In 2003, he officially assumed the additional duties of communal rabbi and has recently been appointed rabbi to Terenure Synagogue.

Rabbi Lent's regular activities for the comparatively few Jewish children left in Dublin include a children's service on Saturday mornings for the under-tens in

Rabbi Zalman Lent with President Mary McAleese and her husband, Dr Martin McAleese, at Áras an Uchteráin following an inter-faith meeting at Farmleigh House (April 2008).

the foyer of the Samuel Taca Hall, which he was instrumental in having attractively renovated, and an annual summer camp. The Lents also organise social activities for children and special community events to mark religious Festivals, which additionally attract a number of short-term residents and those families who normally socialise outside the community. A children's *Purim* Fancy Dress competition in the Samuel Taca Hall can have up to seventy entries, while imaginative carnivals, displays of magic or fire-eating, communal *menorah* lighting and other 'get-togethers' periodically engender a welcome spirit of fun into young and old.

Rabbi Yaakov Pearlman arrived from America in September 2001 and was inducted as Ireland's eighth Chief Rabbi on 30 January 2002. Born and educated in Manchester, he was the youngest rabbi in England in his year to receive *Semicha* (rabbinical ordination). Shortly afterwards he moved to Lakewood, New Jersey, where he embarked on higher Jewish learning and began the secular studies that would lead to an MA in Jewish History and applied human relations and a PhD in Educational Administration. He was rabbi to a community in Rochester, New York, and Jewish chaplain to both a veteran's medical centre and a correctional facility, when he began seeking a new outlet that would develop his personal growth and make his ministry more effective. Suitably mature for the aging community, experienced in counselling and mediation, accustomed to interacting with people of widely differing views and well versed in matters of *kashrut*, he was happy to meet the challenge of becoming Rabbi Broder's successor. From the very beginning he set himself guidelines. Dissention over the synagogues was not his domain. *Halacha* (the legal framework of Jewish tradition) was, and the dearth of kosher products became a top priority.

Though he describes himself as 'a people person', Rabbi Pearlman proved more of 'a person person', preferring to work with individuals rather than committees. Never too rushed to exchange pleasantries, affable but never intrusive, he handled problems with efficiency and discretion. Where they concerned *kashrut* he frequently ended his sermons with welcome announcements of improved communal facilities, sending congregants home a little more cheerful and optimistic than when they arrived. His American wife Sheila is an academic. A Professor of Mathematics and Education, her work in the United States involved the training of principals, superintendents of schools and teachers. Warmly received by both the Jewish and the wider community, the couple adjusted to Irish life quickly. The Rabbi unexpectedly discovered Irish roots when he noticed a plaque in Terenure Synagogue dedicated to the memory of his grandmother, Anne Hymanson, whom he now realises lived with his grandfather, Michael, at 20 Lombard Street from 1912 until they moved to Manchester around 1918. A first cousin, Harvey Hymanson, made his *Bar Mitzvah* at Terenure Synagogue.

Rabbi Pearlman enjoyed the diplomatic and inter-faith aspect of his work while establishing excellent relations with the President of Ireland and heads of State; the *rebbetzin* became involved in many aspects of communal life, acting as advisor to Stratford Schools and the Irish Jewish Museum, holding ladies' study groups from time to time, calling regularly at the Jewish Home to divert the residents with recorded music and some personal story-telling and visiting the sick and the lonely. She devoted her spare time to cultural events and the enjoyment of Ireland's scenic beauty.

Pivotal to synagogue services for the past twenty years has been the melodious voice of South African-born Cantor Alwyn Shulman, who studied *chazzanut* (Jewish liturgical singing) in Israel. Appointed first as *chazzan* to Schoonder Street Synagogue in Cape Town, on the retirement of world-renowned Cantor Simcha Kusevitsky, he was cantor to Adelaide Road Synagogue from 1991 until it closed in 1999. Now the *chazzan* at Terenure Synagogue, he is also responsible for the supervision of *kasrut* at Bloomfield Care Centre and at Irish factories producing goods regarded as kosher. He and his Israeli wife, Nurit, who is the head of the Hebrew Studies department at Stratford National School, reared three sons in Ireland, and describe the warmth and support shown to them as 'remarkable'. They regard the Dublin Jewish community as their extended family.

The rehousing of Cantor Shulman, obliged to vacate his bungalow in the grounds of Adelaide Road Synagogue when the building was sold, and the provision of suitable accommodation for Rabbi Pearlman and Rabbi Lent, have added to the community's assets, and much of the infrastructure of Dublin Jewry is still intact. Stratford National School and Stratford College remain predominantly multi-faith, although Jewish intake is rising slightly through immigrant families or those on contract work in Dublin. Hebrew has been introduced as a spoken language from senior primary level and the Hebrew and Religion curriculums remain under constant review. The twice-daily *minyanim* are now centralised in one synagogue, and an occasional Sabbath-service reminder of obligations in that respect usually ensures the necessary quorum for the following week.

In November 2001, Rabbi Pearlman re-established a kosher meat supply for Dublin Jews by taking advantage of an existing arrangement between King's Meats in Britain and Liffey Meats in Ireland. Once every two weeks *shochtim* travel from Britain to kill Irish cattle and lamb in strict accordance with Jewish ritual at Liffey Meats in Ballyjamesduff, Co. Cavan. Most of the meat then processed at a second plant in Castleblaney, Co. Monaghan, is exported frozen to Britain and France, but it also supplies the Irish market.

In February 2003, discreet negotiations with the new owner of the Bretzel Bakery restored its kosher status for both patisserie and bread, without detriment to Connolly's, which continued to supply its own range of fully supervised bread and cakes from expanded premises that incorporated a kosher coffee shop. In 2006, Irish Pride, one of Ireland's primary bakeries, converted its entire plant to kosher production under rabbinical supervision. For the first time since the heyday of Clanbrassil Street, Dublin Jews could choose between bakeries, a choice further widened by the pre-packed, imported cakes and biscuits on sale at Super Valu. The luxury was short-lived. In 2008, the Bretzel outsourced its patisserie division to an unsupervised bakery, leaving only its bread kosher and Connolly's discontinued its kosher production. Super Valu's monopoly in supplying kosher groceries was breached in 2008 when Tesco opened a small kosher section at its Nutgrove branch, but it was short-lived competition. Recently refurbished, Super Valu now sells kosher products from central aisles which are kept reasonably well stocked. Transport and currency fluctuations combine to keep the prices artificially high but kosher shopping in Ireland was always an expensive option.

A hospital food amenity was introduced in the late 1990s through the good offices of a strictly kosher member of the community with no close family in Ireland, who was admitted in emergency to the Meath Hospital. Her refusal to eat hospital food was so steadfast that the Blackrock Clinic, where she was taken for a test that required her to eat beforehand, sent a taxi to the Meath Hospital to collect a kosher cup cake from her room. Embarrassed at depending for her meals on the goodwill of friends, she wrote to the secretary-general of the Meath Hospital explaining her predicament and urging that kosher food be regarded as a special diet and made routinely available to patients who required it. He readily agreed to provide the service whenever she needed Meath Hospital care. When a later appeal to the Adelaide Hospital on her own behalf proved equally successful, she applied to every major Dublin hospital for its automatic extension to all Jewish patients. Not one hospital refused. Jewish patients unwilling to eat hospital food could request the alternative of unsupervised kosher meals, freshly prepared in her own home by kosher caterer, Hazel Hyman. A later development, through the intervention of Hilary Gross, is the availability in some hospitals of imported frozen kosher meals, prepared under supervision.

On 2 February 1999, as part of the negotiations for the closure of Adelaide Road Synagogue, a legal agreement was entered into between Dublin Hebrew Congregation and Terenure Hebrew Congregation. The two would amalgamate, Terenure Synagogue would be demolished and 'a new synagogue, *mikvah* and community centre' would be erected on the site at Rathfarnham Road, Terenure, with costs defrayed by the sale of Adelaide Road Synagogue.

A replacement *mikva* for the one located at Adelaide Road was erected adjacent to the Samuel Taca Hall in Terenure in 2000; but despite clause 7.1 which specifically states that, 'this agreement shall be irrevocable', no other part of it has so far been implemented. Architects were consulted and outline plans drawn up for a synagogue to seat 200 people, with overflow extension to 400; but every communal meeting held to discuss the proposal ended in disagreement. Though lacking the majestic ambiance of Adelaide Road Synagogue and in need of some modernisation and repair, Terenure Synagogue, commonly admired by visitors, was viewed by many of its regular worshippers as adequate for its purpose. Restoration, preferred by many to replacement and eventually decided upon, seemed on initial investigation to be an expensive option that would deplete capital to no real community advantage; yet few in Terenure Hebrew Congregation wanted to use all the money from Adelaide Road Synagogue in building what most still consider an unnecessary new *shul*. Suggested alternatives ranged through a 'budget' *shul*, a more commodious communal hall, a community centre possibly encompassing a kosher restaurant and shop, sheltered accommodation for the elderly not yet in need of full-time care, a purpose-built home for the aged to include a synagogue, even commercial apartments. Many opted for just holding on to the money. While the councils of both synagogues continued to meet separately with neither able to agree even among its own members as to the best communal use of £6 million there could be no general meeting of minds, but the Adelaide Road council was not ungenerous in its response to communal needs. Even before the two councils merged under the banner of the Dublin Hebrew Congregation it was making substantial contributions to the upkeep of the rabbinate in Dublin as well as funding rabbinate expenses for Cork and supporting the communal functions organised by Rabbi Lent. It financed the replacement *mikvah* in accordance with the agreement, paid for the complete renovation of Rabbi Pearlman's home prior to his arrival, bought the houses now occupied by Revd Shulman and Rabbi Lent and modernised the kitchens in the Samuel Taca Hall. The purchase of the two houses has been the only capital expenditure; everything else is financed from interest on the capital, being kept intact for the future development of the Rathfarnham Road site or some viable alternative communal project.

Dublin Hebrew Congregation sees its prime obligation as the continuation of existing facilities for the Observant, but the cost per head of providing those facilities rises as numbers decline. Unless a substantial number of Jews from other countries can be encouraged to settle in Ireland and share the burden, it could well reach an unsustainable level.

Attracting Jewish immigration to Ireland was an unlikely scenario until the economic boom of the late 1990s reversed the traditional pattern of emigration. On 7 December 2000, the broadcaster Marion Finucane drew the attention of radio listeners to Dublin's growing shortage of labour. A national survey of vacancies carried out for FÁS in 1998 had shown that a quarter of Irish firms, in all sectors, had vacancies for professional and industrial workers and the situation had not improved. A spokesman for Country Quest Potatoes dismissed advertising for staff as a waste of time. Michael Maloney of *An Bord Glas* thought the newly-launched seven-year development plan for horticulture would offer 4,500 more vacancies than there were Irish applicants to fill them. John Brennan from the Park Hotel, Kenmare, said the formerly 100 per cent Irish work force in the hotel industry was now 16 per cent foreign, and likely to rise to 50 per cent. The radio programmeme concluded, 'We can't survive here without immigration.'

An agent bringing foreign workers legally into Ireland explained the procedure and the economic advantages to the immigrants. At least one Jewish listener was fascinated to hear that most of the foreigners were from Eastern Europe, and especially Latvia, home to the forefathers of many Irish Jews. In a letter to the Rep Council she offered her services to research into the feasibility of bringing Jewish workers from Eastern Europe, for the joint purpose of improving their lot and revitalising the Irish-Jewish community. A reply of 24 January 2000 indicated that the 'interesting contents' of her letter 'were under active consideration'.

The person appointed to investigate immigration possibilities was Carl Nelkin, who was independently thinking along the same lines. Initial enquiries to the *Tánaiste* Mary Harney TD, in June 2000 led to a meeting on 6 July with officials from the Department of Enterprise, Trade and Employment. While they were 'favourably disposed' to the rejuvenation of the Irish Jewish community, the officials stressed that the Government could not be seen as 'positively discriminating' in favour of a particular social or ethnic group. Nevertheless, on the basis of existing current legislation and practice, there was no reason why the proposed scheme should not be successfully implemented. Carl was especially interested in targeting South African Jews, who were well-educated, English-speaking, of the same Lithuanian background as Irish Jews and anxious to leave South Africa for political reasons. With FÁS about to launch a travelling 'job fair' to recruit workers from around the world, the Irish Jewish community could advise Jewish communities in South Africa to attend.

An early obstacle was the refusal of the South African Jewish press to carry any advertisements encouraging emigration unless the destination was Israel, but a professionally-designed, comprehensive portal called *Moving to Ireland*, incorporated into the Irish Jewish Community website, encouraged Jewish attendance at the FÁS job fairs and invited further enquiries. About 100 people responded. Of those who were seriously interested, few were willing to reduce their professional status even temporarily, making it difficult to place them in employment. The low exchange rate of the South African rand imposed financial problems. The recruitment drive was still in its infancy when the Irish economy began to lose buoyancy and the economic situation worsened to a point where Irish employers were discouraged from using foreign labour. They had to prove that the vacancy could not be filled by an Irish worker and apply for the immigrant's work permit at a cost of €400. A minority, nonetheless, achieved successful re-settlement.

Brian Gresak is one South African immigrant who had no compunction about changing careers. An architect by profession, he arrived alone in 2001 and was employed within three days as a contract manager. A year later he changed companies for a more senior post with additional benefits. His wife Alice and their two young children have since joined him and they have a home of their own. The family has integrated well and Brian is 'very happy' to be in Ireland. In common with Carl Nelkin, he sees the Irish Jewish community as 'not dying, but evolving', a reflection of how the world is changing.

Equally successful immigrants are the Bondi family. Originally from Zimbabwe, Ray Bondi, a brother of Alice Gresak, arrived in Ireland in 2008 to be joined soon after by his wife Cheryl and teenage son. Self-employed, he makes regular business trips back to South Africa but regards Ireland as his home. The Gresak and Bondi cousins attend Stratford College; Alice and Cheryl assist at *Kiddush* rotas, with Cheryl sometimes arranging the flowers in the Leslie Golding Hall on special occasions. Both families are members of Terenure Synagogue and Brian and Ray are stalwart supporters of the often hard-pressed daily *minyanim*. On *Simcha Torah* of 2010, Brian concluded the reading of the Torah for that Hebrew year (*Chatan Torah*) and Ray restarted it (*Chatan Bereshit*), honours rarely applied to newcomers.

Even more involved are Riva and Moti Neuman. Seconded to Ireland in 1998 by Amdocs, the international software company to whom he was contracted, Moti spent one whole year travelling back and forth to Israel every weekend to spend Shabbat with his wife. When he returned to Ireland for an Amdocs project in 2001, Riva joined him. Neither expected to be away from Israel for more than a few years but when his Amdocs contract expired in 2004, Moti founded his own company with local partners. It is a measure of its success that the Neumans are still in Ireland.

To Roumanian-born Riva, a teacher in basic computer skills, Ireland was something of a cultural shock. Compared with Israeli sunshine, she found Irish weather grey, wet and depressing and fumed at the heating, electric, water and drainage problems that constantly plagued their rented accommodation – but she had no problem with the local Jewish community. Invitations and offers of friendship followed hard upon their first appearance in *shul* and Moti and Riva responded by participating in almost every facet of communal activity. A committed member of WIZO, Riva chaired the committee that organised one of its most successful, and possibly its last, annual lunch. She sews with the Sewing Circle for the Holy Burial Society, helps with Kiddush rotas and acts as sometime guide at the Irish-Jewish museum. Arriving with good basic English, she has talked to a group of teachers about Holocaust survivors and given a public account of her recent trip to Poland. Moti seems indefatigable. Besides being a member of the Holy Burial Society, he is chairman of the Irish-Jewish Museum committee, and serves on both the Rabbinate and the *Kashrut* committees. He fills in for both Rabbi Lent and Cantor Shulman in their absence, frequently leads the congregation in prayer and gives a weekly *shiur* (study group) on the Talmud.

Settling equally well for a while were Israelis Tzour Vaish and Bettina Strelitz. Tzour, a civil engineer, read *Moving to Ireland* on the website. His first visit with his wife in May 2001 was by way of exploratory vacation. Two more visits made alone secured him suitable employment and his wife and baby joined him in their own home. Bettina Strelitz found employment with a pharmaceutical company but none of them remained in Ireland. Paul Tollman did. A native of South Africa, he studied in Israel, met his wife in Cork, married in England, and has since lived in both Cork and Israel, where he still has a home. At present settled in Cork where his son, Ilan, made his *Bar Mitzvah*, he misses the support and facilities of a larger Jewish community. With only four other permanent Jewish families, Jewish social life in Cork is confined to Festival times when surrounding migrant Jews join the locals in celebration. Like Rabbi Lent, he believes outreach hospitality is the way forward. The perennial Jewish call for a return to Zion makes it inappropriate to encourage Israeli emigration, but enquiries initiated by Israelis interested in settling in Ireland are on-going. Ireland has also welcomed two Polish families, since the enlargement of the European Community.

For a time Argentina seemed a possible future source of immigration; its economy had collapsed and many thousands of Jews were anxious to leave. Mostly poor people, they were less concerned about their future in Ireland than by the logistics of gaining admission. The Hebrew Immigrant Aid Society (HIAS), established in New York over a hundred years ago to assist Jews immigrating into the United States, had broadened its activities to encompass immigration elsewhere. With an office that screens applicants and a budget that covers air fares, it was well-placed to act as intermediary for the 100 or so enquiries it received every day from Argentineans wanting to leave. Placements have been made in Italy and England but the prospective applicant must apply from his own country for work authorisation which is valid for only two years with no guarantee of extension. He must also have a prospective employer willing to do the paper work and bear the cost of the work permit. HIAS ear-marked six or seven families whose area of expertise matched Irish requirements but Carl Nelkin believed it would take a full-time, professional recruiter and administrator to bring the different strands of the scheme together.

In July 1991, Harold Smith, then president of the Belfast Hebrew Congregation, deplored the situation that left Northern Ireland Jews with no minister and no *shochet*. Buying meat from 'outside' was subject to 'a lot of bureaucratic clearances' and he concluded that, 'In terms of morale, we are about as low as we have ever been.'

With only eighty-five paid up members of the synagogue, most of them elderly, few people are actively involved in the Belfast Jewish community. Without an influx of some kind, it faces a bleak future. Similar to Dublin, it once looked towards Argentina for immigrants but it took no steps beyond the establishment of Project Horizon to investigate the general situation. With only one 'umbrella' synagogue covering all degrees of Orthodoxy, the Belfast community has no inter-congregational disputes but problems arise where *halacha* is challenged. Rabbi

Brackman and his wife enrich the religious and social life of the community as best they can. The rabbi takes the synagpge services and visits the sick; the *rebbizin* provides *kugel* for the special kiddush that marks the first *Shabbat* of every Jewish month. On Sundays she teaches the two children who comprise her Hebrew class. Socially, Belfast has a Wednesday Club which encourages members to bring their non-Jewish friends; they listen to speakers on various topics and enjoy soup and sandwiches served by Linda Coppel, who founded the Wednesday Club, and her friends. The community also hosts a very successful WIZO lunch once a year.

Establishing the exact number of Jews in Ireland is difficult. Some arrive with non-Jewish partners and identify little or not at all with the local Jewish communities; others, seconded to Ireland for indefinite or set periods by firms such as Google, the web search engine, and Intel, manufacturers of semi-conductors for the computer industry, can be equally elusive. Itai Pront, English-born with an American wife, lived in Israel for ten years before Intel sent him to Dublin as a contract and materials manager for a maximum period of two years. Orthodox in religious practice, his initial reaction was one of shock at the lack of kosher facilities and what he termed 'exorbitant food prices'. He missed the vibrancy of Israeli social life and urged a more liberal attitude by the community towards adaptation and change.

Though a crowd of Israelis may appear at one of Rabbi Lent's festive events, and both a first-night *Seder* and a *Chaucah* party in Cork in 2002 attracted more than 100 people that included Israelis, British, Americans, Argentineans and an Afro-American convert from Chicago, many newcomers remain on the periphery of Irish-Jewish life and some disassociate themselves entirely. The *Chabad-Lubovitch* movement in America sends newly-ordained or final year rabbinical students each year to the out-lying towns and villages of different countries in a search for Jews living completely within the wider community. In 2008, Rabbi Baruch Davidson from America and Rabbi Pinchas Raitmen from Australia visited Ireland. In their first two weeks, they made contact with forty such people in diverse locations from Donegal to Cork, bearing out Chief Rabbi Mirvis's contention that there are Jews living in every county of Ireland.

With Adelaide Road Synagogue now closed, its *Aron Kodesh* (the Holy Ark which had housed the *Torah* scrolls), its *bimah* (the lectern from which both clergy and congregants had led the service) and its pulpit from which the rabbi had preached, were defunct. Too historically valuable to discard, they were placed in storage pending their need in the future by some other synagogue with an Irish connection. The future became the present in 2008 when, through the strenuous efforts of Estelle Menton and Martin Simmons, the artifacts were shipped to Israel, restored by Martin and his wife Rebecca in memory of their parents and incorporated into *Kehillat* (community) *Ahavat Tzion* (Love of Zion), a new synagogue, at Ramat Beit Shemesh in Israel. The Irish connection could not have been more pronounced. The rabbi of *Ahavat Tzion*, Dayan Menachem

Copperman, is the son of former congregants of Adelaide Road Synagogue who emigrated to Israel, while Eli Shaw, son of Keith Shaw, a lay leader of *Ahavat Tzion*, was able to make his *Bar Mitzvah* standing on the same *bimah* that his grandfather, Rikki Shaw, had used when called to the reading of the Law many years ago in Adelaide Road. The dayan addressesd the *Bar Mitzvah* boy from the same pulpit used in Adelaide Road Synagogue to address his grandfather. Isaac Herzog, a cabinet minister in the Israeli government, speaking from the same pulpit at the re-dedication service, recalled that it had also been used by <u>his</u> grandfather, Chief Rabbi Herzog, to deliver a *Bar Mitzvah* address to his own son, Chaim Herzog, twice President of Israel and Isaac Herzog's father.

When Martin Simmons, as its last president, closed the doors of Adelaide Road synagogue for the last time, the entire Dublin Hebrew Congregation mourned

Stuart Rosenblatt leans on the stack of books he has produced about Irish Jewry.

its loss; six years later, there was rejoicing in both Dublin and *Ramat Beit Shemesh* when Martin and Seton Menton, his presidential predecessor at Adelaide Road, were the first to open the new synagogue's *Aron Kodesh* at the ceremony for its official rededication. The already special occasion acquired an even greater significance for Keith Shaw when Martin unexpectedly presented him with the decorated scroll mantel donated in 1988 by the Dublin Hebrew Congregation to Adelaide Road Synagogue to commemorate the first anniversary of the death of his grandfather, Eli Schwartzman, the *shul's* one-time honorary financial secretary and a life vice-president. In what Estelle Menton called 'the epitome of Jewish continuity', the circle had been closed around what the Irish Ambassador referred to as 'a little piece of Ireland in Israel'.

The thousands of Irish Jews who chose to make their home elsewhere look to Ireland only for their roots. In 1999, Stuart Rosenblatt, son of the tailor Martin Sidney, established the Irish Genealogical Society, now a division of the Irish Jewish Museum. Begun as part-time searching in museum archives, synagogue records and Jewish cemeteries for his own family background, his interest in genealogy developed into a record of 45,000 Jews, born, bred or settled anywhere in Ireland since the nineteenth century. Both the list and the data are still growing. A computer programme specially designed for him over a period of eleven months enables Stuart to cross-reference the seventy fields of information tabulated for each entry and an email to srosenblatt@irishjewishroots.com is all it takes for Jews with Irish connections to receive all he knows about several generations of their family history, in family tree format. He receives about twenty enquiries a day from around the world.

Personal interviews and extensive research have led to his discovery of historically valuable documents such as Ada Shillman's Birth Register and the Aliens' File. He found records of the marriages solemnised at Mary's Abbey and Adelaide Road Synagogues from 1845 to 1905 in the General Register Office in Roscommon and derived particular satisfaction from codifying the graves in Dolphin's Barn cemetery by name, section, row and plot. 'Now they are at peace,' he told himself, each time he succeeded in connecting a deceased person with no apparent relatives to other family members. The hobby, which occupies about thirty hours of his time per week, has become almost an obsession. Now professionally qualified with a Diploma in Family History, he is internationally recognised as an expert on Irish Jewish genealogy and acted as consultant for the television documentary, *Who Do You Think You Are?* when the actress Dervla Kirwan sought her own Jewish roots. From 1999-2002 he was honorary vice-president of the Genealogical Society of Ireland.

The sixteen volumes of data relating to Irish Jews that Stuart has self-published over the last six years are available for reference in Dublin at the Irish Jewish museum, the National Archives, the National Museum and the Genealogical Society of Ireland. Belfast and Cork also have copies. Most of them record births, marriages, deaths, school records, occupation and family history over the last 300 years. His *Irish Garden of the Dead* traces burials in Dublin, Belfast, Cork and Limerick from 1748. Stuart describes his research of the last thirteen years as a 'one-stop, all-embracing family quest never performed anywhere in the world.'

It was a genealogical enquiry in 1999 addressed to Stuart Rosenblatt and three others – Ann Rabinowitz, an American with Irish connections, and Dublin expatriates Davida Noyek Handler and Frank Baigel – that initiated the computer-based IrishJIG (Jewish Irish Group), known to its 460 members simply as the JIG. Dr Saul Issroff, a South African living in London, was trying to trace Irish connections. Davida in America passed the request to five other Dubliners, variously domiciled in Israel, Canada, South Africa and Ireland. After the Israeli source, Len Yodaiken, had supplied the required information, Davida, president of the Litvak SIG (Special Interest Group) asked, 'Doesn't anyone want to start an Irish SIG?' The South African contact, Anne Lapedus Brest, who welcomed the idea, helped to launch it and kept it alive through constant contact with all the members until it gave way to 'Shalom Ireland', a second Irish-Jewish channel of communication, which is still active.

The daily digests issued by 'Shalom Ireland', to which any member can contribute, are filled with inquiries, anecdotes, reminiscences, greetings, invitations, expressions of congratulation and sympathy, local news from around the world and general chit-chat. Twice there have been JIG reunions in Dublin but the main function of 'Shalom Ireland' is to preserve contact worldwide among those who once shared a way of life unique to Irish Jews.

Now in abeyance due to pressure of work, Rabbi Lent's twenty-first century 'newsletter of the Irish-Jewish community', *L'Chaim Ireland*, proves Irish-Jewry was never static. Well-laid out, entertaining and informative, the ten issues distributed detail the occasional *Shabbatons* (communal celebrations of *Shabbat*), organised in conjunction with Shiela Pearlman, Hinda Bloom's kosher restaurant open for business in the Samuel Taca Hall (originally on Sundays from 12 a.m.– 3.30 p.m. but currently on Thursday evenings), lectures on subjects that ranged from *Kabbala* (Jewish mysticism) to a crash course in basic Judaism, a children's summer camp, a toddlers' group, the over-80s club, and a range of other activities. Irish firms continue to seek a kosher licence for their products; McConnell's smoked salmon, McCambridge's bread and Broadway Bagels have all recently added variety to the kosher goods available. Terenure Synagogue and grounds have been tastefully restored. Cork doggedly holds on to its synagogue with a Friday night service once a month and, with the help of Rabbi Lent, 'imports' from United Kingdom *yeshivot* as many adult males as are needed to provide a *minyan* for High Holy days. The rabbi also helps arrange a communal seder which can still attract seventy or eighty people.

The then Irish ambassador to Israel (seated second row aisle)
hears Dayan Menachem Copperman lead the service at
Kehillat Ahavat Tzion in Ramat Beit Shemesh, new home to
the reconstructed Aron Kodesh, bimah and pulpit formerly
used at Adelaide Road Synagogue.

The possibly 2,000 or less native and immigrant Jews scattered around Ireland, many of them students or technologically skilled young people attracted to Ireland by its growing reputation as an international centre for multi-lingual, online support, form a very small percentage of the island's overall population, estimated in 2010 at five-and-a-half million. Depleting numbers tend to go hand in hand with diminishing influence. Eminent and able an advocate as Alan Shatter TD is in the promotion of Jewish interests, his is now the only Jewish voice in Dáil Eiranne where once there were three; Ireland's sole surviving Jewish judge has long-since retired and its prominent and often colourful medics, academics and exponents of the arts are largely gone. Ireland has no Chief Rabbi.

Replacing Chief Rabbi Pearlman was a contentious issue even before he left Ireland. Some already considered the community too depleted to warrant the appointment of a new Chief Rabbi whose duties could largely be fulfilled by Rabbi Lent; others, despite Rabbi Lent's proven and acknowledged achievements, still believe a Chief Rabbi is important to Ireland for external diplomatic relations, for the rabbinical supervision of kosher products whose licensing fees help the community survive financially, and for the self-esteem of a community that has always been proud of having its own Chief Rabbi.

The Russian Jews who came to Ireland in the 1880s found a small, English-speaking Jewish community, well-educated, influential beyond their numbers, reasonably affluent and more traditional than religious. Jews coming to twenty-first century Ireland would find pretty much the same thing. To re-build their community, the remnants of Irish Jewry would have to wait until Ireland's current economic situation improves and then invest in people rather than property. The Court Order that extended the use of the Maccabi Trust Fund left it applicable only to Irish Jews. A second Court Order could be sought to sanction its use for foreign Jews. Arriving with nothing, such immigrants would have the same incentive as the nineteenth century Russians to build and prosper. Argentinean immigration could still be pursued and the possibility of a *kollel* reviewed. Recommendations of this kind have so far fallen on deaf ears and the local, aging community seems generally content to watch its decline with apathetic resignation. Attempts to attract non-participating Jews, indigenous and immigrant, into synagogue membership and communal activity have largely failed and there is minimum communication among the Jews of Dublin, Belfast and Cork.

At the last synagogue council election in 2010, several traditional, committed stalwarts were voted out of office in favour of other generally younger and less Orthodox, but possibly more dynamic, nominees. In electing Bertha Cohen as honorary secretary, the re-constituted council gave Dublin its first ever female executive member to serve an Orthodox synagogue. In an effort to stimulate community participation, it has also begun organising innovative and successful social events and has instituted a Monday morning coffee rendezvous in the Samuel Taca Hall, free of charge, for anyone wishing to socialise. Rabbi Lent continues to reach out to newcomers as well as to permanent residents through the communal celebration of festive occasions. Anything that gives the community a focus and a profile can only be beneficial in a land where it is now likely a Gentile will grow up without ever meeting a Jew..

At the re-dedication ceremony at *Kehillat Ahavat Tzioin*, Martin Simmons told the congregation, "In the diaspora communities grow, flourish, bloom but ultimately either fade from their former glory or, in most cases, just wither." Should that be the fate of Ireland's Jews, they will have left a wonderful legacy both in Israel and around the world, wherever they chose to settle – but it's far from over yet. Jewish people will not disappear from Ireland. That they still mourn the destruction of their temple 2000 years after the event is evidence of their long memories. Succeeding generations will go on recounting the glories of Irish Jewry for many years to come; historical accounts will continue to be written and a people that never forgets its past will always have a future.

APPENDIX

DUBLIN SYNAGOGUES

Those underlined are still functioning

Dublin Hebrew Congregation, Mary's Abbey (founded 1839) moved to Adelaide Road
(1892–1999)

Lennox Street Hebrew Congregation, Lennox Street (1876-1974) then located at Stratford
College (1974–81)

St Kevin's Parade Hebrew Congregation, St Kevin's Parade (founded 1876) renamed
Machzikei Hadass when it moved to Terenure Road North (1968)

Camden Street Hebrew Congregation, Camden Street (1892-1916)

Lombard Street Hebrew Congregation, Lombard Street (1900-60)

Walworth Road Hebrew Congregation, Walworth Road (1912-81)

United Hebrew Congregation, Greenville Hall (1914-84)

Rathmines Hebrew Congregation, Grosvenor Road (1936) renamed Terenure Hebrew
Congregation when it moved to Rathfarnham Road (1953). Renamed Dublin Hebrew
Congregation on closure of Adelaide Road Synagogue (1999)

Knesset Orach Chayim, Dublin Jewish Progressive Synagogue (founded 1946)

Jewish Home of Ireland Synagogue, established 1950 and re-located within the Home until
its closure in 2005

JEWISH ORGANISATIONS IN DUBLIN BASED MAINLY ON *IRISH-JEWISH YEAR BOOKS* (1955–2003)

Those underlined are still functioning

COMMUNAL

Jewish Representative Council of Ireland (founded 1936)
Committee of the Chief Rabbinate in Ireland (1947–93)
Holy Burial Society (1898) renamed Dublin Jewish Holy Burial Society (1994)
General Board of *Shechita* of Éire (1915–93)
Ritual Baths Committee renamed *Mikveh* Committee in 1980
Kashrut Commission for Ireland (1962–89)
Kashrut Committee (1965–80)

RELIGIOUS

CHevra Gomorrah (pre-1955) renamed Dublin *Chevra Gomorrah* (1963–78)
Chevra Mishnayoth (1957–63)
Torah Study Circle (1961–78)
Choverei Torah Group (1964–9)
Ladies' Jewish Study Group (1971–2)
Chevra Torah (1973)

EDUCATIONAL

Dublin *Talmud Torah* and Jewish Day Schools: Zion Schools (1932–80)
Stratford College (founded 1953)
Talmud Torah Ladies' Committee (1961–5)
Zion Schools and *Talmud Torah* Parents' Association (1964–80)
Stratford College Parents' Association (1965–80)
New Schools Development Committee (1972–5)
Dublin *Talmud Torah* and Stratford Jewish National School (1980) renamed Dublin Talmud Torah incorporating Stratford College and Stratford National School (1981)
Stratford Parents' Association (founded 1981)

CHARITABLE AND WELFARE

Dublin Jewish Board of Guardians (founded 1889)
Dublin Jewish Philanthropic Loan Fund (1890s–1980)
Dublin Jewish Ladies' Charitable Society (founded 1894)
Dorcas Society (1903–67)
Dublin Jewish Brides' Aid Society (1926) incorporated into the Dublin Jewish Ladies' Charitable Society (1975)
Dublin Jewish Hospital Aid Society (1928–80)
Home for Aged and Infirm Jews in Ireland (founded 1950) renamed Jewish Home of Ireland (1973) and transferred to Bloomfield Care Centre (2005)
Jewish Students' Aid Society (1954–c.1960)
Combined Israel Charities Fund (1955–80)
Dublin Jewish Friendship Club (1963–90) re-established as Over 55's Friendship Club (1994)
Jewish Marriage Counselling Service (1982–4)
JAFA Ireland, Jewish Association for Fostering, Adoption and Infertility (1984–94)

ZIONIST

Dublin Daughters of Zion (1900–77)
Jewish National Fund (founded 1901)
Ziona (1937–2001)
Emunah Child Resettlement Fund–Dublin Women's Mizrachi (1946–91)
Hulda (1946–86)
Children and Youth *Aliyah* (1946–80)
Mizrachi Federation of Ireland (1948–73)
Friends of the Hebrew University (founded 1948)
Regional Council of Women Zionists (1949–79)
Joint Palestine Appeal later United Jewish Israel Appeal (founded 1951)
Dublin Zionist Council (later Zionist Council of Ireland) (1951–80)
South Dublin WIZO (1956–93)
Dublin Mizrachi Society (re-established 1958–90)
Zionist Revisionist Organisation (*Herut*) of Ireland (1959–66)
JNF Younger Commission (1961–81)
Hadassah (1959–2000)
Hannah Senesh Young WIZO Group (founded 1961) incorporated into *Hadassah* (1987)
Children and Youth *Aliyah* Younger Committee (1961–6)
Chug Aliyah (1963–5)
Achdut (1970–6)
Magen David Adom (1971–80)
Left-Zionist Forum (1972–4)
Jewish Child's Day Committee (1973–89)
WIZO Ireland (1993)

YOUTH

Dublin Jewish Students' Union
Dublin Jewish Youth Leaders' Council
Dublin *Torah V'avodah* (1927) renamed Terenure *Torah V'avodah* (1959–63)
Tifereth Bachurim (1937–7)
Dublin *Bnei Akivah* (1945–90)
Hechalutz (1954–5)
Boy Scout Movement (1925–2002)
  16th Dublin Jewish Scouts
  Rovers
  Cubs
  Beavers
Girl Guide Movement (1932–2002)
  23rd Dublin 1st and 24th Dublin 2nd Company Guides
  Rangers: 23rd Dublin Company
  Brownies: 23rd and 24th Dublin Packs
Habonim (1929–68)
Jewish National Fund Youth Section (1941–62)
Agudist Youth Movement (1961–6/7)
Dublin Jewish Youth Leaders' Council (founded 1972)
Jewish Youth Voluntary Service (1974–90)
B'nai B'rith Youth Organisation (founded 1976)
Federation of Zionist Youth (1977)
Youth Jewish National Fund (1987–90)

FRIENDLY SOCIETIES

Grand Order of Israel: Dr Max Nordau Lodge No. 27 (1904-80)

Order of Ancient Maccabeans: Mount Carmel Beacon incorporating King Solomon Lodge, Beacon No. 57 (1907-78)

B'nai B'rith Dublin Lodge (founded 1954) and *B'nai B'rith* Dublin Women's Lodge No. 2609 (founded 1968) amalgamated into Dublin *B'nai B'rith* Unity Lodge (1978-92)

GENERAL

New Jewish Literary and Social Club (early 20th century) renamed The Jewish Club (1956-88)

Friends of *Habonim* (post 1929-69)

Friends of *Bnai Akivah* (1953-7)

Dublin Jewish Dramatic Society (1909-57)

Dublin Maccabi Association (1954-98)

Edmondstown Golf Club (founded 1944)

Judaic Study Group (1945-57)

Ladies' Study Circle (ended 1957)

Dublin Jewish Musical Society (1950) renamed Hazamir Choral Society (1956-7)

Dublin Hebrew Speakers' Circle (revived 1952) renamed Hebrew Speakers' Circle (1963), renamed Hebrew Speakers' Circle '*Chug Dovrei Ivrit*' (1983)

16th Jewish Scouts Parents' Committee (1962) renamed Friends of Scouting (1974-80)

258 Shalom Ireland

Ireland-Israel Friendship League (founded 1967)

Irish Soviet Jewry Committee (1975-80)

35s Group (1976-90)

Dublin Yiddish Circle (1977-82)

Federation of Jewish Women's Societies of Ireland (1983-90)

Irish Jewish Museum and Holocaust Education Centre (established 1984)

Dublin Maccabi Association Charitable Trust (founded 1998)

PROFESSIONAL

Association of Jewish Clergy and Teachers in Éire (1947-84)

National Union of Hebrew Teachers of Great Britain and Ireland, Dublin Branch (1946-81)

Jewish Medical Society of Ireland (1950) renamed Jewish Medical Society (1963)

TRADERS AND RESIDENTS IN LOWER CLANBRASSIL STREET 1892–2001 IN ACCORDANCE WITH THOM'S DIRECTORY WHICH LISTS ONLY PROPRIETORS AND PRIMARY LEASE-HOLDERS

No. 2
Mrs Sharpe   1892-9
S.H. Danker   1965-82

No. 18
S. Miller, picture framer 1895-1904, moved from No. 98

No. 23
Joseph Daniels 1924-8

No. 26
Samuel Pushinsky 1898-1900
David Spiro, draper 1902, moved to No. 45
Abel Philips Spiro 1903-4
J. Taylor 1905
G. Hool, draper 1921–32

No. 30
H. Myerson 1895-1902
Margolis, family grocer 1903-12
Baigel, tea, wine and spirits 1913-39
Freedman 1940-3

No. 31
S. Rubinstein, butcher 1939-80
Suissa's delicatessen 1981-96

No. 32
M. Wolfe, draper 1913-37
Jacob Gredstein, draper 1938-48
L. Goldstein, draper 1949-55

No. 33
L. Gittleson 1912-15
D. Solomons, butcher 1917-21
E.S. Dorsky, butcher 1922-3
Annie Zamsky, provisions 1929-36

No. 34
M. Leventhal 1897
S. Yodaiken 1899-1906
M. Wolfe 1907-41
S. Kronnberg 1943-8

No. 35
A. Rosenthal 1907, moved from No. 43
Mrs Gorsky, draper 1910
M. Shulman, bootmaker 1912-14
S. Levi, baker 1915-19
Freedman, grocer 1920-51
L. Erlich, butcher 1952-2001

No. 36
A. Kahan 1907-8
D. Lewis 1910
M. Wolfe, greengrocer 1912-13
Jackson, greengrocer 1914-17

No. 37
J. Rubinstein 1905
J. Jaffey, greengrocer 1917-24
Israel Vard, tobacconist 1925-31
Barron (first H. then Mollie) 1932-58

No. 38
Mark Herman 1894
H. Ginsberg 1895-1903
Mrs Stein, greengrocer 1922-3
J. Goldberg 1924-7
Betty's Draper 1933-74

No. 39
Morris Robinson 1901-3
M. White 1905
L. Gittleson 1907-11
B. Marcus 1912
Rudstein, tobacconist 1913-27
C. Jackson, provisions 1828-1974

No. 40
J. Glass 1905-6
Sigman, dairy 1907-23
J. Fine, dairy 1924-69

No. 41
J. Fletcher 1913-14

No. 42
Mrs Solomon, greengrocer 1910-13
H. Buchalter, greengrocer 1914-36
B. Davis, grocer 1937-71

No. 42A
M. Weinrouck, bakery 1904-43
A and M, victuallers 1946-71
Suissa's delicatessen 1977-80

No. 42B
M. Weinrouck, bakery 1905-43

No. 42
M. Freedman, stores 1935-6
B. Werzberger, stores 1937-61

No. 43
J. Cohen 1896-1902
Aaron Rosenthal 1903-6, moved to No. 35
A. Weinrouck 1907-17
M. Bookman 1918-43

No. 44
J. Barron 1898-1918
H. Posner 1919-27
P. Davis, butcher 1928-43
Leslie Cohen 1946
Werzberger 1947-63

No. 45
David Spiro, draper 1903-6, moved from No. 26
Mrs S. Clein 1907-11
H. Baigel 1912
J. Rubinstein, butcher 1913-15
Max Garber 1920-53
Saul, then Celia Robinson 1953-71

No. 46
Marks Brass 1899-1903
Louis Barron 1911-59
Mollie Barron 1960-7

No. 49
John Glickman 1896-7

No. 50
H. Glasser 1910

No. 57
S. Smullen 1955-67

No. 58
Jacobs 1954-82

No. 59
Mirrelson, turf accountant 1957-85

No. 62
A H.M. Gross 1972-80

No. 69
J. Solomon 1905-9

No. 71
M. Brodie 1935-44

No. 72
Mrs M. Barron 1923-44

No. 74
J. Bernstein 1906

No. 76
R. Rosenovsky, draper 1911-12
Goldwater, butcher 1936-62
I. Goldwater and Chaiken 1940-77

No. 78
Abel Mann 1904-5, moved from No. 98
A. Leopold 1947-57
Leah Leopold, dressmaker 1958-9

No. 80
Baigel, forage stores 1914-15
H. Ordman, greengrocer 1916-44

No. 81
Citron, chemist 1936-44
S. Waterman, grocer 1947-55

No. 82
J. Rubinstein, butcher 1905-79

No. 84
E.B. Barron, tobacconist 1901-10
H. Posner 1911-15
Mrs A. Rosenthal 1917-23

No. 86
J. Jaffa, grocer 1909-15
H. Smullen 1957-8

No. 87
A. Eppel 1895-8
L. Hershman 1899-1904
J. Brennan 1911
H. Atkin, bootmaker 1917-44

No. 88
Isaac Noik (Noyck) 1891-1903
M. Guinsburg 1904-44

No. 97
Abel Mann 1898-1903
M. Jacobson 1904

No. 98
S. Miller, picture framer 1892-3, moved to No. 18
S. Rubin 1894, moved to No. 112
Solomon Bloom 1895-8
N. Cristol 1904-11
T. Goldberg 1921-29

No. 98A
S. Yodaiken, rubber merchant 1907-33

No. 102
A. Freedman, draper 1898-1902

No. 112
S. Rubin 1895-1911, moved from No. 98

No. 115
A. Jacobs, draper 1923

SOME IRISH-JEWISH ACHIEVERS IN SPORT AT INTERNATIONAL LEVEL

ATHLETICS
Jonathan Kron (Long-jump)

BRIDGE
Rosalind Barron
Harry Bridberg
Sonia Britain
Dr Frankie Fine
Harry Fine
David Jackson
Adam Mesbur
Monty Rosenberg
Harry Robinson
Barbara Seligman
Don Seligman
Marcus Shrage

CHESS
Danielle Collins

CRICKET
Elya Berstock
Rodney Bernstein
Louis Bookman
Mark Cohen
Dr Sonny Hool
Dr Louis Jacobson
Greg Mollins
Jason Mollins
Mervyn Yaffey

LADIES CRICKET
Lara Mollins

FENCING
S. Elliman
Martin Simmons
Edward Solomons
Leslie Spivac

GOLF
Mark Bloom

MOTOR RACING
Cecil Vard

TEN PIN BOWLING
Marcia Goldwater
Karen Vard

RUGBY
Dr Bethel Solomons
Louis Bookman

TABLE TENNIS
Harry Collins
Mick Collins
David Marcus
Hubert Wine

WRESTLING
Ernie Cantor
Jackie Vard

CAPTAIN IRISH CRICKET TEAM
Jason Mollins

INTERNATIONAL REFEREE (WRESTLING)
Michael Coleman

INTERNATIONAL UMPIRE (HOCKEY)
Karen Eppel

List compiled in asssociation with Alan Shaper

HEBREW AND YIDDISH GLOSSARY

Jews in Ireland traditionally used Ashkenazi pronunciation of Hebrew; modern Hebrew, based on Sephardi pronunciation, came into more general use after the foundation of the state of Israel. Where two versions are given in the glossary such as *bris* and *brit* (circumcision) the 's' ending is Ashkenazi, the 't' ending is Sephardi

Aishit Chayil: woman of worth

Aron Kodesh: Holy Ark

Ashkenazi Jews (Ashkenazim): Jews from eastern and western Europe

Bar Mitzvah: initiation into adult religious status for boys aged thirteen

Bat Chayil: form of religious initiation for girls aged twelve in Orthodox Judaism

Bat Mitzvah: equivalent of *Bar Mitzvah* ceremony for twelve-year-old girls within Progressive Judaism

BCE: before the common era

Beth Din: ecclesiastical court

bimah: rostrum in synagogue

B'nai Akivah: children of Akivah

bris, brith, brit milah: the ritual circumcision of male babies

challahs: plaited or round loaves traditionally used for bread benedictions on Sabbath and festivals

Chanucah: the Feast of Lights, an eight-day festival commemorating the re-taking and re-dedication of the Holy Temple by Judah Maccabee in 165 BCE

Chatan Bereshit: person who re-commences the reading of the Torah for the new Hebrew year

Chatan Torah: person who concludes the reading of the Torah for the out-going Hebrew year

chazan (plural *chazanim*): a synagogue cantor

chazzanut: Jewish liturgical singing

cheder: Hebrew and religion classes

chevra gemorrah: study circle

Chevra Kadisha: Holy Burial Society

Chollent: meat, potato and bean dish baked overnight

chometz: leaven or foodstuffs containing leaven, forbidden on the Passover

chrane: horseradish sauce

Chumash: the five books of Moses plus sections from the Prophets

chuppah: wedding canopy or wedding ceremony

din Torah: arbitration based on Jewish law

frümkeit: degree of religious observance

gefülte fish: chopped fish, fried or boiled in brine

Gemarrah: commentaries on the *Mishnah*

glatt kosher: the highest level of *Kashrut* that can be applied to meat

goldene medina: land of dreams

goy (plural *goyim*): a Gentile

Haganah: pre-State Jewish underground movement

Haggadah: book containing the Passover *Seder* service

halacha: the legal framework of Jewish tradition

hechsher: the stamp on food that certifies it is *Kosher*

heim: the country of origin of Jewish immigrants

heimische: homely

imberlich: Passover sweetmeats

Irgun Z'vai L'umi: pre-State Jewish underground movement

Kabbalah: Jewish mysticism

Kaddish: prayer recited during synagogue services and by mourners

kaese: soft cheese

kashering: the process of making utensils and ritually- slaughtered fowl and animals KOSHER

kashrut: a code of dietary laws imposed on observant Jews

kehillat: community

kichlach: biscuits

kiddush: benediction on wine and bread on Sabbath and Festivals

Kohen (plural *Kohenim*): a descendent of ancient priests

Kol Nidre: the prayer chanted at the start of the *Yom Kippur* Service

kollel: a settlement based on religious learning

kosher: conforming to the dietary laws imposed on observant Jews

kugel: pudding

landsleit: friends or relations from one's native district

lockshun: vermicelli

losh inhora: precepts against slander

macher: community decision-maker

Magillah: Book of Esther read on *Purim*

mandel bread: almond cake

matzo: unleavened bread used during Passover

menorah: originally a seven-branched candelabra; term now applied to the eight-branched
    candelabra used at *Chanucah*

mensch: a considerate person worthy of respect

mikvah: ritual baths

milchige: yeast cake

minyan: a quorum of ten post-*Bar Mitzvah* males, required for certain prayers

Mishnah: oral *Torah*

mohel (plural mohelim): a person qualified to perform ritual circumcision

nedan: a dowry

perogin: meat pasties

Pesach: Passover

pidyon ha-ben: festive Redemption of the Firstborn who is otherwise dedicated to
    the service of G–d; applies only if firstborn is a son and there has been no previous
    miscarriage

Purim: a day of celebration, commemorating the downfall of Haman, an arch-antagonist
    who sought the destruction of the Jewish people *c.* 500 BCE

Rav: rabbi

Rebbizin: rabbi's wife

Rosh Hasannah: the Jewish new year Festival, generally falling in September

schmaltz: fatty

Seder: Order of Service on the first two nights of Passover

Sefer Torah: *Torah* scrolls

Semicha: rabbinical ordination

Sephardi Jews (plural *Sephardim*): Jews from the Iberian Peninsula, the Mediterranean lands,
    and North Africa

Shabbat: the Sabbath

Shabbaton: communal celebration of Shabbat

Shabbos goy (Sabbath gentile): a friend or neighbour who performs tasks forbidden to
    Observant Jews on the Sabbath

shadchen: a matchmaker

shechita: the ritual killing of fowl and cattle

sheilahs: queries regarding both the ritual fitness of food and general Orthodox practice

sheitel: a wig traditionally worn after marriage by highly Orthodox Jewish women

Shevuot: Pentecost or the Feast of Weeks, a festival commemorating the end of harvesting
    and the acceptance by Moses at Mount Sinai of the *Torah* and the Ten Commandments

shidduch: an arranged marriage

shiur: study session

Shiva: seven days of prayers and condolences from friends and relations following a
    bereavement

shnoddering: charitable offerings from worshippers called to the Reading of the Law shochet (plural shochtim): one qualified to perform *shechita*

shofar: a ram's horn, blown to mark the end of *Yom Kippur*

shomer: a supervisor who ensures compliance with dietary laws at kosher functions

Shtetl: a small town in central or eastern Europe where Jews predominated

shul: a synagogue

simcha: celebration

Simchat Torah (Rejoicing of the Law): the day after *Succot*, when the year-long reading of the *Torah* Scrolls is concluded and begun again

smetena: sour cream

spiel: a play

succah: a decorated booth roofed with leaves and branches, erected by Orthodox families and used for meals and entertaining during *Succot*

Succot: the Feast of Tabernacles, a harvest festival celebrated five days after *Yom Kippur*

tagelich: Passover sweetmeats

tallis (tallit): prayer shaw

Talmud: rabbinic commentaries on the *Torah*

Talmudist: expert in *Talmud*

Talmud Torah: organisation responsible for religious education

Tashlikh: a ceremony whereby sins are symbolically cast into running water

Tenach: the entire Hebrew Testament, including the Prophets

Torah: the body of law and doctrine contained in Jewish scripture and oral tradition

tzedakah: charitable offering

tzimmis: carrot-based compote

wurst: form of salami

yarmulke: a skull-cap

yeshiva: a Jewish religious seminary

yichis: prestige

Yid: a Jew

Yiddish: the traditional language of *Ashkenazi* jews, originally a dialect of German

Yiddishkeit: Jewish ethos

Yom Kippur (Day of Atonement): the last of the ten days of penitence that begin on Rosh *Hashannah* and end with the blowing of the *shofar*

IRISH GLOSSARY

ardfheis: general congress

An Bord Glas: marketing board for fruit and vegetables

An Cosantóir: magazine of the defence forces

AnCo: training council for adults

An Droichead: magazine

An Post: Department of Post

Aosdána: academy of artists

An tÓglach: Irish Republican Army (IRA) underground newspaper

An Tóstal: national Arts Festival

Áras an Uachtaráin: President of Ireland's official residence

Baile Átha Cliath: Dublin

Bord Fáilte: Tourist Board

Céilithe: dances

Clan na Gael: nationalist organisation

Clan na Poblachta: political party

Cumann Gaelach: Irish language Society
Cumann na mBan: Women's Auxiliary of the Irish Volunteers
Dáil: lower house of Parliament
Dáil Eireann: Irish Parliament
FÁS: Government training scheme
Feis Cheoil: music competition
Fianna Éireann: revolutionary youth movement
Fianna Fáil: political party
Fine Gael: political party
Gael Linn: agency for promoting Irish language
Gaelteacht: Irish speaking districts, mostly in the West of Ireland
Garda: policeman
Garda (Siochána): police force
Oireachtas: houses of Parliament
Páirc: park
Radio Éireann: Irish broadcasting service
RTÉ: Irish television service
Saoirse: freedom
Sceilg: Steep rock
Seanad: Senate, upper house of Parliament
Sinn Féin: political party
Sinn Féiner: supporter of Sinn Fein
Tailtean:national sports festival
Tánaiste: second minister in the Government
TD: member of Dáil Éireann
Taoiseach: leader, Prime Minister
Tuairim: Ideas

INDEX